HERMANN GILIOMEE

Maverick Africans

The shaping of the Afrikaners

TAFELBERG

Tafelberg
An imprint of NB Publishers
A division of Media24 Boeke (Pty) Ltd
40 Heerengracht, Cape Town, 8000
www.tafelberg.com
© 2020 Hermann Giliomee

Cover design by Michiel Botha
Book design by Nazli Jacobs
Edited by Russell Martin
Proofread by Camilla Lloyd
Index by George Claasen

Set in Dante
First edition, first impression 2020

Printed and bound by CTP Printers, Cape Town

ISBN: 978-0-624-08908-7
Epub: 978-0-624-08909-4
Mobi: 978-0-624-08910-0

Small nations. The concept is not quantitative; it points to a condition; a fate; small nations lack that felicitous sense of an eternal past and future; at a given moment in their history, they all passed through the antechambers of death. In constant confrontation with the arrogance and ignorance of the mighty, they see their existence as perpetually threatened or with a question mark hovering over it; for their very existence *is* the question.

– Milan Kundera, *Testaments Betrayed* (1993)

CONTENTS

PREFACE

This book is a companion volume to *The Rise and Demise of the Afrikaners*, published early in 2019 by Tafelberg. The collection of essays in that book focused
on the apartheid era and the transition to a negotiated settlement. The first
part of this volume deals with the long-term historical forces that shaped the
Afrikaner people: the powerful position that Afrikaner women enjoyed in their
marital relationships under Roman-Dutch law, the expanding frontier which
gave rise to individualism and later to republicanism, the struggle of the Dutch
Reformed Church to remain racially exclusive while spreading the gospel to
black people, and the rise of the nationalist movement that carried the Afrikaners
to power in 1948.

The second part of this book covers key aspects of the political history of
the past quarter of a century, some of which are still controversial. Chapter 5
examines the real and alleged politicisation of the civil service subsequent to
regime change in 1948. Rumours of improper political interference abound,
but the fact is that until 1994 a stable and professional service supervised by the
Public Service Commission was one of the country's strengths. Although
Afrikaners dominated the political system, it was only in the mid-1960s that
the upper levels of the civil service reflected the division between Afrikaans- and
English-speakers in the composition of the white population. Expertise was retained despite political divisions. Within thirteen years after 1994, however, the
civil service reflected the county's racial composition but at the cost of an enormous loss of experience and expertise.

As I argue in chapter 6, the struggle between African and Afrikaner nationalism
was not, as the leadership of the ANC has portrayed it, between the ANC's

non-racialism and the National Party's apartheid policy but between two different communities. The one, led by Afrikaners, stressed a form of self-determination over issues like education, culture, language, the market and property rights. On the other hand, while proclaiming itself to be a non-racial movement, the ANC was in fact a typical populist movement that wanted to gain full control of the state and the land.

Chapter 7 deals with corruption perpetrated by or condoned by the state. This has been a key issue from the start of ANC rule. In a counter-attack, some ANC leaders have charged that the NP government either initiated or condoned corruption on a substantial scale under its watch. The chapter examines the famous 'lifeboat' issue involving state aid to Bankorp during a serious financial crisis in the 1980s.

The subject of chapter 8 is Piet Cillié, long-time editor of *Die Burger*. He was regarded by several of his peers as the most formidable opponent of Prime Minister Hendrik Verwoerd in Afrikaner nationalist ranks. Surprisingly, his critical voice became quiet when John Vorster became leader. Chapter 9 discusses the leadership qualities of people at the helm of the apartheid state. Finally there is a chapter on the current fractured state of the Afrikaner community.

I wish to thank Annette for giving me the mental space to write, Erika for her unwavering support, Albert for exchanging ideas on history and university life, and my children and grandchildren who have not yet read any of my books but whose energy and *lewenslus* are a source of great pleasure. It is to them that I dedicate this book in the hope that they will one day read it.

HERMANN GILIOMEE
Stellenbosch, 21 November 2019

AUTHOR'S NOTE

Some of chapters in this book have been published before as articles or have appeared on a blog. They are published here with permission of the publishers and are substantially unchanged.

Chapter 1: *New Contree*, vol. 59, 2010

Chapter 2: From Howard Lamar and Leonard Thompson (eds), *The Frontier in History: North America and Southern Africa Compared* (New Haven: Yale University Press, 1981)

Chapter 3: *South African Historical Journal*, vol. 19, 1987

Chapters 5 and 7 were posted on the blog www.politicsweb.co.za

Chapter 6: From Hermann Giliomee and Lawrence Schlemmer (eds), *Negotiating South Africa's Future* (New York: St Martin's Press, 1989)

Chapter 9: From Robert Schrire (ed.), *Leadership in the Apartheid State* (Cape Town: Oxford University Press, 1994)

PART ONE

An exceptional history and the growth of a maverick community

The emotional debate about South Africa's past of colonialism and apartheid draws heavily on the assumption that our history differs little from that of other Western colonies. Where, similarly to South Africa, the land was forcibly taken from an indigenous population that was decimated or completely marginalised. Any comparative study of colonialism would, however, reveal features that have made South Africa exceptional.[1]

South Africa's uniqueness starts with the position of women of European descent, which is discussed in chapter 1. It is a topic that has received scant attention in the historiography despite its fundamental importance. In most other halfway or refreshment stations, like the Dutch trading posts in the Far East, European men cohabited with or married slave women or women from the indigenous population. As the saying goes, necessity is the mother of invention and the father of the Eurasian. This was the pattern at the Cape in the first four or five decades after the establishment of a settlement in 1652.

But in the ranks of the parties of French Huguenots who arrived in the late 1680s were many fecund girls. Increasingly a pattern of racial endogamy developed at the Cape among the burghers. Under Roman-Dutch law women enjoyed an exceptional position. The universal community of property was the basis of matrimonial property rights, with each party's portion merging into the common property. A surviving partner inherited half the estate and each child regardless of sex inherited an equal portion of the rest. Further strengthening the position of women was the fact that the Dutch Reformed Church allowed divorce, including on grounds of adultery.

It was not the Calvinist conception of an exclusive calling that was decisive in shaping the racial character of the Dutch Reformed Church at the Cape but rather the determination of European women to live as Europeans and as Christians in a slave society. A case study of the Stellenbosch district in the eighteenth century shows that women became confirmed members of the church in great numbers well before the men. They would insist that a suitor of any of their daughters become a member of the church too. As a church of slave owners, the DRC made no special effort to challenge slavery or to promote racial equality within its congregations.

The relatively strong position of women had profound consequences. It was one of the major reasons for the development of an endogamous white community, for the decision of many frontier farmers to leave the colony on what came to be called the Great Trek, and for the heroic struggle of the *bittereinders* during the Anglo-Boer War. In the 1890s the novelist Olive Schreiner painted a remarkable picture of the 'Boer woman'. She noted that the Boer woman on the farm had already attained what the 'women's movement' in Britain was then striving towards, namely to stand beside her man as his full co-labourer, and hence as his equal. Referring to Roman-Dutch law, she stated: 'The fiction of common possession of all material goods . . . is not a fiction but a reality among the Boers, and justly so, seeing that the female as often as the male contributes to the original household stock.'[2]

Schreiner argued that the Boer woman had no intention of becoming a 'drone of society' like upper-class women in Europe, leading a parasitic life in which she was 'fed, clothed and sustained by the labours of others for the mere performance of her animal sex function', while employing other women to raise her children. There was no mental chasm between the Boer woman and her male comrade, Schreiner concluded; she instead enjoyed a position of 'intellectual equality with her male companion, a condition which seems to constitute the highest ideal in the human sexual world'.[3]

Chapter 2 deals with the different frontiers opened up by the Afrikaner trekboers and the Voortrekkers. In these frontier zones a new society was formed from a combination of the indigenous population, European settlers and slaves from both Asia and other parts of Africa. The history of the frontier was marked not only by dispossession and discrimination but also by economic growth and social development. The trekboers and the trekkers kept cattle just as the Khoikhoi and Bantu-speaking Africans did. Because their economies were compatible, the different communities did not try to wipe each other out but sought to find ways in which they could coexist. Unlike other colonies settled by Europeans, the indigenous population here was not decimated but instead grew strongly.

A quick look at the populations of Australia and the United States demonstrates the different patterns of development. In Australia the aboriginal population today is about half a million strong and forms just under three per cent of the population. In the US there were by 1890 about 248 000 Native Americans (0,4 per cent of the total population). By 2010 they formed just under one per cent of a total of 309 million people.

By contrast, in 1910 Africans in South Africa numbered just over 4 million and formed about two-thirds of the total population of 6 million, while there were 1,2 million whites, representing about one-fifth of the country's population. The African population would grow to 12,6 million by 1951 and to 45 million by 2018, when they formed nearly four-fifths of the country's population.

Decimation of the indigenous population, as happened in countries like Australia and the US, only occurred in South Africa in the north-eastern divisions of the Cape Colony at the end of the eighteenth century. Here a relentless battle was waged between burghers (later called Afrikaners) and Bushmen (later called San). Records show that burgher commandos killed 2 480 Bushmen and indentured 654 of them, while Bushmen captured 19 161 cattle and 84 094 sheep from the colonists and killed 276 of their herdsmen. In the final years of the century the Sneeuwberg was considered to be in a state of perpetual warfare.

A remarkable figure now appeared among the frontier burghers. He was Field-Commandant J.P. van der Walt, who in 1793 settled in a division largely abandoned after Bushman attacks. He received a free hand from the government 'to eradicate and extirpate the robbers'.[4] Initially, he did not question commandos shooting as many Bushmen as possible and forcing their women and children to return with the colonists to work on their farms.

Five years later, however, Van der Walt changed his views. The commandos had been unable to prevent the Bushmen from staging attacks along a broad swathe of country, as a result of which many burghers abandoned their farms. Van der Walt now asked the landdrost to refuse permission for commandos to attack the Bushmen and capture their children since 'the burghers would also give their all if they were robbed of their children'.[5] Under Van der Walt's leadership the burghers in his division donated 283 sheep and supplies of tobacco and beads to the local Bushman clans to induce them to live peacefully on land of their own. The *veldwachtmeesters* of Mid-Roggeveld and Hantam also collected sheep and other gifts to hand over to the raiders to persuade them to stop stealing. In 1809 a British officer, Colonel Richard Collins, noted how pleasing it was 'to observe the anxiety evinced by the farmers of the north-eastern districts to preserve peace with that people [the Bushmen] rather by conciliation than by terror'.[6] During the 1820s the landdrost Andries Stockenström and the missionary James Clarke expressed similar sentiments.[7]

On the eastern frontier government attempts at enforcing territorial separation between the colonists and Xhosa were undermined because so many farmers insisted on retaining the services of their Xhosa herdsmen and on trading with the Xhosa beyond the colonial boundary.

In the meantime, a community of wine and wheat farmers had begun to prosper in the western Cape. While the economy of Cape Town was based on trade, that of the rural Cape, west and south of the first mountain ranges, was based mainly on wine and wheat production on land given out as freehold farms. Production expanded steadily: between 1720 and 1790 the number of vines increased more than fourfold, the wheat crop trebled, and the average net value of cultivators' estates grew nearly threefold. Historians have used the term 'gentry' to describe the stratum of wealthy plantation owners and reasonably well-off farmers that emerged in the western Cape so as to distinguish them from the great majority of hard-working yeoman farmers in the rest of the colony.

Chapter 3 discusses the development of a white community in South Africa which from the early nineteenth century increasingly called themselves Afrikaners. Among them were the western Cape gentry, who by second half of the eighteenth century had amassed sufficient wealth to engage in conspicuous consumption. Large houses built in the 'Cape Dutch' style were a splendid example of this. By the 1780s visitors began to comment on signs of affluence and prosperity on several farms in the south-western Cape. Houses were filled with elegant furniture and the tables were decked with silverware and served by tidily clothed slaves.

In this respect the history of South Africa was not fundamentally dissimilar to that of the American colonies founded at roughly the same time. But the Cape was different in that it was ruled by a commercial company which looked at everything from the perspective of its own interests. Even when the burghers were consulted, the Company considered its own interests as of paramount importance. In the eighteenth century, however, the burghers rejected the Company's plan to replace the importation of slaves with subsidised white immigration from Europe. They wanted to have as much land as possible available for their children so that they could also engage in extensive farming.

In the society that developed at the Cape, members of the gentry preferred to intermarry, but the shortage of European women made this impossible, so instead they married across class lines. Burghers of all classes attended the four churches in the rural western Cape (Stellenbosch, Paarl, Roodezand and Swartland). Both wealthy and poor burghers participated in the same militia exercises and rode out on commando together. So, too, the extension of credit helped to tie the burghers to one another. In the absence of banks, the gentry granted credit on an extensive scale to the middling and poor burghers.[8]

The other part of the community was commonly known as 'Boers' but some observers also called them Afrikaners. They lived in the interior beyond the first mountain ranges, where a form of community developed in the course of the eighteenth century that was quite different from that in the south-western Cape. C.W. de Kiewiet, a truly exceptional historian, describes the origin of the trekboers of the interior well: 'In the long quietude of the eighteenth century the Boer race was born.'

Unlike the Dutch- or Afrikaans-speaking white community of the south-western Cape, 'they had left the current of European life and lost the economic habits of the nations from which they had sprung . . . They had the nomad's appetite for space and possessed the hardness and courage of men of the saddle who watched their flocks and hunted their meat . . . Their life gave them a tenacity of purpose, a power of silent endurance, and the keenest self-respect.' But their tenacity could develop into obstinacy, their power of endurance into resistance to innovation, and their self-respect into suspicion of foreigners and contempt for their inferiors.[9]

By the mid-1830s the Afrikaner farmers of the eastern frontier had come to realise that on their own they would not be able to defeat and push back the

Xhosa. Only the British army was capable of defeating and subjugating the Xhosa chiefdoms. In what became known as the Great Trek, the Afrikaner farmers of the eastern frontier pulled up their roots and outflanked the Xhosa, moving into the thinly populated central interior of South Africa. They settled in areas that would become known as the Free State and Transvaal. The model of land settlement adopted here was the loan farm system of the Cape Colony of the eighteenth century. This did not embrace the English system of exclusive, private property rights but rather encouraged a farmer to attract white and black employees to help him look after his cattle and defend his farm.

As a result of a decision by the British government to retreat from direct control of the interior beyond the Cape borders, two republics were established here: the South African Republic, or Transvaal (1852), and the Republic of the Orange Free State (1854). The two republics experienced different paths of development. In the so-called British Sovereignty, which existed between 1848 and 1854 prior to the establishment of the Free State, British farmers who moved there tended to appeal to the British imperial state to back up their land claims, provide roads, create markets, and subordinate the local Africans. On the other hand, many Afrikaners in the territory attached no priority to creating a state, much less a British colonial state. Nor did they want a firm border separating white-occupied territory from black-occupied or a severing of contact with or expulsion of the Sotho; some indeed made their living by exchanging Sotho wheat for lead and gunpowder. They did not mind asking the Sotho leader Moshoeshoe for papers ratifying their land claims.

In his book *Colonial South Africa and the Origins of the Racial Order*, Tim Keegan notes that Richard Southey, the highest British official in the territory, admitted that burghers in the contested area along the Caledon River in the east preferred the rule of the Sotho chief Moshoeshoe to that of the British government. Southey's appeals to the burghers 'to put down the common enemy of the white man' went unheeded. Josias Hoffman, who would become the first Free State president, objected to a plan to expel some 3 000 Sotho from the Caledon River Valley. 'The natives will not consent to remove and will revenge such unjust treatment,' he wrote and added: 'If Southey thinks that he can bind the Boers to the British government by giving them all the land, he is mistaken and knows neither the Boers nor the natives.'[10]

Within three decades of its establishment in 1854, the Republic of the Orange Free State achieved a remarkable degree of stability. This can be attributed to its agrarian character, its relatively homogeneous electorate, and the absence of large concentrations of wealth. English-speakers and the few Germans who dominated commercial and professional life in the towns had a leavening effect. There was no xenophobia, and even in the 1890s the state welcomed foreign settlers. The Free State combined republicanism with an inclusive sense of nationhood, similar to that espoused by the Afrikaner Bond in the Cape. It was, as Lord Bryce, the British constitutional expert, remarked, in many ways 'an ideal commonwealth'.[11]

But at the same time it was not a modern, liberal order. There were no political parties and only whites could vote. As the great liberal historian Leonard Thompson once commented, if the Free State had not been dragged into the war between the Transvaal and Britain in 1899, racial exclusion might well have been phased out in the Free State. In his testimony before the South African Native Affairs Commission (1903–5) C.H. Wessels, who had served as chairman of the Free State Volksraad, advocated extending the vote to intelligent coloured people and to black property-owners.[12]

Unlike the Free State, the republic between the Vaal and Limpopo was for all practical purposes a failed state until Paul Kruger became president. Leading by personal courage, strong conviction and passionate oratory, Kruger spread the message that without republican independence the Transvaal Afrikaners could not survive as a people with their own language, beliefs and livelihood. But Transvaal leaders prized the Republic's control over its own destiny much more than pan-Afrikaner unity. One progressive opponent of Kruger, Schalk Burger, chairman of the first Volksraad, declared that 'the word Africander should be interpreted as Transvaler. Everyone from beyond the borders of the Republic must be viewed as a stranger, no matter if he came from the Free State, the colony, England, or Holland.'[13]

Few would have predicted at the time of Union in 1910 that the colonial Afrikaners of the Cape and ex-republican Afrikaners would come together in a formidable nationalist movement that dominated South African politics until 1994. It was not Calvinism or racism that was decisive in the formation of Afrikaner nationalism but the Westminster-style electoral system, which favoured the largest ethnic group in the electorate.

Chapter 3 analyses the earliest manifestations of nationalism among the Afrikaner. The literature on this topic was long dominated by F.A. van Jaarsveld, who in his book *The Awakening of Afrikaner Nationalism* (1961) argued that its first manifestation was the revolt of the burghers of Transvaal against British annexation in 1880–1 and the expressions of solidarity by Afrikaners in the Orange Free State and Cape Colony. But this response was short-lived. No structures of co-operation were put in place and, after the discovery of gold on the Witwatersrand in the mid-1880s, economic competition between the Transvaal and the Cape eroded the feelings of solidarity among Afrikaners across South Africa.

Chapter 3 argues that it was the establishment of Afrikaner financial institutions in the western Cape, in particular the Stellenbosch District Bank, that provided the spur for the earliest manifestations of Afrikaner nationalism. It is significant that the decision to establish Nasionale Pers took place in the home of the manager of the District Bank. Nasionale Pers (now Naspers) has been publishing *De Burger* (later *Die Burger*) since 1915. Almost exactly a century later it was the biggest company in Africa measured in terms of market capitalisation.

During the twentieth century the mines and industries replaced agriculture as the dominant sectors of the economy. While other colonies also had rich mineral resources, there was nothing that could be compared to the vast mineral wealth of the Witwatersrand. The discovery of gold transformed South Africa. But much of South Africa's gold ore is low-grade. Because it was sold at a low, fixed price it could only be mined by very cheap labour. Furthermore, low-grade land, together with poor and uncertain rainfall, was responsible for many of the problems in agriculture.

Despite the deposits of gold, South Africa's economic development remained stagnant until the early 1930s. In 1931 Jan Hofmeyr, who would soon become minister of finance, wrote that it was an illusion to believe that South Africa was a rich country with vast mineral resources and boundless agricultural possibilities. The gold mines, the only reliable source of foreign exchange, were a wasting asset, the manufacturing sector was sluggish, and agriculture was 'no easy oyster for man's opening'. The country was in a race against time to provide food and work for a rapidly growing population.

Hofmeyr warned that the future of 'white civilisation' was at risk if the country failed to develop a modern manufacturing sector speedily. He concluded that 'from the shadow that these things bring . . . South Africa in our day does not find it easy to escape'.[14] In a despairing mood Jan Smuts, leader of the South African Party, wrote: 'There has never been such a test to our economic civilization, and it is still a question whether we can pull through without serious challenge to our spiritual heritage.'[15] But a sudden jump in the gold price would put South Africa on a quite different level of growth and development.

It was at this point, in the year 1929 to be precise, that the word 'apartheid' appeared in print for the first time. This occurred in a pamphlet reporting on a conference held in Kroonstad to discuss ways in which the Dutch Reformed Church could intensify its efforts to promote Christianity among Africans. The DRC's dilemma was that it was then lagging far behind other churches in this field. DRC leaders were keen to expand the church's work among Africans but they also knew that a steady flow of African members into existing congregations would cause major tensions. The church tried to deal with this by accepting what Richard Elphick calls 'the equality of believers' while rejecting the equality of all individuals regardless of colour in secular life.

As chapter 4 explains, it was in fact a decision by the DRC in 1857 condoning segregated worship that set the Afrikaner churches and the Afrikaner community on this road. Hence in explaining how apartheid became part of the South African political system, we need to consider not so much what the National Party did to the Afrikaner churches but what these churches did to the NP. Chapter 4 considers the ecclesiastical origins of apartheid policy in detail.

1.

'Allowed such a state of freedom':
Women and gender relations in the Afrikaner
community before enfranchisement in 1930

The history of Afrikaner women remains a neglected field.[1] The main reason is the absence of diaries, letters and other written records at a time when rates of literacy were low. Historians have not deliberately suppressed the role of women in the history of the Afrikaners, but because of the absence of documentation they have missed a lot. Significantly it was not a trained historian but Karel Schoeman, a novelist, who, in his published biographies of extraordinary women, highlighted the important role of women in pre-industrial South Africa.[2]

This chapter analyses the status of Afrikaner women with particular reference to institutional factors such as the law of inheritance, slavery, and church membership. It also discusses the role Afrikaner women played in the rise of racial domination and anti-imperialism in pre-industrial South Africa. It ends with a brief discussion of the responses of Afrikaner women to the campaign for the vote for women in South Africa.[3]

English and Roman-Dutch law

An investigation should start with a brief comparison between the English law of inheritance and family law, and Roman-Dutch law in early modern times.

English law

Marriage in English law was all about property, with the husband becoming the owner of the wife's moveable property. The wife lost all claims to it even if she survived him. A recent study states bluntly that English women enjoyed a status only a little higher than slaves. A husband could beat her as long as the stick was not thicker than his thumb.[4] The historian Edmund Morgan formulated the position of women in the American colonies as follows: 'Women were excluded from any share in formal public power even in the privacy of the family. A woman's very identity was subsumed in her husband's; any property she brought into the marriage was his, any debt she owed was his, almost any tort she committed was his.'[5] Under the rule of primogeniture, as applied in England and her colonies, the eldest son inherited everything. People in England did, however, have testamentary freedom, and they could leave money and estates to daughters if they so wished, provided that there was no entail. But there was a strong tendency to favour males. What Jane Austen refers to as 'a daughter's share' was characteristically a small portion of the total estate.[6]

Roman-Dutch law

Roman-Dutch law, as applied in the Netherlands and also at the Cape, went further than other legal codes in recognising that all free people – men and women – had rights. In the words of the great jurist Voetius, it preserved equality and bound the citizens equally. This 'legalised egalitarianism' had profound social and political consequences. Among its expressions were a lack of respect for the aristocracy and officialdom, the weakness of ecclesiastical authority, and the absence of clearly demarcated hierarchies.[7]

Although Britain became master of the Cape Colony early in the nineteenth century, it did not abolish Roman-Dutch law, except for some amendments to the criminal law. Roman-Dutch law was virtually the only legal system in Europe that retained universal community as the basis of matrimonial property, with each partner's portion merging into the common property. The rule of partible inheritance, applied when one of the partners died, stood in stark contrast to the primogeniture rule. Under partible inheritance, the surviving partner retained half the estate and each child, regardless of sex, inherited an equal portion of the rest. These inheritance portions could be changed in a will but this rarely happened, and no spouse or child could be disinherited of more than half his or her 'legitimate portion'. The British authorities disliked this rule, but because the Dutch colonists at the Cape considered partible inheritance an intimate part of their culture, they were very reluctant to change it.[8]

No farm could be subdivided under the loan farm system that held sway under the Dutch East India Company, but the surviving spouse and the children received their share of the property, including the slaves. Afrikaner women normally outlived their partners and many widows gained control over substantial amounts of property consisting of both land and slaves.[9] This gave rise to what has been called a 'widowarchy'. A widow who had been left half the estate of a farmer could consider the options for a subsequent marriage just as an astute modern investment manager today would. Many widowed Cape women remarried several times, thereby accumulating a small fortune.[10]

The Roman-Dutch law of inheritance also had another important effect. Since each child, regardless of sex, had to receive his 'legitimate portion', parents were compelled to divide the farms among them. The subdivision of farms into uneconomical units was widespread. Many families ended up in chronic debt as a result of the mortgaging of land in order to pay out the younger sons and daughters. Often entire farms were sold and the proceeds divided, forcing sons to seek new land elsewhere or become *bywoners*.

The divorce law that was applied in most of the Netherlands and also at the Cape strengthened the position of women. It provided for several legitimate reasons for divorce or a separation from 'table and bed', which effectively annulled the marriage. Among the reasons were adultery, malicious desertion and gross physical cruelty. In the case of divorce, the wife received half of the estate. The wife could also recover the moveable assets donated by a husband to a concubine.[11]

The status of women under Roman-Dutch law should not be exaggerated, as is revealed by the indignant remark made by Petronella van Heerden, perhaps the first Afrikaner feminist, who came of age just after the South African War. She wrote: '[A woman] is classified among children and idiots, when she marries she becomes a minor; she has no control over her things and children, and she could do nothing without the permission of her husband.'[12] While hyperbolic, this is not devoid of some truth. A woman who married within community of property in most respects acquired the status of a minor and was subject to the authority of her husband. A father had the final say over the children. There were indeed few legal limits on a husband in the disposal of common assets or the discharging of debts out of the common assets during the existence of the marriage.

First-generation women

The married European women of the first generation were primarily drawn from the Netherlands and their numbers were later supplemented by Huguenot refugees from France. In addition, manumitted slave women made up a sizeable proportion of married women during the seventeenth century.

Dutch women

Women in the Netherlands could sign commercial contracts and notarised documents and could carry on a trade, business or profession without the express consent of their husbands. They were closely involved in their husbands' jobs, particularly if he was in business or commerce, often enjoying full recognition for their role.[13] Many of the first Dutch women at the Cape were from orphanages, but they were not unaware of the relatively strong position of women in the Netherlands. Women could not hold what was called a burgher office, like that of *heemraad*, or an ecclesiastical office, like that of minister or elder, but when they married burghers they shared the general status of burghers. Their children were considered burghers as well under Roman-Dutch law, which decreed that women enjoyed the status of their husband.

European women at the Cape quickly became active in the hectic trade that characterised the port city. Women received licences to keep guesthouses or taverns or to engage in any other business. C.P. Thunberg, who visited the Cape during the 1770s, wrote: 'If the father does not trade, but carries on some handicraft business, his wife, daughter or son must.'[14] Some European travellers to the Cape were shocked by the rough methods lower-class women used to escape from poverty. In *Working Papers in Southern African Studies* one wrote: 'Many of the evil burghers and burgher women (who had come out in male attire as stowaways) milk the poor sailors not only of every penny they own, but when cash runs short seize on anything else they possess.'[15]

French women

There is no evidence of a distinctive influence exerted by French Huguenot women, but they had behind them a traumatic history of religious persecution and political struggle. This was likely to make them more fiercely determined to resist unjust authority. Without a fatherland to which to return, the Huguenots had to take root or go under. Simon van der Stel, governor at the Cape, soon became disenchanted with the French immigrants, describing them as insolent and inclined to plotting.[16]

The Huguenots greatly strengthened the pattern of white endogamy that was becoming established at the Cape. When the first party arrived at the Cape in 1688 there was still a severe shortage of European women in the settlement, prompting many men to take half-caste slaves as brides or stable partners outside wedlock. The Huguenots, by contrast, were generally already married when they arrived, and their daughters young and fecund. A cursory glance will show that a surprisingly large proportion of established present-day Afrikaner families had a Huguenot as *stammoeder*.[17]

Between 1705 and 1707 women were prominent in the struggle of the farming burghers against the governor, Willem Adriaan van der Stel, and other high officials. In violation of the strict Company policy some officials farmed for the market, increasingly squeezing the burghers out of business. Discontent and rebelliousness became rife in the Cape and Stellenbosch districts. The landdrost Johannes Starrenburg, a well-read and well-travelled man who knew his Cicero, Dio Cassius and Grotius, was deeply disturbed by what he saw as the open contempt the burghers displayed towards the government. He was most upset by a demonstration in 1706 in the town where some burghers danced around him, vowing that they would not abandon the struggle. He took refuge in his house, where he wrote to Van der Stel: '[The] women are as dangerous as the men and do not keep quiet.'[18] The stiff resistance persuaded the Company directors in the Netherlands to recall Van der Stel and other officials.

Significantly it was a French woman who played a key role in the establishment of the commando system, which was crucial to the way the farmers subjugated the indigenous people and defended their property. For the first 50 years of European settlement the government allowed burghers only to go on military expeditions that were led by soldiers employed by government and based in Cape Town. For burgers farming in the interior, the Company's soldiers invariably arrived far too late to recover any stolen cattle.

In 1716 Gertruida du Toit, wife of Pierre Rousseau, a *heemraad* of Drakenstein, became exasperated after San raiders had killed her Khoikhoi herder and carried off several head of cattle. Although she lived as far away as the site of the present

Wemmershoek Dam near Paarl, she travelled all the way to the Castle in Cape Town to ask senior government officials to allow burghers to assemble a commando to pursue raiders without waiting for the government's permission. The commandos were an essential part of Boer conquest and settlement for nearly two centuries.

Inevitably the system was wide open to abuse. Many of the commandos not only retrieved the stolen cattle, but also raided cattle and forced Khoisan women and children to accompany them back to their farms and work there against their will.[19] The commando system experienced its finest hour in the Anglo-Boer War (1899–1902) when it pinned down the British forces despite their vastly superior numbers.

Slave-born women

Although there was a correspondence between legal status, colour and religious identity, there was no rigid racial division, particularly during the first 75 years of Company rule. People of mixed racial origins were prominent both as burghers and free blacks and did not appear to suffer any racial discrimination. The frequent racial mixing was due in the first place to the huge gender imbalance in the white population. By 1700 there were in the Cape district twice as many men as women in the adult burgher population, and in the interior the ratio was three to one. Marriages between white men and fair-skinned non-white women were common during the first 75 years. Many stable mixed liaisons occurred outside wedlock, and there was also large-scale miscegenation in the form of casual sex, especially in the Slave Lodge frequented by local European men as well as sailors and soldiers.

J.A. Heese, a genealogical researcher, has estimated that seven per cent of modern-day Afrikaner families have a non-European *stammoeder* or progenitress.[20] During the early years the situation was fluid enough for some children born from unions of non-European parents to be accepted into the European community. There were two particularly striking cases. The slave Armosyn Claasz was born in 1661 at the Cape. Her mother was presumably a slave from the west coast of Africa; the identity of her father was unknown. She gave birth to the children of four different fathers in the Company's Slave Lodge; some of them were described as *halfslag* (half-caste), which means that the father was white. Many of these children and their descendants were absorbed into what became prominent Afrikaner families, like the Volschenk, Coorts, Du Plessis, Pretorius, Horn, Myburgh and Esterhuyzen families.

The other case relates to the liaison between Louis of Bengal and Lysbeth van de Caab, both considered non-European. Three daughters were born out of this liaison, and Lysbeth had two daughters from another relationship with a European. All the children entered into relationships, either marital or extra-marital, with Europeans, and most of their descendants were absorbed into the Afrikaner community. Those most directly involved were the Brits, Van Deventer, Slabbert, Fischer and Carstens families.[21]

Genealogies include a few instances of European women marrying non-Europeans. The most striking case was that of Marguerite de Savoye, the daughter of Huguenot parents, who in 1690 married Christoffel Snyman, who, according to oral tradition, made a living from pruning vineyards. He was the son of Anthony of Bengal and a non-white mother. The well-known Snyman family is descended from them. Another case was that of Maria Roos, who in 1794 married David Simon Hoon, the son of a slave from Madagascar and his wife, Rachael, of Indian descent. Other 'Coloured' males entered 'white' society, including the progenitors of the Antonissen, Jonker, Jacobs and Serfontein families.[22]

Confident women

From an early stage the European women at the Cape displayed a considerable degree of social self-confidence. Girls not only shared equally with their brothers in the estates of their parents, but also received the same elementary education. Women did not show undue respect to people in political or clerical office. Some visitors to the Cape expressed the view that they were more intelligent than the male burghers and better informed.[23]

The pattern of women acting as a strong force in the family became firmly established in the agrarian western Cape rather than the port city. Slave owners on farms or in small settlements allowed very little manumission or slave baptism in order to enhance their control over their slaves. Consequently the number of slave women who could compete with European women as stable partners of European men remained extremely small.

O.F. Mentzel, an astute German who lived at the Cape for most of the 1730s, considered the Cape Town women too glib and status conscious. By contrast, the women in the patriarchal community of the rural western Cape impressed him. He wrote that a girl was not pampered but often put to work in both the house and in the fields. She 'looked everybody straight in the eye . . . and [was] unabashed'. As married women they 'understand more about their husband's business than the latter do themselves; when this is not the case the affairs are seldom well conducted.'[24]

He passed this general judgement:

> In general, farmwomen surpass the men in nature and intelligence, good behaviour and ability to understand anything, wherefore they are almost always held in higher esteem by the Europeans than the women of Cape Town. They are unusually industrious, good housekeepers, and excellent mothers. They are not so ambitious as the townswomen; they do not quarrel over precedence, and it is immaterial to them whether they are seated at the table to the left or the right, or whether they were served first or last.[25]

By contrast, Robert Semple, the son of a British merchant who visited the Cape in the early nineteenth century, expressed a favourable impression of the women of the town. He wrote:

> There exists not at all at the Cape that marked difference in the manners of the two sexes that we find in Europe. In conversation the women are free and unreserved, and very often listened to, but make use of expressions by no means to be reconciled with English ideas of decency and propriety. They are not the disciples, they might be the models of the school of Mrs Mary Wollstonecraft, they call everything by its right name, and seem in general to think that actions which men might perform with impunity ought equally to be allowed to themselves.[26]

Often called the first British feminist, Wollstonecraft argued that women were naturally equal to men but only appeared to be unequal due to a lack of education. In her *Thoughts on the Education of Daughters* she argued that the mind was not tied down or dictated by gender, and that the pace of learning had to be adapted to each pupil, regardless of sex.[27]

Some Afrikaner women in Cape Town enjoyed considerable free time because they left the task of suckling and rearing their children to a slave woman.[28] A visitor wrote: 'They [the Afrikaner women] seldom suckle their children, the most prevailing practice is to consign them over in a manner to a faithful female slave who suckles them, overlooks them, brings them up, and in a word becomes a second mother.'[29] The practice made it possible for the biological mother to ovulate sooner and have children at shorter intervals. Thus wet nurses and nannies shared the burden of the prodigious growth of the burgher population at the Cape. Wet-nursing was controversial and it was certainly frowned upon in Holland. Some historians argue that it was widespread at the Cape.[30] Analyses of the pattern of manumission show that it was European women rather than men who manumitted slave women who had been wet nurses or 'foster mothers'.[31]

Slavery was not widespread on the frontier and life here was much tougher for women. A traveller offered a glimpse of what settling in the deep interior entailed:

> A soldier living in a tent during a campaign is not so badly off as a young couple who settle in such a distant wilderness isolated from all human society . . . Imagine the situation when such a wife should in time become pregnant, and have no assistance other than that of a Hottentot woman, without being able to understand one another.[32]

But except for the poorest households, women could generally rely on servants to perform most of the mundane tasks of the household.

Marriage and divorce

Parties who wanted to marry had to appear before the Matrimonial Court. The court, consisting of four commissioners (two officials and two burghers), sat in Cape Town. The court asked the following of them: (i) if they appeared voluntarily, (ii) whether they were perfectly free to marry, (iii) if their parents were alive and had given their consent in the case of men under 21 years and women under 18, and (iv) if they were related to each other. If the commissioners were satisfied, the banns were published and the celebration of the marriage took the form of a religious ceremony in the church.[33]

The right under Roman-Dutch law for a woman to file for divorce in certain circumstances protected women against an abusive husband. In the Netherlands both the state and the Reformed Church viewed marriage and the family as the bedrock of ordered society and neither was in favour of divorce, except in extreme cases. In the eighteenth century, however, there was an explosion of separation suits in the Netherlands.[34] It is not known what the divorce rate was, but a visitor to the Cape declared: 'Most domestic quarrels have their set and fixed remedies provided by the law. If a husband and a wife disagree, it is easy [for them] to separate.'[35]

At the Cape there were always married European men prepared to risk divorce by having sexual relations with slaves. There was the case of Willem Menssink, a brewer, who early in the eighteenth century carried on affairs with female slaves in his household. His wife was unable to get a divorce settlement.[36] However, this happened before endogamous marriages between Europeans had become the social bedrock of society, particularly outside Cape Town. A little more than a century later there was a quite different outcome in the case of Carel Greyling. His slave, Clara, gave birth to a child, believed by his wife to be Carel's. He tried to shift the blame to his son, but his wife left him immediately. She asked for, and received, an order for the dissolution of her marriage and a property settlement.[37]

A woman living on an isolated farm who did not enjoy active support from her parents or siblings would find it difficult to take on a husband who had sexual relations with slave women. Pamela, the wife of Galant, a slave who led a rebellion in the Koue Bokkeveld in 1825, had to sleep in the bedroom of Willem van der Merwe, his master. No mention was made in the court record of how Pamela or Van der Merwe's wife reacted to this. The rebel slaves killed Van der Merwe and a few other white men but did no harm to the white women.[38]

The Cape and Brazil compared

To highlight the place of white women in Cape society we can compare it with another slave society, namely Brazil. Portuguese law, as applied in Brazil, recognised universal property as the basis of matrimonial property, but in the Catholic Church no divorce was possible. A European woman could do little if her husband wanted to bring the offspring of a liaison with a slave into the household and have them baptised in church. In the words of the great scholar Gilberto Freyre, the settler families in Brazil were enlarged by great numbers of 'bastards and dependants, gathered around the patriarchs, who were more given to women and possibly a little more loose in their social code than the North Americans were'.[39] One has to allow for the fact that Freyre was engaged in the ideological project of making Brazilians proud of the heritage of racial mixture, but for at least some parts of Brazil, like Pernambuco, his description is accurate.

During the first 70 years of the Cape settlement many European men married slave women who had been freed. As noted before, this tendency had declined sharply by 1730, but extramarital sex between European boys or men and slave women was rife. Writing about the Cape, Mentzel reported that European boys more often than not got entangled with a slave belonging to the household without incurring the wrath of their parents.[40] For a child born outside wedlock to be legitimised, both child and father had to be present at the celebration of the marriage and the father had to publicly acknowledge that he had procreated the child. This rarely happened if the mother was a slave or a free black.

After 1730 there was some anxiety among the top officials in and around Cape Town that the trekboers who had spread out over the deep interior would become degenerate. Mentzel observed that the frontier colonists had accustomed themselves to such an extent with 'the carefree life, the indifference, the lazy days and the association with slaves and Hottentots that not much difference may be discerned between the former and the latter'.[41] The more affluent burghers in Stellenbosch and Cape Town also expressed the fear that morals on the frontier could become 'bastardised', leading to a 'completely degenerate nation'.[42] These fears were unfounded. Between the 1720s and 1790s the settler population was transformed from one that had no firm racial boundaries and was far from strict in religious observance to one in which endogamous marriages were the norm throughout the colony. A premium was now put on membership of the church, which had itself become increasingly racially exclusive.[43]

Women and endogamous marriages

What role did European women play in this? Before this question is addressed, one must also look at some other factors at work. The first was cultural influences. Like all colonising people of the period, the Dutch were convinced of the superiority of their culture and religion. Cultural chauvinism was an important component of social attitudes. Even before 1652 the Dutch had shown a strong cultural aversion to Africans, attributing to them sexual licence, savagery and a diabolical religion.[44]

Secondly, there was the legal factor. There was a high incidence of sexual intercourse outside wedlock between Europeans and slaves but, as we have seen, children born from such liaisons were not taken into the burgher's family, but were incorporated in the slave population. Another legal obstacle to the advancement of women or children of mixed origins was the regulations covering marriages. It is a supreme irony that slave women, with their extremely low social status, were in fact very expensive to marry. The prospective husband first had to buy a female slave from the owner. As part of the manumission regulations he also had to pay a sum to the authorities as a guarantee that she would not become a burden on society. From the remarks of a traveller one can deduce that many a poor European male would have manumitted a slave and married her but for the price of 800 to 1 000 rixdollars that some fetched.[45] For instance, in 1810 the burgher Willem Klomphaan was charged 950 rixdollars for his slave mistress and their twins – the price of some farms in Graaff-Reinet. He died after having paid 600 rixdollars.[46] By contrast, eligible European girls or women, thanks to the rule of partible inheritance, often had dowries.

Thirdly, demographic forces were at play. The ratio between European men and European women stood at 260 to 100 early in the eighteenth century and declined to 140 to 100 by 1770. Mixed marriages began to decrease from the 1730s, and men who could not find a European wife tended not to marry. A study of the 1731 census shows that 59 per cent of European men in Cape Town and 51 per cent of those in the rural western Cape never married.[47] In 1807 only five per cent of a sample of 1 063 children baptised in that year in the Reformed and Lutheran churches had a grandparent classified by genealogists as 'non-European' (invariably a female). At this time the proportion of marriages that were obviously racially mixed in the Tulbagh and Graaff-Reinet districts was one and three per cent.[48] A rigid pattern of racial endogamy had been established in the course of the eighteenth century. The offspring of European men who had engaged in illicit liaisons almost all passed into the ranks of the slave or free-black community.

The church was crucial to the rise of endogamous marriages and the strong position women acquired in society. The role of religion in the first century of the settlement is overstated in popular history, where Van Riebeeck's official prayer is often cited as evidence of the Europeans' piety. The fact is that for most of the period of Company rule the burgher community was not regarded as devout. In 1726, only in the case of one-fifth of burgher couples in Stellenbosch were both partners confirmed members of the Reformed Church. In 1743, after touring the colony, the Dutch official G.W. van Imhoff noted 'with astonishment and regret how little work is done with respect to the public religion'. He added that the 'indifference and ignorance in the frontier districts is such that they have the appearance more of an assembly of blind heathen than a colony of European Christians'.[49]

It was women who took the lead in becoming confirmed members of the church. In the first 50 years of the Stellenbosch district three times more European women than men were confirmed. By 1770, 90 per cent of the adult European women in the very large Stellenbosch congregation were confirmed members of the church, against only a third of the male burghers.[50] By the end of the century the men had stepped into line. Observers now generally considered the burghers of the outlying districts to be devout. Couples travelled enormous distances, sometimes involving a journey of five to six weeks, to have children baptised in Stellenbosch and to partake of Holy Communion. Henry Lichtenstein, one of the best-informed travellers, testified to this: '[We] never heard from the mouth of a colonist an unseemly word, an overstrained expression, a curse, or an imprecation of any kind . . . The universal religious turn of the colonists, amounting almost to bigotry, is, perhaps, a principal cause to which this command of themselves is to be ascribed.'[51]

It had become the norm that a European man who wanted to marry had to find a European woman. Eligible European women or their mothers probably demanded that a suitor be confirmed in the church before giving their consent. Married couples accepted that it was their duty to baptise their children. A historian who closely analysed the data for the Stellenbosch district has remarked: 'It is quite possible that pious people mainly sought a partner through the church, but we must seriously consider the possibility that marriage and family were important factors in finding the way to belief.'[52]

Why did women stress membership of the church so much? Two reasons suggest themselves. Church membership was virtually the only thing that set people in the dominant white community apart from those who served them, and it also connected them to the wider European world beyond the colony's shores. The pattern of endogamous marriages limited membership of both the family and the church to Europeans. A church that was racially exclusive was a major step towards a racially exclusive community that upheld and even idealised the status of white women.

Mistresses and slaves

With her central place in the household assured by the end of the eighteenth century, the woman became the equal partner of her husband in the running of the household. According to P.B. Borcherds's account of Stellenbosch life, the internal arrangements of the household were considered the wife's department exclusively. Members of her household and several servants were 'generally well employed' in needlework and other necessary tasks. He added: 'The rest of the house, such as the bedrooms, nurseries, pantry, kitchen etcetera, was of course the exclusive domain of the mamma.'[53]

The dominant image of life in the eighteenth century is usually that of the spacious and elegant Cape Dutch homes of the Afrikaner gentry in the western Cape, but in the newly settled regions conditions could be quite rough. Hendrik Swellengrebel wrote at the end of the 1770s that the houses in the area of Camdeboo (Graaff-Reinet) were sheds 40 feet long and 15 feet wide. Here 'chickens, ducks and young pigs swirled around' and two or three families shared the house. An account of the same period of life in the Sneeuwberg declared that houses 'nearly all comprised a single low-walled room without any privacy'.[54]

In the ideology of paternalism the myth was propagated that slaves and servants were members of the household and even part of the extended family: this consisted of the patriarch's immediate family, some brothers or sisters and their families, one or more *bywoners* (white tenant farmers) and their families,

Khoikhoi servants, and slaves. The master saw a slave or a servant as part of his *volk* (people) or as 'a sort of child of the family'.[55] The concept of a bonded extended 'family' was emphasised by the practice of *huisgodsdiens* (family devotions). By the end of the eighteenth century it had become common practice for masters to admit their most trusted slaves and servants, usually squatting or standing against a wall, to the family prayers held every day. In the master's mind the act of inviting the slave briefly into the inner sanctum of his family demonstrated his benign, paternal intent. This 'benevolence' was a counterpoint to the violence inflicted on erring servants, and it boosted the burghers' self-image as Christian colonisers of the land.[56]

Invariably, the most stable forms of paternalism were not to be found in the relationship between a master and a male slave but between a mistress and a female slave, particularly one born into the household. Slave women at the Cape seldom did hard manual labour in the fields, as happened in many other slave societies. They had duties within the home, as wet-nurse, nanny, cook, cleaner and confidante of the mistress. A senior official depicted African-born female slaves as 'the favourite slaves of the mistress, arranging and keeping everything in order'. They were 'entrusted with all that is valuable – more like companions than slaves; but the mistress rarely, and the slave never, forget their relative situations, and however familiar in private, in the presence of another due form prevails.'[57]

No slave system was ever humane and it would be a mistake to consider Cape slavery as anything but brutal. While slave women, especially, developed bonds of allegiance and trust with their 'family', they remained perpetual minors who had to sacrifice an independent family life of their own. Slave women, moreover, had to endure the sexual advances of the master class. For them the suffering of slavery was most acute, exposed as they were to both the intimate and the harshest side of the Cape form.[58] It was probably slave women who most often felt betrayed by the paternalistic relationship.

Paternalism challenged

Except for the criminal records, we do not know much about what happened when things went wrong in the paternalistic relationship. The documentation is much richer in the case of the American South. Eugene Genovese, author of a masterly account of paternalist slavery in the American South, makes a plausible distinction between the responses of house slaves and field slaves. If a master and a field slave fell out, the latter could, as Genovese puts it, 'lower his eyes, shuffle and keep control of himself'. By contrast, the house slaves lived in close daily contact with the mistress and the master. The mistress knew them well enough 'to read insubordination into a glance, a shift in tone, or in a quick motion of the shoulders'.[59]

Genovese is firmly of the belief that no evidence suggests that house slaves more readily accepted slavery than the field slaves, while much evidence exists to suggest the reverse. Psychologically and physically the house slaves were much more dependent on the master and the mistress, but they were also much more aware of their weaknesses and flaws than the field slaves. Their masters' dependence on their black slaves went hand in hand 'with gnawing intimations of the blacks' hostility, resentment and suppressed anger'.[60]

At the Cape, slavery was much more widespread than in most of the other slaveholding societies. Half the colonists owned slaves. By 1770 approximately 70 per cent of the burghers in Cape Town and of the farmers in Stellenbosch owned at least one slave. There were few very large farms with supervisors, and control was mostly very personal and direct. While there was no mass slave uprising at the Cape, apart from one in 1808, there were several cases of docile slaves suddenly erupting in a murderous rage.[61]

The British, having acquired the Cape early in the nineteenth century, reformed slavery, first by ending slave imports and then by giving government far more power to protect slaves. In 1823 the government laid down minimum standards for food, clothing and hours of work and the maximum punishments permissible, and in 1826 it made the recording of punishments compulsory and introduced a further limitation on them.

Slave women submitted many of the complaints received by the newly appointed guardian of slaves. On the eastern frontier some slaves took their mistresses to court. These developments represented a body blow to the whole paternalist order. Owners craved nothing so much as the gratitude of a slave or a servant. For a master or mistress a servant's withdrawal from a relationship presumed to be benevolent, not to mention an accusation made in court of maltreatment, was almost impossible to comprehend, except in terms of instigation by malign forces.

Developments on the eastern frontier produced a fury among white frontier women against British rule that would not abate for many decades. For them there could be no compromise with the British, no willing subjugation to their rule. The women had not left the colony as mere adjuncts of their husbands; the decision was one they had helped to make. In some cases it had been precipitated by what had happened to them personally. The Voortrekker leader Piet Uys only became politically disaffected after the arrest of his wife on charges brought by an indentured slave, which he considered malicious.[62] At least fifteen families headed by widows participated in the different trek parties.[63]

The government also intervened in ecclesiastical matters. As part of its attempt to do away with all status distinctions in order to achieve equality before the law, the British government in 1829 put an end to the widespread practice of Communion being served separately to people who were white and not white. Significantly, it was a woman, Anna Steenkamp, a niece of Piet Retief, who lodged the strongest protest. She complained that slaves were placed on an 'equal footing with Christians, contrary to the laws of God, and the natural distinction of race and religion . . . wherefore we rather withdraw in order to preserve our doctrines in purity.'[64]

It was also a woman, Olive Schreiner, later a major feminist figure in England, who realised that the expression of racial superiority by British officials towards the Afrikaners on the frontier fundamentally alienated them from the government. As a governess on farms in the districts of Colesberg and Cradock three decades after the Great Trek, she heard stories of how the trekkers had been estranged from the government by overbearing officials. She wrote:

> [What] most embittered the hearts of the colonists was the cold indifference with which they were treated, and the consciousness that they were regarded as a subject and inferior race by their rulers . . . [The] feeling of bitterness became so intense that about the year 1836 large numbers of individuals determined for ever to leave the colony and the homes they created and raise an independent state.[65]

The feeling of being scorned as inferior or ignorant incensed women in particular. They appear to have had a leading hand in the radical decision of the

Voortrekkers to sell up at a cheap price and take the risk of leaving the Cape and settling in the far interior. A British settler on the frontier wrote while the trek was getting under way: 'They fancy they are under a divine impulse', adding that 'the women seem more bent on it than the men.'[66] The resentment of a section of Afrikaner women towards the British would cast a long shadow on South African history.

Republican women

The women on the Great Trek made their presence felt in 1838 when a British force briefly annexed Port Natal (later Durban), where a section of the Voortrekkers had settled. The British commander, Major Samuel Charters, wrote that among them there were families who had been living in 'ease and comfort' but were now reduced to squalid 'poverty and wretchedness'. However, they 'bore up against these calamities with wonderful firmness, and, with very few exceptions, showed no inclination to return. They considered themselves as unjustly and harshly treated by the Colonial Government while under its jurisdiction and all they now desired from it was to leave them to their own resources and not to molest them again.' Dislike of English rule was particularly strong among the women. Charters added: 'If any of the men began to droop or lose courage, they urged them on to fresh exertions and kept alive the spirit of resistance within them.'[67]

In 1839 these trekkers proclaimed the Republic of Natalia under a Volksraad (Assembly), but in 1842 the Cape government sent a force of 250 men to Port Natal to annex the territory. In their ranks was Henry Cloete, an anglicised Cape Afrikaner, dispatched as a commissioner with the task of reconciling the trekkers to the British occupation. He announced that the Volksraad would be allowed to administer the interior districts until the British government had made a final decision about the territory's status. In July 1842 the Volksraad invited Cloete to Pietermaritzburg, and, while a hostile crowd gathered outside the building, deliberated with him. The men eventually decided to submit to British authority.

After the meeting a delegation of women subjected Cloete to a baptism of fire, with the redoubtable Susanna Smit[68] playing a leading role. She headed the delegation that confronted Cloete. He reported that the women expressed 'their fixed determination' never to yield to British authority. Instead they 'would walk out by the Draaksberg [Drakensberg] barefooted, to die in freedom, as death was dearer to them than the loss of liberty'. Angered by the men as well, they told Cloete that as a result of the battles they had fought alongside their husbands, 'they had been promised a voice in all matters concerning the state of this country'. Yet the all-male Volksraad was now submitting to the British despite the women's protests. The women's fury dismayed Cloete; he considered it 'a disgrace on their husbands to allow them such a state of freedom'.[69]

Clearly something exceptional had happened. During the nineteenth century women on both sides of the Atlantic were denied the vote, either because they owned no property or were poorly educated, or because of a supposed natural lack of aptitude for public affairs. It was only in 1893, when New Zealand granted the vote to women, that a national or colonial state enacted women's suffrage in national elections.[70] It is against this background that Henry Cloete's bewilderment must be understood.

Women were also at the heart of the early expressions of Afrikaner nationalism. The first was the uprising in 1880–1 of the Transvaal Afrikaners against the British occupation of their country, leading to a crushing British defeat at Majuba and their withdrawal from the Highveld. Olive Schreiner wrote in the early 1890s that the war was largely a 'woman's war'. Women urged their menfolk to actively resist the British authorities. 'Even in the [Cape] Colony at the distance of many hundreds of miles Afrikaner women implored sons and husbands to go to the aid of their northern kindred, while a martial ardour often far exceeding that of the males seemed to fill them.'[71]

In 1890 Schreiner painted her famous picture of the 'Boer woman'. She noted that the 'Women's Movement', as she called feminism, always desired nothing more and nothing less than to stand beside the man as his full co-labourer, and hence as his equal. The Boer woman on the farm had already attained this. Referring to Roman-Dutch law, she stated: 'The fiction of common possession of all material goods . . . is not a fiction but a reality among the Boers, and justly so, seeing that the female as often as the male contributes to the original household stock.'[72] On the farm all the domestic arrangements were her domain – slaughtering, cooking, making clothes, educating the children, and instructing them in the Christian faith and Boer traditions.

Schreiner concluded that the Boer woman 'retained the full possession of one full half of the labour of her race'. She had no intention of becoming the 'drone of society' like upper-class women in Europe, leading a parasitic life in which she is 'fed, clothed and sustained by the labours of others for the mere performance of her animal sex function', while employing others to raise her children. There was no mental chasm between the Boer woman and her male comrade, Schreiner concluded. She enjoyed a position of 'intellectual equality with her male companions, a condition which seems to constitute the highest ideal in the human sexual world'.[73]

Thus the woman not only brought to the common household an equal share of material goods, but – and Schreiner thought this infinitely more important – 'she [also] brought to the common life an equal culture.'[74] In her view there were few societies in which 'the duties and enjoyments of life are so equally divided between the sexes' as in Boer society. The Boer woman even stood side by side with the man, facing death in fighting enemies. She remarked that it was the Boer woman 'who still today [the 1890s] has a determining influence on peace or war'.

Ten years after she wrote these words Boer women, to use her phrase, did indeed play a major role in the *bittereinder* phase of the South African War. The Republican forces had suffered some disastrous defeats in the first year of the war, and by June 1900 the Transvaal burghers were ready to surrender. Rejecting this option, President M.T. Steyn of the Republic of the Orange Free State propagated the idea of a war to the bitter end. So did many of the Boer women in the two republics.

The great suffering and privation that women were prepared to endure baffled the men, both Boer and British. They hid in mountains, forests or reed-infested rivers, or wandered across the land in so-called *vrouwen laagers*, all to avoid capture and being sent to the concentration camps. Most insisted that their husbands and sons had to continue fighting, even to the death. Soldiers setting their houses on fire did not cow them. Some candidly declared that they preferred their houses to burn down than to see their husbands surrender. A British officer noted after two months of farm burning that, without exception, the women said that they would not give in.[75]

As early as March 1900 the historian G.M. Theal, who had written extensively about South African history, warned that Eurocentric gender stereotypes did not apply in South Africa: 'The women are the fiercest advocates of war to the bitter end. For independence the Boer women will send husbands and son after son to fight to the last.'[76] General Kitchener, commander-in-chief of the British forces, wrote just after assuming his post in November 1900: 'There is no doubt the women are keeping up the war and are far more bitter than the men.'[77]

Women scorned men who had given up the fight. After the British had over-run the Orange Free State in mid-1900, a Boer woman noted: '[We] think the men should be on commando instead of meekly giving up their arms to, and getting passes from, the English.'[78] In one camp the British authorities consid-ered separating *hendsoppers* (Boers who had surrendered) and women. A British officer wrote: 'The feelings between the families of men still on commando and those who have surrendered appear to be very bitter . . . and the men of the latter class have to put up with a great deal of abuse . . . from the women who call them slaves of the British and "handsoppers".' In another camp a *hendsopper* wrote of being 'unmercifully persecuted by the anti-British sex'.[79]

J.R. MacDonald, a British visitor, concluded: 'It was the *vrouw* who kept the war going on so long. It was in her heart that patriotism flamed into an all-consuming heat. She it is who returns, forgiving nothing and forgetting nothing.'[80] For many women and children, the camp was a searing experience that stayed with them for the rest of their lives. When an English woman exhorted Boer children at Maria Fischer's camp to develop a spirit of forgiveness and love for one's enemy, Fischer grimly commented: 'To my mind it is not only impossible but also undesirable.'[81]

Defeat in war also made women cling tenaciously to their culture. Indignation about British war methods prompted a Bloemfontein woman to wonder aloud whether she should continue letting her children speak the English language. Reflecting on what separated her from the English, another Free State woman came up with an answer: republicanism, history, the *taal* (language) and 'hatred of the [British] race'.[82]

In the early stages of the war the British high commissioner, Alfred Milner, remarked that the Boers loved their property more than they hated the British and would never fight for a political system; but the *bittereinder* stage of the war changed the course of South African history. At stake were the character of the

Boer people, their republican commitment, and their willingness to pay the highest price for their freedom. It was the valour of the *bittereinders* and, above all, the grim determination of the Afrikaner women to persevere until the bitter end that won the Boers universal respect as freedom fighters. Smuts and General Kitchener observed that this stand had made a vital difference. It meant, as Smuts pointed out, that 'every child to be born in South Africa was to have a proud self-respect and a more erect carriage before the nations of the world'.[83]

The Women's Monument erected outside Bloemfontein is virtually unique in paying tribute to the sacrifice of women in war, particularly the deaths in the concentration camps. It seems particularly inappropriate to consider the monument as a symbol of female subservience. It was rather the manifestation of a deep sense of indebtedness on the part of the Boer leaders, who erected it after consultation with women like R.I. (Tibbie) Steyn, the wife of former President Steyn.[84]

The women's resistance during the *bittereinder* phase is such an extraordinary event that the search for an adequate explanation will continue.[85] Here one can only note that it cannot be understood without giving full weight to the extraordinary position Afrikaner women enjoyed in the household as a result of Roman-Dutch law, their partnership with their husbands in running the farms, and the development of what Jan Smuts called 'the Boers [as] an intensely domestic people'.[86] The violation of their domestic space and the wilful destruction of the farms made it impossible for women to conceive of defeat and subordination to British rule.

Women's political activism did not subside after the peace treaty had been signed. When Union was formed in 1910 the nationalist leader J.B.M. (Barry) Hertzog noticed the large number of Afrikaner women in his audiences. He concluded: 'They stood firm in maintaining language, life, morals and traditions.' They 'feel more than the men', he remarked.[87]

After the Rebellion of 1914–15, Afrikaner women marched in protest against the jail sentence passed on General C.R. de Wet and other leaders of the rebellion and the stiff fines that were imposed on many of their followers. Prominent Afrikaner women had initiated the protest, including Hendrina Joubert, wife of Commandant-General Piet Joubert, and F.G. (Nettie) Eloff, a grandchild of President Paul Kruger. They called on 'mothers and sisters' to assemble in

Church Square in Pretoria. Some 4 000 women marched to the Union Buildings, where they presented a petition to Lord Buxton, the governor-general.[88] After the rebellion Hertzog declared: 'Perhaps they were the greatest rebels.' He concluded with a warning: 'If one ignores the voice of Afrikaner women, one would land this country in a political hell.'[89]

Women and modernisation

South Africa entered its period of industrialisation with the discovery of minerals in the last quarter of the nineteenth century. There was a rapid growth of towns and cities, an expansion of trade and industry, and the modernisation of the education system. By the early 1870s three distinct categories of Afrikaner women could be discerned. The first were girls and women in affluent families who were educated in English and were increasingly using English in their correspondence. The second category included poorly educated women in towns who were unable to read or write properly in either English or Dutch. Thirdly, there were the large majority of women, living mainly on subsistence farms, who had little schooling and spoke only Afrikaans.

Afrikaner women were all profoundly affected by developments between the 1870s, when modernisation began to accelerate, and 1930, when white women received the vote. The most important was a change in the law of inheritance in order to promote the stability of landownership and capital accumulation. In 1874 the Cape government abolished partible inheritance, based on the rule of equal shares, and replaced it with primogeniture. Alfred Milner introduced primogeniture in the ex-republics after the Anglo-Boer War, despite considerable opposition.[90] Although the convention of equal shares persisted for some time, it was no longer obligatory to have children equally share half the estate. Invariably the result was that the daughters received a smaller share than had been the case under Roman-Dutch law. Increasingly they had to move to the towns and cities in search of a livelihood.

Another development was the modernisation of education. Until the early 1870s the level of education provided to Afrikaner girls was very low, while that of boys, with the exception of two or three schools, was not much better. The leading figures in the Dutch Reformed Church interested in educational reform believed that an English-medium education was the only realistic option.

Insisting that girls had a right to a proper education, N.J. Hofmeyr, professor of the Theological School at Stellenbosch, in 1874 pleaded for government assistance in view of the fact that 'the civilisation of a people depends more upon the culture of the women than the men'.[91]

The leading reformer of education was the British-born Andrew Murray, moderator of the DRC and minister of the Wellington congregation, who attracted excellent American teachers to the private schools for Afrikaans girls belonging to his church. He also helped to found the Huguenot Seminary which opened in Wellington in 1874. This institution would later establish Bloemhof High School for girls in Stellenbosch and would also acquire a girls' high school in Paarl, later called La Rochelle, as a branch institution.

The Afrikaans journalist and writer MER, who was in high school in the early 1890s, argued that there was a clear difference between the British and the American female teachers sent out to teach in South Africa. American teachers would never break down a child's self-respect by regarding with contempt the language he or she spoke. British teachers, by contrast, were inclined to be status conscious and were quick to disparage Afrikaans.[92]

From the 1890s education for Afrikaner girls made rapid strides. Growing numbers enrolled in secondary schools, and by the end of the century some were going on to college where they received BA degrees. With men reluctant to become teachers, teaching was one of the few careers open to women. In 1905 the senior official of the Cape education department reported: 'In truth it has become the proper thing among the fairly well-to-do farming class that the daughters of the family on completing their education should go out and teach for three or four years.'[93]

Yet another development was the rise of nationalist organisations and publications. It is instructive to conceive of nationalism as built on the ideas of a patriarchal family and a fraternity or brotherhood of men. In this scheme of thought the traditions of the 'forefathers' are passed down through the generations to young men, who are deemed to be the heroic protectors of women and of the purity of the nation. Women were seen as the reproducers of the nation and the protectors of tradition and morality. Men had the obligation to shield them from public controversy and embarrassment, while women had to devote themselves to the welfare of their husbands and children.[94]

The architects of the first Afrikaner political movement were nationalists in this mould. It was led by S.J. du Toit, minister in the town of Paarl in the western Cape, who, together with seven other men, founded the Genootskap vir Regte Afrikaners (GRA) in 1875. The GRA published the Afrikaans paper *Di Patriot* and several Afrikaans books, including a history and a volume of poems. From the outset *Di Patriot* refused to publish poems submitted in Afrikaans by women, which raises the question whether the decision was informed primarily by misogyny or the special circumstances in which the GRA operated.

Misogyny characterised the thinking of Du Toit, who wrote the following, citing Nehemiah 13 verses 23–28:

> Seduction and degeneration usually slips in by means of the woman. Virtually every heresy counts women among its first adherents and most fiery disseminators. When they could not eradicate our nationality openly in our church and the state they directed their fire at our families. They took our daughters and educated them in American and other schools, in order to denationalise the future mothers of our generation and their children.[95]

Du Toit was influenced by conservative Protestant Dutch literature of the nineteenth century which was suffused with old-fashioned biblical misogyny.[96] However, his comments must also be seen against the background of the GRA's objectives of elevating Afrikaans to the level of a literary language and of rehabilitating lower-income white Afrikaans-speakers. Poems sent from Huguenot Seminary in the neighbouring town of Wellington were unlikely to serve any of these purposes. Almost all the girls there came from upper-class homes. At best they considered Afrikaans as a medium for light-hearted fun; at worst they saw it as an impure language fit only for working-class or Coloured people.

The manifestation of an aggressive British imperialism in the Jameson Raid and the South African War shocked Cape Afrikaner girls who attended English-medium private schools. Among them were Petronella van Heerden, who would become a physician and feminist, and M.E. Rothmann, who would later write under the name MER. Later in life they each gave an account of how they suddenly discovered that underlying the actions of imperialist politicians was a profound contempt for 'Boers' or Afrikaners. Both of them turned to a variant of Afrikaner nationalism that rejected the misogyny of Du Toit and some of his allies.

During the South African War some 10 000 Cape Afrikaners became rebels by joining the republican forces, but the Afrikaner men were quiescent. It was Afrikaner women who organised and attended the fourteen protest meetings in the Colony that took place during the war at which imperialism was denounced. After the war the women regrouped first. Well before men founded the first cultural organisations, they established welfare organisations to address the needs of poor Afrikaners. These were the Afrikaanse Christelike Vrouevereniging in the Cape Colony, the Oranje Vrouevereniging in the Orange River Colony, and the Suid-Afrikaanse Vrouefederasie in the Transvaal Colony. Women ran these organisations entirely separately from the Dutch Reformed Church's all-male hierarchy.[97]

Women and the vote

Although Afrikaner women held a strong and secure place in the family, particularly on the farms, their public position was weakened by a long history of discrimination. From the beginning of European settlement at the Cape a gendered definition of political rights and offices applied, with access to office in the state and church open only to European men. This continued under British rule. Women were excluded from the vote in both the liberal Cape constitution of 1853 and the constitutions of the Boer republics.

By the end of the century opposition to women's rights in South Africa had grown. It was probably a response to growing assertiveness by women in other parts of the Empire. In 1898 laughter greeted a suggestion in the Cape Parliament that women be allowed to vote.[98] Paul Kruger never contemplated enfranchising Afrikaner women, thus creating a clear electoral majority, which would have been a masterstroke against the efforts of Milner to provoke war. John X. Merriman, a leading liberal politician, made what a historian called the 'characteristic assertion' that women were quite unfit to exercise the vote.[99] Of all the leading politicians President Steyn stood virtually alone as a strong and outspoken champion of the vote for white women.[100]

By the turn of the century Merriman made an intriguing statement: 'Oddly enough in South Africa the [Afrikaner] women have always exercised a great influence. I say "oddly" because they are so utterly opposed to the modern view of "women's rights".'[101] By 'the modern view' he meant the views of the suffragette movement, which originated in Britain in the last decades of the nineteenth century. Frustrated by pervasive gender discrimination, the suffragettes formed a mass movement of predominantly urban, middle-class women to win equal rights and opportunities for women.

Very few Afrikaner women joined when English-speaking women in South Africa began to campaign for the enfranchisement of women early in the twentieth century. For a start they suspected that the suffragettes in South Africa were above all interested in projecting the extension of the vote to women as part and parcel of the programme of imperial reform which had served as a justification for the war in South Africa.

Afrikaner women only began pressing for the vote in the late 1920s. Both Olive Schreiner and MER, who had become one of the first full-time social workers, made revealing comments about the reason why women in some societies refrain from insisting on political rights for their own sex. After telling the story of an illuminating conversation she had with a traditional African woman who had stoically endured polygamy and other disadvantages, Schreiner recorded this important observation: no women of any race or class would ever rise in a revolt or attempt to bring about a revolutionary adjustment to their situation in their community while the community's welfare required their submission. That stance would only end when changing conditions in a society made women's acquiescence in the discrimination against them 'no longer necessary or desirable'.[102]

In 1922 MER wrote that Afrikaner women believed there were greater priorities than getting the vote. Of overriding importance were regaining the freedom of Afrikaners as a 'conquered people', the taalstryd, and addressing the impoverishment, 'neglect and degeneration [of Afrikaner people]'. The vote for women did not appear to be an important factor in addressing these grave crises. MER added that the campaign to enfranchise women had been imported from Britain, and that in South Africa it had been propagated by English-speaking women who 'cared little about the issues of vital concern to Afrikaners'.[103]

Afrikaner women refused to join the suffragette movement in great numbers but many gave enthusiastic support to associations for women's rights founded within the framework of the Afrikaner nationalist movement. After the Vroue Nasionale Party had been formed its mouthpiece, *Die Burgeres,* remarked that the NP leadership had not anticipated the force it would unleash when it called on women to organise their own political party.[104]

In 1930 white women were enfranchised, but this important step was soon eclipsed by Fusion in 1934 and the rise of a radical Afrikaner nationalist movement dominated by men. Men now led the struggle for the advancement of Afrikaans and the rehabilitation of the poor, leaving church membership, charity work and domestic chores to Afrikaner women. Between 1934 and 1994 fewer than ten Afrikaner women went to Parliament and Rina Venter, the first woman to become a cabinet minister, was only appointed in 1989, the same year that the men in her party decided to give up exclusive white power.

Conclusion

Along with other women on both sides of the Atlantic, Afrikaner women were denied public office and the vote for more than two centuries after the founding of the settlement at the Cape. Nevertheless their legal position was probably stronger than that of any women in Europe or the European colonies. They could claim a fixed part of the estate and played a major role as partners of their husbands in running the farms. Their role was crucial in the forging of a racially exclusive Afrikaner people and a predominantly white church. Women demanded a share of the decision-making on the Great Trek. The last two years of the South African War were above all characterised by the unbending refusal of the republican women to surrender, something unique in the history of European settlement.

From the 1870s onwards several developments, especially the introduction of primogeniture and urbanisation, undermined their position. Afrikaner women, however, refused to join in the suffragette movement as a separate cause, because they considered the *taalstryd* and the rehabilitation of the Afrikaner poor as more important than promoting women's rights.

2.

Afrikaner frontiers

This chapter discusses the main frontiers opened up by the Afrikaner[1] settlers in southern Africa. These frontiers were zones where processes of colonisation occurred in a situation marked by a weak political authority and quite often by conflicting claims to the land of two or more distinct societies existing there. The Afrikaner frontier is best understood by contrasting it with the American West of the nineteenth century and with the gradual westward expansion of the Xhosa people between the Mbashe and Sundays rivers on the south-east coast of southern Africa in earlier centuries.

The American West in the nineteenth century was predominantly the scene of capitalist expansion. Initial white settlement was quickly followed by commercial and capitalist development and the growth of new communities, backed by the Federal government and connected with the heartland through the transportation revolution. With the help of these resources, the indigenous peoples of America were quickly expelled or exterminated. By contrast, the indigenous Xhosa people of southern Africa extended their particular social order and mode of subsistence production in a process of inclusive expansion. A self-sufficient pastoral people whose land was controlled by the community rather than by the individual, the Xhosa gradually established mastery over new territory and incorporated previously independent Khoikhoi herders into their society. During the initial stages of absorption, the Khoikhoi were relegated to a subservient role, but biological mixing occurred freely and the Khoikhoi did not develop into separate caste; rather, their descendants became Xhosa.[2]

The Afrikaner frontier fits in somewhere between the American West and Xhosa expansion. It was a mixed capitalist and subsistence frontier but with the

subsistence element heavily predominant. The Afrikaners introduced the concept of individually owned land and the idea of the family existing separately
as a patriarchal unit while at the same time regarding itself as part of a distinct
European cultural group and kinship network.

In southern Africa the initial occupation by near-subsistence farmers was
only very gradually followed by commercial development, in some cases after
50 years or more. Few in numbers and not backed by a strong central government, the near-subsistence farmers lacked the resources to sweep away before
them the developed and organised Bantu-speaking indigenous peoples; indeed,
extensive subsistence farming practised by a small white settler population dictated the incorporation of large numbers of black workers into their society.
These Africans formed a client and, later, a labouring caste; their descendants did
not become Afrikaners.

The American, Xhosa and Afrikaner variants of frontier expansion are by
themselves enough reason to make any generalisations about the nature of
political institutions or class relations on the frontier questionable, if not invalid.
The focus should much rather be on different frontier processes which accompanied different types of settlement and colonisation. Even if the focus were
limited to the Afrikaner frontier experience, generalisations would be difficult to
make. For it is clear that within the ambit of European expansion in southern
Africa different frontier societies were produced that had to contend with different
political and economic environments. A distinction can be made here between
three classic types of white frontiersmen.

Firstly, there was the transcolonial frontiersman who existed, as it were, beyond
the frontier. Here one thinks of the small number of English traders who established a trading post at Port Natal in 1824[3] and of Coenraad de Buys,[4] an Afrikaner who became the patriarch of a distinct mixed group, the Buys Bastaards.
Living on their own among Bantu-speaking peoples far beyond the colonial
border, these white men married black wives, adopted indigenous customs, and
built up followings like African chiefs. A loss of European identity occurred, as
these whites lacked the numbers and institutions to withstand the pressures of
a vigorous indigenous culture.

Secondly, there was the pioneer Afrikaner frontier society living on the frontier
that was opening up. There a community of Afrikaners coexisted in a frontier

zone with other ethnic groups competing for the land and its resources. There was usually a rough balance of power between the groups, and for a considerable period no group succeeded in establishing undisputed control over the area. Such a phase existed during the first three or four decades of intense contact between the Afrikaners and the Xhosa on the Cape eastern frontier of the late eighteenth century.[5]

Thirdly, there was the settled frontier society living on what can be called the closing frontier. Here the consolidation of settlement had advanced much further, though both the pioneer and the settled societies should be considered as frontier societies in the sense that they were involved in processes of settlement and colonisation in a context marked by a relative lack of established power. From the Afrikaner point of view, settlement embraced notions of occupation of the land and control over all its resources; colonisation involved not only the conquest of land but also the incorporation of the indigenous peoples; while lack of power usually had two dimensions: ineffective control by the white government over its own frontier offshoot (the periphery) and the inability of any one of the communities to establish its hegemony in the frontier zone.

For Africans, as Martin Legassick has pointed out, the frontier meant something quite different: it was the first stage of a process in which their political power was eroded as they were absorbed into plural communities, and in which their material and social bases were transformed through their integration into a market economy linked with the industrialising and capitalist economy of Europe.[6]

This chapter is concerned with the most significant processes related to the opening and, more importantly, the closing of the frontier – the transition from a pioneering frontier to a settled frontier. On the pioneering frontier, with its seemingly abundant land, the Afrikaners could start farming without much capital. Because it was far away from settled white society, they could take political and military action with the minimum of interference from the government. This situation gradually changed as the frontier began to close. The closing of the frontier cannot be reduced to a series of dates or a set of processes that came in any given chronological order. It is more accurate to think of a multiple closure or a series of closures based on different aspects of the frontier.

These included a growing scarcity of land and other resources which in some cases led to farmers leaving their land and in other cases to a shift from subsistence to commercial farming; growing social stratification in the society as discrete 'races' or ethnic groups merged into a plural society with a given set of caste or class relationships; and political closure, involving the imposition of a single source of authority. Although not always interconnected, there was some link between the various 'closures', as will be seen below.

My generalisations about the frontier processes draw mostly from my research on the Cape eastern frontier during the period 1770 to 1812. In the prevalence of near-subsistence farming and the absence of a strong political authority, the frontier which opened up there between 1770 and 1800 was in many ways similar to the Transorangia frontier pioneered by the Bastaards from 1800 to 1830 and the Afrikaner frontier in Transorangia and the Transvaal from 1830 to 1870. From about 1800, the Cape eastern frontier began to close after a much-stronger central government had assumed control and land became scarce. These conditions were also found in the Free State (Transorangia) and Transvaal after the conquest of the African chiefdoms there in the second half of the nineteenth century.

The opening of the frontier: Pioneering Afrikaner society

Land and near-subsistence farming

The opening of the Afrikaner frontier had to do, above all, with the initial occupation of land in order to start near-subsistence farming in a most extensive way and with the first phases of incorporation of labourers from indigenous societies, either through inducements or local controls. The crucial feature of the pioneering stage of the frontier was abundance of land, near-subsistence farming, and the absence of regional markets. For whites, land was abundant during the first 130 years of the settlement because the Khoikhoi could be easily dispossessed. In fact, dispossession occurred almost from the beginning of European settlement. For the Khoikhoi, the loss of land was not sudden or dramatic. In the Cape Peninsula and its vicinity the Europeans practised extensive agriculture and so the transhumant, pastoralist Khoikhoi could exist on productive land lying between European farms. Gradually, however, the Khoikhoi were squeezed out, and by the end of the seventeenth century those who wished to retain their independence had to retreat into the interior, beyond the first range of mountains.

In 1717, when the granting of freehold land ceased, there were just over 400 European farms occupying an area of 75 square miles out of a total landmass of 2 500 square miles.[7] Yet the Europeans considered the colony fully settled and began to speak of a land crisis. But a safety valve opened when the government started to issue grazing licences to stock farmers and lifted the ban on Europeans and other freemen bartering cattle with the Khoikhoi. Out of these licences evolved the loan-farm system, which allowed a stock farmer the use of a minimum of 6 000 acres of land for a small annual fee of 24 rixdollars, which was equal to the value of two cows. The *opstal* (fixed improvements) of a loan farm, though not the land, could be purchased. The average price of a loan-farm *opstal* during the mid-eighteenth century ranged from 300 to 500 guilders, compared to 6 000 to 10 000 guilders for an arable farm. Whereas the average cost of a working arable farm before 1770 was 15 000 guilders (including the price of the land), a stock farmer needed only about 1 000 guilders to get started.[8] For Europeans without any capital, the pioneering frontier offered the opportunity of becoming *bywoners*. These were tenant farmers who looked after their patrons' stock on a system of shares, which was often a first step towards an independent farming career.

On this frontier a peculiar lifestyle evolved after the beginning of the eighteenth century which, in some remote regions, lasted until the 1940s. A special class of colonist, called trekboers, came into existence, who practised an economy in which hunting was intimately connected with transhumant stock farming. In a country where game abounded, the pioneer could penetrate the interior with the assurance that he would always find food. Through hunting he also often obtained almost his only cash income from the sale of ivory and ostrich feathers, whips, *sjamboks*, hides and horns. These trekboers regularly trekked during the dry season to other pastures. Often accompanied by their families, they lived temporarily in wagons and tents, or in simple huts of reed or rush mats.[9]

In conditions of land abundance, European pastoral farmers could set themselves up on the frontier with little capital, practising near-subsistence farming on a most extensive scale and drawing on the indigenous peoples for labour.

The opening of new frontiers was propelled by a complex mix of political, economic and social factors. Politically, expansion offered a refuge from the controls
of government and the wealthy farmers in the Cape Peninsula and vicinity.
Socially, it was an escape from a potentially catastrophic loss of status: with
slaves providing the manual and skilled labour in the western regions of the
colony, the European who entered service lost not only his independence but
also his standing as a member of the dominant class.

There was also an economic incentive. Expansion into near-subsistence farming was, as Leonard Guelke has shown,[10] not profitable from a commercial point
of view. However, apart from all the political and social advantages, the pioneer
farmer who directly exploited the existing resources and abandoned them when
they were exhausted could support himself with much less effort than the commercial farmer, who had to increase yields through manuring and weeding. As
long as the frontier was still open, it was more cost-effective for the frontiersmen to expand production by enlarging the size of their grazing lands than by
using the already occupied area more intensively.

As a result of all these considerations, the Afrikaner outside Cape Town considered independent farming as the only suitable career for a freeman. As an
administrator remarked, 'One sends no children away from home . . . prejudice
prevents one's children from serving another. They intermarry and then they
must have a farm.'[11] Until the late nineteenth century, whites nurtured the expec-
tation that cheap land would be acquired on the open frontier. In 1812 the first
circuit court which visited the frontier reported that 'all the young people of
which many of the houses are full, have no other prospect than the breeding
of cattle . . . all look forward to becoming graziers, and no person forms for
himself any other plan of livelihood.'[12]

The northward expansion of the trekboers in the nineteenth century and
subsequently the Great Trek, which started in 1834, create a vast new pioneering frontier. In the Voortrekker states of the Orange Free State and the Transvaal, the Cape system of land tenure was retained. The recognised method of
initial settlement was the occupation of land not yet taken up by other whites.
The new occupant would subsequently register his farm with the authorities;
his title was subject to the payment of an annual quitrent. In the South African
Republic (Transvaal) the quitrent was ten shillings for a farm up to about

8 000 acres, which was the average size, and a further two shillings and six-pence for every additional hundred morgen. Under this system some colonists soon appropriated vast tracts of land. However, there were also considerable numbers of trekboers, especially in the Transvaal, who chose not to take up land, although the first settlers in Natal and the Transvaal were entitled to two farms as their 'burgher rights'.

Landholders welcomed men who could assist them in defence, increase their income on a sharecropping basis, and provide some company on the isolated farms. As one such trekboer later explained: 'There were many men, owners of good farms, who were only too glad if you came and stayed with them. You might very well be wealthier than the owner, and "you were equally boss".'[13] These men did not even consider themselves *bywoners* since their position was clearly not associated with social or economic inferiority as long as land was plentiful.

Caste and class relationships

On the pioneering frontier a plural society began to develop with its own caste and class relationships. Here farmers had to find labour in a situation where there were no market incentives or government-driven labour compulsion. This meant that they were dependent on their own resources to attract labourers and induce them to stay in their service. However, this was especially difficult because the low man–land ratio enabled the indigenous societies to coexist independently with the pioneer settlers in the frontier zone. In the absence of any institutional resources, the pioneer farmers were generally unable to command unfree labour on a large scale. However, at the same time, the very absence of institutional controls enabled them to exercise a great degree of local control over their few clients and servants.

The rapid expansion of the trekboers in the eighteenth century extended a slender European superstructure over a vast area. On their unenclosed farms the trekboers needed dependable labour to herd their large flocks of sheep and cattle. They could not always acquire this by mere coercion as the opportuni-ties for flight or theft were too great. Often a patron–client relationship evolved in which there was some quid pro quo for the contribution of the master in dealing justly with his clients and protecting them, and that of the client in the services he rendered. Trekboers would entrust a portion of their stock to a Khoi-khoi clan, or clansmen would work for a year or two on a farm before returning to their people.[14]

As a way of inducing indigenous people to serve them, frontiersmen could offer security in a country where beasts of prey roamed freely and where San (Bushmen) 'raiders' threatened the small herding communities. In the clientship tradition of Khoikhoi society it was common for a poor and insecure man to seek the protection of a patron to enable him to build up his livestock. A Khoikhoi client entering a colonist's service retained his livestock, and this was supple-mented by payments in kind which he received for tending his master's cattle and accompanying him (or going in his place) on commando against Xhosa and San.

Three decades after trekboers had begun to settle in the frontier region of Camdeboo (Graaff-Reinet district), the Khoikhoi still possessed considerable numbers of livestock. An *opgaaf* (census) of 1798 lists between 1 300 and 1 400 Khoikhoi in the district, owning 140 horses, 7 571 cattle and 30 557 sheep. One of these clients later told an official that until the turn of the century he and his clansmen living with the trekboers had nothing to complain of – 'until that time the Hottentots were boors [farmers] and kept on their masters' land large flocks of their own'.[15]

In such cases the transition from independent herder to client of a trekboer was not traumatic. The client retained his stock and maintained the bonds with his clan or kinsmen, preferably settling with them on the same farm. The latter arrangement evidently occurred on a large scale, for one of the major problems of the trekboers was the uneven distribution of labour. This happened because Khoikhoi refused to separate from their kinsmen who had settled with them on a farm. Thus the pioneering frontier, rather than being a place where new social and cultural institutions originated, was one where the disparate groups were often successful in maintaining conditions and institutions similar to those exist-ing before contact.[16]

Ultimately it was the prevailing balance of power which determined whether on a particular frontier Africans could retain a large measure of independence or whether whites could impose the forms of involuntary labour known in the settled parts of the colony. Because this power balance differed so sharply from one frontier to another, there existed a whole spectrum of labour relationships, ranging from those which involved almost a form of parity in status to others which rested purely on local coercion.

There is evidence of the former especially in the northern Transvaal, where Afrikaners began to settle in the 1840s. Here the sparseness of the pioneer population and their inability to subjugate the stronger African chiefdoms strengthened the bargaining power of African labour. Consequently, the frontiersmen had to provide considerable incentives to Africans in order to acquire their services. In their hunting and raiding activities the Soutpansberg frontiersmen employed Africans in what can be called partnership relations. *Swart skuts* (black marksmen) were entrusted with guns by white patrons to engage in elephant hunting. H.W. Struben, who arrived in the Soutpansberg in 1857, gave the following description: 'Each hunter, according to his recognised value, was given a certain number of carriers to take his truck in, and the ivory out, and the hunters got a percentage on the ivory delivered. Some of these men were good elephant shooters and made lots of money.'[17]

By the 1860s so many Africans had acquired guns that they formed a distinct stratum of the hunting community of the Soutpansberg. The problem facing the whites was to ensure the loyalty of these *swart skuts* at the head of hunting teams, something which could be secured if the system was allowed to evolve into some permanent form of clientship, with rewards roughly commensurate with the services rendered. Conflicting interests within the white community, based on competition for labour, often prevented the formation of such stable relationships. The desertion of black marksmen who kept their masters' guns indicated that the reward of hunt labour was insufficient. Eventually they transferred their allegiance to Venda chiefs, who launched a series of raids on the white settlement. Having lost their monopoly of guns, the Europeans were forced by the late 1860s to abandon the entire Soutpansberg district in the northern Transvaal.

However, the Soutpansberg experience was unusual. When Afrikaners had settled an area more fully, it was easier to dictate terms to labourers, maintain control, and track down those who absconded. But the increase in the number of employers also brought in its wake a greater element of competition and the risk of desertion to other masters. One of the perennial problems of white frontiersmen was the shortage of labour amid an apparently abundant supply. With labour unevenly distributed, employers constantly tried to entice servants from other farms.

By the end of the eighteenth century, when the eastern frontier was fully settled, the Graaff-Reinet local authorities issued the first pass regulations to control Khoikhoi labour. They were directed specifically at countering the practice of farmers enticing servants away from other farms.[18] However, because the district authorities did not have the means to enforce these controls, the master's dominance over his servants depended mainly on the extent to which he could offset the labourer's economic mobility with his own power.

The *inboek* system (indentureship) evolved out of the need to acquire a more stable labour force. Indentured labour was quite distinct from client labour and much nearer to mere coercion on the spectrum of labour relationships. It sprang from the incorporation of conquered Khoikhoi people into a society used to slave labour. Since children of a Khoikhoi mother and a slave father were legally free, frontiersmen in 1721 petitioned the government that such children should be indentured for a number of years. The government did not respond to this request, but in 1775, when labour shortages became critical in the south-western Cape, it allowed the indenturing of such children in the Stellenbosch district until their twenty-fifth year. By the end of the eighteenth century, the informal indenturing of all Khoikhoi children (including those who did not have slave fathers) was widespread.

The indenture system can be regarded as a quasi-institutional form of labour. As with slavery, the government legitimised the indenturing of legally free indigenous children. However, the masters' enforcement of their legal claims on indentured labourers depended on their own resources. Because they were so personally involved in the indenturing of children, frontiersmen tried to give the system a cloak of paternalism. The rationalisation in which this paternalism was rooted was that binding native children (and, indirectly, their families as well) to a period of service was justified because their destitute condition required the care and protection of a master; in exchange for this trouble and expense they could be assumed to have incurred the duty of protected service.

Frontier paternalism was soon extended from child to adult labour, with the master arguing that they could make claims on their adult dependants in return for accepting responsibilities towards them. Their claim 'he is mine' in fact meant 'he is my responsibility, he is attached to me, he works for me'. In turn, among labourers there was a paradoxical mixture of, on the one hand, resentment towards an oppressor who had taken away their land and exploited their labour, and, on the other, respect for their master's superior wealth and power. The words 'he is *my baas*' could indicate as much an identification with the master as a subservient relationship.[19]

However, especially where adults were involved, this subservient relationship ultimately rested on coercion. When the Afrikaners were faced with the Xhosa and Zulu people, who were much more resilient than the Khoikhoi, they acknowledged that paternalist inducements were not enough: force was needed to acquire labour. As a frontiersman in Natal expressed it: 'There are no other means to rule the [Africans] but by fear; and [Africans] will not work for the white men unless they know that they will be punished when they refused.'[20]

The pioneering frontier was thus the scene of local coercion, different from the institutional coercion of the closing frontier, where the state and the market played a growing part in providing labour. Commandos were raised on the pioneering frontier in the first instance to retrieve stolen cattle, but soon the procurement of child labour became an important additional activity. Sometimes paternalist assumptions were involved. On the eastern frontier, where commandos were mounted to exterminate the San, frontiersmen brought back San children and indentured them on the grounds that their parents had been killed and that this would prevent them from starving.[21]

In other cases the paternalist assumptions were absent. In Natal, where the Voortrekkers settled in the late 1830s, the 300 or so burghers who participated in the so-called Cattle Commando received permission beforehand to capture four native children each.[22] On the open frontier of the Transvaal, the Voortrekkers also resorted to indenturing not only orphans but also children captured on raids by commandos or bartered by chiefs or their parents in periods of poor harvests and starvation. In parts of the Transvaal, the trade in indentured children was common practice.[23]

In some cases there was also coerced adult labour, particularly in areas where the Voortrekkers had established control over small and broken chiefdoms that were only gradually beginning to recover from the ravages of the Difaqane the wars accompanying the rise of Shaka's Zulu kingdom. A particular form of adult forced labour in these conditions was tribute labour extracted from smaller homesteads, which for short periods were compelled to provide additional hands for agriculture.

But because the power resources of the pioneering farmers were weak, purely coercive relations were unstable and often the means defeated the ends. Fear and intimidation as the basis of labour compliance meant both a pervasive insecurity for workers confronted by their masters' power and, for that reason, frequent desertions. Labour relations without any bond of interest or loyalty gave rise, in the words of a frontier landdrost, to 'the faithlessness of such Hottentots towards those whom they regard not as their masters but as their executioners, and whom they serve only through hunger or fear'.[24] Thus a vicious circle arose in which the very consequences of forced labour required further coercive measures.

Frontiersmen unable to assert themselves sometimes looked to the government for help. By the end of the eighteenth century, a field-cornet, writing on behalf of some remote Stellenbosch farmers, proposed to the governor a solution which was unusual but reflected a common frustration:

> It is my humble request to your Honour to enact an ordinance prohibiting the Hottentots who are presently in this district from maintaining their kraals, and expelling them from there . . . Thus I request that the Hottentots who have entered service should be put in leg-irons for a time when they steal or desert so that this nation can be tamed a little, as they are extremely devious. Once their conduct has improved sufficiently, the leg-irons might be removed.[25]

However, in a colony where there was just a small market for agricultural produce, near-subsistence farming predominated. The market was so small that the frontiersmen did not make a concerted effort to find long-term solutions to their labour problems. It was only when commercial opportunities became available on the closing frontier that they sought to harness the labour of Africans more effectively.

The social stratification of the pioneering frontier was weakly developed.

Khoikhoi and San, and, to a lesser extent, those Bantu-speaking Africans over whom control had also been established, were compressed into an undifferentiated servile caste regarded as belonging to an inferior order of people. However, blacks who had not yet been subordinated were considered more as alien than inferior. Predominant in the Afrikaner frontiersmen's perception was cultural chauvinism rather than an immutable belief in their biological superiority. The Voortrekkers most commonly regarded Bantu-speakers as cunning and cruel 'savages' and 'heathens'.[26] They strongly objected to mixing, but this was because they feared above all that social equality would have dangerous political and economic consequences. This sentiment was well expressed by the Lydenburg authorities in 1860, when they rejected the position of missionaries that all Christians are equal. They declared that 'to expound the doctrine that confirmed Christian natives are of equal status with white men will only have the result that converts, and those who are not converts, will become yet more arrogant, haughty and untameable [*ontembaar*] than previously'.[27]

But even all white men were not equals in the full sense of the word. At the pinnacle of white society was a dominant class of landholders who were fairly successful in ensuring that their progeny acquired a similar status. They tended to look down upon the landless poor in white society. However, they preferred to take on landless whites as *bywoners* rather than Bastaards or Africans; at the same time these poorer whites tended to identify vigorously with the dominant Europeans and to secure their protection.[28] It was only when land became exhausted that class strains became prominent in white society.

The political order

The political order on the pioneering frontier was characterised by the lack of a single controlling authority. The expansion of near-subsistence farmers over a vast area ruled by a commercial company only interested in the Cape as a halfway station for its ships had profound implications for the political order. In order to maximise profits, the Dutch East India Company kept its complement at the Cape as small as possible. In the 1790s, the last years of Company rule, there was a garrison of only a thousand men stationed at Cape Town. Any attempt by the government to improve political control was frustrated by the dispersed state of the population, which made tax collection a difficult task. Consequently, the government was unable to provide services and afford protection to the pioneering frontier, and the pioneers had to rely on themselves for political and military action.[29] This in turn produced a great measure of individualism and some frontier anarchy. Thus the lack of government control was directly related to extensive subsistence farming and low (white) population densities.

The establishment in 1786 of the Graaff-Reinet district, an area as large as Portugal, only nominally increased the government's control over the frontier. The landdrost of Graaff-Reinet was assisted by only four or five *ordonnantie ruiters* (mounted police). He had to rely on local burghers called *veldwachtmeesters* (later field-cornets) to ensure compliance with the law in their respective divisions. But the field-cornets were dependent on their fellow colonists and normally chose to uphold the latter's interests. In a situation where colonists had free access to guns and considered it their right to fire on raiders, the landdrost could not remotely claim to monopolise the use of force. The first landdrosts of Graaff-Reinet despaired of instilling in the colonists a respect for their office and the law. In 1786, Landdrost Woeke remarked that unless he was aided by 50 or 60 soldiers, 'the rot will continue . . . and if not suppressed will increase to such an extent that everyone will act arbitrarily and do everything of his own sweet will'.[30] In fact, the only lever the government had was its monopoly of the ammunition supply. This was used to quell rebellions and forestall frontier wars, but effective control over the Afrikaners on the eastern frontier was not established until 1800 when the British government, which had taken over the Cape Colony in 1795, stationed a contingent of troops there.

The lack of government control was compounded by the fragmented nature of both African and Afrikaner societies. An African chief identified primarily with his own small community. In matters of trade and external relations, he frequently regarded the interests of his chiefdom as being in conflict with those of other chiefdoms in the region. Like the Native Americans on the New England frontier, the Khoikhoi or Bantu-speaking people lacked a community of interests or a feeling of racial or national unity.[31]

There was also disunity in Afrikaner society, but not of the same sort. Although there is a danger of overemphasising it, Afrikaners had a sense of belonging to a distinct group comprising individuals with a common racial and cultural background and a similar legal status as freemen. This was both cause and effect of a high rate of endogamy, a sense that physical appearance was a badge of group membership, and an identification with European (Christian) civilisation.[32] The disunity that did exist was the result of the disintegrative effect which the expansion of subsistence farming had on frontier society. Afrikaners on the frontier had little to bind them together politically except the commandos assembled to capture land, to seize cattle or retrieve those which were stolen, and occasionally to acquire child labour. The South African frontier certainly did not produce the same loyalty to a national government which F.J.Turner argued the American frontier did. In the eighteenth century, frontier colonists' requests for the extension of the colonial borders had limited objectives: they wanted a school and a church so they might remain part of the European cultural and kinship network; they desired to be incorporated into the landholding system of the colony in order to legitimise their occupation of the land; and they needed the government's sanction and its supplies of ammunition for commandos against indigenous enemies. They certainly did not intend to invoke a strong government which might protect their labourers against abuse or prevent them from acting against their enemies as they wished.

Government weakness meant that Afrikaner landholders on the frontier sought to establish some local control in order to secure their property and pursue their political goals. Occasionally they collaborated with Africans, sometimes against other Africans but on occasion against whites, since there was some uncertainty of status on the pioneering frontier. As Martin Legassick has phrased it, 'White frontiersmen expected all their dependants (save their families) to be non-white; they did not expect all non-whites to be their servants.'[33]

To achieve their objective of expelling some 'rebel' Xhosa chiefdoms from the Zuurveld, on the colonial side of the boundary, colonists on the eastern frontier formed an alliance with the Xhosa paramount chief. This alliance fought together in 1793 but then fell apart, allowing the Zuurveld Xhosa to launch a counter-attack. When frontiersmen rebelled in 1795, 1799, and 1801 because the government would not allow further attempts to expel the Zuurveld Xhosa, both sides attempted to enlist non-white allies.

The rebels tried to bring in the Xhosa, while Landdrost Maynier planned to use Khoikhoi troops against the rebels. In 1803, when Governor Janssens made his first visit to Graaff-Reinet, he told the colonists frankly that if disorder in the

district did not cease, 'he would have to adopt such measures as would exterminate those who were the cause of the turbulence, even if it were possible only
with the assistance of [Africans] and Hottentots.'[34]

The leaders of the various parties of emigrants – Bastaards, trekboers and
Voortrekkers – that left the Colony in the late eighteenth and early nineteenth
centuries also sought to form alliances to strengthen their weak political bases.
They often did so by intervening successfully in African succession disputes, as
when the Voortrekkers supported Mpande against the Zulu king, Dingane. But
Africans could also play this game. On the hunting frontier of the Soutpansberg
in the northern Transvaal, Africans intervened effectively in disputes between
white factions. Africans as much as whites had a clear perception of how cleavages within the other society could be turned to their own advantage.[35]

The Afrikaners' involvement in African politics could not occur without putting some strain on the cohesion of their own society. That whites would always
stick together was not a foregone conclusion. Ever since the end of the eighteenth century, large Afrikaner landholders in settled areas had dreaded the rise
of an armed and rebellious class of poor freemen of mixed racial origin who
might threaten their predominance. In the 1780s some leading western Cape
farmers expressed concern about frontier miscegenation and warned of the rise
'of a completely degenerate nation who might become just as dangerous for
the colony as the Bushmen-Hottentots are'.[36] Soon afterwards Coenraad de
Buys, having established a liaison with the mother of the Xhosa paramount,
invaded the colony at the head of some Xhosa intending to expel the British
troops from the frontier zone and set himself up as ruler. And the Slagtersnek
episode of 1815 was in a sense a rebellion of poor, landless whites who threatened to form a cross-racial alliance against the propertied class. The rebels
sought Xhosa help to challenge British control and warned that those frontiersmen who refused to join the rebellion would be killed and their families and
property given over to the Xhosa.[37]

Even Voortrekker leaders sought the help of blacks against whites. There is
evidence that Hendrik Potgieter, leader of the northern Voortrekkers, enlisted
the help of Sekwati of the Pedi against his Voortrekker adversaries. Andries
Pretorius considered King Moshoeshoe as a potential ally in his struggle against
the British in Transorangia, and his son Marthinus sought the help of the

Basotho leader in his attempt to secure Transvaal control over the Afrikaners in the Free State.[38]

In peripheral frontier zones there is evidence of strategies that went further than temporary cross-racial alliances and that tried to incorporate Africans in other than a merely labouring capacity. Hendrik Potgieter was poised ambivalently between a policy of establishing an exclusive white society and one aimed at setting himself up as an African chief, absorbing non-Europeans as subjects and allies in a larger political community. After his death the Soutpansberg settlement, which he had founded, emphasised the latter trend. R.G. Wagner observes that it began as a tight Voortrekker society; however, as its hunting activities expanded, it incorporated other hunter-traders such as Albasini, a Portuguese trader, to develop its trading links with the outside world. It also incorporated African allies, such as the personal followings of the Buyses and Albasini, who helped to ensure its military domination over Venda villages from which tribute was exacted. Lastly, it incorporated the *swart skuts*, Africans to whom it gave guns to expand its hunting and commercial activities.[39]

However, there was a distinct difference between the Afrikaner and Portuguese frontiersmen in southern Africa. Unlike the Afrikaners, who with a few exceptions remained tied to their culture and kinship network, the prazeros of Mozambique largely abandoned their European affiliations, became absorbed through intermarriage into the indigenous population, and shifted their loyalties to them.[40] Among both Portuguese and Afrikaner frontiersmen there was a constant interplay between cultural traditions, material conditions and political goals which shaped their actions and attitudes with respect to land, labour and the social order. But what ultimately separated them, especially when they lived in isolation in a peripheral area such as Angola, was a different worldview or ethos. Among the Portuguese, with their Catholic roots, there was a much fuller acceptance of Africans and mulattos as part of the family, as marriage partners and as church members, and a general acceptance of the emergence of a mixed society.[41] Among the Afrikaners, the Calvinist church adapted to existing cleavages between white and black and formed no bridge between them. Afrikaner frontiersmen turned to African or Coloured sexual partners when expedient; however, persons with a black ancestry were stigmatised and mulattos were denied the prospect of securing the status of whites. As the number of whites increased in a particular zone, the dominant families imposed the hegemonic values of a separate society.

To sum up: the first free burghers on the seventeenth-century frontier inherited and in turn transferred to their descendants the value of private landownership. The opening of the frontier encouraged them and their descendants to abandon the intensive methods of Dutch agriculture in favour of extensive ones. Seventeenth-century Dutch agriculture was based on free labour; but because slavery was common in the Dutch colonies and because the sons of near-subsistence farmers preferred to have their own farms, slaves were imported to solve the labour shortage at the Cape. The trekboers of the eighteenth century brought to the interior the cultural tradition of slavery and were gradually able to transform free indigenous peoples into unfree labourers. Nineteenth-century white frontiersmen sought to implement these two principles – individual instead of communal holding of land, unfree instead of free labour – in the societies they were to found. To merge with African societies would put these principles, and also their goal to establish a separate society, at risk. At times the Boer state in the Transvaal was too weak to establish a political order on such principles. But once military and political supremacy was achieved, they became the core values of the new society.

The closing frontier: The development of a settled society
Land, markets and towns

A distinct feature of the closing frontier is the change from abundant land resources and near-subsistence farming to a shortage of land, leading to the more intensive exploitation of existing land resources and the gradual rise of commercial farming. In the place of long trips to a distant market and *smousen* (itinerant traders) came regional markets and towns. This in turn affected caste and class relations and the political order.

To Europeans with little capital at their disposal, the pioneer frontier of southern Africa seemed to offer almost the same abundant opportunities to make an independent living as the original settlements in North America. It was only when the frontier began to close that the differences between the two settlements became starkly clear. With the exception of areas like the Piedmont plateau and the Appalachian Mountains, commercial development quickly followed initial settlement on the North American frontier. On the southern African frontier, farming largely outside the market continued for much longer. Compared to the abundant resources of North America, those in southern Africa were limited. Until the 1860s, land and game were virtually the only natural resources known to the colonists, and these fairly soon were exhausted. Also, compared to the settlement in America, capital was scarce. After the primary stage of land exploitation, little was available to finance the improvement of pasture. There was no rapid secondary phase of settlement based on the exploitation of resources such as coal and minerals, with which North America was blessed, to invigorate the frontier economy.[42] As a result, markets, towns, communications and an industrial economy were slow to develop.

What is more, southern Africa never received the steady flow of European immigrants that North America did. Early in the eighteenth century the Dutch East India Company decided against a policy of assisted immigration of European artisans, agricultural labourers and farmers who would work their own lands. Instead, slaves were imported, which meant that the arable part of the colony did not develop a large internal market. For long periods the pastoral farmers with their near-subsistence economy were dependent on Cape Town, the only town in the colony, for guns and ammunition, sugar, coffee, and cloth, but for the rest they had only tenuous links with the urban market. Their labourers were rarely paid in cash and remained largely outside the market system. Before the second half of the nineteenth century there were no African peasant communities which sold their surplus to the towns. African societies lived in isolation, conducting only a trickle of trade with the colonial markets.[43]

After the pioneer stage of settlement on the southern African frontier, there was no economic abundance, no people of plenty with a uniquely democratic vision as in North America. There was a lack of capital and of money, growing cleavages between rich and poor, and a weakly developed institutional structure which struggled to provide a sense of national cohesion or to promote economic growth through administrative efficiency and political stability.

When land and game became exhausted, farmers who wished to retain their independence and wealth had either to find land elsewhere or to make the transition from their near-subsistence operations to a more intensive exploitation of resources, developing into commercial farmers involved in a specialised exchange economy. Because the conditions for sustained economic growth were lacking, capital investment in more intensive land use did not pay off immediately. Thus the closing of the frontier was a time fraught with insecurity for the Afrikaners as they tried to adapt to the new economic imperatives.

In southern African history there were three occasions when this process impinged in a traumatic way on whites, who perceived it as nothing less than a survival crisis. These were the closing of the frontier of agricultural settlement in the south-western Cape at the end of the seventeenth century; the closing of the pastoral frontier in the eastern Cape from the end of the eighteenth century to the period of renewed trekboer expansion in the 1820s and the Great Trek; and the closing of the Transvaal and Free State frontier towards the end of the nineteenth century. This discussion of the closing of the frontier will focus on these cases.

Two decades after the founding of the Cape settlement it was clear to the colonists that intensive agriculture had failed, and from then on the expansion of the settlement would be based on extensive agriculture. By the end of the seventeenth century the colony was facing an economic crisis. With a small market that was easily glutted, there was chronic overproduction. The poor roads and low prices for agricultural products made it impossible for those on the fringes of the area of arable farming to compete with commercial farmers near Cape Town.

For more than a century the position was to remain the same: it was estimated that a wheat farmer who had to make a return journey of more than three days to Cape Town was unable to market his produce at a profit.[44] Not only the distances and quality of the roads but also the nature of the Cape market worked against the frontier farmer. Because there was no large domestic market, the farmers had to rely on passing ships to sell their surplus produce. Since such visits by ships were irregular, profits were made either by those who could sell first or by those who could hoard their produce to sell at the most favourable prices.

During the first 150 years of white settlement, loans were exceedingly difficult to obtain. It was hard to find the capital for farming near Cape Town or for hoarding produce. The closing of the frontier of agricultural settlement at the end of the seventeenth century saw poor farmers sinking into debt as they failed to receive an adequate return on their capital. A young man without much capital could still set himself up as a stock farmer on the fringes of the settlement, but droughts, epidemics and Bushman raiders could easily wipe out his stock. Land was ever more difficult to find. There was none available within the limits of the colony as defined by the government, which in the 1690s strictly forbade settlement beyond the borders or even journeys into the interior.

The government's decision in 1703 to grant grazing permits beyond the colony's limits made possible the expansion of pastoral farmers into the interior. By the 1770s the eastern frontier zone extended as far as the Fish River, nearly six hundred miles from Cape Town; but this zone, in turn, was confronted with serious economic problems. Firstly, it was too far from the market, which in any case was not very large, to allow the commercialisation of the pastoral economy. An observer who visited the Graaff-Reinet district at the end of the eighteenth century commented as follows:

> The distance is a serious inconvenience to the farmer . . . If he can contrive to get together a waggon load or two of butter or soap, to carry with him to Cape Town once a year, or once in two years, in exchange for clothing, brandy, coffee, a little tea and sugar, and a few other luxuries, which his own district has not yet produced, he is perfectly satisfied. The consideration of profit is out of the question. A man who goes to Cape Town with a single waggon from the Sneuwberg must consume, at least, sixty days out and home.[45]

Secondly, the increase of population in a newly settled area led to a steady decline in the wealth of near-subsistence farmers as the available resources diminished. The number of pastoral farmers increased almost twelvefold between 1721 and 1780.[46] Nevertheless, unlike the American frontier, this increase was not large enough to support the development of a specialised exchange economy.[47] Nor could it provide the tax base for the improvement of transport facilities. The dispersion of the population made it even more difficult for the inefficient Company administration to raise money to improve the transportation system. The large and virtually self-sufficient farms also precluded the growth of towns, which might have attracted people and encouraged them to start careers outside farming.

Thus, while frontier expansion was an escape hatch for a European lower class with diminishing opportunities, in the long run it only transplanted the poverty of the seaboard to the outer reaches of the settlement. The deterioration of resources combined with the increase of population was well summed up in 1776 by a visitor to the eastern frontier:

> In the Camdebo [Graaff-Reinet] there are about 30 farms of which about 25 are inhabited. If they will not begin to conserve artificially the grazing for their cattle, it is to be feared that the luxuriance of the grass that has already started to deteriorate markedly, though settlement in the area only began 7 or 8 years ago, will not last long, and this veld will become wholly deteriorated just like that which is nearer the Cape. This has already gone so far that one Jacobus Botha has had to move to the Great Fish River because he had no pasture for his cattle here; and A. van den Berg spoke of wanting to trek elsewhere because he could not maintain himself on his own farm.[48]

After 1780 the eastern frontier began to close rapidly, with further expansion blocked by the Xhosa in the east and temporarily by the San in the north. During the 1770s it was still possible for a young man with little or no capital to acquire land and start raising cattle. But by 1798 only 26 per cent of the adult men listed in the *opgaaf* of the frontier district of Graaff-Reinet owned farms. By 1812 this had shrunk to eighteen per cent.[49] Large extended families stayed on the farms, leading to heavy overstocking of the land. In 1809 Colonel Collins found people almost everywhere in the colony devoid of farms, some living with relatives, others wandering from place to place.[50]

As land became scarce, the strategies open to frontier farmers were few and unattractive. Firstly, some tried 'forcing in', that is, finding land between existing loan farms, but that did not help much. Cattle farming needed waterholes and all the good ones had been occupied at an early stage. Secondly, some hoped to mobilise support for driving back the Xhosa and San, and thus to continue expansion. However, white frontier society lacked the military resources to launch a successful expedition. In the frontier wars of 1793 and 1799 to 1802, the farmers suffered heavy livestock losses and were forced to abandon a large area of the frontier district of Graaff-Reinet. Thirdly, colonists could attempt to increase the carrying capacity of the land. The Colebrooke–Bigge commission of inquiry, which visited the colony from 1823 to 1826, expressed the hope that the increase in the population 'will at last compel them to contract the ranges of their cattle and to provide for them by raising artificial food'.[51] But in the 1820s this transition was still too difficult to make for all but a few. The water supply was scarce and technical equipment, such as windmills, primitive. The distance from the market and the absence of easily marketable commodities did not justify a more intensive application of capital and labour.

Of the three alternatives, the Afrikaner frontiersmen strongly preferred the second – expansion of the area of subsistence farming in the eighteenth-century mould. However, this was resisted by the much stronger British government, which realised that such expansion would only lead to the duplication in other areas of the same cardinal problems of frontier settlement. As early as 1797, an official argued:

> As long as one may infringe upon the countries of the [Africans], Bosjesman, etc. to take their lands and to live upon the breeding of cattle, so long no person will be anxious about the state of his children, so long no sufficient number of hands will be obtained in the country itself to carry on the tillage, so long the inhabitants will never enter into the service of each other; and finally so long the importation of slaves will be necessary for the sake of the culture of grain. While on the other hand, one will never scruple to settle himself throughout the whole country of Africa among all the nations, and by so doing become like those wild nations.[52]

Andries Stockenström, landdrost of Graaff-Reinet and arguably the greatest authority on the eastern frontier, clearly realised the implications in the 1820s, when trekboers in large numbers began to expand beyond the limits of the colony in search of better grazing:

> Every stretch of migration throws the mass of our borders back in point of improvement, as long as it is not forced by a redundant population, or scarcity of food, which is far from being the case . . . It is a curious fact that the complaints of the diminution of stock are accompanied by as loud a one that there is no market whatever for the little which remains, so that however unpalatable I know the theory to be to my countrymen, I think it would not be unfortunate for the colony if the present distress of graziers were to throw numbers out of that line of life into more active ones, which we cannot expect to take place as long as a hope of the extension of the boundary exists.[53]

From this perspective, the Great Trek was a dramatic escape, not only from the political controls which the British government imposed on frontier society, but also from all the difficult social and economic adjustments which the closing of the frontier required. It would remove both the threat of disastrous frontier wars and the calamitous loss of status entailed by entering someone else's service. It transplanted to the deep interior the pioneering frontier of the mid-eighteenth century, with its near-subsistence farming, undiversified economy, and lack of political controls.

In fact, just at the time of the Great Trek the frontier economy was slowly emerging from its depression and there was an acceleration in the transition from subsistence to commercial farming. This was the long-term result of the increase of the colonial European population from 25 000 in 1800 to 237 000 in 1865. Together with the British drive (unlike that of the Dutch East India Company) to promote economic development and intensify the collection of taxes, the population increase stimulated the development of roads, markets and towns in the colony.

The economic history of the frontier town of Graaff-Reinet, established in 1786, provides a case study of the gradual transition towards the post-frontier stage of settlement and trade. In 1811 an official report noted the beginnings of trade in the town where 25 tradesmen had recently settled.[54] Townsmen were making a living from the produce of their vineyards and orchards situated near the Sundays River. The arrival of the more commercially oriented 1820 British settlers, the presence of military garrisons on the eastern frontier, and the development of a new harbour at Port Elizabeth promoted the growth of a regional market. By the 1830s the farmers of the district were bartering their produce for manufactured goods at Graaff-Reinet and had stopped obtaining supplies in Cape Town or from the *smousen*.[55]

It was wool that finally heralded the beginning of commercial farming. In the 1830s Graaff-Reinet was still producing very little wool and had hardly made a start with the breeding of merinos as a substitute for the thick-tailed Cape sheep. Gradually a switch toward cash-oriented farming took place as the prejudices and doubts of conservative farmers were broken down by the success which the newly arrived British settlers were achieving with wool.[56] Loans were becoming more readily available from institutions in Cape Town and even England. This led to greater activity in the building of dams and to experiments with new ploughs and reaping machines. The wool production of the district increased from 150 000 lb in the mid-1840s to 1 282 168 lb in 1855. By then Port Elizabeth was exporting nearly four times as much wool as Cape Town. In some areas land values multiplied by more than six times between 1843 and 1857. There was increasing agitation for improvement in the quality of the roads, but without much success. However, in 1879 the opening of a rail link between Graaff-Reinet and Port Elizabeth helped to assure the Graaff-Reinet market of a share of the wool and meat production in the area north of the Cape Colony.[57]

By the 1850s the transition of Graaff-Reinet from 'frontier' to 'Midlands' was complete. In 1800 it was a cauldron of frontier conflict; by the mid-1850s the frontier had passed by. In some senses the frontier had closed much earlier: no more free land was available after the 1780s and the government had established full political control over the Afrikaner frontiersmen by the first decade of the nineteenth century. However, in other senses frontier closure only progressed gradually over the next four decades.

There was the slow development of commercial farming and a regional market, and of control over 'Hottentot vagrants' and Xhosa 'raiders'. But by 1850 Graaff-Reinet was politically and economically settled. The expansion of the colony, the increase of the European population, and the establishment of new districts to the north and east protected the Midlands region from frontier turmoil. It was now a leading producer of wool, a place where the Mosenthal

Brothers bought or bartered wool and 'all description of produce' and extended credit to farmers through the financing of local storekeepers.[58]

The Graaff-Reinet case also applies in some respects to the frontier development in the area north of the Orange River, where Afrikaners began to settle in the 1830s. There was a short mini-boom in wool, especially after the British established control over Transorangia in 1848.[59] For the Griquas (previously named Bastaards), the boom in wool spelled the end of their independent existence in the Transorangia area as they were edged out by trekboer and Voortrekker immigrants.[60] However, the British withdrawal from the Highveld in the 1850s ended the mini-boom and also reduced the extent to which the Free State economy was integrated with that of the Cape Colony. Despite the trade boost provided by the discovery of diamonds and gold, the Free State only gradually made the transition towards agricultural specialisation and commercialisation in the second half of the nineteenth century.

In terms of open conflict over disputed land, the Free State ceased to be a frontier region in 1868 when Britain assumed control over Basutoland. There were no large African reserves within the Free State borders. Neither was there a large disparity in numbers between white and black: the 1890 census put the white population at 77 000 and the Africans at 128 000. However, lacking real commercial development and an effective government machinery, the Free State was still partly in the frontier stage until the late 1880s. Economic isolation resulted in largely subsistence farming; settlers waited for an improved transportation system and an increase in population density before they would embark on farm improvements. Until 1870 there were no public highways to speak of, and the first bridge over the Orange River was only built in 1879. The population density gradually increased from 2,65 persons per square mile in the 1850s to 4,23 per square mile in 1890, with the highest densities in the east where there was a large concentration of Africans. Some wool was exported but wheat had to be imported from Basutoland and the Cape Colony. Agriculture consisted mostly of subsistence farming; and barter, with *smousen* playing a prominent role, formed the bulk of trade.[61]

Eventually it was the Witwatersrand market, the railways and the revenue from customs which ended pre-capitalist, near-subsistence farming in the Free State. The Transvaal mines spurred agricultural development in the northern

Free State where land values increased sharply. Transport riding became an attractive alternative career for whites. In 1889 the Free State for the first time received revenue from customs. This enabled the government to strengthen its control over its subjects and to launch economic development projects. When the Free State entered the South African War in 1899, commercial farming was rapidly replacing subsistence farming. Farmers no longer relied primarily on barter to procure necessary items such as guns, building materials and clothing, but aimed to sell a growing part of their produce for cash in the market while still depending on unfree labour in their farming operations. But it would take several decades before sufficient capital and coercive apparatus appeared to complete the full transition to capitalist farming, involving maximisation of profits, wage labour, and conducting agricultural production as a business enterprise.

Throughout the second half of the nineteenth century, the Free State and Transvaal governments tried to attract white immigrants to promote economic growth and expand their tax base. But both governments had at early stages squandered their only real asset, land, through their liberal grants of it. In the Free State this land policy did not have the same disruptive effect on settlement as in the Transvaal. In 1874 the Bloemfontein *Friend* stated: 'The country is filling up rapidly – in some of the older districts there being scarcely an unoccupied farm to be had.'[62] By the end of the century, land was much better distributed among Afrikaners there than in the Transvaal. To be sure, there were large absentee landlord estates at one end of the spectrum and, at the other, numerous small farms, the result of subdivision among heirs according to the Roman-Dutch law of inheritance. But there was never the overcrowding of land, the acute poverty and the *bywoner* problem which Afrikaner society in Transvaal began to experience from the 1870s. Instead, a viable white middle class had developed in the Free State rural areas by the end of the nineteenth century, which enabled twentieth-century Afrikaner nationalism to draw its first leader and initial support from this region.

If there is some resemblance between the Free State and the American frontier, particularly as far as the formative impact of the frontier on democracy and nationalism is concerned, the Transvaal represents a different case. In its political development it lies somewhere between the individualist democracy of the

United States and the paternalist authoritarianism of Latin America. Its settlement pattern is reminiscent of the Latin American frontier where, as Alistair Hennessy has written, the 'filling in' process did not occur because big landowners controlled the distribution of land. On both the Transvaal and the Latin American frontiers the white population was too sparse and the commercial links too weak to encourage the development of regional economies.[63]

Afrikaner occupation of the Transvaal was a slow and haphazard process. In the 1850s there were mainly two small strips of settlement – in the west from Potchefstroom to Rustenburg and in the east from Utrecht to the Soutpansberg. Large areas, including the Highveld proper, were unoccupied by whites. Settlement in the north had to be abandoned in the 1860s. Even as late as 1886 there was a population density of less than one white per square mile in the Transvaal. The overwhelming majority of the roughly 60 000 Afrikaners of the Transvaal – an area of about 71 600 square miles – were concentrated in the southern half of the republic.[64] A filling-in process did not occur. By the end of the century, half of the land to which whites laid claim in the Transvaal was unoccupied, being in the hands of absentee landlords or land companies.[65] In 1871 the government had temporarily stopped issuing land in an attempt to counter excessive land speculation, which left large areas of the country unoccupied, and to restore the credit of the state.[66] But by that time the chance of systematic colonisation had been lost and the detrimental effects of the existing pattern of settlement were closing in on Afrikaner society.

The way in which the Transvaal had been occupied by whites made it very difficult to incorporate the region into the economic heartland of South Africa. Ports were too far away and the land was not suitable for the production of wool. A class of large landholders remained wealthy, but most farmers faced a crisis as the resources for extensive subsistence farming became exhausted. In most of the area, trade was reduced to a minimum and consisted largely of barter. In the absence of exports the money supply was soon exhausted and the pioneer society became heavily dependent on merchant capital. In 1886, when gold was discovered, the Transvaal was still not self-sufficient in agriculture. D.M. Goodfellow, an economic historian, wrote some 50 years later: 'It became a commonplace, and a true commonplace, that the Transvaal scarcely responded to all the demand for foodstuffs created by the new industry . . . The country had existed too long without markets and without commerce to be able to respond instantly to the great market which appeared with such suddenness in its midst.'[67]

The great difficulty which the Afrikaners experienced in becoming cash-crop producers in the nineteenth century must be partly ascribed to their heritage of near-subsistence farming. Certainly, factors such as the absence of a well-regulated labour force and the instability of agricultural prices weighed heavily, but the slow reaction of Transvaal farmers to the new market can only be fully understood by taking into account the long-standing tendency among the average and the small farmer to produce only as much as was needed to purchase essential commodities.[68]

By the turn of the century there was no more cheap land available and game was all but wiped out. In terms of the availability of these easily exploitable resources, the frontier had closed. A new resource in the form of gold became available in the 1880s. However, most Afrikaners on the Witwatersrand sold mineral options cheaply. Some Afrikaners seized the opportunity of transport riding to the new towns. But the farming community as a whole was crushed in the 1890s by the rinderpest, which wiped out a large proportion of cattle,[69] and by the devastation of the South African War (1899–1902). Although the problem had existed long before, the term 'poor white' was first used in 1890.[70] The 'poor white problem' was soon to become a spectre of white politicians, as the Afrikaner poor flocked to the cities in their last trek. Just as the seaboard in the eighteenth century had exported its poor to the frontier, the frontier exodus of the early twentieth century exchanged rural poverty for urban indigence and squalor. During the second and third quarter of the century a maze of segregation and apartheid laws would be passed to protect the poor whites whom the frontier had pushed out.

Caste and class relations

Relationships between white and black on the pioneering frontier were shaped by the abundance of land, the lack of market incentives, and local rather than government recruitment and control of labour. On the closing frontier these relationships were mainly affected by declining land resources, a growing state role in the regulation of labour, and the demands of commercial farming. These variables influenced the treatment of labourers, but equally important was the extent to which the indigenous Bantu-speaking African society, as distinct from the Khoisan people, survived the impact of European colonisation, withstanding not only their firepower but also European diseases and alcohol as means of conquest.

For the Khoikhoi the south-western Cape changed unmistakably from the 1670s to a rapidly closing frontier. The area became fully occupied by Europeans and slave labour was readily available. Khoikhoi who stayed in the area sank rapidly to a position where their status was not much higher than that of slaves. Indeed, by the turn of the century there were settlers who spoke of them in the same breath as slaves.[71] As the Khoikhoi became poorer and unable to find alternative means of subsistence, farmers cut back on their meat and other provisions and their small livestock holdings became depleted.

By the end of the eighteenth century, the Khoikhoi had been squeezed out by whites and by the expanding Xhosa from the few remaining unoccupied spaces on the eastern frontier. Without land they lost the option to refuse their labour and exist outside someone else's service. Local coercion had become increasingly effective. Once a Khoikhoi had become an apprentice or a debtor to a farmer, it was difficult to leave the farm. Colonel Collins, an observer sympathetic to the colonists, reported in 1809:

> A Hottentot can now seldom get away at the expiration of his term. If he should happen not to be in debt to his master . . . he is not allowed to take his children, or he is detained under some frivolous pretence, such as that of cattle having died through his neglect, and he is not permitted to satisfy any demands of this nature otherwise than by personal service.[72]

After Britain reoccupied the Cape in 1806, the government tried to substitute contractual arrangements for the arbitrary power of the masters. But the coming of the British also linked the Cape more strongly to the channels of world trade, and the new government, much more than the Company, sought to provide producers with a docile and regulated workforce to supply an expanding market. Therefore it sanctioned some of the existing labour-repressive practices such as the indenture system. Within two decades the government reversed its position. The growing humanitarian movement in Britain and local pressure by reformers such as Dr John Philip and Andries Stockenström made it impossible to condone any longer the ill-treatment of indigenous peoples and involuntary servitude. A recent interpretation suggests that the Cape government was also prompted by its conviction that large supplies of unfree labour were tied down on Afrikaner farms while the newly arrived British settlers were suffering acute labour shortages.[73] Ordinance 50 of 1828, which lifted the restrictions on Khoikhoi mobility, aimed at countering labour repression and increasing the flow of labour.

After 1828 there was for a short period a sharp increase in what frontier farmers termed 'vagrancy'. But because the Khoikhoi had no land of their own and could seldom find alternative employment in towns, they were unable to improve their position materially in society. Andries Stockenström, the reformist frontier official, observed in 1836 that the Khoikhoi were subjected to the same regime as slaves, except that they could not be sold and were not bound to their master except by contract. Far removed from the magistrate, Stockenström went on, they existed in a state of moral debasement and physical misery, because a farmer valued his slave more than his Hottentot servant, who could not be sold.[74]

The farmers, on the other hand, received increasing institutional support for the control of labour. The Masters and Servants Ordinance passed in 1841, three years after slaves in the Cape had been emancipated, to a large extent erased the legal distinction which had formerly been maintained between slaves and Khoisan. Through this ordinance, the government put all labourers, who were almost all non-white, in a position of legal subordination to the masters. In 1856, two years after the colony received representative government, the Cape authorities even further tightened the control that masters could exercise over their labour. For African farm labour this law remained in force for more than a century.[75]

The steady deterioration of the status of Khoikhoi labourers was closely linked to the decline of Khoikhoi society during the first century and a half of European colonisation. After the frontier began to close, Khoikhoi culture disintegrated; Khoikhoi and their descendants, the 'Coloureds', became a labouring caste without the psychological support that tribal affiliation and a vibrant culture of their own could provide. Disease and alcohol consumption completely debilitated many.

In contrast, European diseases and alcohol made little impact on the Bantu-speaking societies. They recovered quickly from military defeat, with the temporary exception of the Xhosa who, during the first half of the nineteenth century, suffered several severe defeats at the hands of the British army and then dealt themselves a crushing blow with the Cattle-Killing of 1856–7. Further north, however, Africans soon recovered from the devastation of the Difaqane. Their populations increased rapidly, and the Zulu and Pedi states became focal points of power until they were conquered by the British towards the end of the 1870s. African culture remained an integral part of the lives of the majority of farm labourers. Compared to the Khoikhoi, African society entered the twentieth century strong in numbers and in spirit, not because of the benevolence of the whites, but because the Boer states were too weak to smash it militarily and because other means of conquest also proved ineffective.

On the closing frontier of the Orange Free State there was virtually no land that was not occupied by whites. What first worked in favour of Africans was the real shortage of labour, for according to the census of 1890 there were only some 70 000 African men to 40 000 white men in the republic. (Whites held the view that at least five African men were needed to work an average farm.) Secondly, while the market was still small and unstable, some large farmers considered African tenants paying rent in kind a more attractive proposition than investing capital in agricultural production. Thirdly, the Free State government only gradually developed the means to coerce African labour. It issued pass laws to restrict the mobility of Africans, it levied taxes to force them to work, it legalised the apprenticeship of children, and after 1872 it passed several laws which aimed at limiting the number of heads of families on a farm to five. But despite all such efforts the government was unable to ensure a sufficient supply of labour to all farms. It did not have an efficient police force to execute its decrees. Especially in the north, wealthy whites with many Africans on their farms were powerful enough to resist the regulations limiting numbers, as repeated discussions in the Volksraad and complaints from frustrated small farmers showed. The government also realised that if its African population was harassed too much, many would leave and settle in neighbouring territories such as Basutoland and Natal. In 1893 the Bloemfontein *Friend,* a Free State newspaper, succinctly summarised the situation: 'The native is as much at liberty to sell his labour at the best terms he can make as the farmer is to dispose of his crops. If the master is too exacting, the native leaves him and goes to one who is an easier man to get on with. If the laws are too oppressive, the native leaves the country altogether.'[76]

'Squatting' emerged on the closing frontier as a working compromise to reconcile the needs of Africans and white farmers. For an African, a squatter farm provided a refuge from unfavourable working conditions, a place where he could pasture his cattle and reap his own harvest, and live together with his family and friends. By the end of the century, with the gold mines and railways paying wages four times higher than farm labour, farmers often had no option but to offer acceptable conditions to Africans. In particular, farmers responding to the Witwatersrand market by switching from subsistence to commercial farming needed a large supply of seasonal labour as well as a class of workers who would work the land they could not exploit themselves.[77] Two systems then evolved: farming-on-the-half, where Africans handed over half the crop to the farmer in return for the right to cultivate, graze stock, and live on the land; and tenant farming, in which absentee landlords let their land to rent-paying Africans.[78]

On the pioneering frontier, conflict occurred between whites and Africans over land and cattle. On the closing frontier of the Free State, the issues were labour and the response of a new class of Africans to the markets then opening up. The smaller white farmers deeply resented the competition for the market which came from African peasants. In the 1890s a group of farmers from the eastern Free State demanded that the Volksraad prohibit 'the large-scale grain-growing' of African peasants, since it was 'impossible for white grain-farmers to compete against Coloureds'.[79] Co-operation between European landholders and African peasants also undermined white solidarity. Because poor whites and *bywoners* were not prepared to do the same work as Africans and therefore set too many demands, white landholders increasingly considered replacing them with African peasants.[80]

It was in the Transvaal that the closing of the frontier produced the greatest transformation in social relations. In the Cape Colony the labour legislation of the 1840s and 1850s made all rural labourers legally subordinate to their masters.

The Cape interior was ruled by a largely solidified white caste, with colour the main marker of subordination. The Transvaal of the late nineteenth century, on the other hand, began to move towards a society which, compared to the rest of South Africa, was characterised more by a class and less by a caste relationship, with Africans enjoying greater mobility. To be sure, there were areas of the Transvaal where landholders could exercise sufficient local control to keep large numbers of black unfree labourers in a rigid, caste-like condition of immobility and inferiority. By the end of the century, their numbers were swollen by the indenturing of newly defeated peoples. However, in this period too a new class of Africans was emerging between white landholders and African labourers, while in white society increasing class conflict was developing between landholders and *bywoners*.

To a large extent these developments were the result of the weakness of the central government and of white society at large in the Transvaal, in a period marked by the discovery of gold and the rise of commercial agriculture. The political autonomy of the Transvaal Republic was considerably eroded during the last two decades of the nineteenth century. For fear of British intervention the Transvaal government did not feel free to pass legislation that would force Africans to work. In terms of the London Convention of 1884, it was also obliged to demarcate reserves for the large African chiefdoms, taking into account the existing claims of these chiefdoms.[81] Besides the reserves, living space was also provided to Africans by the vast tracts of land held by absentee landlords or companies and by mission stations. Africans were also free to leave the territory and settle beyond its borders. And after the discovery of gold, a vast new field of alternative employment was open to them. According to an estimate of the South African Republic, there were 131 539 male Africans under its jurisdiction in 1895; of these, approximately 70 000 were working in the mines.[82]

In such conditions the coercive relationships between masters and unfree indentured or tributary labourers were gradually transformed into what Stanley Trapido calls a 'variety of unstable landlord–tenant linkages'.[83] They were unstable because Africans had acquired a considerable degree of mobility and bargaining power. African tenants paying rent in cash or labour for living on a farm preferred to attach themselves to prosperous farmers owning fertile land where they could sow and pasture their cattle. They were often able to demand favourable terms in sharecropping arrangements. One farmer, for instance, had to accommodate 40 families and provide pasture for their 400 cattle, but could only draw on the labour of three young Africans for the full year and an additional twenty for two months per year.[84] A mission journal wrote that 'the Natives are not bound to the soil . . . The Boers are obliged in self-defence to treat their people leniently.'[85] Africans living together in the reserves or on large farms secured a considerable measure of psychological and cultural autonomy.

At the same time, economic differentiation and class strains began to appear in white society. As we have seen, half of the land to which whites laid claim in the Transvaal was unoccupied by the end of the century, being in the hands of large absentee landlords. Lands that were occupied were often heavily subdivided among as many as 40 whites to a single farm. In some cases, subdivision of a farm led to the impoverishment of more than 100 whites within three or four generations – the start of the so-called poor white problem. In the distribution of land a key role was played by the field-cornets. They inspected claims to the land before it was given out as farms and also auctioned land for which taxes had not been paid. Having prior access to information about land on the market, they often acquired substantial tracts and could attract large numbers of tenants. Towards the end of the century they constituted a class of notables that was well represented in the Volksraad.[86]

The obverse of the large number of Africans living on the farms of the wealthy was the labour shortage experienced by the small farmer. Obviously Africans would have to work harder on these farms; moreover, there was no status attached to working for a poor man. 'It is known throughout the world that the poor rarely want to serve the poor,'[87] was a field-cornet's comment on the constant complaints of labour shortage. The Transvaal government responded by passing legislation limiting the number of African families on a farm to five. These laws had some restrictive effect on African mobility but did not prevent the wealthy from having as much labour as they required; neither did they supply the poor with the workers they wanted. Toward the end of the Transvaal Republic, the government was both unwilling and unable to use effective measures to compel Africans to work or to redistribute African labour, and the small farmers began complaining vociferously that they were forced to work themselves and to 'use their children as [Africans] in order to hold their own'.[88] With little land and hardly any labour at its disposal, the poorer section of white society was unable to survive economically in the rural areas. In 1899 the young Jan Smuts, who came from the caste society of the rural south-western Cape, warned that if laws were not passed to protect the white farmer, their sons would have to become labourers, and the real (*eigenlijke*) nation of the republic would become a labouring class.[89]

The inequality of land and labour resources as the frontier closed transformed what had previously been a fairly egalitarian Afrikaner society. It was a phenomenon that repeated itself. When the south-western Cape frontier closed in the seventeenth century, poor whites were forced to enter the service of wealthy farmers. There was a minimum of social intercourse between landholders and white labourers. Significantly, white *knechten* (overseers) addressed their employers as 'baas',[90] which was to become the classic term denoting racial and class superiority. However, on the open frontier of the eighteenth and nineteenth century, wealth was fairly evenly distributed among whites, with a tendency to become still more evenly distributed in the largely subsistence economy.[91] 'That there is still no real class division among the true inhabitants of this colony [the whites] provides proof of the slight progress made in the welfare of the colony,'[92] W.C. van Ryneveld had observed in 1805.

White egalitarianism came under pressure towards the end of the nineteenth century when there was no more free land in southern Africa and farmers had to use their land more intensively. In 1879 a special commissioner on the northern frontier of the Cape Colony wrote: 'it is the poorer class of farmers who, pressed out by their richer neighbours, move on in search of *vrygrond*'.[93] Their time of crisis came at the end of the nineteenth century when there was no more *vrygrond* (free land) and farmers were rationalising their operations to meet market demands. Also weakening their position was the fact that, whereas on the pioneering frontier the landholder needed his tenant farmers to join him (or go in his place) on commando, supervise his labourers, and provide company in his social isolation, on the closed frontier the government could provide protection while legal controls and the market compelled Africans to work.

Although a sense of 'white solidarity' remained, it was constantly being eroded, especially in the Transvaal, by landholders who exploited their tenant farmers by paying them even lower wages than non-white labourers, or who pushed them out to the cities because they preferred black peasants, who were generally regarded as better labourers and producers. Unable to exist as independent producers and unwilling to work as manual labourers, *bywoners* had little status. A Dutch visitor to the Transvaal remarked in 1890 that a man living on the farm of someone else 'does not count for much and is not held in esteem'.[94] Early in the twentieth century the following definition of the *bywoner* was current: 'everyone on a farm who is white but not a *baas*'.[95] Black labourers on the farm no longer addressed and treated the *bywoner* as a *baas*. The social distinction between the farmer and the landless white grew. R.W. Wilcocks, a member of the Carnegie Commission of the 1930s investigating the poor white problem, expressed a sentiment that had been strongly felt during the preceding four decades: '[The farmer] often finds it difficult to strike a happy mean between treating his European hand as a European, and so in a sense as still his equal, and at the same time as his subordinate.'[96] To Wilcocks, the increasing economic equality between the large lower stratum of white society and the black population spelled the danger of poor whites losing caste and becoming 'the social equals of the great mass of non-Europeans'.[97]

How far the class cleavages within Transvaal and Free State white society had developed became starkly clear when more than a fifth of the Afrikaners in the field came to fight on the side of the British by the end of the South African War. Of the roughly 5 000 'joiners', the vast majority had been *bywoners*. In some sense this act of treason was a rebellion against class exploitation. A recent study cites evidence of serious pre-war *bywoner* discontent. In the 1880s and 1890s they had to go on commando against Africans without any recompense to defend the property of landholders, while their own families were destitute. The 'joiners' of the Boer War clearly hoped that the British would offer them a better dispensation.[98]

In the end the Transvaal did not become a class society like Brazil. But its caste society might have been transformed had there not been such a short period between the 1880s, when land resources became exhausted, and the birth of a new order dominated economically by the rapid industrialisation of South Africa and politically by the Union constitution of 1909, which enfranchised all white men, thereby entrenching not only white supremacy but also white egalitarianism. Without this new order, the frontier that had made white egalitarianism possible might also have been instrumental in reordering society on the basis of class rather than race. Certainly, the dominant class of land-holders in Transvaal would have found it much more difficult than the Southern planters of the US to ensure that lower-class whites retained a sense of racial caste and solidarity.

The political order

Two overlapping trends characterised the political order of the closing frontier. Firstly, there was a decline of regional strife and the establishment of control by the centre over the periphery with its anarchic tendencies. Secondly, the central government with its modern bureaucracy took over the local administration in which the field-cornets had played a pivotal role. As we have seen, the British imperial government established a considerable measure of control over the Cape frontier during the first half of the nineteenth century. In the Free State and Transvaal this occurred only towards the end of the nineteenth and the beginning of the twentieth century, when a coalition consisting of the imperial power, Britain, and Afrikaner landholders finally closed the frontier.

On the pioneering frontier the authority vacuum produced endemic conflict, which the frontiersmen attempted to resolve locally through the commando system. The decentralised nature of the commando system, in which regional commandants co-ordinated the activities of field-cornets under their command, made prompt action possible in the frontier zone but it also bred regionalism and anarchy. When trekboer expansion was halted in the late eighteenth century, the government appointed two commandants, one for the northern frontier, where the Bushmen had forced the evacuation of several frontier divisions, and the other for the eastern divisions, which were intent on expelling the Xhosa over the Fish River. During the rebellions of the 1790s, Afrikaner society in the Graaff-Reinet district split along these regional lines. The northern frontier divisions wished to concentrate the district's military efforts on the conflict against the Bushmen. The south-eastern divisions ignored calls to enlist for commandos against the Bushmen and demanded an attack on the Xhosa. The rebellions of the 1790s were in fact nothing but a thinly disguised take-over of the district authority by the south-eastern division, and they failed primarily because the northern frontiersmen first remained neutral and then opposed the rebellions.

Such conflicting regional loyalties often undermined the effectiveness of the commandos. One of the chief reasons why the frontier colonists were unable to maintain themselves against the Xhosa in the period 1793 to 1811 was the continual bickering among military leaders and the general disunity which characterised the commandos. The expulsion of the Xhosa from colonial territory in 1811–12 was due not so much to the presence of British troops, who only brought up the rear, but to British military officers who led the attacking force consisting of burgher militia and Khoikhoi. British intervention ended regional strife and radically changed the nature of the commandos on the eastern frontier. In the days of the pioneering frontier, commandos were often raised without the direct involvement, and sometimes even without the sanction, of the authorities. After the British had taken over, commandos were still called up, but they served essentially as auxiliary forces subordinate to the British military and acted under much more effective government control. The constraints under which commandos then had to operate added to the sense of grievance and frustration that gave rise to the Great Trek. In 1836 Walter Currie recorded the comment of a frontier farmer on the turmoil in his division: 'He thought they were worse off than fifty years ago; in those old times when they were robbed they redressed themselves, but now their hands are tied while the [Africans] were loose.'[99] These words caught the essence of the transition from the pioneering frontier to a situation where the conduct of frontier warfare had shifted from the periphery to the centre, largely because the government was determined to control what John Galbraith has called the 'turbulent frontier'.[100]

In the Transvaal, regionalism based on personal loyalties to the various commandants-general had long thwarted attempts to establish central control. From 1845 onwards there were continuous clashes between various groups of burghers, and several regional 'republics' were created in the 1850s by discontented factions before all the burghers in the region were brought together under one flag and one constitution.[101] It was only in the 1870s that the Transvalers started to coalesce under a stronger executive presidency, which developed under Burgers and Kruger, and power began to shift from the localities to the centre.

The gradual end of regional strife and anarchy was linked to another trend: the replacement of a 'government of men' exercising arbitrary power, by a 'government of laws' executed by a modern bureaucracy and a civilian police force. What law and order existed on the pioneering frontier in the Cape, Free State and Transvaal had to be maintained by local agents acting according to their own lights and means. Police action in each division was the task of the field-cornets, who not only called up men for commando duty but also acted as constables to arrest suspects, register labour contracts, resolve disputes between masters and servants, and investigate unnatural deaths. But while the field-cornets exercised some restraining influence, the landlords on their farms largely supplied their own interpretation of the law.

Gradually the pioneers' conception of government and the law changed as the central government began to make its views felt. The change often came as a shock, as it did for a pioneer charged with murder after he had shot an African on his farm:

> I have a letter from my field cornet . . . in which he instructed us to 'put out of the way' any such creatures who do not want to surrender themselves. From our worthy commandant we have the same, also in writing. Indeed, this has been the law of the frontier since time immemorial. And now, for obeying the law and doing as has been done many times to my knowledge and as every frontier resident does in such cases, we face the accusation of murder. This is intolerable.[102]

After the second British occupation in 1806, the government of the Cape Colony wished to establish a modern polity with efficient military and administrative machinery. For a considerable period, however, the lack of financial resources prevented the attainment of this objective. The government hoped to take an important step towards this goal in 1828 when it replaced the courts of land-drosts and *heemraden* with resident magistrates. In terms of Ordinance 50, which granted the Khoikhoi legal equality, the power to register labour contracts was given to two new officials, the justice of the peace and the clerk of the peace, of whom there was one for each district. The contracting of all servants was thus transferred to the district's capital. For a considerable period this system failed to have significant impact. A justice of the peace in the Beaufort West district remarked in 1845 that most of the farms were seventy to a hundred miles from the district headquarters, which made it too difficult for complainants to obtain redress: 'Parties either submit to the evils . . . or in cases of petty thefts, ill conduct of servants, etc., they take the law into their own hands, and inflict such punishment as they think fit.'[103]

In another respect, however, Ordinance 50 signalled an important phase in the closing of the frontier. Before 1828 field-cornets played a major role in the system of labour coercion through enforcing the pass laws and stopping 'vagrancy'. After 1828 the Khoikhoi were no longer required to carry passes and vagrancy was no longer a crime. The resident magistrates and justices of the peace then supervised much more closely the way in which the field-cornets exercised their police duties, and the main responsibility for patrolling the border and tracking down stolen cattle came to rest on government troops based at the military posts.

From the point of view of the colonists there was a major breakdown of law and order in the decade after 1828, with a sharp increase in 'vagrancy' and also cattle thefts by Khoikhoi and, on a larger scale, by Xhosa who had lost large tracts of land since 1811. The vagrants were men who were looking for better employment or refused to work in view of the extremely low wages offered by the colonists. Instead they squatted on farms and lived from cattle they stole.[104] In an important sense the Great Trek sprang from the fact that the frontier had not yet completely closed in the far eastern part of the colony. It was no longer a pioneering frontier where the frontiersmen could impose their will through vigilante action. But the alternative forms of control of a modern industrial and capitalist society – the imperative of work or starve, which forces people into productive activity, and an efficient police force compelling the lower classes to comply with the prevailing notions of law and order – were still virtually non-existent. Commenting on the desirability of a vagrancy law, in 1829 the judges of the Supreme Court pointed out that the police force and prison discipline were insufficient to combat crimes arising from vagrancy.[105]

The weakness of the frontier administrative apparatus can be illustrated by looking at the Albany district, from which many of the Voortrekkers came. Some 4 800 square miles in extent, the district in 1834 contained 4 202 whites, 5 949 free blacks, and 156 slaves. At the district capital there resided a resident magistrate, a clerk of the peace, and eight constables; there were also six field-cornets in the district.[106] Neither the military stationed at Grahamstown nor the field-cornets were able to act effectively against cattle raids and petty thefts. It was only in 1855 that a modern police force was established in the eastern part of the colony. This was the Frontier Armed and Mounted Police, which had an original strength of seventeen officers and 500 men.[107]

In the Voortrekker republics there was, by the end of the century, not nearly the same amount of government control as in the Cape Colony, which could draw on the expertise and resources of Britain. In the Free State the increased revenue flowing from the discovery of diamonds made possible some expansion of the bureaucracy. In 1889 there were nineteen districts in this comparatively small territory. However, the state remained unable to enforce its laws with respect to 'vagrancy' and the maximum number of African families on farms. Often the landdrosts and field-cornets were farmers who opposed these laws or feared resistance if they tried to enforce them. By the 1890s the Rijdende Dienstmacht, a mounted police force consisting of some 90 men who patrolled the districts, ensured a somewhat greater measure of government control and compliance with the laws.

In the Transvaal the field-cornets and commandants, who were all locally elected, were until the 1870s the chief sources of authority in the districts. It was mainly they who commandeered and distributed African labour; it is probable that much of the tax Africans paid ended up as their property.[108] At first the state's machinery for raising taxes from its own citizens was hopelessly inadequate. However, administrative efficiency gradually increased. From the 1870s the landdrost, the only appointed official, began to replace the field-cornet as the government's agent in the rural areas. After 1886, although the executive machinery improved considerably as a result of the increased revenue from the gold mines, there was never any effective police force in the interior, and the commando remained the main instrument for police as well as military action in the Transvaal.[109] On the Witwatersrand the administrative apparatus was unable to meet the demands of a growing industrial economy.

It was a coalition between Afrikaner commercial farmers and British capitalist interests which finally completed the closure of the southern African frontier. This sprang from the strongly increased demand for cheap and abundant indigenous labour as the region began to industrialise rapidly after the discovery of the Witwatersrand gold fields.[110] Between 1886 and 1899, when war broke out, there was sharp competition for labour between commercial farmers and mining capitalists. Great tensions developed when it became clear to the mining capitalists that the Transvaal state, representing largely the interests of the commercial farmers, lacked the means to ensure a sufficient supply of labour to the mines or even interfered with its flow to the towns.[111] Some historians have rooted the origins of the South African War in the British desire to rationalise the control of the labour force and remove other obstacles to industrialisation. After the war an uneasy alliance between 'gold and maize' took shape. Although African peasants contributed a substantial part of the locally grown crops in the Transvaal, British imperial interests then chose to rely on the dominant class of Afrikaner society, not only for agricultural production but also to control the Africans in the rural areas and the white and black urban proletariat. State subsidies and credits enabled this class of large landholders to accumulate even more land and increase their profits at the expense of poor white and black peasant farmers.[112]

With the frontier finally closed, the decade after the war witnessed an assault on Africans who had succeeded in avoiding white demands for cheap labour. In the late nineteenth century it was the small white farmers who objected to African squatting; now it was the great landholders supplying a large but unstable market who insisted that the competition from African peasants be eliminated.[113] Land passed from the hands of absentee speculators and African tenant farmers to commercial farmers who demanded labour service instead of rent from African tenants and curtailed the number of cattle they were allowed to hold. The Land Act of 1913, which prohibited African land purchase, tenancy and sharecropping, reflected the new dominance of the commercial farmer. For the African peasant farmer it had become 'a fool's errand to find a new home for his stock and family'.[114] Severely restricted in their rights of movement, African tenants were transformed into wage or serf labourers. Also in the first two decades of the twentieth century, the 'Great Flight to the Cities'[115] of the Afrikaner rural poor began.

Conclusion

The southern African frontier differed in three major ways from the moving American frontier. What North America had, and southern Africa lacked, was the ferment of a frontier moving along with the ferment of industrial development from an early stage of settlement. Until the 1870s there was in southern Africa no major industrial and capitalist revolution occurring simultaneously with frontier settlement, each shaping and controlling the other. Nor before the

1870s was there the transportation revolution of America to link the frontier with the sources of technological and governmental change. On the frontier of the Cape Colony, and in the Free State and Transvaal, the initial settlement of near-subsistence farmers was only gradually followed by the development of commercial farming and the rise of markets and towns. The frontier in a particular area lasted much longer in southern Africa than in North America before it finally closed.

Secondly, unlike the North American frontier, which entailed the conquest of the land through the expulsion of the indigenous peoples, white expansion in southern Africa involved the colonisation of the indigenous population as well as the land. On the eastern frontier of the Cape Colony, which opened in 1770, not all the land was expropriated, and Xhosa society did not disintegrate. In the Transvaal, where there was a resurgence of African chiefdoms in the second half of the nineteenth century, the land was won but many of the indigenous people were not entirely vanquished. In fact, peasant farming, an essential feature of this frontier, was situated in the context of an 'uncompleted colonisation'. The competitors for land on the frontier would meet again in the cities to compete for work and living opportunities.

Politically, the 'frontier' conveys different meanings. Europeans think of a frontier as a borderline between countries or a line between antagonistic nations where the struggle for survival is the most intense. For American historians it means the moving line of settlements between established, organised society and the wilderness or desert beyond,[116] an area where opportunity beckoned and men lived as equals. To an Afrikaner, and perhaps also an African, the term 'frontier' had both these meanings.[117] The pioneering frontier was a place where poor men could settle and escape subordination, where they could live as equals within their own community, relatively free from threats to their political and economic survival. But as the frontier began to close, the lower classes experienced impoverishment, subordination and proletarianisation – the heritage of the vast majority of Africans and at least a quarter of the Afrikaners by 1930. Thus the closing of the frontier in all its economic, social and political dimensions had much more profound implications for twentieth-century southern Africa than it ever had for North America.

3.

Becoming Afrikaners

Recent studies have investigated the political economy of Afrikaner ethnic nationalism and political mobilisation in its 'secondary' phase of growth, starting in the 1930s and leading to the establishment of apartheid after the victory of the National Party (NP) in the election of 1948.[1] Far less is known of the economic and social bases of the political mobilisation of Afrikaner ethnicity during the second half of the nineteenth century. Analyses of Afrikaner ethnic consciousness in this earlier period have generally been concerned with identifying its 'awakening' or its 'origin'. Particularly influential has been F.A. van Jaarsveld's study, *The Awakening of Afrikaner Nationalism, 1868–1881*, which concludes that it was British imperialist interventions, particularly the annexation of the Transvaal in 1877 and the subsequent revolt of 1880–1, that triggered a nationalist response among Afrikaners all over South Africa.[2] Van Jaarsveld argues that without this awakening, the Afrikaners in the Cape Colony would have become absorbed in the English stream and Dutch/Afrikaans would have disappeared as a local language.

This study avoids both the 'awakening' and the 'origin' approaches in explaining the growth of Afrikaner nationalism up to 1915. As Ernest Gellner points out, the use of a concept such as 'awakening' comes close to accepting 'the nationalist ideologue's most misguided claim, namely that the "nations" are there, in the very nature of things, only waiting to be "awakened" (a favourite nationalist expression and image) from their regrettable slumber by the nationalist "awakener"'.[3] There is also a problem with the concept of 'origin'. In a different context, Marc Bloch remarked that in popular usage an origin tends to be regarded as a complete explanation.[4] In fact, there can never be a complete explanation as to why Afrikaner ethnic consciousness originated. At best, we can only start to give a broad explanation of its slow and tortuous beginnings.

Both Van Jaarsveld and Rodney Davenport have stressed the cultural and political aspects of the early manifestations of Afrikaner ethnic consciousness.[5] My approach attempts to situate the development of nineteenth-century Afrikaner ethnic consciousness within a socio-economic context as well as within a political and cultural framework.

Ambiguous identities before 1850

The group that ultimately became known as the 'Afrikaners' was drawn from disparate elements, particularly people from a Dutch, German or French background in the seventeenth and eighteenth centuries. Genealogists also calculate a six to seven per cent contribution from 'non-Europeans'. By 1870 it was possible to identify a distinct group of people, all of whom spoke Dutch or a variant of it, had a common religion, and maintained a fair degree of racial endogamy. Yet the development of a distinct Afrikaner ethnic consciousness that could be mobilised readily for political purposes was slow in emerging. In fact, the gradual and often tentative growth of Afrikaner cultural and political ethnic awareness was rooted firmly in historical changes that occurred after 1870. To understand the absence of an ethnic consciousness before 1870, one must explore the nature of the economy, the form of politics, and class and political cleavages in society.

Before 1850 membership of an Afrikaner ethnic community was seldom invoked as a political claim. In their dispute with the Dutch East India Company government, the supporters of the Patriot Movement of the western Cape, which arose between 1778 and 1784, made their claims in terms of their role as indispensable producers of trade goods and of their privileges as burghers. In their rebellion of 1795–6, the Graaff-Reinet burghers on the frontier depicted themselves as burghers and producers legally occupying loan farms and entitled to protection by the Company. The Voortrekkers did not see the Great Trek of 1835–8 as a positive expression of an Afrikaner political ethnicity but rather conceived of themselves as 'emigrants' and 'expatriates'.[6] Furthermore, there are no convincing historical grounds for the later, widely held belief that they tended to consider themselves as a uniquely chosen people who had a covenant with God.[7]

Among the Dutch-Afrikaner[8] colonists who did not trek we also find little evidence of an ethnic consciousness being articulated or of ethnic strategies being pursued. During the 1830s a small group of Cape Town professionals tried to stimulate a sense of cultural identity based upon recognition of a shared language and history. They supported a periodical, *Het Nederduitsch-Zuid-Afrikaansch Tijdschrift*, a college for advanced education, the Zuid-Afrikaansche Athenaeum, and a society for the promotion of arts and letters. These efforts did not succeed. The periodical folded in 1843, the society soon ceased to function, and the college became anglicised. The group of professionals was too small and the neighbouring farming population too apathetic to secure success.[9]

Even the name of the group as a whole remained highly ambiguous until the twentieth century. The term 'Afrikaner' was employed in different ways by various groups. In the early eighteenth century it was used for slaves or ex-slaves of African descent. From the late eighteenth century onwards the literature also records whites using the term. But this usage had a colonial (or regional) rather than an ethnic connotation. The *Zuid-Afrikaan*, the most widely read Dutch publication by 1830, defined Afrikaners as those 'whether English or Dutch who inhabited the land and were bound by duty and interest to further the well-being of their country'.[10] In subsequent decades the *Zuid-Afrikaan* proposed this identity as one that encompassed both Dutch- and English-speakers and that would in the course of time replace the discrete Dutch and English identities of the settlers at the Cape.

This term and definition were found acceptable by non-jingoist English-speakers who propagandised for the amalgamation of all groups of colonists in order to press political and economic claims upon Britain. Depending on the political strategy chosen, politicians used it in both an exclusive and inclusive sense. Some British imperialists appropriated it, but others spurned it because, in the words of the *Cape Times*, 'The name was originally applied to the half-bred offspring of slaves, and even in a word the mark of slavery is detestable.'[11] Indeed an official list of Cape Town prostitutes, taken in 1868, was headed by the term 'Africanders', meaning people of mixed descent.[12]

Apart from the ambiguous term 'Afrikaner' or 'Africander', there also existed the notion of a 'Boer' people. Dutch-Afrikaners generally acknowledged that they were of Boer descent, but it was usually the pastoral farmers in the interior who applied the term to themselves. Finally, there was the term 'Cape Dutch', but this was an English description rather than a self-concept. English-speakers tended to distinguish between the better-educated and more 'civilised' Cape Dutch of the western Cape or interior towns and the Boer people, whom they considered ignorant and illiterate.[13]

Although the Dutch-Afrikaners did possess by 1850 certain common cultural traits in the form of generally endogamous marriage patterns, membership of the Dutch Reformed or Lutheran churches, and a common language (or variants of it), it is difficult to find any self-conscious sense of ethnic unity among them. Indeed, from the 1850s the cleavages already existing within the group began to intensify, making the task of establishing an ethnic coalition for political purposes extremely difficult.

During the second half of the nineteenth century two interlinked forces impeded the development of such an ethnic consciousness. Firstly, there was the accelerated integration of the entire South African region into Western, and particularly British, capitalism. Secondly, the informal empire operated by Britain in the region constrained the development of Afrikaner ethnic consciousness.[14] In South Africa, unlike Australia or Canada, Britain could not count on the weight of racial kinship to keep the colonists closely tied to the metropole. When the Cape Colony received representative government in 1853, fewer than a quarter of the white inhabitants were British. In the Transvaal and Orange Free State, which became independent republics in 1852 and 1854 respectively, there was only a small scattering of British merchants, professionals and prospectors. Consequently Britain used the stratagems of informal empire and economic control to prevent these states from moving out of the imperial orbit. From the Voortrekkers a promise was exacted to support free trade and accept British control over the coastal ports upon which they depended for essential supplies. Britain could thus relax formal political control over the two Voortrekker states, secure in the anticipation that their economic dependence would achieve the same purpose.

British merchant capitalism soon assumed a dominant position in all the South African states. From the merchant houses based in the Cape Colony and, to a lesser extent, Natal, there poured forth a constant supply of indispensable articles such as wagons, firearms, gunpowder and lead. These were necessary for defence and also for hunting, an important activity in the frontier economy. The low population densities in the Boer republics, with only 15 000 to 20 000 whites in each, the lack of capital, and weak transportation links ensured that hardly any industries developed before 1875, while the transition from subsistence to commercial farming occurred at an extremely slow pace. The Free State was soon hopelessly in debt to foreign creditors.

The British cultural imperialism that went hand in hand with informal empire further hampered the development of an explicit ethnic consciousness. The towns of the Free State and the Transvaal, where one would expect ethnic movements to start, were dominated by English or Jewish merchants who were hostile or indifferent to local nationalisms and who promoted English culture. In the Transvaal they established private schools which drew as many pupils as the state schools. Eager to master the language of commerce, Dutch-Afrikaner children also preferred to attend the English section of the parallel-medium schools which the state established. Because of the greater availability of English-speaking teachers, four of the eight state-supported schools in the Transvaal used only English by 1876.[15] In the Free State the realities of merchant capitalism and cultural imperialism together similarly frustrated the development of an autonomous Dutch-Afrikaner cultural and political life. While English was accepted as the language of commerce and intellectual discourse in the town, it also penetrated the rural areas. The wealthiest farmers usually founded rural schools, and more often than not they chose English as the medium of instruction. Finally, virtually all the teachers and civil servants came from either the Netherlands or the Cape Colony. 'We are dependent on foreigners and are still ruled by foreigners', a member of the Volksraad remarked in 1873.[16]

Other stumbling blocks to a developed ethnic consciousness were internal class conflicts in Dutch-Afrikaner society, decentralised power structures, and regional rivalries. Power in both the Free State and the Transvaal was effectively in the hands of the large landholders, sometimes called patriarchs, who established patron–client relationships with both their family dependants and *bywoners*, or landless Afrikaners. The Boer–bywoner relationship, and the spirit of paternalism which infused it, was full of contradictory tendencies. In a wider sense the poorest white could participate in the political process and claim equality with the wealthy, but on the farms the *bywoners* soon became subservient to the patriarchs. Moreover, the local field-cornets, who allocated land to new-comers, distributed African labour among the individual farmers and settled labour disputes. Chosen by all the burghers in a particular division, they were invariably drawn from the ranks of, or were beholden to, the larger land-owners. Although there were exceptions, field-cornets generally favoured the larger farmers in performing their duties, and this worked against a feeling of ethnic solidarity.[17]

Furthermore, there is evidence that the burden of commando service, which every burgher was expected to perform in the Transvaal and the Free State, tended to fall unevenly on the poor. This was because of the practice which permitted a man who had been called up for service to send someone in his place. Many rich farmers abstained from commando duty, sending *bywoners* or other poor whites as their substitutes. A reader's letter in a Free State paper dis-tinguished between the *meer gegoede* (well-off) and the *minder gegoede* (less well-off) in the commandos, and this was confirmed by another who stated flatly that the war against the Sotho between 1866 and 1868 was fought mainly by the poor burghers and their children.[18] In the Transvaal the situation was much the same. By the late nineteenth century, this division gave rise to serious class conflict. Of the roughly 5 000 'joiners' – men who supported the British in the Anglo-Boer War of 1899–1902 – the vast majority were *bywoners*, some of whom were bitterly discontented because in the 1880s and 1890s they had to go on commando without payment to defend the property of the landholders at a time when their own families were destitute. They clearly hoped that the British would offer them a better deal as a reward for their collaboration.[19]

Instead of the growth of a unifying ethnic consciousness, extreme individu-alism, self-aggrandisement, and even anarchy prevailed in the early years of the Transvaal and Free State. The field-cornets often displayed great contempt for Pretoria and its representative in the district, the landdrost (magistrate). Land-drost A.F. du Toit once remarked that the field-cornets acted as if they were 'Emperors of the state'.[20] They identified primarily with their division, then with their region, and only in a nominal sense with the state or the ethnic group. Regionalism was a powerful force in the years 1850 to 1880.[21] During the late 1850s and early 1860s three regional factions – based at Lydenburg, Soutpans-berg and Potchefstroom – tried to establish their own separate sovereignties and on occasion clashed in military skirmishes.

By the end of the 1860s regional strife had subsided, but the state remained weak and religious schisms compounded the political divisions.[22] The Dutch Reformed (Hervormde) Church (NHK), established in 1853, was the state church with a privileged position. Disputes over the singing of hymns led to the establishment in 1859 of the fundamentalist Reformed (Gereformeerde) Church (colloquially known as the Dopper Church). By the 1870s the Doppers, among them Paul Kruger, had become known as a group imbued with an acute ethnic consciousness, strongly anti-British, and keen to develop a distinct political, economic and social life along their own lines.[23] Thirdly, there was the Dutch Reformed (Nederduits Gereformeerde) Church (DRC), which was initially small but had grown to ten congregations by 1870. It was doctrinally more orthodox in its doctrine than the Hervormdes, but it was politically in favour of close ties with the Cape Colony, and some of its ministers promoted English cultural influences by establishing English-language seminaries.[24] The armed civil strife of the late 1850s and early 1860s had a definite religious dimension in that the feuding factions were largely divided along religious lines and exploited religious differences for political gain.[25]

In the Orange Free State the prospects for state-building and fostering a community consciousness were not appreciably better than in the Transvaal. The state was even more dependent on British merchant capital. The Free State's leaders in its first decades often despaired of saving the state and its people. In 1858, for example, President Boshof said that it was doubtful that the Free State could sustain itself because 'patriotic feelings' were still not wide or strong enough, and he was instructed by the Volksraad to negotiate with the Cape Colony to form a federation.[26] Militarily weak, the Free State faced a formidable enemy on its eastern flank, where the Sotho resisted white expansion. The Free State's war against Moshoeshoe plunged it still deeper into crisis, and its very survival was thrown into doubt.

Ultimately, however, this war was crucial in forging a stronger sense of national identity. War, as Anthony Smith remarks, stimulates a sense of community and territory and also helps to concentrate the apparatus of physical coercion at the centre by undermining the status and power of regional leaders.[27] Moreover, war propaganda strengthens a sense of national identity. Yet as the Free State did not have an intellectual elite of its own, foreigners acted as the articulators of nationalist feelings.[28] As editor of one of the first journals, *De Tijd*, a Dutch immigrant, H.A.L. Hamelberg, set himself the task of 'cultivating a true citizenship atmosphere' by composing a folksong which soon became the republic's national anthem, sung by the burghers on commando. After the war the Volksraad thanked him for his efforts 'to cultivate a spirit of nationalism in our midst'.[29]

Although British rule in the Cape Colony had eliminated earlier frontier anarchy, the patriarchs in general and the field-cornets specifically still wielded considerable local power in large parts of the colony as well as in the republics. The introduction in 1853 of representative government at the Cape saw the replacement of the old ruling coalition, which comprised top officials, a few large estate owners, and the great merchants. In its place came a commercial middle class – the progressive sheep and cattle ranchers, the village storekeepers and artisans, the accountants, attorneys, newspaper editors and professional men who ministered to local business.[30] Indeed, English-speakers almost completely dominated the world of commerce. The commercial life of South Africa rested on a structure of mercantile credit extending from London to the country's remote rural towns. Closely associated with partners and correspondents in Great Britain and Europe, the merchant houses of the Cape extended credit on a large scale to wool producers, who were their customers in the eastern Cape, Transvaal and Orange Free State. Based on this wool trade, Port Elizabeth, with some 30 merchant houses, was the centre of South Africa's commercial world, with exports worth twice as much as those of Cape Town in 1870.

Yet, apart from some localised tensions between British and Dutch-Afrikaners centring on Grahamstown and Graaff-Reinet, there was little ethnic rivalry in the Cape Colony. The Dutch-Afrikaners did not covet the British commercial predominance while the English-speakers, except in the eastern Cape, left farming to the Dutch-Afrikaners. The so-called Boers on their isolated farms impassively resented British rule and cultural imperialism, but the Cape Dutch in the interior towns, acting as political and economic brokers, performed an important cushioning function. Neither the Boers nor the Cape Dutch resisted the dominant English role in politics. Although Dutch-Afrikaners accounted for roughly 70 per cent of the Cape's white population, the proportion of Dutch-Afrikaner representatives in Parliament ranged from only 32 to 36 per cent between 1850 and 1870. At the constituency level great apathy reigned. In 1869 a canvasser found that nine-tenths of young farmers under the age of 26 in his area had not troubled to register as voters. Jan Hofmeyr, who founded the first political interest group, remarked about this period that 'the Dutch were very apathetic as to their political privileges. Even if they registered and voted, they simply did so for their English shopkeeper or agent, or for someone recommended by them.'[31]

Parliamentary politics largely played out within patron–client relationships manipulated by the merchants, the large landholders, and the influential Cape Dutch. They faced little opposition. Many of the constituencies were not even contested, with nearly half going unopposed in the 1869 election, for example. Where there was a real contest, it was usually a small number of men who mobilised a majority with their family connections, colleagues and friends. There was no secret ballot and men of influence expected their tenants, clients, debtors and other dependants to vote for them and also had the means of ensuring that they did so. With their prominent position as financial middlemen in the towns, the Cape Dutch were strategically placed to control the vote of the wealthy Boers in rural constituencies and deliver seats to merchants who were, as a group, over-represented in Parliament. The same patron–client relationship operated with respect to careers in the civil service, entry to which was regulated in most cases by the exertions of parents or patrons rather than by any system of merit and qualification.[32]

The reason for this lack of political interest of the Dutch-Afrikaner farmers is simple: the colony's Parliament hardly touched their daily lives. It had a limited ability to tax, and its greatest topic of discussion was the budget deficit and the need for retrenchment. There was indeed little room for ethnic politics in the colonial state during the 1850s, 1860s and early 1870s. The wealthier class of Dutch-Afrikaner farmers in the western Cape had no serious quarrel with the British connection or with English-speakers' political domination of the Cape. They unquestioningly accepted the need for British military protection of the colony. They hoped against hope that Britain would again grant preferential tariffs on Cape exports, eagerly enlisting English allies in their campaign for pro-tective tariffs against imported wine and other products. Their chief mouthpiece, the *Zuid-Afrikaan*, wrote in 1857 that the colony was witnessing 'the gradual amalgamation of the Dutch and the English nationality which will, however, take many years'. In the meantime the colonists should promote the many interests they had in common, and 'the less we speak of nationality the better'.[33]

Early stimulants of Afrikaner ethnic consciousness

It would become increasingly difficult to maintain such a phlegmatic posture. From the 1850s onwards, the Dutch-Afrikaners in the Cape faced a twin assault on their cultural and spiritual values in the form of the so-called liberal movement and intensified British cultural imperialism. Springing from the eighteenth-century Enlightenment in Europe, but only gathering force in the Cape from the 1850s, the liberal movement stressed personal autonomy, personal self-sufficiency and personal sovereignty. Considering itself the antithesis of absolutism, it championed democracy and the separation of state and church. It challenged the authority of the Scriptures, the Protestant Confessions, and the ruling ecclesiastical bodies. From the 1860s some young ministers in the DRC in the Cape started to preach a liberal theology which questioned some of the fundamental tenets of the Confessions. Two were deposed in 1864 on account of heterodox teaching but were restored to office by secular courts. In 1865 the liberal movement scored a major breakthrough when instruction in the Christian religion was barred from state schools, which now became fully secularised. In 1875 a final separation between church and state was effected with the triumph of the principle of voluntarism in respect of religion. Disestablishment brought about the end of the state's financial support for the DRC, which in the mid-nineteenth century had received some £7 000 annually for paying salaries. The result was that each parish had to assume sole responsibility for providing for its minister's remuneration.[34]

British imperialism increasingly expressed itself in its political, economic and cultural forms. Even more ominous was the growing challenge of British cultural imperialism. To protect its commercial and strategic interests in the Cape Colony, it seemed vital for Britain to reshape the white colonists in its own image. The Dutch-Afrikaners were 'the ideal prefabricated collaborators' in helping to secure British power and influence.[35] Although a very large number of Dutch-Afrikaners still existed on a subsistence basis and had little or no knowledge of English, the government in 1865 abolished Dutch as a medium of instruction in government schools and imposed English as the sole medium. This decision flowed from a recommendation by an education commission of seven members, three of whom had Dutch names. They belonged to the relatively small number of 'Anglo-Afrikaners' in and around Cape Town who wanted English to become the sole official language and the colony to assume an English identity. By the 1860s it appeared as if their wish was gradually coming true – certainly as far as Cape Town and its immediate environs were concerned. Several observers reported that Dutch-Afrikaner youth in this area were becoming estranged from their language and customs. With a good command of English being a prerequisite for a career in the civil service, law and commerce, there were powerful forces at work in favour of further anglicisation. Even the most prestigious DRC congregation, the 'Moederkerk' in Cape Town, yielded to the demand for English services to be held in the Groote Kerk on some evenings. The Moederkerk was preceded or followed in its example by several rural congregations. In effect, this legitimised the Anglo-Afrikaners' position.[36]

No one watched these developments with more concern than the Rev. G.W.A. van der Lingen of Paarl. Van der Lingen realised that what was happening at the Cape was a vital ideological battle between, on the one hand, the state and the liberal movement, both of which emphasised rationalism and secularism, and, on the other, the authority of religion and the clergy. If they lost the battle, the church and its ministers would steadily find themselves losing control over their members and would be confronted by dwindling support and dwindling status. Anthony Smith has acutely observed that in situations such as these, neo-traditionalists not only strongly defend traditional values and dogma but also try to use political means to revive religious heritage, faith and authority. What they do, in short, is to turn their religious congregations into ethnic communities, as happened with the Jews.[37]

After his studies in the Netherlands, Van der Lingen became the leading force among those who rejected the call for freedom, civilisation, enlightenment and progress. He was also in the forefront of the fight against liberal theology in the DRC. Deeply concerned by the rapid advance of English culture and the alien influences of the state education system, Van der Lingen established schools under the auspices of the church council which gave a prominent place to the teaching of Dutch and religious instruction. But he seemed to be waging a losing struggle and his influence did not extend much beyond Paarl and Stellenbosch, where he served as chairman of the Theological Seminary council. Even in the seminary there was a distinct trend towards anglicisation.[38]

By 1870 the traditional Dutch-Afrikaner world of subsistence farming as well as the sway of patriarchal local or regional leaders was slowly coming to an end. With the advent of commercial farming, the increased dependence on credit, and the development of an infrastructure of roads and markets, a new kind of politics appeared. It assumed different forms in the two republics in the north and in the Cape Colony. In the Orange Free State and the Transvaal mobilisation around the state began to develop and, over time, became the basis of local nationalisms. In the Cape Colony the Dutch-Afrikaners began to articulate ethnic sentiments and started to explore political strategies based on ethnic mobilisation. An emotional attachment to the Dutch-Afrikaners as a cultural group with shared beliefs about descent and history began to be channelled into a movement that made political claims on behalf of this group. Initially it was an amorphous type of ethnic consciousness, quite different from the radical twentieth-century Afrikaner ethnic movement of the 1930s and 1940s, which would insist on political supremacy and which would define the group exclusively in terms of an elaborate ethnic ideology.

The context in which such a mobilisation occurred in the Orange Free State was supplied, firstly, by the response to the British annexation of Basutoland (1868) and the diamond fields of Griqualand West (1871), to which the young republic had expressed strong claims, and, secondly, by accelerated economic development, which made increased resources available to the state. The British annexation of the diamond fields made the burghers feel that they had been wronged as an ethnic group by Britain and by English-speakers, who were now seen as 'the other'. But as important was the growing prosperity brought by the discovery of diamonds and the rise of a market in Kimberley, a town which already by 1871 had a population of more than 40 000 whites and 20 000 Africans. This prosperity, which spilled over into the Free State, enabled the struggling republic to develop its institutions and infrastructure. It was able, for example, to set aside funds for commissioning a Dutchman, H.J. Hofstede, to write a history of the Free State. This book aimed to stir and 'uplift national feelings', by telling of the 'trials and tribulations' of the people's forefathers and the numerous grievances of the Afrikaners.[39] This was not so much 'the product of an awakening of national feeling' as a deliberate attempt by the government to cultivate such a feeling for the sake of state-building.[40] Yet, these efforts encountered considerable stumbling blocks. In the Volksraad merchants and professionals closely tied to British merchant capital were well represented. While J.H. Brand was president (1864–88), they were able to promote a bicultural consciousness in which English was predominant as the language of commerce and intellectual discourse.

Nevertheless, with many burghers in a state of indebtedness, both local and ethnic sentiment could, from the early days of the republic, feed on a financial anti-imperialism which expressed itself in strong resentment against their main creditor, the Standard Bank. The bank sent large dividends abroad and was accused of charging excessive interest rates. Against it stood the local bank, the Bloemfontein Bank, which had several members of the Volksraad as shareholders. They had no qualms about spreading the word that the avaricious foreign bank would drive the Free State burghers over the Vaal River or into the sea. In 1865 the Volksraad expelled the Standard Bank from the republic and in 1882 it rejected the bank's petition to be readmitted. In a report to London the general manager complained that 'while the President . . . is friendly, we cannot expect that he will exert himself in our favour and the [Volksraad] itself is at present extremely anti-English'.[41]

In the Transvaal the development of a local nationalism was less advanced than in the Free State. Subsistence farming, linked only tenuously to the market, continued to reinforce established networks of patron–client relationships, and extreme individualism was still scarcely diluted by the integrative effects of trade. The influence of regional leaders was too strong and the interests of the regions too diffuse for any national cohesion to develop. The Rev. F. Lion Cachet, head of one of the three Reformed churches in the Transvaal, aptly remarked in 1872 that the Transvaal burghers were so divided 'that they appeared to be four or five nations instead of one nation'.[42]

Ironically, it was under T.F. Burgers, president of the Transvaal from 1872 to 1877, that the greatest factionalism and disintegration occurred. More than any Dutch-Afrikaner leader of the time, he advocated the unity of all 'Afrikaners whether by birth or adoption' across the political boundaries of South Africa, the teaching of a national history to counteract English cultural hegemony, and the development of a railway line to Delagoa Bay to lessen their dependence upon the Cape Colony.[43] Yet while Burgers propagandised on behalf of these ideas, his state became heavily indebted to foreign banks, particularly the

Cape Commercial Bank, which granted low interest rates to obtain a political grip on the state. The parochial Transvaal burghers had little enthusiasm for allowing Cape Dutch-Afrikaners open competition for jobs in the Transvaal and refused to pay increased taxes for constructing a railway and waging war against local African chiefdoms. By the time the British agent, Theophilus Shepstone, arrived in the Transvaal in 1877 to annex the state, it was utterly bankrupt and politically paralysed by the divisions between the Kruger and the Burgers factions.[44]

In the Cape Colony political ethnic self-consciousness also began to develop. This occurred within the context of, firstly, the rapid economic expansion consequent upon the opening of the diamond fields in 1869; secondly, the introduction in 1872 of responsible government, which created a new arena for political contest; and, thirdly, the growing concern, articulated by intellectuals and professionals, about a major economic and cultural crisis impending for a large section of the Dutch-Afrikaners.

Even before accelerated economic development started around 1870, there had been a considerable improvement in communications. Cape Town's penny post was extended to the rest of the colony in the 1860s, telegraph cables were flung eastwards and northwards to beyond the colony's borders, and newspapers proliferated. By 1871 there were some 34 newspapers in the colony of which 24 were published outside Cape Town. Most of them appeared twice a week with pages in both English and Dutch. While these innovations bound the Dutch-Afrikaners closer together, this was counterbalanced by the fact that more than 90 per cent of them still lived on the land, mostly on widely dispersed farms.

The economic boost which the diamond fields gave to the colony did not immediately destroy the isolation of subsistence farming. It did, however, make farmers in particular and Dutch-Afrikaners in general much more aware of new opportunities, existing constraints, and the uneven nature of economic growth. The two most important branches of agriculture in which Dutch-Afrikaners were engaged benefited little from the diamond boom. Wine production, the most important economic activity in the region and the one dominated almost exclusively by Dutch-Afrikaners, faced exceedingly difficult times. A period of growth and prosperity for the industry had ended in 1861 when the British preferential tariff on Cape wines was abolished. Total wine exports plummeted from 319 146 gallons in 1863 to only 57 942 in 1875.[45] Wine surpluses increased annually, prices dropped, and by 1878 the economic position of the wine farmers caused deep pessimism.[46] Wool farmers also gained little from the opening of the diamond fields. The value of wool exports had peaked at more than £3 million in the early 1870s, but by 1885 it had dropped to less than half that in value.

Dutch-Afrikaners slowly moved into industry, but they found it difficult to compete with the more skilled English-speakers. During the 1870s and 1880s most of the wine distilleries established by Dutch-Afrikaners in the rural western Cape became bankrupt. The Dutch-Afrikaners also entered in considerable numbers into the world of finance and property speculation which burst upon South Africa in the 1860s and 1870s, coming into competition with British interests. The banking monopoly had ended by the middle of the nineteenth century, and in its place came district banks, of which there were 29 by 1862. Dutch-Afrikaners invested heavily in these banks and some became involved as directors. In the early 1860s, strong London-based banks opened branches in South Africa. Soon there was a surfeit of investment capital chasing far too few sound investment opportunities. Many of the district banks went bankrupt as a result of incautious lending and over-speculation, and by 1882 there were only eight left. In contrast the Standard Bank's dividend rose steadily from 1865 to 1881, most of it being distributed overseas.[47]

Severe barriers also faced Dutch-Afrikaners who contemplated entering central and local government, which by 1875 employed some 4 500 people in the colony. Every candidate had to be fluent in English, the only official language, and the informal system of patronage was dominated by English-speakers, who virtually monopolised the senior ranks of the service. Against this general economic background, Dutch-Afrikaners began to agitate for protectionist policies to aid farmers, for a national bank to counter the imperial banks, and for equal status for the Dutch language. In general, English-speakers, with their base in commerce and industry, opposed these demands.

The introduction of responsible government in 1872 also stimulated ethnic mobilisation as it created an arena in which effective contests for state patronage and revenue could take place. While there was little to contest in the 1850s and 1860s, the state's resources and capabilities began to expand rapidly by the 1870s. Between 1854 and 1874 the value of exports (including diamonds) increased eight times, that of imports three times, and revenue five times. While the government had previously been preoccupied with keeping expenditures down, its main concern in the 1870s and 1880s was to secure credit to develop the diamond fields, to construct railways and other public works, and to procure labour from the Transkeian territories. The Cape government worked hard to maintain a flow of credit, especially from London. To gain access to that credit and to benefit from state expenditure and patronage was vitally important for the fortunes of landowners, commercial farmers, local businessmen, commercial middlemen, and those active in the import-export sector.[48] It was along these avenues that the Cape Dutch-Afrikaner leader, Onze Jan Hofmeyr, would pursue his career.

Responsible government also made possible an amendment to the Cape constitution. In the 1850s Dutch-Afrikaner leaders had supported the low, colour-blind franchise, hoping that it would counteract 'the fictitious inequality of wealth' which existed at the Cape. During the 1860s this hope gave way to disillusionment. Coloured and African voters supported English merchants and traders rather than Dutch-Afrikaner candidates, who mostly represented farmers who generally paid low wages to their workers. This prompted Dutch-Afrikaner leaders to turn away from the non-racial democracy and increasingly resort to racist politics. After the introduction of responsible government, Hofmeyr and the *Zuid-Afrikaan* would more and more engage in discussion of the constitution in terms of 'Africanderism', which meant a curtailment of the non-white franchise and the promotion of farming interests.[49]

Dutch-Afrikaner political mobilisation was encouraged by the political decline of merchant hegemony and the incorporationist strategy of Cape liberalism, which was aimed especially at Coloured artisans and progressive African peasants. The merchants were unable to consolidate their own class position largely because of a bitter conflict between the Cape Town and Port Elizabeth mercantile communities over railway extensions and the improvement of harbour facilities. Neither group of merchants tried to establish a regional political base by attracting the support of farmers and professional men. Moreover, with the rise of Kimberley and the Witwatersrand, the Cape merchants lost their grip on the mainspring of the southern African regional economy.[50] Their political and ideological dominance receded as the Cape's English-speakers tied their fortunes to the gold-mining industry of the Transvaal, based as it was on low-paid African wage labour. Inevitably these changes undermined Cape liberalism. The tide now clearly turned in the direction of a restrictive franchise and state intervention to meet the labour needs of farmers, a change which well suited Dutch-Afrikaner politicians.[51]

It was of course not inevitable that a colony-wide Dutch-Afrikaner political movement based on ethnic awareness would emerge. Another possibility was a farmers' party, but that went aground upon the antagonism between English farmers and merchants in the eastern Cape and the economically less advanced Dutch-Afrikaner farmers in the east. That there emerged an Afrikaner party conforms to the general observation that in societies where class and ethnic ties tend to coincide rather than cross-cut, political entrepreneurs usually establish a following by relying on emotive ethnic distinctions between 'us' and 'them'.[52] Senior English officials sensed that responsible government could mean the demise of the English ascendancy at the Cape. The attorney-general wrote to London in 1871 that the Boers, forming the majority of the white section in the constituencies, 'desire to keep Africa for themselves and keep down English interests and institutions'.[53]

In the framework of Cape politics, however, such sentiments had to be reinforced by the perception of a viable common culture before a specifically Dutch-Afrikaner political platform could be constructed. This brings us to the last dimension of the context in which a politically oriented ethnic consciousness developed, namely the recognition among Dutch-Afrikaner professionals that a large section of their ethnic group faced both economic and cultural decline.

Accelerated economic development had greatly widened the class cleavages within Dutch-Afrikaner society. At the top were the large landholders and commercial farmers and the Cape Dutch in the towns, who prospered as financial agents and auctioneers; then came a large number of middling farmers who managed to make ends meet; and finally, at the bottom, there were the small farmers and *bywoners*. From the 1870s onwards a large class of poor and often destitute small farmers began to form. They were unable and unwilling to do anything but farm – and they formed almost an underclass that in Marx's terms was 'passively rotting away'. Some of the most desperate of these small farmers began to migrate to the towns where they found casual employment, but others resorted to vagrancy, begging and crime. In towns all over South Africa, blacks and whites were now working and living together and, in small but growing numbers, having sexual relations.

This economic crisis was accompanied by a grave cultural crisis. At its apex, Dutch-Afrikaner society was losing some of its brightest minds through the steady process of anglicisation. At its bottom there was the even greater threat of large numbers of the poor becoming proletarianised. The cultural crisis sprang from the economic crisis facing poor farmers. In the eastern Cape many Afrikaner farmers could not afford to send their children to school because their labour was needed on the farms. Some Boer farmers in 1875 even demanded a bonus for each child they sent to school to compensate for the loss of labour that schooling involved.[54] The result was child illiteracy of alarming proportions. In the 1875 census it was estimated that only 43 per cent of children between the ages of 5 and 15 in the Cape Colony could read and write, and for Dutch-Afrikaners it must have been considerably lower, assuming that English-speakers probably attained the level of their counterparts in Victoria, Australia, and New Zealand, where the figure was about 60 per cent. It was true that almost everyone older than 15 learned to read and write, but the level of these skills was in most cases extremely rudimentary. It was generally known that a large section of Boers never read any books apart from the Bible.

By the 1870s this cultural degeneration began to alarm government officials. In 1873 a series of anonymous articles appeared in the *Cape Monthly Magazine*, obviously the work of a well-informed person:

> I would ask the ministers of religion, the promoters of education, and the responsible rulers of the Colony, if they are satisfied with things as they are? – if they realise the fact of the children of Dutch-speaking, European parentage growing up with less care bestowed upon them than upon the beasts of the field – without the ability to read or write even their mother tongue, without any instruction in the knowledge of a God that made them, having at their command no language but a limited vocabulary of semi-Dutch, semi-Hottentot words, and those only concerning the wants or doings of themselves and the animals they tend?[55]

The author delivered a searing indictment of 'state-paid ministers' who were unconcerned about this situation and whose only visible activity was a Sunday sermon in the village church. He warned that if no remedy was found, a growing criminal class would develop.

In 1867 diamonds were discovered, beginning a period of economic transformation of South Africa. The accelerated industrialisation of South Africa in the wake of the mineral discoveries did not immediately transform people's self-conceptions. Invariably, collective memories persist in institutional forms when the social conditions that originally gave rise to them have evaporated. As long as they remained tied to the land, the Afrikaners retained a primary loyalty to their church and faith and to regional and other subgroupings rather than to the state or a pervasive culture. Nevertheless, a slow movement towards ethnic identification did begin, initially undertaken by ethnic culture-brokers and then stimulated by catalytic political events, ultimately producing concrete expressions in a politically articulated ethnic consciousness. In the western Cape a few clerics and teachers tried to deal with the cultural crisis of Dutch-Afrikaner semi-literacy and illiteracy; in the same region wine farmers mobilised against a tax that adversely affected their industry; and in the Transvaal near-subsistence farmers rose against the British annexation of their state.

The culture-brokers of the western Cape during the 1870s

It was in the Paarl–Wellington area that the first conscious attempts were made to develop a specific ethnic ideology for the Dutch-Afrikaners. The leading role was taken by two Dutch school teachers, A. Pannevis and C.P. Hoogenhout, who had settled in the area in the 1860s, and a Dutch Reformed Church minister, S.J. du Toit, the son of a Paarl wine farmer. A complex set of concerns drove these men. In the first place, they were deeply disturbed by the way in which industrialisation and the secularisation of education were affecting Dutch-Afrikaner society. They wished to encapsulate Dutch-Afrikaners in their own institutions and culture so as to deflect alien influences. Secondly, they were motivated by a concern with the more general cultural crisis.

Ironically, the initial attempts at upliftment were not directed at Dutch-Afrikaners. A part-time missionary, Pannevis was at first moved by the plight of the Coloured population of the western Cape, whose educational opportunities

were even poorer than those of the Dutch-Afrikaners. He was greatly concerned
that thousands of them were unable to understand the Bible in either Dutch or
English. In 1872 he made a plea in the *Zuid-Afrikaan* that for their sake the Bible
be translated into Afrikaans, a language spoken by the vast majority of them.

Before Pannevis made his plea, Afrikaans had been used in religious pam-
phlets and magazines directed at Coloured Muslims and Christians. Some three
hundred letters in Afrikaans, mostly written by whites, had appeared in newspapers. However, whites used Afrikaans as a dialect – or the 'lowest vernacular' –
to amuse or to poke fun at the lower classes. 'Afrikaans' was a collective term
denoting all the corrupted versions of Dutch in the colony. Pannevis realised,
however, that Afrikaans was an excellent medium for making the Bible accessible
and for providing education to poor and uneducated people. This proposal to
render the Bible in Afrikaans for the Coloureds soon lost force, and from the
mid-1870s Pannevis and Hoogenhout used all their efforts to persuade the Dutch-
Afrikaners that Afrikaans was a language in its own right and that it was the
true language of white Dutch-Afrikaners.

It was Hoogenhout who saw the potential of Afrikaans as the basis of a cultural ethnic awareness to oppose English hegemony. Like Van der Lingen before
him, Hoogenhout stressed the link between industrialisation and anglicisation,
and condemned both. English was for him the language of corruption, bred at
the billiard table and in the drinking den. The *volk* was being bastardised by the
way in which English had completely usurped everything in the name of progress. In his novel *Catharina* he wrote of the evil and corruption of the anglicised society of Cape Town and contrasted it with the worthiness of the
patriarchal social relations typical of the rural Dutch-Afrikaners. In 1873 Hoogenhout appealed in the *Zuid-Afrikaan* for an Afrikaans translation of the Bible
'not only for Coloured people but also for many whites, because there are really
many whites who do not understand half of the Dutch language'. He added
that 'the Lord would not tolerate that the Bible should remain unintelligible to
many poor people in South Africa'.[56]

Building on the work of the two Dutchmen, Du Toit declared war against
British cultural hegemony, the secularisation of education which undermined
traditional authorities, and the corrupting influence of industrialisation. He
devoted all his efforts towards making Afrikaans the cardinal ethnic symbol

which encapsulated the history and singularity of the Afrikaner people. In three newspaper articles published under the pseudonym 'A true Afrikaner', he argued that language expressed the character of a people (*volk*) and that no nationality could be formed without its own language. Secondly, he argued that Afrikaans should be accepted as a language in its own right by Afrikaners. Thirdly, he criticised the process of anglicisation taking place in Parliament, the courts, schools and churches, and was particularly scathing about the DRC clergy who delivered sermons in English and who set up English-language educational institutions in the principal towns.[57]

In 1875 Du Toit, Hoogenhout and six others founded the Genootskap van Regte Afrikaners (GRA) (Fellowship of True Afrikaners) in Paarl. By the mid-1870s a strong section within the dominant class considered Dutch-Afrikaners and colonial English-speakers as all members of a nascent Afrikaner nation. The *Volksblad*, for instance, remarked in 1875: 'When we speak of "Afrikanders" we do not mean Dutch-speaking or English-speaking South Africans, but the people who have been and still are being moulded into that distinct nation.'[58] In contrast, the GRA employed the concept of the Afrikaner people to denote a distinct ethnic group within the population. It divided Afrikaner people into three groups – those with English hearts, those with Dutch hearts and those with Afrikaner hearts, and only the last were considered to be true Afrikaners. The GRA declared itself in favour of Afrikaans and resolved not to rest before it was recognised as the national (ethnic) language. To this end, it published a newspaper, *Di Patriot*, a nationalist history, a grammar, and some school texts in Afrikaans. The GRA's use of Afrikaans had several dimensions: it was a political language which embodied Afrikaner ethnic self-awareness and expressed opposition to imperial rule; it was an educational instrument, which would uplift large numbers of backward children; and it was a vehicle for the dissemination of the Bible among large numbers of poor and ignorant Coloured and white people.

Yet this emphasis on the Afrikaans language embodying the singularity of the Afrikaners obscured the fact that the great majority of Coloureds – people of slave, European and Khoikhoi descent – also spoke Afrikaans and did so much less self-consciously. No attempt was made to embrace all Afrikaans-speakers as members of a new *volk* participating in a developing nationalist movement.

The class divisions between white and Coloured Afrikaans-speakers were too acute for this. Whites prided themselves on being part of a master or 'aristocratic' class, and even its poorest members considered themselves too superior to accept employment in someone else's service, to do manual labour, or to work as artisans. Dutch-Afrikaners generally treated Coloured Afrikaans-speakers as a class of servants still bearing the taint of slavery.

Growing segregation widened the gulf. A trend, starting in the 1830s, to segregate Coloured members of the Dutch Reformed Church found expression in the establishment of separate Coloured congregations and culminated in the founding of the Dutch Reformed Mission Church in 1881. Schools were racially segregated in 1893. No statutory residential segregation existed, but the great majority of Coloured people lived together in the poorest sections of the towns. The main Afrikaner political movement did not formally exclude Coloured members but it did reject applications at branch level.

Thus Afrikaner ethnic consciousness from the beginning contained both a strong racial dimension and a considerable measure of self-delusion about the origins of both the ethnic group itself and the Afrikaans language. Despite the fact that a considerable proportion of marriages had occurred across the colour line in the eighteenth century, *Di Patriot* and *Zuid-Afrikaan* spoke only of the ethnic group's white or European ancestry. In championing Afrikaans, *Di Patriot* was at pains to declare that Afrikaans was a pure Germanic language without 'Hottentot' words, and that the 'Hottentots had abandoned their language and adopted ours'. While there was still little direct economic competition between white and Coloured Afrikaans-speakers, this racially exclusive ethnic mobilisation resulted in the increasing alienation of the Coloureds.[59]

The political mobilisation of Dutch-Afrikaners after 1870

The second major development stimulating growing ethnic awareness was the rise of Dutch-Afrikaner farmers' associations (*boeren vereenigingen*). During the 1870s several were formed in the north-eastern and eastern part of the colony. Like their English counterparts, they started as agricultural organisations but soon began to speak out on political issues. The Albert Boeren Vereeniging, where *Di Patriot* found an avid readership, in particular demanded the right to speak Dutch in Parliament and proposed a colony-wide Afrikaner Bond based

on common interests and loyalties. In 1878 the wine producers of the western
Cape were roused by an excise bill which threatened to injure them further,
and, in response, Onze Jan Hofmeyr established the Zuid-Afrikaansche Boeren
Beschermings Vereeniging (BBV). It was initially an organisation of wine producers established to oppose the new bill. It was also a western Cape political
formation against a government dominated by English-speaking politicians of
the eastern Cape. Most importantly, it was an ethnic movement that championed
Dutch-Afrikaner interests in matters as diverse as farmers' control over labour
and Dutch language rights. To broaden his political base Hofmeyr defined the
group as one that included 'patriotic' English-speakers. Coloured Afrikaans-
speakers were, however, hardly mentioned and were usually treated as a separate category.

The BBV scored a remarkable success in the 1878–9 elections, winning nine
of the 21 upper house seats and a third of those of the lower house. Soon after
the elections, however, enthusiasm dwindled. The BBV failed to attract more
than a thousand members and barely extended outside the western Cape. Efforts
to link up with the eastern Cape farmers' associations were not successful, and
those associations themselves failed to form their own co-ordinating body. In
1880 Du Toit seized the initiative by founding the Afrikaner Bond, which aimed
at co-ordinating the activities of the GRA, BBV and eastern Cape *boeren vereenigingen* and linking them with Dutch-Afrikaners in the Boer republics. The Bond's
principles represented a compromise between Du Toit's exclusive and Hofmeyr's
inclusive strategies. On the one hand, there was Du Toit's attack on speculators,
foreign banks and traitors in Parliament, criticism of the education of Dutch-
Afrikaners while 'millions of pounds' were spent on the education of the
English, and complaints about the sacrifice of 'Africa's interests to England, or
those of the Farmer to the Merchant'. On the other hand, the Bond's definition
of the 'Afrikaner' was the one favoured by Hofmeyr: all those who recognised
Africa as their fatherland and wanted to work together for the good of a united
South Africa.[60]

In the Transvaal Dutch-Afrikaner ethnic awareness was politicised by the
successful revolt in 1881 of the burghers against the British occupation of their
state. As De Kiewiet aptly puts it: the unity of the Transvaal burghers when it
finally came 'was not really proof of a slow cementing into consistency and

durability of their opinions and practice, but a more rapid fusing in the heat of the clash with the British government'.[61] The resistance of the Transvaal burghers indeed became a remarkably vigorous ethnic mobilisation. Mass meetings were held where large numbers of burghers camped out for several days to listen to speeches by their leaders. Petitions against the annexation were signed by between a half and two-thirds of the total population of some 8 000 burghers. In this mobilisation all political divisions were temporarily transcended. The annexation had, as Judge Kotze put it, 'given birth to a strong national feeling among the Boers; it had united them and all were now for the state'.[62]

After the war, the Boer generals, using their new status as 'national leaders', appealed to the burghers to end their political and religious divisions. In Paul Kruger the Transvaal had a president who succeeded far better than Burgers in becoming the focus of a loyalty to the Transvaal and in developing a sense of community. In his speeches and in several history books that appeared after the war, a new basis for historical consciousness was propounded. This history was, as Van Jaarsveld notes, 'a tabulation of grievances and a story of clashes be-tween Boer and Briton'. Its spirit was 'that of "wrong", "injustice" and "oppres-sion"'. The Great Trek was interpreted as a 'sacred passion for freedom' and the Battle of Blood River, where the Voortrekkers in 1838 had won a major victory over the Zulu, began to occupy a central place in Afrikaner historical mythology.[63] After the war the commemoration of this battle became a truly national festive occasion for the first time. The five-yearly festivals at Paardekraal were great events that celebrated the vow made by the Boers prior to their revolt against the British. In 1881 a crowd estimated at between 12 000 and 15 000 listened with rapt attention to the patriotic speeches of Kruger and others.

These three developments – the founding of the GRA and the so-called First Afrikaans Language Movement, the establishment of the BBV and the Afrikaner Bond, and the Transvaal revolt – are often considered by historians as constitut-ing the 'awakening' of Afrikaner nationalism, and there is indeed some evidence to support this view. The writings of *Di Patriot* encouraged the Transvaal bur-ghers to resist British imperialism actively, and their successful revolt in turn boosted ethnic initiatives in the western Cape and elsewhere. *Di Patriot* had struggled to survive with a circulation of only 500 in 1877, but after the war of 1880–1 this jumped to 3 000. Du Toit himself thought that the glorious Boer victory at Majuba had given birth to the Afrikaner nation. In 1881 a pan-Afrikaner ethnic movement really seemed to have taken off. In many places in the Cape Colony and Free State Dutch-Afrikaners expressed their solidarity with the Transvaal burghers. They saw the revolt as a struggle which affected everyone of Dutch and French descent with 'a true Afrikaans' spirit. In Hofmeyr's words, 'it filled the Afrikanders, otherwise grovelling in the mud of materialism, with a national glow of sympathy for the brothers across the Transvaal'.[64]

The Afrikaner Bond greatly benefited from this upsurge of ethnic emotions. At the end of 1880 it had only three branches, but after the revolt branches were founded in numerous towns, particularly in the eastern Cape, and also in the Orange Free State and Transvaal. In 1883 the BBV and Bond were merged after Hofmeyr outmanoeuvred the Du Toit faction, and the Bond emerged as the strongest bloc in the Cape Parliament, increasing the proportion of Dutch-Afrikaner representatives from approximately a third in the years between 1854 and 1885 to just under a half in the last sixteen years of the century. It easily secured formal approval for Dutch to be used in Parliament, in the courts, and as the medium of instruction in schools.

The faltering of ethnic consciousness in the 1880s

Yet despite these early accomplishments, Afrikaner political ethnicity failed to sustain its momentum. Three forces worked against it: firstly, continuing British imperial hegemony; secondly, deepening class cleavages within the Dutch-Afrikaner group; and, thirdly, intense inter-state rivalry between the Cape Colony and Transvaal. All of these contributed to an incoherent and inconsistent ideological conception of 'Afrikanerhood'.

The inhibiting force of British political hegemony was evident in the Cape Colony even at the time of the Transvaal protests and revolt. Despite their strong feelings of solidarity with the Transvaal burghers and resentment at British imperial arrogance, the Dutch-Afrikaners – particularly the Cape Dutch – were reluctant to engage in any kind of politics that challenged the dominant consensus. This consensus demanded an almost unqualified political loyalty to Britain and to the ideal of a common nationhood for the two white groups. While Hofmeyr and several branches of the BBV in 1880 protested against the annexation, only one branch received a Transvaal deputation seeking to rally the support of the Cape. The BBV in general acted in an uncoordinated and un-convincing way.[65]

After Britain granted a qualified independence to the Transvaal, Hofmeyr declared in Parliament: 'The generosity of the terms had strengthened the loyalty of the Dutch in the Colony . . . [and] had given it a warmth and heartiness which it never had before.'[66] In the course of the 1880s Hofmeyr came to reject the Afrikaner Bond's call of 'Africa for the Afrikanders' and South African political unity under its own flag, in favour of a political union under the British flag. President Brand of the Orange Free State also sought to maintain close politi-cal and economic ties of unity with the Cape Colony and, by extension, with Great Britain, and to promote Dutch-Afrikaner and English unity. He thus strongly attacked Du Toit's Afrikaner Bond. Only Kruger in the Transvaal took an opposite approach. Even he, however, espoused a Transvaal nationalism whose point of departure was loyalty to the Transvaal state and which was not based on an 'organic' Afrikaner unity.[67]

English cultural hegemony reinforced British political rule. Despite the formal recognition of Dutch, the English language maintained its dominant position in the Cape's schools, courts and Parliament. In growing numbers, better-educated Dutch-Afrikaners spoke English in public debates and used English for correspondence and even in their personal diaries. The situation was little differ-ent in the Free State. Its rural schools were usually started by wealthier farmers who set a premium on English as the language of commerce and intellectual discourse and who deliberately sought out English teachers. In the early 1880s a school inspector found that only a third of the schools he visited used Dutch as the sole medium of instruction. A cleric reported: 'I cannot neglect mention-ing how much talking and writing in English has become prominent in the Free State, especially in the towns. Nowhere else did I have to speak so much English as there.'[68] Before the end of the nineteenth century public and social life in Bloemfontein was almost exclusively English.

A major problem in the Transvaal was illiteracy. In 1877 it was estimated that only eight per cent of white children of school age were attending classes, as opposed to 50 per cent in the Cape Colony and twelve per cent in the Orange Free State. The opening of the gold fields in the 1880s brought with it deep cleavages in the community over the question of education as well as fresh opportunities for capital accumulation. A group of Dutch-Afrikaners, often the products of English education in the Cape, demanded the inclusion of much more English in the syllabus. Against these 'progressives' stood President Kruger, who made Dutch the medium of instruction and who was strongly supported by Dutch immigrant civil servants and school teachers and by the Dopper Church. S.J. du Toit, who had become head of Kruger's education department, sided with the 'progressives' against Kruger and his 'Hollanders' and was remarkably lax in enforcing the language ruling. When Dr Nicolaas Mansvelt, a Hollander, became superintendent of education in 1892, an attempt was made to enforce Dutch as the medium of instruction in all higher standards. This sparked an outcry from the 'progressives', who saw English as a prerequisite for their economic advancement, as well as from the substantial English population of Johannesburg. Mansvelt was forced to back down, and the state continued to subsidise schools where Dutch was taught at least four hours a week.[69]

Potential ethnic solidarity was further undermined by the deepening class divisions within Dutch-Afrikaner society. In the Cape Colony there was in fact little in common between the well-educated Cape Dutch, acting as financial middlemen in the towns, and the common, lowly Boers. In the competition between Hofmeyr's BBV and Du Toit's Bond there was a distinct class dimension. The BBV appealed to the upper or middle class in contrast to the more populist Bond, which criticised the large sums expended on railway extension and attacked British banks and merchants as alien fortune-seekers.

While the BBV members spoke what passed as High Dutch or simplified Dutch, the GRA and Du Toit's Bond deliberately chose Afrikaans, then regarded as the language of both Coloured workers and the poor and ignorant class of Dutch-Afrikaner society. The BBV's mouthpiece, the *De Zuid-Afrikaan*, haughtily commented that 'brandy and *Di Patriot* have this in common: that they are enemies of civilisation'.[70] There was surprise when it was discovered that *Di Patriot* was read not only by *bywoners* but by 'civilised people' as well.[71] While the GRA busily tried to invent a national culture, the BBV's membership did not care much for culture and worried rather about their class interests. In 1878 a speaker at a Paarl dinner for parliamentarians expressed the hope that the enthusiasm for a 'nationality' would lead to the establishment of brandy as a national drink and that the moment would soon arrive when there was a South African nation and a South African national drink.[72]

After Hofmeyr took over the Bond he toned down the nationalist strains of his organisation. The Bond accorded a prominent rhetorical place in speeches to the lowly Boer farmers, but its true base was the town-based businessmen, rich landholders and commercial farmers. The leadership of Hofmeyr's movement was derived from such groups, and they increasingly looked to the state to further their interests, not least through the provision of public works. In towns they organised petitions for the building of courts, magistracies and local railways. The large flow of credit from London cemented the Bond's collaborative relationship with British imperialism.[73] The less affluent whites on the farms and in the towns shared little of this enthusiasm for development and modernisation. In Graaff-Reinet the poor, known as the 'backstreet people', at one stage refused to pay municipal rates. But over the longer run there was little the poor could do against the dominant position of the Bond and the commercial stranglehold of English-speakers. Du Toit's proposals for a national bank, *boerewinkels* (farmers' cooperative stores), and consumer boycotts all came to nothing.

In the Transvaal and Orange Free State the rapid commercialisation of farming during the 1880s and 1890s created a growing gulf between landless and landed Dutch-Afrikaners. The large farmers accumulated wealth through their access to office and their ability to exploit the labour of large numbers of Africans living on their land. They successfully resisted demands from the 'levellers' – usually poor and middling farmers – that African labour be evenly distributed among the farmers. By the end of the century many farmers, having lost patience with *bywoners* desperately clinging to their status as whites, chose to have rent-paying or sharecropping Africans on their farms. That growing numbers of poor whites had little interest in ethnic appeals was shown by their large-scale defection to British ranks during the Anglo-Boer War.

The final reason why Afrikaner ethnic consciousness did not develop as a political force transcending parochial territorial boundaries lay in the interstate rivalries of the 1880s. The root of the problem was the Cape's desperate search for revenue to meet its rapidly growing liabilities, while attempting constantly to extend its trade and railway network beyond its northern boundaries. Despite the fact that the Bond was the strongest party in Parliament, it did little or nothing to ease the financial distress of the republics and more than once rejected requests that the inland states be allocated a share of the customs duties collected at the Cape ports. A recent study describes the Bond as blinkered, selfish and parochial in this respect.[74]

The discovery of gold confronted the Cape with the sudden prospect of becoming the 'poor relation' in South Africa. Kruger blocked the extension of the Cape railway system to the Rand, the new powerhouse of the South African economy, threw obstacles in the way of trade in agricultural products, and made it as difficult for Cape Dutch-Afrikaners in the Transvaal to obtain citizenship as it was for other Uitlanders. At the same time, Hofmeyr and his Bond began increasingly to act as British imperial agents by supporting British-backed expansion, which aimed at the encirclement and isolation of the Transvaal. In 1887, amid growing tensions over railway and trade policies, four Cape Town Bondsmen, including Hofmeyr, wrote to Kruger:

> We must admit having noticed a cooling off of the warm feeling of attachment to the cause of our Transvaal brothers that showed itself from 1877 to 1881. We fear that unless events take another course, it will soon be almost impossible to obtain in the Cape Colony a similar expression of sympathy for you, as on that occasion . . . [Once] a division arises between kinsfolk, one cannot foresee where it will end, and the Africander cause is far from being strong enough to be able to face division between Transvaal and Colonial sons of the soil.[75]

But division did grow. By 1890 Hofmeyr was so much under Cecil Rhodes's influence that he was willing to travel to Pretoria to tell Kruger that he could not unconditionally claim Swaziland.[76] Kruger thundered at him: 'You are a traitor, a traitor to the Africander cause.'[77] Yet, despite his objections to the Transvaal's stringent franchise qualifications for Uitlanders – particularly Cape-Afrikaner Uitlanders – Hofmeyr continued to profess his sympathy and affection for the Transvaal with the words 'blood is thicker than water'.[78] These words, and Kruger's too, certainly suggest an awareness of Afrikaners as members of a common ethnic community. However, for Kruger and Hofmeyr the basis of political action and the definition of the concept of 'Afrikaner' were quite different.

Indeed, during the last quarter of the nineteenth century the very notion of 'Afrikaner' remained highly ambiguous. At the one end of the spectrum there was the GRA and *Di Patriot*, which defined the term in the ethnic sense of a people with a common descent and history. For Hofmeyr and the Zuid-Afrikaan, Afrikaners were a volk or a nation-in-being comprising both Dutch-Afrikaners and English-speakers who were loyal to the Cape and believed in the need to maintain white supremacy vis-à-vis the Africans.[79] While James Rose Innes, a leading Cape liberal, did not consider himself an Afrikaner, who in his view were people belonging to the oldest section of the white population or new-comers holding specific views on the 'native question', Rhodes for his part embraced the inclusive concept of Afrikanerhood.[80] Eagerly availing himself of the political base that Hofmeyr's Bond offered him, he stated in 1890 that his government would be an 'Afrikander' one, and said he shared the Bond's views on labour and African policy.[81] Edmund Garrett, editor of the *Cape Times*, coined the phrase 'John Bull Afrikander' in asserting that Britain by 1890 was acting only in the interests of South Africa as a whole.[82] Finally, there was the conception of leading Transvaal burghers, such as F.G. Wolmarans and Schalk Burger, who both served as chairman of the Volksraad. They defined the term Afrikaner in narrow, republican terms. Propagating a distinct Transvaal nationalism, Burger stated flatly that 'everyone from beyond the borders of the republic must be viewed as a stranger, no matter if he came from the Free State, the Colony, England or Holland, etc.'.[83]

Despite these divisive forces, a degree of ethnic awareness and commitment had been attained by the 1880s. The catalytic forces that produced it did not fade away. Indeed, they would intensify over the next twenty to thirty years. British imperial policy did become more conciliatory in the 1880s (leading to the waning of Hofmeyr's ethnic fervour), but the mid-1890s saw the emer-gence of an aggressive British imperialism that threatened to sweep aside Dutch-Afrikaner political and cultural autonomy. In the meantime the conflicts arising from the changing political economy increased as did the cultural strug-gle waged by people whose livelihoods depended on mastery of a foreign lan-guage. By the turn of the century Dutch-Afrikaners would, on a much broader level, see themselves as a distinct political group and would attempt to develop a separate culture – they had become Afrikaners. The task of extending and in-stitutionalising Afrikaner ethnicity differed in the Cape and the two republics.

In the Transvaal and Orange Free State the state preceded the nation, and political expressions of ethnic consciousness could accordingly feed on the idea of national self-determination in addition to responding to class needs. In the Cape Colony, however, it had to grow from a shared culture and common economic concerns.

The institutionalisation of ethnic consciousness in the Cape to 1915

It was in the western Cape, and in particular the Stellenbosch–Paarl region, that the first viable Afrikaner ethnic movement took root and grew. For various reasons, Du Toit and the GRA in the 1870s did not appeal to the intellectual class of Dutch-Afrikaners. Du Toit was a controversial figure, disliked by the church hierarchy, and *Di Patriot's* Afrikaans was considered too vulgar and banal to have any appeal. Nevertheless, clergy and teachers in growing numbers recognised the need for an alternative culture. The modernising colonial state was obliterating the old distinction between the public sphere and the private life of family and church, posing the threat not only of anglicisation but also of undermining the authority of Dutch-Afrikaner clergy and teachers. What made the matter all the more pressing for the clergy was the state's decision in 1874 to disestablish the church. Ministers of religion could no longer look to it for their salaries but had to rely instead upon their parishes. It can hardly be a coincidence that from 1874 onwards the church took a greatly increased interest in the education of Dutch-Afrikaner children and in ethnic issues. Clergymen figured prominently in the establishment of BBV and Bond branches. And in the early 1880s the church suddenly became prominent in the agitation for the recognition of Dutch as an official language. In growing numbers ministers of religion and teachers rejected the inclusive definition of Afrikaner and asserted a close link between language and nationality.

In the 1870s and 1880s Hofmeyr had argued that Dutch was merely of instrumental value in educating the Dutch-Afrikaners to enable them to claim equal rights with English-speakers. Always sensitive to any movement in his constituency that might outflank him, Hofmeyr began to emphasise from the 1890s the close links between language and ethnic identity and argued that they were mutually dependent. But Hofmeyr's bland ethnic formulations had already been overtaken by a more radical ideology espoused by a new generation of relatively well-educated ministers of religion and teachers who were eager to invent and elaborate an ethnic culture. By the turn of the century they were taking a leading role all over South Africa in commemorations of the Battle of Blood River and the founding of debating societies. Both served to heighten ethnic consciousness at a grassroots level among the rural population.[84] In the Cape Colony the new movement would find its leader in Daniel François Malan, a DRC clergyman who returned to South Africa in 1905 after studying theology in the Netherlands and who was to become leader of the National Party in the 1930s. In the Netherlands Malan had watched Abraham Kuyper implementing the *verzuiling* (segmentation) of Dutch society along religious and class lines. Once back in South Africa, Malan spread the new gospel that religious, cultural and political separatism could be the only basis for co-operation between the Afrikaners and the English.

In isolation these clergymen and teachers could not achieve much. For their ethnic movement to acquire momentum it was necessary to link up with farmers, in particular men of some wealth, who also found ethnic identification both materially and psychologically rewarding. Obvious candidates were the wine farmers who belonged to the 'best of families' and who were possessors of 'old' wealth. There were two main reasons why the wine farmers of the western Cape by the turn of the century were increasingly attracted to ethnic strategies, and not only in the economic field.

Firstly, the structural relationship between Dutch-speaking farmers and English-speaking merchants virtually built an ethnic dimension into the political process. Before the BBV was formed in 1878, some wine farmers and wine merchants had been joined in a wine producers' association, but it soon fell apart because of conflict of interests: the merchants did not buy enough wine, which they considered inferior, and they failed to protest against the Excise Bill, which they did not see as a threat to them. Conflict within the wine industry continued in the decades before Union. Although there was generally a huge local wine surplus, the wine producers had to endure strong competition from wine and brandy imports, which the merchants found more profitable to handle. Figures for retail sales of foreign spirits were 44 per cent of that of Cape wine and brandy in 1892, rising to 69 per cent in 1895 and over 80 per cent in 1897 before declining to 72 per cent in 1904.[85] In that year the Cape government of

Dr Jameson, known for its lack of sympathy for Dutch-Afrikaner causes and interests, imposed a tax on Cape brandy that was 67 per cent higher than the import tax on the foreign product.[86] Wheat farmers found it equally difficult to compete with cereals imported from Australia and the regions north of the Cape Colony.[87] The Bond constantly sought government protection for wine and other agricultural products. The desire for agricultural protection was one of the main reasons why the Dutch-Afrikaner farming population supported the Afrikaner Bond almost to a man in the last Cape election before unification in 1910.

Secondly, the farmers' financial situation prompted them to turn to local banks and trust companies. From the 1890s these local institutions began to attract a growing flow of funds from both the rich and the poor, farmers and professionals. As local sentiment turned into ethnic sentiment, these institutions facilitated the encapsulation of classes within the ethnic group and the accumulation of resources that was necessary before major ethnic projects could be launched. By the turn of the century an ethnic establishment had emerged, comprising some affluent farmers who were also shareholders or directors of local financial institutions, professional men, and leading figures in the DRC and the university college in Stellenbosch.

The British-backed Standard Bank, which started doing business in both Paarl and Stellenbosch by 1880, did not covet the average wine producer as a client. In general, wine farmers were heavily in debt as the bulk of the wine sold fetched prices not much higher than their production costs. Increasingly farmers began to turn to local financial institutions. It is sometimes suggested that Afrikaners were manipulated by ethnic entrepreneurs into supporting ethnic enterprises. The Paarl Board of Executors, the Stellenbosch District Bank and other institutions in fact offered real services. Because they were small and ran the risk of collapsing, they had to offer much better rates than the Standard Bank in order to compete. In the 1880s the District Bank was paying 5 to 5,5 or 6 per cent on fixed deposits and 2 per cent on current accounts, compared to the Standard, which paid an average of 3,5 per cent on fixed deposits and no interest on current accounts. In contrast to the Standard, the District Bank made no charge for country cheques and ledger fees. The same applied to credit. The branch manager of the Standard Bank had to apply the head office's well-tried general rules in extending credit. In general it preferred to extend long-term credit to sound commercial and speculative enterprises. In this respect a district bank suited the farmers' needs much better. The farming operations of Stellenbosch and Paarl did not require long-term credit but short-term, seasonal credit based on the assumption that the harvest would cover production costs. This introduced a risk factor, which the manager of a local bank could better assess than his Standard Bank counterpart.

All this worked to the disadvantage of the Standard Bank. On top of all this came the Jameson Raid of 1895–6 and the Anglo-Boer War, which were not only major blows to Hofmeyr's political collaboration with imperial policies but also greatly strengthened financial anti-imperialism. The District Bank, which had weathered a serious crisis in the late 1880s, capitalised on this and on the economic boom which the colony enjoyed from 1895 to 1904. It was patronised by both large and small farmers, professionals, the university college, and the town council. In 1904 the Standard Bank inspection report noted that the District Bank had the best of all the advance business and all farm mortgages. It described the directors of the bank as local magnates. In the 1880s, the Standard Bank had expected the imminent collapse of its local rival. By 1908, however, its own branch was running at a loss and District Bank showed a profit of £2 400 for the first six months after writing off £4 000 for bad debts. A Standard Bank inspection report blamed it on the bitter feelings towards the British and 'the few loyalists of their own nationality'. The report of 1909 was more explicit:

> At the present time we can hardly hope to do much here, our rivals the Stellenbosch District Bank receiving a large measure of support from the local populace and institutions. The causes of this support appear to be largely in sentiment and the clannishness of the Afrikander under the lead of a few influential men. No doubt they often accept risks also which we ourselves would never care to take.[88]

This mobilisation of financial assets along ethnic lines was accompanied by a large-scale cultural mobilisation. The Anglo-Boer War, the disenfranchisement of the Cape Afrikaner rebels and the retrogressive post-war policy regarding language rights stung Dutch-Afrikaner politicians and intellectuals into action. In 1905 Hofmeyr delivered a major speech in Stellenbosch in which he attacked the neglect of Dutch in schools and among Dutch-Afrikaners. Language equality was a fiction, he declared. The younger generation of intellectuals vigorously sympathised with the call for equal language rights, but they no longer had any enthusiasm for Dutch. Even in the 1880s and 1890s there had been a growing belief among the clergy and teachers that to insist on Dutch as an educational medium would mean writing off the large lower class of Dutch-Afrikaners, who would never be able to master the language properly. They now believed that the answer lay in making Afrikaans a respectable spoken and written language by professionalising it, by using simplified Dutch spelling rather than the ultra-phonetic spelling of the GRA, by creating a true literature rather than a collection of simple rhymes, and, in general, by shedding its image of being the language of the poor. In 1908 Malan stated: 'Raise the Afrikaans language to a written language, let it become the vehicle for our culture, our history, our national ideals, and you will also raise the people who speak it.'[89]

In founding the South African Academy for Arts and Sciences in 1909, the Dutch-Afrikaner leaders still compromised by promoting both Dutch and Afrikaans. But among students from Stellenbosch, Afrikaans had already won the day and they would enthusiastically carry it forward as the ethnic language of a new people, 'the Afrikaners'. This new concept had still many obstacles to conquer, but the merger of culture and economic concerns had created a formidable force. A key figure in the new ethnic establishment was J.H. (Jannie) Marais. He had made a fortune on the Kimberley diamond fields before returning to Stellenbosch in 1891 to take up farming just outside the town. After the war he became the largest shareholder of the Stellenbosch District Bank. Marais's financial backing provided a vital breakthrough for institutions that were to play a role in the development of Afrikaner ethnic consciousness.

One such institution was the University of Stellenbosch. After the establishment of the Union of South Africa in 1910, there was a strong move to set up a single, overarching teaching university in Cape Town. This would have posed a severe threat both to Stellenbosch's Victoria College, which was in danger of becoming merely a high school, and to Afrikaner ethnic aspirations. It would also have entailed a devastating blow to the town of Stellenbosch generally and to the District Bank in particular, as it was estimated that by 1915 £130 000 was spent in Stellenbosch by the various educational institutions as compared to the £60 000 to £100 000 brought in by wine and brandy production. Local businessmen and leading figures in the Dutch Reformed Church and the University of Stellenbosch strongly protested against any downgrading of Victoria College. But the move to establish 'an authentic Dutch-Afrikaans university' in Stellenbosch only acquired real momentum after Marais (who died in 1915) bequeathed £100 000 to Victoria College.

Marais – and, to a lesser extent, the District Bank – also played a decisive role in the establishment of Nasionale Pers and its newspaper, *Die Burger*. The decision to start a publishing house and a nationalist newspaper was taken at the end of 1914 in the house of Hendrik Bergh, manager of the District Bank. Apart from Bergh, there were fifteen men present – including four academics, two lawyers and Bruckner de Villiers, a businessman who also served as Marais's private secretary. The remainder were active or retired farmers. As far as can be ascertained, the twelve Stellenbosch men were all clients of the District Bank. Unable to raise the £8 000 required to start a newspaper, they approached Marais, who took out 5 000 one-pound shares. Six months later the first issue of *Die Burger* appeared with D.F. Malan as editor.

There was no immediate swing in the western Cape to the new National Party of J.B.M. Hertzog, founded in 1913. Farmers in this region had consolidated behind Hofmeyr's Afrikaner Bond, which at the time of unification in 1910 was absorbed into the South African Party of Generals Smuts and Botha. As both this party and Hertzog's breakaway party based their programme of principles on that adopted by the Afrikaner Bond in 1889, the National Party initially failed to make headway in the Cape Province. But the rebellion in 1914–15 of dissident Afrikaner generals who objected to South Africa's participation in World War I and its suppression by the Botha government prompted Marais to take a stand against the pro-Empire policy of the government and to support a newspaper which would give priority to the rights of '*eigen land en volk*', as he put it, and not to demands and wishes emanating from Johannesburg and elsewhere.[90]

The growing support for the National Party between 1915 and 1929, when it captured the Stellenbosch and Paarl constituencies, was complementary to the channelling of Afrikaner farming capital into Afrikaner institutions such as the Paarl Board of Executors and the Stellenbosch District Bank. They had been turned into vigorous enterprises by the 1920s. Political anti-imperialism thus had its parallel in financial anti-imperialism. At the same time the difficulties wine farmers experienced in marketing their wine made them increasingly inclined to support parties and schemes which favoured intervention on behalf of the farmers. In 1918, two years after the wine price had slumped to an average of £2 per leaguer, the Koöperatieve Wijnbouwers Vereniging van Zuid-Afrika (KWV), an overarching wine cooperative, was founded.[91] However, the KWV had only limited success until the promulgation of the Wine and Spirit Control Act of 1924, which prohibited the purchase of wine for distilling purposes without the permission of the KWV or below a price fixed by it. The fact that the tasks of marketing and distilling were now taken out of their hands freed the wine farmers from the necessity of incurring large capital expenses. On a far larger scale than before, they could now invest their savings. A considerable share of this capital found its way to the District Bank and institutions like Sanlam and Santam which unambiguously projected themselves as specifically Afrikaner enterprises.[92]

These developments point to the socio-economic base of the 1929 Nationalist electoral victory in the 'wine seats' of Paarl and Stellenbosch. The active involvement of Stellenbosch and Paarl farmers in local financial institutions and ethnic projects laid the groundwork for the Cape Afrikaner economic and cultural advance during the 1920s and 1930s. This was the main support base of the 'purified' Afrikaner nationalist movement that was launched in 1933 under the leadership of D.F. Malan and other Cape Afrikaner nationalists, and of the southern wing of that party.

Ethnic revivals in the Free State and the Transvaal, 1890–1915

In the Free State the sway of patriarchal leaders began to break down in the 1880s. Here the land had filled up much more evenly than in the Transvaal. There were few notables who could flout the authority of the central government, as could happen north of the Vaal. A relatively modern state, free from anarchy and graft, was in place by 1890. With the opening of the gold fields in 1886 South Africa's economic centre of gravity shifted towards the Transvaal. The Free State now began to move out of the Cape's economic orbit and turned itself politically and economically towards the Transvaal. British imperial aggression against the Transvaal was seen by the Free State as an attack on its own autonomy, for which it was prepared to go to war in 1899.

However, even before the war there were signs of a more vigorous ethnic self-awareness being cultivated by an alliance of intellectuals and commercialising farmers. During the 1890s ethnic entrepreneurs saw the Free State as being under attack economically as well as politically. Unable to adapt to the market created by the gold fields, many subsistence farmers in the northern and eastern Free State sold out to English-speaking farmers who produced commercially for the market. M.T. Steyn, who became president in 1895, warned the Free State burghers that if this continued, their sons would in due course become tenants on their fathers' land.[93] After the sluggish 1880s, during which the British had been generally conciliatory to the republics, politics seemed to come alive in the 1890s, as tension with the British increased. Debating societies and farmers' associations sprang up in many towns. In 1896 the OVS Boeren Beschermen (Orange Free State Farmers' Protection Society) presented itself to Steyn as the 'national party' and requested lower taxes and improved labour legislation. One of its offshoots was the Vrystaatse Jongelingsvereeniging (Free State Youth Society), which expressed the need for a newspaper that would expound an 'Afrikaner nationality . . . and would use no other language than Afrikaans or Dutch'. They wanted this nationality to be like a wall around them to protect them against foreign intrusion.[94] In the build-up to war, Steyn, who had married an English-speaking woman and moved easily in the bicultural society of Bloemfontein, also began to fear the demise of his state and his people. He stressed the vital importance of language: 'The language is the people and if we neglect our language we would have to expect the gradual atrophy of our national existence.'[95]

After the Anglo-Boer War, Hertzog would make ethnic politics the cornerstone of his Orangia Union movement. In a colony where the great majority of the white population was Dutch/Afrikaans-speaking there was little need for a party devoted to reconciliation with the English on the model of the Cape's Afrikaner Bond. Reconciliation was in any case made extremely difficult by the devastation of the war and an aggressive post-war British administration which closed down Dutch private schools and made only minimal concessions towards Dutch-medium education in state schools. The sentiment expressed by many

Free State English-speakers that they were Afrikaners – but not Boers – began to fade away. A politically active ethnic consciousness, with Hertzog as its champion, was thus intensified by the experiences of the war and the British assault on language and culture. Yet Hertzog did not develop a coherent ethnic ideology. Even after his breakaway from the South African Party in 1912 he used the term 'Afrikaner' both in its exclusive sense and in Hofmeyr's inclusive sense.[96] When and from whom he adopted his policy of racial segregation and of Afrikaner cultural separatism has not yet been properly investigated. But both in Stellenbosch and Potchefstroom intellectuals had been attracted to these ideas before Hertzog thought of breaking away. Hertzog himself remained an ambiguous leader, uniting people behind him on the basis of personal loyalty rather than through deeply shared convictions. This was as true in 1913 when Hertzog led the Free State out of the South African Party as in 1933 when he merged his National Party with the pro-Empire South African Party of Jan Smuts.

The development of Afrikaner ethnicity as a political force took a different course in the Transvaal. In the 1890s there was a growing commitment in the independent Transvaal to promoting the Afrikaner and republican character of the state. There were, of course, political divisions among the burghers. On the one hand, there was the conservative faction of traditional Boers, headed by Kruger. On the other, there were the 'progressives' representing modernising commercial farmers and a new generation of better-educated professionals and civil servants, the most able and senior of whom came from the Cape. To some extent, this division was once again between an exclusive and inclusive conception of nation and state-building. Kruger and his followers put a low premium upon education and bitterly resented the use of English in schools as something which undermined the national culture. As a Transvaal nationalist, he was reluctant to enter any alliances that might possibly compromise the state.

After the Jameson Raid, the Free State proposed closer unity between the two republics, Kruger waited eight months to respond. The 'progressives', on the other hand, were more inclined than Kruger to regard 'patriotic' Uitlanders as potential burghers and Afrikaners. They were modernisers who attacked the nepotism, corruption, incompetence and maladministration under Kruger's patriarchal state and proposed thoroughgoing reforms. But they could be equally exclusivist, and this was especially evident in their attacks on the Dutchmen appointed by Kruger to senior positions in the civil service. It is notable that in their opposition to Kruger, the 'progressives' took care to distance themselves from the *Uitlanders* and presented themselves as acting in the best interests of local Afrikaner society.[97]

The Jameson Raid and the impending war produced a closing of political ranks and ended any chance of the 'progressives' toppling Kruger as president. Yet during the war the Transvaal leadership changed drastically. The older generation of patriarchs and incompetents yielded to a new class of leaders, much more efficient and successful agriculturally, professionally and militarily than their predecessors. Identified with the pre-war opposition, they were recruited from wealthy landowners, such as Louis Botha, Schalk Burger and Koos de la Rey, and from professional men, such as Jan Smuts, Christiaan Beyers and Louis Esselen. It was this new leadership who took charge of the politics of reconstruction after the war's end in 1902. Against the background of a devastated countryside and acute poverty, they saw their first task as building an ethnic political base in a situation where Dutch-Afrikaners formed half of the white population but only a third of the potential voters.

An ethnic consciousness was greatly facilitated by the post-war policies of the British administration under Lord Milner. Instead of reconciliation, Milner deliberately used education to form imperial citizens. Yet, despite this, he made no attempt to exploit in Britain's interest the class and ideological divisions among Dutch-Afrikaners by diverting government resources to the patronage of the *bywoner* class which had supported Britain in the war. The political expression of ethnic awareness was also fostered by the constitutions which Britain granted first to the self-governing Transvaal colony and then to the Union of South Africa. The provision of white manhood suffrage meant that it was in the interest of Dutch-Afrikaner leaders to mobilise the *bywoners* behind them. And the exclusion of Africans from the franchise effectively ended the relations between white landlords and African tenants and other cross-racial linkages that had grown up in the decade or so before the war.[98]

It was in such circumstances that these leaders, with the help of the various Dutch Reformed churches, addressed the acute divisions between the *bittereinders* (generally the men who fought until the 'bitter end' of the war) on the one hand and the 'joiners' and '*hendsoppers*' on the other. These divisions were soon sufficiently healed to allow for the formation of Het Volk, a mass Dutch-Afrikaner party. It won the 1907 election handsomely, as well as the first election under Union before being absorbed by the South African Party in 1911. Lords Selborne and Milner, the British high commissioners in South Africa in the 1900s, clearly realised that this was not the manifestation of an organic ethnic unity but the work of cultural brokers who had constructed a set of alliances with an ethnic framework. In a report of 1905 Milner distinguished between the bulk of the Boer people and the 'political Boers, the Afrikander party' whose ideal was the doctrine of 'a separate Afrikander nation and State'. He concluded:

> The Afrikander doctrine emanates essentially from the towns and the non-agricultural middle class, and is 'pumped into' the country Boers . . . It is quite certain that, but for the influence of parsons, doctors, attorneys, law agents, journalists, and the more educated and town-frequenting of their own class, the country Boers as a body would not be irreconcilable.[99]

Declining support was now given to the tendency to define Afrikanerhood in inclusive terms. A knowledgeable observer noted in 1906 that the dictionary meaning of 'Africander' was still 'one born of white parents in South Africa'; however, he added, 'the Dutch have arrogated to themselves the title of Africanders, which has come to have a political meaning'.[100] In his view the country had become an 'Africander land'.

Revived ethnic mobilisation after 1910

In the end Botha and Smuts as leaders of Het Volk failed to harness the support of this separatist political ethnic consciousness. Once in power, these leaders increasingly were drawn into the developing state–capital complex. This symbiosis depended on industry providing an environment which ensured profits and attracted an expanding supply of finance capital from abroad. Locked into the international capitalist system, Botha and Smuts embarked on policies of reconciliation calculated to attract investors and political support from beyond their ethnic base. This meant dropping the popular anti-(British) capitalist plank of Het Volk and shelving the idea that the mines should solve the acute white unemployment problem by using unskilled whites in the place of blacks. It also entailed giving only lukewarm support to Dutch-Afrikaner cultural aspirations, about which neither Botha nor Smuts cared very much.[101]

The period between 1905 and 1915 witnessed the emergence of the constituent parts of the subsequent nationalist alliance in the Transvaal. In the vanguard was the Afrikaner educated stratum, particularly ministers of religion, teachers and journalists. This stratum saw the danger of one large section of the *volk* lapsing into what Gustav Preller, one of their spokesmen, called 'an ignorant, uncaring proletariat while another part was leaning to English'.[102] Like their counterparts in the western Cape, Preller and other intellectuals in the north believed that English could be countered only by Afrikaans. But Afrikaans should be promoted as a professional, 'civilised', white man's language, with a proper body of literature. Occupationally these men were often insecure. As teachers, they faced a distinct trend towards anglicisation in the schools; as clergy they were painfully aware of the loss of members of their congregations as a result of poverty and proletarianisation; and as writers they saw the market being flooded by English newspapers and cheap English novels. This educated stratum had an overriding interest in creating Afrikaners who would refill Afrikaner churches, attend Afrikaner schools and buy Afrikaans books.[103]

This was a massive task. A prominent part was played by the Doppers of Potchefstroom. Deriving their theories from Dutch neo-Calvinists, they built 'Christian national' schools and disseminated the message that the Afrikaners were a unique people whose strength lay in isolation with the freedom to practise apartheid vis-à-vis both the English and the Africans.[104] The Doppers, however, represented only one strand. The principal cultural entrepreneurs were the journalists and writers who, in newspapers and journals such as *Die Brandwag* and *Die Huisgenoot*, presented Afrikaner history as a heroic epic and tried to redefine almost every aspect of everyday life in Afrikaner terms. This message found a particular resonance among women and in the family context.[105]

When the National Party was founded in 1913, the educated stratum was the first of the disaffected groups that flocked to the banner of Hertzog. The intellectuals sought allies among Dutch-Afrikaner workers but found that they were a difficult class to mobilise by ethnic appeals, which failed to meet their material demands for employment and relief. A recent study concludes that the workers were unwilling to try on 'the yoke of a nationalist-dominated labour movement'.[106] The Dutch-Afrikaner workers only turned away from the English-dominated Labour Party after they had been shunned persistently by the formal trade union movement. They were rarely elected as leaders.

The poor farmers were another group that proved hard to mobilise. Botha and Smuts represented the gentry class of farmers who just before and just after the war bought out large numbers of the poorer farmers and pushed many *bywoners* off the land. Many small farmers became alienated from the rich land-holders. One spoke in 1905 of 'these selfish, self-righteous blood-suckers . . . Even our great generals who make such grand speeches oppress the poor in private and enrich themselves from the impoverished.'[107] After the National Party was formed, the rural poor gradually rallied behind its banner, particularly after the Rebellion of 1914–15. The National Party's open identification with the rebels persuaded the poor that the party might challenge not only imperialism but also the entire capitalist order. The rural poor were equally attracted to the explicit racism of the National Party, believing that only a tough policy towards blacks would solve their acute labour problems. After a tour of the Transvaal rural districts in 1921, Smuts noted that 'the landless *bywoner* is very definitely attaching himself to the Nationalist cause'.[108] Accused by the exclusive nationalists of being traitors because of their pro-British stance during World War I, Botha and Smuts bitterly responded that those who accused them had been '*hendsoppers*' and '*joiners*' in the Anglo-Boer War.

Building an Afrikaner ethnic consciousness that could assert itself as a decisive political force remained a long-term project requiring hard ideological work by politicians and cultural entrepreneurs. Before the day was won, class interests had to be redefined as ethnic interests and the invention and popularisation of an Afrikaner national culture had to proceed much further. It is clear, however, that the Rebellion of 1914–15 was a crucial event which allowed the National Party to unite the anti-imperialist and anti-(British) capitalist strands in Dutch-Afrikaner history and present them as the main thrust of the new ethnic ideology.

It was also in the aftermath of the Rebellion that the most powerful of the churches, the DRC, really began to rally behind the ethnic movement and ideology. At a special conference of DRC clergy in 1915 the church did not censure the rebels (as the government would have wanted). Instead it accepted Malan's view that the church had a distinct calling with respect to the 'Dutch-speaking' group and consequently had the duty to be 'national' and maintain 'national interests'.[109] Andrew Murray, champion of the once-dominant church tradition of Evangelicalism with its universalistic message, was deeply troubled by these developments, but he sensed that it was impossible to stem the nationalist tide.[110] In the general election held at the end of 1915, Hertzog's National Party made a net gain of fifteen seats country-wide. The astute politician John X. Merriman noted gloomily that only the richer and older Afrikaners still supported Botha and Smuts.[111] An exclusively defined ethnic consciousness was passing them by as a political force.

Conclusion

This chapter has argued that the construction of an Afrikaner political ethnicity must be sought in broad economic and social processes and not merely in the realm of cultural innovations. At the heart of such economic and social changes lay the attempts first to define the group of Afrikaans-speakers exclusively and then to mobilise them for political and economic goals. This process took different courses in the western Cape and the Transvaal.

In the Stellenbosch–Paarl region of the western Cape, with its history of a rigid slave system, political mobilisation of the Afrikaners excluded Coloured Afrikaans-speakers but initially attempted to incorporate non-jingoistic English-speaking whites. Conflicting political and economic interests together with imperialist aggression widened the gulf between Dutch-Afrikaners and English-speakers. For a complex set of reasons Dutch-Afrikaner farmers were drawn to local financial institutions, which in time became ethnic institutions. By the turn of the twentieth century an Afrikaner ethnic establishment, comprising farmers, teachers and professionals, had arisen which possessed the funds and the motivation to launch specifically ethnic projects such as Nasionale Pers, the National Party and the University of Stellenbosch. While Afrikaners and Coloureds lived in close proximity to each other and while both spoke what was basically the same language, political and economic forces drove them apart. Indeed, to counter the anglicisation of the upper class, the Afrikaans language was appropriated in the first two decades of the twentieth century as an ethnic language of which every Afrikaner should be proud. This stood in stark contrast to the late nineteenth century when in towns like Bloemfontein and Cape Town lead-ing Dutch-Afrikaners shunned Afrikaans, spoke English in public and generally conducted their correspondence with other Dutch-Afrikaners in English or, in isolated few cases, in High Dutch. J.H.H. de Waal, one of the main protagonists of Afrikaans, later remarked that by the turn of the century only the (Coloured) Muslim community was loyal to Afrikaans in the Cape Town area. When Du Toit made an about-turn after the Jameson Raid and became a supporter of Rhodes, Afrikaans suffered a great setback, for he had become identified with the language. At the end of the Anglo-Boer War, De Waal noted, 'Our language as a written medium was almost completely dead.'[112]

In the Transvaal and the Orange Free State the Anglo-Boer War shattered the political institutions on which local Afrikaner political ethnicity had been built. Ethnic entrepreneurs now had to assume the task of what a recent analysis has called 'building a nation from words'. The architects came from a fairly isolated educated stratum and had to undertake hard ideological work to persuade the lower class – workers and poor farmers – and also those of more affluent classes to see their political destiny in common Afrikaner terms. It was a task not yet completed by World War II; and perhaps only in the early 1960s, when a republican form of government was in place and apartheid imposed at almost all levels of society, was it finally achieved.

4.

'The weakness of some':
The Dutch Reformed Church
and white supremacy

This chapter investigates key moments in the history of the Dutch Reformed Church of South Africa and also offers a critique of existing work which holds that extreme racist beliefs such as those disseminated in Nazi Germany played an important role in Afrikaner nationalist thinking. I argue that there is no evidence that Nazism significantly influenced D.F. Malan and other members of the Afrikaner nationalist intelligentsia of the western Cape, who were mainly responsible for the formulation of the apartheid ideology.[1] A more fruitful comparison can be made between the Afrikaner churches in South Africa and the Protestant churches in the American South.

The views of white Southerners in the United States were remarkably similar to those the Afrikaners held in the 1940s and 1950s. From the early 1960s the views of white South Africans on race begin to diverge markedly from those of people in Europe and the US. The main influence on Britain and Europe was the process of decolonisation, which gathered pace in the 1960s. In the United States the Federal government accelerated the process of racial integration. American views are presented in the accompanying table.[2]

Table 1: Percentage of American whites approving integration

Issue	1942	1956	1963
Public school integration			
Southern whites	2	14	30
National whites	40	61	75

Issue	1942	1956	1963
Public transport			
Southern whites	4	27	51
National whites	44	60	78

Residential areas			
Southern whites	12	38	51
National whites	35	51	64

When Eben Dönges, minister of the interior, in 1949 tried to justify a law banning all marriages between whites and non-whites in South Africa by pointing to what he said was the practice in the US, there were at that point 30 American states with similar laws; with a marriage officer to administer them.[3] In 1962, when President Barack Obama's mother married a black man from Kenya, 30 of the 50 states of the US still banned such 'mixed marriages'. As late as 1971 the state of Louisiana passed a law decreeing that a person with one black ancestor out of 32 would be classified as black. At the Cape in the seventeenth and eighteenth centuries slaveholders defended the almost total control they wielded over their slaves as a pivotal part of their own liberty, dignity and honour. In the American colonies too, whites collectively defended the symbolic distinctions that underpinned the gulf between freemen and slaves.

White racism and white egalitarianism

In the literature there is a failure to come to grips with the real nature of racism. Far too often it is ascribed to mere greed or selfishness or to defective thought processes, something that sound theology or an enlightened education or legal sanctions would remedy.

In the hierarchical systems of the Spanish and Portuguese colonies in America, race was simply yet another form of inequality. The ruling elites here invariably used class or cultural ethnocentrism as the main justification of exclusivity and privilege. It was because Protestant whites were so much more egalitarian in their own ranks than Catholic-based societies that they so desperately sought a doctrine to justify racial discrimination. If, however, notions of equality and brotherhood are absent in the dominant group in a slaveholding society, such as in Brazil or Mexico, slavery can be easily justified.[4]

The racism of white Southerners in America and Afrikaner Protestants in the Cape Colony took root in societies characterised by a pronounced egalitarianism in the dominant group. In South Africa white egalitarianism developed over time. At the Cape of Good of Hope under the rule of the Dutch East India Company the higher Company officials and the wealthy burghers enjoyed greater status and power than the common burghers, but the further the burghers moved into the interior the less these distinctions counted within the white community. Early in the nineteenth century a traveller remarked: 'Every man is a burgher by rank and a farmer by occupation and there is no one so poor that he would not consider himself degraded by becoming the dependent of another.'[5]

Within white society at the Cape a genuinely egalitarian church took root. At the beginning of the twentieth century John X. Merriman, a leading Cape liberal politician, wrote: 'I am more sure than ever that in their democratic church lies the salt of the Afrikaner character. Many things they lack – imagination, education, energy – but faith they certainly have and that keeps them strong and sound.'[6]

In both the American South and the Cape Colony the churches condoned slavery as a system decreed by God. In both there was 'a coolness towards the conversion of blacks'. One of the main reasons was the fear that slaves would be much more difficult to discipline if they had been baptised.[7] Those parishes that did admit freed slaves seated them at the back of the church to highlight their inferiority.

With few exceptions the churches in both the United States and the Cape opposed the movement to abolish slavery because it would cause discord in the church. After the abolition of slavery in 1864 in the US, blacks left the mainstream churches in droves and formed their own. In 1866 even the Catholic bishops recommended that, wherever possible, separate churches had to be built for black Catholics.[8]

As the result of some ambiguous government proclamations slaveholders at the Cape wrongly concluded that they would be compelled to free baptised slaves. This was detrimental to their investment in the slaves. Slaves not baptised were more marketable.[9] The virtual absence of any significant police or military force outside Cape Town until 1806 made security a vitally important issue for slaveholders and the larger burgher community. The burghers believed that any form of *gelykstelling* (levelling), between people who were free and those who were slaves, would seriously undermine public order.

The stock farmers in the interior of the Cape Colony brought with them the slave owners' obsession with maintaining status distinctions and extended this to their Khoikhoi servants and later also to Xhosa labourers. They expressed outrage about *gelykstelling* – 'being put on an equal footing with servants or slaves', as they called it – when servants or slaves or their immediate descendants violated the markers and symbols of status and honour in society.

On the frontier the opposition to *gelykstelling* could even include preventing the Khoikhoi from becoming literate or receiving the Christian sacraments. In 1801 the missionaries Johannes van der Kemp and James Read began to offer instruction in religion and literacy to about a thousand Khoikhoi who had converged on the town of Graaff-Reinet at a time of great instability. This caused outrage among the burghers. According to Van der Kemp, the rebel burghers declared that the government 'protected the Hottentots and [Xhosas] and were instructed by us [the missionaries] in reading, writing and religion, and thereby put upon an equal footing with the Christians especially because they were admitted to the church of Graaff-Reinet'.[10]

The British, who took over the Cape first in 1795 and then again in 1806, were no social revolutionaries. Nevertheless, the British settlers of 1820 were not allowed to own slaves and very few members of the English churches were slaveholders. Consequently, the English churches in the Cape Colony did not have to make the fatal compromises between slavery and membership of the Christian church, or between the norms of slaveholders and the egalitarian thrust of the New Testament. Against this background some of the pivotal events in the DRC's history can be revisited.

'The weakness of some': The 1857 decision

For much of the nineteenth century the question of how baptised slaves and other people who were not 'born Christians' could be incorporated into the established churches of the Cape Colony remained unresolved. The policy of the Reformed Church at the Cape was emphatic: the church was open to all who had been baptised and Communion had to be served to all those who were confirmed, regardless of whether they were free or enslaved. Yet while open to all, the Reformed Church showed no enthusiasm for admitting large numbers of non-white converts into the local congregations.

This was how things stood in 1850. At that point NJ Hofmeyr and the two Murray brothers, Andrew and John, had just returned to South Africa from their theological studies in the Netherlands. They were full of evangelical fervour for missionary work as an inescapable obligation of the church. Hofmeyr, who had a high regard for Van der Kemp, found the DRC's poor record of missionary work an embarrassment. Using the pseudonym I.T., he addressed the issue of missionary work in a series of articles in 1853 and 1854 in the official church journal, *De Gereformeerde Kerkbode*.[11] (The use of pseudonyms was customary in the journal.) He did not want to bring about *gelykstelling* or social levelling by disturbing the status differences that had developed under slavery. His priority was the need to bring the Gospel to souls who would otherwise be lost.

Hofmeyr investigated three possible options for the Reformed Church's missionary activities. Firstly, he rejected a policy of *afscheiding*, which would later be known as 'segregation', the practice of setting up completely separate mission stations or 'congregations' for Coloured Christians. Second, he rejected as unsuitable the 'fusion' of white and Coloured Christians through identical treatment. Coloured people, he said, had a lower level of social development; the Gospel must be brought and taught to them in a simple way. It was important that Coloured Christians should understand their place in the status hierarchy and should not challenge the social order. He observed that ministers who admitted into their congregations people who were not white found that they promptly forgot their 'station' or position in life.

Hofmeyr declared himself in favour of a third or 'middle way' as a means of overcoming the barriers to missionary work and the fear of *gelykstelling*. Every parish would have both a minister and a missionary, and both a church and a separate *gesticht* or chapel. Like a mother and her daughter, they would be intimately bound together while remaining separate. The minister would conduct the services in the church, which Coloured members would also attend, and the missionary would use the *gesticht* for religious instruction, tailored to the needs of the Coloured Christians. In the *gesticht* the minister would perform all baptism and confirmation ceremonies and administer Holy Communion.[12]

Hofmeyr quoted no biblical sources or authorities on mission policy in support of his position, but pointed instead to two successful models in Cape Town. One was St Stephen's, a parish of mainly ex-slaves in Cape Town, who shared a minister with a white Lutheran parish nearby; the other was the Presbyterian Church, which held white and Coloured services in the same church but at separate times. Hofmeyr was a practical man and wanted a 'serviceable' policy.

Nobody writing in *De Gereformeerde Kerkbode* during this period favoured *afscheiding* or segregation. The debate came to a head at the Cape synod of 1857. In the town of Ceres there was a dispute between an elder who wished to establish a *gesticht* to bring the Gospel to Coloured people, mostly ex-slaves, and a church minister who argued that this was in conflict with the 1829 synod decision that stressed the unity of the church. Andrew Murray senior, the minister in Graaff-Reinet, was aware of a dispute in the parish of Stockenstrom on the eastern frontier where there was a small white minority in a largely Khoikhoi congregation. The former wished to receive Holy Communion separately.

Significantly, also at this synod, a special commission reported that the time was not yet ripe for a co-ordinated effort to extend missionary work. In response, the synod appointed a new committee, composed of Hofmeyr, the Murray brothers, and P.K. Albertyn. It promptly informed the synod that, with the necessary zeal, progress would indeed be possible. A formula was needed and this was what Hofmeyr's scheme would provide.

In the synod debate on the issue of whether to permit segregated facilities, several participants called for a reaffirmation of the church's policy of non-discrimination. Hofmeyr, one of the last two speakers, insisted that there was a more important issue than addressing prejudice. This was to identify the most effective way for the church to promote the Christianisation of the heathen. According to newspaper reports, after he spoke the debate took a new turn.

In the end the synod accepted a compromise resolution, proposed by Andrew Murray senior, who was a prominent evangelical and mission enthusiast. The resolution declared that it was 'desirable and in accordance with the Scriptures to absorb members from the heathen population in existing congregations' wherever this was possible. However, in cases where 'the weakness of some' hindered the spreading of the Gospel, the synod agreed that people might practise their Christian faith in a separate building.

This resolution sanctioned separate facilities but not segregated parishes, and it was not in conflict with what other Protestant churches were doing at the time. The church had no intention of drawing a rigid colour line. Indeed, the same synod decided to accept the St Stephen's parish of ex-slaves as a full member of the DRC.

The 1857 decision introduced Hofmeyr's 'middle way'. However, the resolution was poorly formulated and the inclusion of the phrase 'the weakness of some' a fatal mistake. It soon became clear that it would be used to sanction racist practices. The 'pious intentions of honest idealists' were no match for the 'callousness of the sinful'.

In the parish of Swartland (Malmesbury) a group of lay members, some of whom were undoubtedly descendants of slaves, waged a struggle to be treated as equals in the church. In response the church effectively prohibited Coloured members from receiving sacraments in the 'big church'. It was now expected of them to use the 'small church' (*gesticht*). The 'may enjoy' of the 1857 synod resolution had become 'have to enjoy'.[13]

Only a few ministers realised in the immediate aftermath of the 1857 synod what a fateful step this was. One was the Rev. D.P.M. Huet, a recent immigrant from the Netherlands and a rather eccentric man, based in Natal. Here he had worked among the Voortrekkers and their children, who in the preceding twenty years had experienced the traumas of massacres and armed clashes between white and black. In this situation of racial polarisation he had found it virtually impossible to have a black person confirmed and accepted in the church.

In the aftermath of the 1857 synod, Huet analysed the objections he encountered to the presence in church of people who were not white. One was a biblical justification for excluding 'Basters' or bastards. Another was a form of biological racism, which proposed keeping Coloured and African people separate because they were supposed to represent a different human species marked by their different colour and hair. According to this line of thinking, Coloured and African Christians stood on a much lower level of 'civilisation' and often understood only the simplest of services. Yet another argument held that people who were not Europeans formed a separate 'nation', and, like the French or the Dutch, they should form their own church.[14]

Huet himself did not object to separate church buildings or *gestichten*, as they were called, if they could accommodate the special needs of people who were not white, but he believed that the synod had erred. It had focused on white prejudice and had elevated the 'weakness of some' almost to the level of a principle, thereby extending a blanket authority to 'the powerful and the proud' to exclude the truly weak and vulnerable – the very persons about whom the church ought to be most solicitous. As he put it, the rejection of *gelykstelling* – 'that terrible, secret word viewed by so many as the greatest of evils' – had been carried over into the realm of ecclesiastical organisation. Huet sensed that the church would have to take a much stronger stand against racial prejudice if it did not want to be overwhelmed by it.[15]

Although the decision seems to have been a pragmatic response to circumstances, it was a turning point for the DRC. At this time American and British missionaries in South Africa insisted on their missions becoming self-financing, self-governing and self-propagating 'native churches'. The DRC was none of these; the congregations were black and all their ministers were white, while the funds for mission work were overwhelmingly from the white church. The 1857 model of segregation without independence became the model for all the missions that the DRC would set up.[16]

The establishment of the Dutch Reformed Mission Church in 1881 involved some of the same paradoxes that were present in 1857 and that had led to the condonation of segregation. Once again it was not reactionaries who were behind the move. One of them was a DRC missionary, Jacobus Pauw, who urged the DRC either to absorb all mission congregations fully or establish a separate church for them. The person most opposed to any form of segregation in the church was the Rev. Philip Faure of the Wynberg parish in Cape Town, the most integrated of all DRC congregations.

In 1880 the DRC synod decided to make it possible for its mission parishes to join together in a new segregated structure. In 1881 five congregations, including one that stemmed from Faure's Wynberg congregation, formed the first synod of the Dutch Reformed Mission Church. Faure had not protested against the synod's decision but neither did it force Coloured members to leave the church. None of those who left publicly complained of discrimination. They clearly believed that their own parish would give them greater scope. No one at this stage could anticipate that the DRC would later be so miserly and authoritarian in its control of the Mission Church that relationships in the DRC 'family' would be severely strained. Segregation in this case produced conflict rather than the other way round.

The political philosopher Hannah Arendt once remarked that evil does not have depth but is extensive: it does not so much grow from premises and principles but spreads like a fungus. It is very difficult to stop because those in positions of power and influence rarely have the capacity to reflect from the point of view of another person.

Missions among Africans

By the 1920s the DRC was engaged in little mission activity among Africans living in South Africa, except in the Orange Free State where a separate black DRC with its own synod was founded in 1865. By the turn of the twentieth century there were two areas in particular where the DRC was far behind the other mainstream churches. One was in ordaining black ministers. By 1911 English South African churches had 341 missionaries in the country and 171 ordained black ministers; the DRC had 225 missionaries and only one ordained black minister.[17]

The other area was in the provision of education to African and Coloured children. In the decade after the end of the First World War there was a surge in the African demand for education. By 1920 education in South Africa was fully segregated. With the help of state subsidies, church or mission schools provided almost all the education for African and Coloured children. Most African education was in the hands of the Roman Catholic Church and the Anglican Church. From the 1920s the English churches, both local and foreign, steadily moved towards the ideal of a common society and promoted this through an education that stressed Westernisation and command of the English language. A major reason why the DRC lagged behind was political. As in the case of Cape slavery there was a strong white perception that better-educated blacks would demand to be put on an equal social and political footing with whites. If the DRC was to expand into this area it needed a formula similar to the one of 1857.

In 1921 Professor Johannes du Plessis edited a volume with contributions from ten leading figures in DRC missionary circles, who tried to defend the DRC against the charge of D.D.T. Jabavu, an influential black academic, that it was 'an anti-native church'.[18] The book admitted that the record of the church with respect to black South Africans was poor, but pointed out that the DRC was the only large church in the country that had to rely exclusively on local funding for missionary work. In his book *The Equality of Believers* Richard Elphick points out that the DRC authors were 'more aware of the ambiguities, contradictions and pitfalls of segregation than many English-speaking theorists'.[19]

Du Plessis developed the intellectual framework for the idea that the DRC was fundamentally a missionary church with a broad social responsibility and that the church should help shape the social policies of South Africa. While Du Plessis was still a dominant figure there was little chance that the church would embrace a form of political segregation with discrimination and exclusion as its main thrust. He could see the need for residential segregation and for a separate franchise. At the same time he was firm in his view that whites and blacks had a common stake in the country and that blacks could not be debarred from any trade for which they had the necessary skills. Morals and character would determine the political future, not numbers.[20]

Yet as a mission strategist Du Plessis was an ambiguous figure. His major work, *Wie sal gaan? Die sending in teorie en praktyk*, first appeared in 1932. Like mission strategists in many other Protestant denominations, he stressed the need to found churches that over time would come to be self-supporting and self-governing. Many of his formulations would find expression and even be repeated in future DRC missions policy documents that proposed the idea of apartheid.[21]

Within the DRC a conservative reaction had made itself felt by the end of the 1920s. This was related to the advance of two black movements. The first was Ethiopianism, a proto-nationalist movement that founded independent churches for those frustrated with the fact that all the main Christian churches were loath to promote Africans in church positions and were unsympathetic towards African national aspirations. The other was the Industrial and Commercial Workers' Union. This trade union mainly concentrated on the urban proletariat, but in some Free State districts it tried to recruit farm workers, to the dismay of the farmers. By the end of the 1920s, for instance, 'the [Kroonstad] district was seething with rumours of pending unrest'.[22]

The first appearance in print of the term 'apartheid', used in its modern sense, dates back to 1929. It must be understood in the context described above. In addressing a conference of the Free State DRC on the 'native question', held in the town of Kroonstad, the Rev. J.C. du Plessis (no relation of the professor) said: 'In the fundamental idea of our missionary work and not in racial prejudice one must seek an explanation for the spirit of apartheid that has always characterised our [the DRC's] conduct.' He rejected a missions policy that offered blacks no 'independent national future'.

By 'apartheid' Du Plessis meant that the Gospel had to be taught in a way that strengthened the African 'character, nature and nationality' and developed Africans 'on their own terrain, separate and apart'. Du Plessis wanted a missions policy for Africans that concentrated on the '*selfsyn*' – being oneself. Implicit in this was the view that only by identifying with one's ethnic community could one be authentically oneself. Du Plessis envisaged the development of autonomous, self-governing black churches as a counter to the English missionaries, who in his view persuaded converts to copy 'Western civilisation and religion'.

Du Plessis could hardly deny that the policy he proposed favoured a racially exclusive DRC. But he saw no problem with that: it was all a question of marrying two different objectives: a 'sound' missions policy coupled with a policy that allowed Afrikaners to worship separately. The latter was necessary to 'ensure the survival of a handful of [Afrikaner] people cut off from their national ties in Europe'.[23] Nearly 50 years later a leading figure in the DRC expressed the policy of the church in almost identical terms. He remarked that the church was faced with the question 'How can we maintain our own people's identity without doing damage to the cause of spreading the Gospel among non-whites?' His reply was: 'The answer came out of our missions policy.'[24]

At the Kroonstad meeting delegates expressed alarm over the spread of Ethiopianism, which was shared by other speakers. One asked: 'Who is today the best friend of the white man in the land?' He gave this answer: 'The native who received his education from the DRC. He is the greatest opponent of political agitators.' For DRC mission strategists like Du Plessis and J.G. (Valie) Strydom, missions secretary of the DRC in the Free State, mission strategy and political strategy had become intertwined. In his preface to the published proceedings of the Kroonstad conference Strydom stated: 'By providing to the native the right kind of Evangelisation and the right kind of learning, the danger of assimilation will be removed.'[25] This was the kernel of the apartheid idea.

This raised the question of the type of education that the church should provide in the schools which it now began to establish for blacks. DRC ministers had strong doubts about the emphasis that most of the other churches and the missionary societies put on the English language to the detriment of African languages and on preparing the child for participation in a common society with whites.

The Kroonstad conference decided to draft a missions policy and submit it to the synod of the Free State DRC in 1931. At this synod meeting the church rejected *gelykstelling*, or racial levelling, but affirmed that Africans possessed a soul of equal value in the eyes of God. To justify its rejection of *gelykstelling*, the church proposed that blacks develop 'on their own terrain, separate and apart'.[26]

At a meeting in 1935 of the Federal Council of the DRC a common missions policy was formulated. The church was firmly of the opinion that 'education must not be denationalised', but must be based on a group's national culture, giving a prominent place to its language, history and customs. It called for Africans and Coloured people to be assisted in developing 'into self-respecting Christian nations'. Two aspects were new. For the first time Coloureds were brought into the scheme as a separate nation. And the church put the stress on the equal worth of all 'self-respecting nations', whereas, before 1935, it had emphasised the equal worth of all individuals before God.[27] Thus DRC ministers and missionary strategists were first in the field to formulate an apartheid ideology and to implement it. Afrikaner nationalism, apartheid and missions policy were becoming a trinity that had separateness as its fundamental principle.

Although a secular justification for apartheid was already in place by 1947, D.F. Malan, leader of the National Party, preferred to refer to the example that the DRC and other churches had set. In 1947 he remarked to a delegation of Afrikaans churches: 'It was not the state but the church who took the lead with apartheid. The state followed the principle laid down by the church in the field of education for the native, the Coloured and the Asian. The result? Friction was eliminated. The Boer church surpasses the other churches in missionary activity. It is the result of apartheid.' It was indeed the 1857 decision of the DRC condoning segregated worship that had set the Afrikaners on this road.[28]

The Afrikaners' 'civil religion'

There can hardly be any doubt that religion and nationalism were the main ideological forces that impacted on the Afrikaners during the twentieth century. The two were interrelated. Without nationalism it is unlikely that the DRC would have remained as rigidly segregated as it was until the final decades of the century; and without the DRC's endorsement of the policy of apartheid, it would never have assumed its extreme form.

The exact relationship between this religion and this nationalism still needs to be analysed properly. Some scholars like Dunbar Moodie see the civil religion – the fusion, in other words, of religion and nationalism – as a form of idolatry. But it is necessary to maintain a sense of perspective. Robert Bellah, on whose description of American civil religion Moodie drew, remarked in 1977: 'I am convinced that every nation and every people come to some form of religious understanding whether the critics like it or not.'[29] The main danger lies in making the Christian faith of the Afrikaners simply an adjunct of their civil religion and their nationalism.

Moodie was unaware of the origins of the concept of apartheid in the missionary circles of the Free State DRC during the late 1930s, as we have described them. For him the key to apartheid was the Afrikaner's civil religion. This involved faith in a God who wanted to save the Afrikaners as a nation along with 'its distinct language and culture, its own history and special destiny'. Separate development was an attempt to impose this policy on Africans as well.

In Moodie's interpretation the Afrikaners' civil religion was a fusion of Kuyperian theology and a 'neo-Fichtean' nationalism committed to history, language, 'blood' and 'land'. Added to this mixture were also the *volkskerk* idea, espoused by D.F. Malan, and Scottish evangelicalism. Moodie saw the *volkskerk* idea as a twentieth-century phenomenon that expressed itself in a commitment to the spiritual and material well-being of the Afrikaners, with a special emphasis on the rehabilitation of the Afrikaner poor and the language movement.[30]

But to see the *volkskerk* as a twentieth-century phenomenon is wrong. As Theron and Durand point out, it goes back much further – to Scottish Puritanism and to Reformed Pietism in the Netherlands during the sixteenth and seventeenth centuries.[31] At the Cape the Dutch East India Company reinforced this by insisting that the church had to promote the Reformed religion and the

Dutch language. When Britain tried to anglicise the Cape in the nineteenth century those political and church leaders who resisted warned that the loss of the Dutch language would also lead to a loss of the Reformed faith.

During the second half of the nineteenth century the *volkskerk* tradition was undermined somewhat by the Evangelical movement. However, when D.F. Malan, along with others, revived the *volkskerk* idea during the Rebellion of 1914–15, he did not turn to Abraham Kuyper but to the early Cape roots. The church, he said, was 'the means by which God guided and forged our people and our church is still the guarantee of our nationality'.[32]

The idea of a chosen people, which is an intimate part of so many nationalisms, also appeared in the course of Afrikaner history. When precisely it did so is a contentious issue. O'Brien makes a useful distinction between nationalism as an ideology, which is only two centuries old and took root first in Revolutionary France and then Germany, and nationalism as a 'collective emotional force'. Appearing first in the Hebrew Bible, the latter was indistinguishable from religion: God chose a particular people and gave them a particular land. In almost all cases of a strong nationalism in the latter sense of O'Brien's distinction there is a tendency to equate the experience of the nation with that of the Jews.[33]

The first people at the Cape who saw their fate as similar to that of the Jews were some Voortrekkers, who left the colony in the 1830s and settled in the far interior. Andrew Murray, who became a DRC minister in Bloemfontein in 1849, noted that some trekkers (he appeared to refer to a party of Doppers) did not distinguish clearly 'between the relations of Israel with the heathen peoples in the time before Christ was born, and their own relations with the indigenous people they encountered on moving into the deep interior. They thought that in going forth to conquer them they were extending Christianity.'[34]

In an academic analysis André du Toit attacked what he called the myth of the Calvinist origins of Afrikaner nationalism. He took issue with the interpretation of some scholars that a seventeenth-century 'primitive Calvinism' remained imbued among the Afrikaners for more than two centuries, prompting them to see themselves as a chosen and covenanted people with a mission to subjugate blacks as hewers of wood and drawers of water.[35] Du Toit argues that during the 1960s Hendrik Verwoerd used a modernised version of the myth to project apartheid as the divine mission of the Afrikaners. In rejecting the myth Du Toit puts forward the view that the Voortrekkers and Afrikaners in general did not see themselves as a chosen people with a divine mission before Paul Kruger started to expound this idea in the 1880s, and that it was only after the Anglo-Boer War (1899–1902) that a significant group of people, with the intellectuals of Potchefstroom in the vanguard, incorporated the idea of a chosen people into their religious and political thought.[36]

This is not a minor issue. If the Afrikaners merged their religion with their nationalism only late in their history, one could agree with Du Toit that 'Afrikaner nationalism is less the product of its unique cultural roots than the ideological labours of a modernising elite' (a reference to the nationalists under the leadership of D.F. Malan and later Hendrik Verwoerd).[37]

One can agree with Du Toit in much of what he says. It is quite wrong to think that the opposition to *gelykstelling* or the belief that the Afrikaners formed a chosen people can be traced directly to the Calvinist doctrine of the Elect. The opposition to *gelykstelling* had its roots in the emergence of status groups in the slave society at the Cape and certain bureaucratic processes that originated in the Company's possessions in the Far East. This was resistance to members of inferior status groups being put on an equal footing with their superiors. The idea of a chosen people was a common nationalist doctrine regardless of whether its adherents were Calvinist or Catholic.

But Du Toit goes too far in dismissing the possibility that some Afrikaners at an early stage considered themselves a chosen and covenanted people. From the early days of the Cape Colony the variant of Calvinism that held sway had at its very core the idea of an omnipotent, sovereign God who intervened directly in the lives of individuals and communities. A covenant theology was reinforced by the sacrament of baptism. The doctrine underpinning baptism held that there was a continuity between God's covenant with the Jews and the one he had with Christians. Accordingly, children of European parents at the Cape were considered 'born Christians' and, as such, deemed saved in the womb, which was symbolised by baptising the child as an infant. It also symbolised the covenant God had with a particular body of people and their descendants.[38]

The children of slaves or servants could be baptised in infancy provided that the head of the household or the Company itself (in the case of its own slaves) undertook to bring up the child in the Christian faith. But in the absence of any patrons the theology of external regeneration through baptism was applied to slaves and Khoisan. It promised that God would save the child later in life provided they could show some knowledge of Reformed doctrines and proved that their life had been exemplary. Often this test was stringently applied with the result that few slaves and servants were baptised. Accordingly, 'born Christians' who was deemed to have a covenant with God and the (white) burgher population became largely synonymous.

We have at least one contemporary source that points to the existence of the idea of a chosen people prior to the departure of the Voortrekkers from the colony in the 1830s and 1840s. In his reminiscences of the year 1858 W.W. Collins, who lived in Bloemfontein, referred to the Doppers as a 'peculiar sect', evidently obsessed with 'Jehovah's wonderful manifestation to his ancient people in . . . the Old Testament'.[39] 'They [the Doppers] seem to be possessed with the idea that they too are a divinely favoured people in the same sense that Israel was, and have been signally endowed by the Almighty with sufficient intuitive knowledge and understanding to undertake any mental or other duties.'

If Collins's reference to the idea of a chosen people had indeed come down 'from father to son', as he phrased it, it means that at least some Doppers had developed the notion in the north-eastern region of the Cape Colony where most of them lived before they emigrated. In the case of Paul Kruger, the most famous of all Doppers, this idea was probably strengthened by the trials and tribulations of the Great Trek, which he accompanied as a young boy. He was instrumental in the decision of the Transvaal burghers in 1880 to renew the commemoration of the vow made prior to the Battle of Blood River of 1838.

A sense of mission was neither widespread nor well articulated among the Voortrekkers. Even among the Doppers there were differences about the nature of their mission – to conquer the land, or to do missionary work, or live by an almost literal understanding of the Bible. Paul Kruger certainly did not subscribe to the heresy that all black people were inferior and eternally doomed. Although Afrikaner nationalism as an ideology developed only in the twentieth century, there was more than enough cultural material with roots in the previous centuries that it could use. The idea of a chosen people was one of them.

Conor Cruise O'Brien distinguishes three kinds of 'holy nationalisms'.[40] The most extreme case is that of a 'deified nation'. The position of the leader is sacro-sanct and there is no entity or law or ethic superior to the nation. Nazi Germany is an obvious example of a nation idolising itself. Then there is in O'Brien's terms a 'holy nation', which 'is still under God, even if basking in his permanent favour'. Finally, there is a third category, that of a 'chosen people', which con-tains within itself 'not only national pride, but also humility, anguish, fear and guilt'. God may bless his people, but he may also punish them and withdraw his protective hand from them. That was the way in which Paul Kruger used the term. D.F. Malan rejected the idea that the Afrikaners considered themselves as a uniquely chosen people. He wrote that 'in his personal fate, as in that of his people, the Afrikaner sees the hand of God. But that he claims this as his exclu-sive right and thus raises his people above others as God's special favourite is a false and slanderous allegation'.[41]

In a collection of sermons delivered at memorial services in the aftermath of Hendrik Verwoerd's assassination in 1966 there is no trace of a holy nation-alism of O'Brien's first two categories or even of a belief in the Afrikaners as a uniquely chosen people enjoying the special grace of God. Like Kruger, several of the presiding Afrikaner clergy expressed the belief that God had taken the volksleier away because the people had sinned or fallen short and had to be taught a lesson.[42] Using the apartheid paradigm in the official memorial service, the Rev. J.S. Gericke saw in Verwoerd's death a message 'not only for ourselves, for our own people, but also for other people'.[43]

Neo-Calvinist ideas developed by Abraham Kuyper began to wield influence in the South African church from the mid-1930s. Kuyper emphasised the diver-sity of peoples, the 'creation ordinances' and the separate social spheres of life – church, state, family, etc. – each of which was sovereign in its own sphere. Unlike 'simple evangelism' and the volkskerk tradition, and their concern with missions and saving souls, the Kuyperians in South Africa emphasised the need for a new Weltanschauung in the church and in politics. God, and the principles derived from his Word, had to be placed at the centre of life and the world.

Irving Hexham argues that the neo-Calvinism of Abraham Kuyper, pro-pounded after the Anglo-Boer War by theologians and other academics from Potchefstroom, was the main ideological influence on the Afrikaner nationalist movement of the twentieth century and on apartheid policy. However, it defies all logic that the small Dopper church and the relatively isolated Potchefstroom intelligentsia could wield such a major influence. The most that can be said is that some neo-Calvinist phrases appeared in the first programme of principles of the National Party founded by J.B.M. Hertzog in 1914. Hertzog, however, was close to being agnostic, often deploring the use of what he called God as an election agent. Christian nationalism, often the code word for Potchefstroom's neo-Calvinism, was little more than a political shibboleth for both Hertzog and D.F. Malan.

Moodie believes that Kuyper's neo-Calvinism became the dominant theology in the Afrikaans churches, but influence is always difficult to measure.[44] Kuyper undoubtedly influenced many academics in Potchefstroom and the theology of the Reformed church, but even here the work of some leading theologians carries few traces of Kuyper.[45] In the DRC Kuyper's emphasis on diversity at the expense of unity was indeed influential, but it would be better to talk of a balance between what Loubser calls ideological and practical approaches or, to put it differently, Kuyperian influences on the one hand and Evangelical, Pietistic and volkskerk traditions on the other.[46]

An effort should be made to distinguish between what were originally Kuyper's thoughts and what were Afrikaner nationalist elaborations of ideas Kuyper had borrowed from others. Among South African Kuyperians there was a strong tendency to speak of the volk or nation as one of the 'creation ordinances' though Kuyper had never done so. And as Schutte remarked, Kuyper was above all concerned with the self-isolation of a religious group on the basis of a specific worldview and distinctive beliefs. Afrikaner nationalists, by contrast, sought mobilisation on an ethnic basis.[47] They tried to bring together Afrikaners in ethnic institutions regardless of their religious beliefs and worldviews.

At a congress held in 1944 J.D. du Toit, a Potchefstroom Kuyperian and professor of theology, presented one of the first published theological defences of apartheid. He argued that racial differences were part of the creation ordinances and that God dispersed the builders of Tower of Babel, who wished to create a single nation, by causing them to speak in mutually incomprehensible languages. For him the lesson was twofold. Those whom God had joined together had to remain united; those whom God had separated had to remain apart, and there could be no gelykstelling or verbastering – no social levelling or bastardisation.[48]

Two central ideas of Du Toit's in this lecture were not originally Calvinist ideas. The idea of *gelykstelling*, as I indicated previously, originated in the status distinctions of the Dutch East India Company. Following Kuyper, Du Toit traced the different nations back to the Tower of Babel. But this idea formed part of the main body of Western segregationist thought and was probably first formulated within the context of slavery. In his work on racial views in early America, Winthrop Jordan mentions two books, one published in 1778 in Edinburgh and the other in 1812 in Philadelphia, both of which linked the Tower of Babel to God's plan to settle different nations in different regions.[49] Although theologically a liberal, D.F. Malan also clung to this outdated interpretation of the Tower of Babel.

Moodie does not argue that the Cape DRC was Kuyperian and correctly points out that Stellenbosch graduates were more attracted to the *volkskerk* position. Moodie is nevertheless of the view that the decisive influences shaping both Afrikaner nationalism and apartheid in the 1930s and 1940s were neo-Calvinist thought coupled with 'neo-Fichtean' nationalism, and that the Afrikaner Broederbond was the main disseminator of these ideas.[50]

But Moodie and several other writers overrate the Broederbond's influence in the making of apartheid. At a 1947 Broederbond conference basic disagreements about key aspects of racial policy surfaced. Speakers resigned themselves to the fact that Africans would remain part of the white socio-economic system for a long time. After the meeting Bond secretary Ivan Lombard called the proceedings 'depressing', because no solutions had been suggested for the numerous problems that were identified. The Bond as a body agreed with, and supported, apartheid, but it did not develop and formulate it. A survival plan grafted as an operational ideology onto Afrikaner nationalism would produce much greater unity. But by 1948 the Broeders had no such plan.[51]

I have argued elsewhere that the main influences of the church on the National Party in its construction of apartheid ideology were the *volkskerk* tradition, the idea of self-governing and self-financing mission churches, and the acceptance by all churches of segregated schools. I have also argued that the centre of political influence in the Afrikaner nationalist movement after 1933–4 was the western Cape nationalist intelligentsia, who considered the work of their Potchefstroom counterparts with some bemusement.[52] The influence of *Die*

Burger, under the editorship of Albert Geyer, far outstripped that of any Afrikaans publication nationally. After 1934 the Cape National Party dominated
the federal NP. As leader of both parties, D.F. Malan enjoyed unrivalled authority.
He rejected the idea of sovereignty in separate spheres, preferring instead to
think in terms of the historically evolved *volk* as the primary unit. According to
D.F. Malan junior, who was himself a minister in the DRC, his father disliked
abstract speculation and was 'not enthusiastic' about Abraham Kuyper's emphasis on doctrine and confession. Apartheid's architects were politicians, journalists,
businessmen and academics in Cape Town and Stellenbosch who, with the
exception of Malan, were resolutely secular people.[53]

Malan became a member of the Afrikaner Broederbond in 1933, but there is
no evidence that it influenced his decisions and thinking. His closest advisers
were fellow politicians Paul Sauer and Frans Erasmus, secretary of the Cape
NP Willie Hofmeyr, chairman of both Nasionale Pers and Sanlam and Albert
Geyer, editor of *Die Burger*, none of whom belonged to the Broederbond. It is
quite implausible that Malan, in developing his political philosophy after Fusion
in 1933–4, would suddenly embrace the views of the Broederbond, an organisation based mainly in Johannesburg and Potchefstroom, of which he had just
become a member, and those of academics steeped in neo-Calvinism, a dogma
which he specifically rejected.

Hendrik Verwoerd had made his mark in Stellenbosch before leaving for
Johannesburg in 1937. Like so many of his colleagues in the south, he was not
attracted by the German academic world and by Nazi thinking. In a visit to the
US in the mid-1920s he was exposed to the new preoccupation in academic
circles with social engineering. Verwoerd's thinking soon ran along social engineering lines but he was never a racist in the way in which the word was
commonly used until the 1970s, that is a belief entailing genetic or biological
inferiority. His lecture notes and memoranda at the University of Stellenbosch
stressed that there were no biological differences between the large racial groups
(or for that matter between Europeans and Africans), and since there were no
differences 'this was not really a factor in the development of a higher social
civilisation by the Caucasian race'.[54] Unlike the historian W.M. Macmillan, who
recommended integrating the reserves into the South African economic and
social system to resolve the problem of poverty, Verwoerd paid virtually no

attention to structures of segregation in the impoverishment of blacks. His focus was on individuals and how, despite adverse conditions, each could be rehabilitated. But the precondition was that no black advancement could occur at the expense of whites. Such advancement could only take place while serving 'their own people' in the reserves and the townships.

An ethnic missions policy and an ethnic racial policy

Apartheid as a policy was not the product of Kuyperian ideas applied to the racial question or a manifestation of the Afrikaners' civil religion. It was rather a response to some practical problems confronting both Malan's National Party and the Afrikaans churches by the mid-1930s. The first was to find a political policy towards Africans in the wake of the removal of Cape Africans from the common voters' roll and in the light of accelerating African urbanisation. The second was widespread Afrikaner poverty (the so-called poor white problem) and the spread of racially mixed slums where many of the poor were living. The third was finding a justification for removing Coloured people from the common voters' roll and from racially integrated suburbs. In the case of the DRC there was a pressing need to address the fact that, inside the borders of South Africa, it was lagging ever further behind other churches in mission work among Africans.

By the second half of the 1930s the United Party government was moving towards segregated suburbs for people who were not white, but some church ministers also wanted the state to go further and proclaim whites-only suburbs, which meant that non-whites would have to be forcibly resettled in many cases. In 1942 G.B.A. Gerdener, professor of theology at Stellenbosch, became chairman of the Federal Mission Council (FMC) of the DRC. Policy towards missions and pseudo-scientific race theory soon became intertwined. In 1942, when the FMC petitioned the government to introduce urban segregation, it inserted in its submission a memorandum by the biologist H.B. Fantham. It maintained that the Coloured offspring of white–black intermixture displayed negative social and mental characteristics. In a 1943 meeting between an FMC delegation and Prime Minister Smuts, the delegation requested a ban on racially mixed marriages. Smuts rejected this, declaring that 'the line between white and Coloured people in many instances could not be drawn'.[55]

In 1944 Gerdener, through the FMC, joined with the Federasie van Afrikaanse Kultuurvereniginge (FAK) to organise a *volkskongres*, or people's congress, on racial policy, which drew on both theologians and secular academics for speakers. The Reformed churches and the full array of nationalist organisations participated. Several proposals for a racial policy were made. They included the prohibition of interracial sex, establishing full control over a 'white South Africa' and extending the policy of urban residential segregation (what D.F. Malan called group areas apartheid) to the reserves. Here black 'nations' would administer themselves and cultivate a feeling of pride in their own tribe or *volk*. It was at this congress that J.D. du Toit presented one of the first biblical justifications of apartheid.

Even Hendrik Verwoerd, who rarely used anything but secular arguments, seemed to be enthralled by the idea that apartheid could be divinely inspired. He wrote that the Afrikaners' survival struggle against millions of non-whites would become ever more difficult. However, the Afrikaners would prevail if they clung to a single idea: 'it was in accordance with God's will that different races and *volke* exist.'[56]

In 1948 the synod of the Transvaal DRC accepted a report that took as its starting point the 1935 missions policy and used the Tower of Babel and the Old Testament history of Israel as justifications for apartheid. There was still no agreement that the Coloured people constituted a *volk*, which made the Cape DRC initially reluctant to use this justification. Increasingly, however, policy towards Coloured people was formulated in virtually the same terms as those used for Africans. An FMC memorandum of 1947 declared that God had ordained separate *volke* and races, giving each a *nasiegevoel* or feelings of nationality, and *volksiel* or national soul. It recognised the Coloureds as one of the races that had to develop separately and on its own terrain, while whites had to help them to become useful citizens.[57]

Missions policy remained intertwined with racial policy and the Afrikaners' quest for political survival. In 1947 the Afrikaner Broederbond initiated a discussion of the question whether the DRC was wise to expend such large resources on missionary efforts outside the country. The meeting, which Gerdener attended along with other church leaders, decided to concentrate on missionary work within South Africa's borders, particularly in the cities. White missionaries had to be replaced by black office-bearers and black churches had to be helped to develop into autonomous churches. Eiselen proposed that the state take over black schools, on which it spent £4 million every year, mainly as contributions to the salaries for the church schools.[58]

In 1959, two years after his retirement, Gerdener still stressed the fundamental importance of missionary work in the struggle to win the hearts and minds of the black majority. He was pleased to quote the response of M.C. de Wet Nel, minister of native affairs in the Verwoerd cabinet, to the question what one's greatest contribution could be to the welfare of South Africa. 'Become a missionary' was Nel's reply.[59]

As Bosch points out, this was no different from the defunct policy of the European colonial powers of using missions to realise their political objectives.[60] Moreover, the DRC's resources were much too limited to disseminate its message. It founded nine new separate black churches between 1932 and 1968. In 1951 there were 297 382 Africans who were members of African churches in the DRC family out of a total African population in South Africa of 8,5 million people. The DRC now embraced only 3,2 per cent of Africans as against 45,3 per cent of Afrikaners and 30,6 per cent of Coloureds.[61] By 1970 there were 1,5 million African, Coloured and Indian DRC members in different DRC 'daughter' churches out of a total non-white population of nearly 18 million people.

The quest for 'absolute and total' apartheid

Church ministers and theologians were much less inclined than secular academics or politicians to express themselves in crude racist terms. For them there could be no question of a hierarchy of souls, churches or cultures. They groped for a bigger idea that could motivate people (and themselves) and ease their consciences. At the same time Afrikaner nationalism, apartheid and missions policy were by the early 1940s becoming a trinity that had separateness as its fundamental principle.

In 1940 the Rev. William Nicol of Johannesburg gave a much-discussed sermon in which he stated that while he worked for the separate survival of the Afrikaner people, he would rather see the Afrikaners swamped by other peoples if they tried to survive without God and his justice. But how was the demand for justice to be met? Nicol proposed that 'self-determination had to be granted to the non-white races on every terrain of life'. Since no limits could be put on the development of blacks, there had to be complete *afskeiding* or segregation, as a solution that combined the Christian demand for justice with 'the need to give to our posterity a future as a European race'. This was, however, not a plea for partition but for the development of the existing reserves.[62]

The church leader who made the greatest contribution to formulating a form of apartheid that went beyond narrow concerns for Afrikaner survival was G.B.A. Gerdener. He had extraordinary influence in Afrikaner mission circles, the Broederbond and among secular academics working on a new approach to the racial problem. Gerdener's father and father-in-law were both Rhenish missionaries, while he himself was one of the founders of the DRC mission church in the Transvaal and of the mission journal *Op die horison*, which he edited.[63]

He combined several strands in the church's thinking about apartheid. Apartheid, he wrote in *Op die horison*, 'required a Christian and generous political approach'. It was not based on race or colour alone but on colour 'paired ... with language, tradition and lifestyle'. It did not imply a social hierarchy but a 'relationship of equals in separate terrains'. He did not go along with biblical justifications of apartheid and would soon deplore the use of the word, but to him *eiesoortige ontwikkeling* (autochthonous development) was the only policy that met the demands of Christian trusteeship, benefited the missionary project and made it possible for all races to make a unique contribution. It also countered 'a process of bastardisation', which he thought vital for Afrikaner survival.[64]

In the early 1940s secular academics and journalists began to take part in the debate on a racial policy that represented a distinctly Afrikaner approach. Three Stellenbosch scholars, P.J. Coertze (a lecturer in anthropology), F.J. Language ('native administration') and B.I.C. van Eeden (Bantu languages) wrote the first book (it was more an extended pamphlet) that propagated a policy called apartheid in social science language. It proposed a policy of 'absolute and total segregation'. Blacks had to be steadily withdrawn from the white economy and transferred to the territories where they 'belonged', with white labour taking their place. Only those 'absolutely necessary' were permitted to remain. The study also advocated the regeneration of traditional institutions in the reserves where Africans could administer themselves, preserve their customs, and restore discipline together with all 'that was healthy in the *volkseie*'.[65]

The authors' acknowledgement in the preface to their book of Gerdener's influence highlights the marriage of the ideas of mission strategists and secular nationalists. But after Gerdener had read the book he sounded a note of caution in his journal. He found the authors too dogmatic and almost authoritarian.[66] The Afrikaners could not hope to solve the racial problem all on their own, staking everything on Afrikaner unity and a resolute Afrikaner nationalist government imposing apartheid despite all obstacles. Time and again Gerdener stressed that the time of white paternalists and submissive servants had gone. He envisaged a solution that called for heavy sacrifices on the part of white taxpayers to establish viable black 'homelands'.[67]

Gerdener endorsed segregated residential areas for Coloured people as well as blacks, but he differed from most other Afrikaner nationalists in urging that Coloured people should not be compelled to move to these townships. He seemed to think that residential segregation could be implemented fairly. At a 1945 conference of the DRC Sendingkerk (for Coloured people) he demanded that Coloured townships had to be 'one hundred per cent with respect to privileges and facilities'.[68]

In 1945 the NP accepted apartheid as its official racial policy and in 1947 D.F. Malan appointed his confidant Paul Sauer to head a party commission to turn apartheid into a comprehensive racial policy.[69] Also on the commission were three NP parliamentarians (one from each of the northern provinces) and Gerdener as the only non-politician. His presence symbolised the fusion of mission policy and apartheid. In rejecting 'equal rights and opportunities for all regardless of colour within a single state structure', the report used terminology very similar to the thinking in mission and church circles: 'It was decreed by God that diverse races and *volke* should survive and grow naturally as part of a divine plan.'

The Sauer report incorporated a section on mission policy, which almost certainly was drafted by Gerdener: 'The Gospel had to be taught to all *volke* and population groups as part of the calling of the Christian church', and the aim of mission work was 'self-governing, self-supporting and self-propagating churches'. These were terms straight from the missiological writings of Protestant missionaries in the first decade or two of the century. The report recommended a strict Christian national education for blacks according to their ethnic nature, aptitude and background that would make it possible 'to cultivate Bantu-worthy [*sic*] citizens'. Werner Eiselen would soon be put in charge of administering such a policy.[70]

The church leaders did not see themselves as engaged in a reckless ideological project that ran counter to the prevailing white consensus. After the 1948 election J.G. Valie Strydom wrote in *Die Kerkbode*, mouthpiece of the DRC, that never had there been more hatred and bitterness between whites and blacks.[71] This was not the result of apartheid but of the racial mixing that was occurring in the town and cities. Apartheid was meant to end that friction. Church leaders believed that the necessary funds would be made available for realising their idealistic conception of apartheid policy. But they were deceiving themselves. It was an illusion that any government would have the resources to build Coloured townships that were 'hundred per cent', to use Gerdener's words. Neither was it able to provide 'the best social, welfare and community services for natives in the reserves', as the Sauer report of 1947 recommended. Gerdener had all along insisted that white taxpayers would have to be prepared to pay a heavy price to make apartheid succeed.

Only a few churchmen voiced a note of caution. Ben Marais warned that 'true apartheid' of the kind propagated by Gerdener would come 'at an enormously high price'.[72] It would face opposition from 'ninety per cent of those who today are supporters of segregation or apartheid'. Like Bennie Keet, Marais objected to the attempt to find any justification for apartheid in the Scriptures. But both accepted it as a practical policy provided that, as Marais phrased it, the policy was implemented with 'a sense of Christian responsibility and not selfishly'.[73] In a political system completely dominated by whites, it soon became clear that it would be all but impossible to satisfy that proviso.

After the surprising NP victory in the 1948 election, Gerdener became the driving force in the attempt to push for apartheid as a policy whose thrust was territorial separation rather than discrimination. In 1950 he organised a church conference on the racial issue which was attended by representatives of the 'mother' and all 'sister' (African and Coloured) churches in the DRC family, as well as of the Gereformeerde and Hervormde churches. Just before the conference, Gerdener published an article that conveyed a sense of his own unease over apartheid. He confessed that he had never liked the word, which had become 'a shibboleth of sinister intentions, misunderstanding and irresponsible talk'. It suggested a static situation, but in actual fact apartheid was intended to mean something dynamic. He formulated the Reformed Church's position as follows: 'If the contribution of every racial group in this, our common father-land, is to be guaranteed, the way of separation and not of integration is the correct one.'[74]

At the conference the Afrikaner church leaders called for 'total separation' and the elimination of Africans from 'white industrial life'. The conference did not specify a territorial base for the plan, but both church leaders and secular academics advocated a policy of separate homelands for the major African ethnic groups. Their argument was that since whites would rebuff black demands for equality in the common area, they would do better to build institutions in their own autonomous states.

In 1950, with the NP government now two years in power, the unrealistic optimism of Gerdener and some other church leaders received a rude shock. Prime Minister D.F. Malan rejected their call for 'total apartheid'. He was, as his son pointed out, never interested in the scheme of separate black 'homelands', only in 'group areas apartheid'.[75] To the church leaders Malan replied: 'If one could attain total territorial apartheid, if it were practicable, everybody would admit that it would be an ideal state of affairs . . . but that is not the policy of our party . . . and it is nowhere to be found in our official declaration of policy.' The next year he repeated his position in even blunter terms: 'The Afrikaans churches' policy of total separation is not the policy of the National Party.'[76] The government's negative response to total separation came as a great disappointment to the apartheid theorists, though they took heart from the fact that the government, in 1950, had appointed a commission to investigate ways of increasing the human carrying capacity of the reserves. It was to be headed by Professor F.R. Tomlinson, an acknowledged expert in agricultural economics.

The church leaders who supported apartheid wanted a policy that guaranteed Afrikaner survival but that did not commit any injustice against Africans and Coloured people. They believed they found such a policy in apartheid. As Richard Elphick remarks, the church leaders were enthralled by their utopian vision and would continue to justify the unjustifiable, thus easing the way for the politicians.[77]

The dynamics of apartheid

The NP election victory of 1948 was not won by apartheid but by a broad Afrikaner nationalist programme in which apartheid was merely one plank.[78] In the 1950s and early 1960s a popular nationalism, striving to attain Afrikaner emancipation from domination by British imperial interests and local English-speakers, provided the dynamism of Afrikaner political life. With the establishment in 1961 of a republic outside the British Commonwealth, much of the dynamism was dissipated. Apartheid, which previously was only the operational policy of Afrikaner nationalism, now became the NP's chief rationale.

To retain the DRC's support it became increasingly important for the NP that the church leadership, forming an intimate part of the nationalist movement, endorse apartheid and that Afrikaners in general continue to see apartheid as a prerequisite for their political survival. The NP leadership was successful beyond its wildest dreams despite criticism from some Afrikaner theologians. In 2001 the Institute for Justice and Reconciliation, founded to continue the work of the Truth and Reconciliation Commission, encountered surprising responses when people were asked to react to this statement: 'There were certainly some abuses under the old apartheid system, but the ideas behind apartheid were basically good.' About 40 per cent of the entire population, 40 per cent of Coloured people and 65 per cent of Afrikaners agreed.[79] Below are the responses in full:

Table 2: Responses to the question whether the basic idea of apartheid was good

	True	Not true	Don't know
All South Africans	39	55	7
Afrikaners	65	29	6
White English	36	60	5
Xhosa-speaking	18	73	9
Zulu-speaking	25	65	10

Why did the twin forces of nationalism and apartheid gain such a tight grip on Afrikaners and the Afrikaner churches in particular? I wish to suggest two answers. The first is material. Tables 3 and 4 highlight the fact that the Afrikaner community was remarkably free from serious income inequalities. In 1946, 90 per cent of Afrikaners were grouped in the income category of R0–R6 000.

If white egalitarianism and white racism go hand in hand, as the theory cited previously suggests, one would expect strong support for apartheid as an ideology that masked a racist programme.

Table 3: Distribution (percentages) of Afrikaner income groups in selected years (1980 incomes)

Afrikaner income-earners (people with no income excluded)				Total Afrikaners		
Income category	1946	1960	1980	1946	1960	1980
R0–R6 000	89,1	61,9	51,4	93,9	85.3	76.8
R6 000–R12 000	9,1	33,7	36,2	5,1	13.0	17.3
R12 000–R18 000	1,3	1,8	8,3	0,7	0.7	4.0

Source: T.J. Steenekamp, "'n Ekonomiese ontleding van die sosio-politieke groepvorming met spesiale verwysing na die Afrikaner', PhD thesis, Unisa, 1989, p. 193

Another material reason for the growing NP support and indirectly for apartheid, which became the party's main plank in the 1950s, was the broad-based nature of the Afrikaners' economic advancement after 1948. Between 1946 and 1960 a large middle-income group emerged among Afrikaners, which helped to blur the divide between the small very rich stratum and the poorest Afrikaners. Table 3 shows that the proportion of Afrikaners earning between R6 000 and R12 000 increased nearly four times, from 9 per cent to 33 per cent. The apartheid system helped to ensure near-full employment among Afrikaners and whites as a whole.

The income inequality in the Afrikaner group was relatively small as measured by the Gini coefficient (a measurement of the inequality between the lowest and highest income groups that takes 1 for complete equality and 0 for complete inequality). A rate of 40 for Afrikaner males in 1960 and 44 for the Afrikaner population is not large if one takes into account that the figure is 0.37 for the population of developed countries in Europe and 0.58 for the present South African population (Table 4). For Afrikaners the inequality rate remained constant between 1946 and 1980 and for male income-earners it even slightly improved. It took more than 30 years before a visible layer of rich Afrikaners developed, with eight per cent earning more than R12 000. The remarkable political solidarity of Afrikaners between 1948 and 1976 probably had less to do with support for apartheid than with the fact that all Afrikaner income groups benefited from NP rule.

Table 4: Gini coefficients for Afrikaner income-earners for selected years

Income-earners	1946	1960	1980
Total	0.464	0.441	0.446
Male	0.443	0.398	0.404

Source: Steenekamp, ''n Ekonomiese ontleding van die sosio-politieke groepvorming met spesiale verwysing na die Afrikaner', PhD thesis, Unisa, 1989, p. 208

Apartheid also enjoyed such durable support because it was a two-faced policy. The report of a commission headed by Henry Fagan, published just before the 1948 election, concluded that the economic integration of the races had proceeded so far that complete segregation was impossible. Fagan was sceptical of the homelands policy but added that 'it could not be stressed enough' that the proponents of this scheme did not mean to commit any injustice towards blacks.[80] It was only from the early 1980s, when the homelands policy had utterly collapsed, that church leaders began to reconsider apartheid.

The ambiguity of apartheid

One could end with a note on the ambiguity of history. Apartheid carried the seeds of its own destruction. In terms of the DRC's missions policy, the churches it founded would become self-governing and independent institutions, with the implication that they could speak on an equal footing with the 'mother church' about the true biblical message for South Africa. In 1982 the Coloured and African 'sister' DRC churches, particularly the Sendingkerk, wielded sufficient influence to have the (white) DRC suspended from the World Alliance of Reformed Churches. It was the international affiliation to which the DRC attached greatest value. Reformed churches in the US and in Europe now all rejected apartheid as heretical. Also in 1982 the Sendingkerk drafted the Belhar Confession, which called on the DRC to confess its guilt for providing the moral and theological foundation for apartheid.

It is noteworthy that the Belhar Confession was accepted about five years after Coloured ministers had become a majority in that church. It dealt a crushing blow to apartheid theology. It is difficult to envisage the Catholic Church in Brazil being rocked to a similar degree by a theological message from those excluded from power.

Table 5: Coloured and white ministers in the Dutch Reformed Sendingkerk (Mission Church)

	Coloured	White
1937	1	62
1946	3	79
1958	11	127
1966	43	122
1970	62	127
1974	90	105
1978	104	98
1982	116	89
1986	134	90

Source: Pers. comm., David Botha,[81] 18 September 2002

By the mid-1970s apartheid as an ideology was beginning to collapse in many areas. Its historiographical foundations had been swept away by the flood of publications by historians, sociologists and anthropologists which challenged the Afrikaner nationalist interpretation. It was now quite unfashionable to argue that the land belonged to the whites, who had planted civilisation in the region.[82] The apartheid view that integration in the workplace or residential areas would trigger major clashes proved to be wrong, although the lack of violence was largely due to the way in which a still reasonably strong state controlled change. Another view that became discredited was that of an incipient inter-tribal war in the African community. Clashes that did take place occurred more along genera-tional or political than along ethnic lines. The steady Westernisation of urban blacks made the call to preserve 'white civilisation' look increasingly threadbare.

The support the Afrikaans churches gave to apartheid was always indispens-able for the NP's ideological cohesion. Polls taken from the early 1970s showed that what counted for Afrikaners was the maintenance of public order and security through a policy sanctioned by the church or in line with privately held moral and religious principles. 'To lead an upright and moral life' was rated first out of nine issues in polls taken in 1974 and 1977.[83] This emphasis remained constant. In 2001 nearly 90 per cent of Afrikaners (versus 40 per cent of English-speakers) indicated that they considered religion more important than politics or money.

But the ideology of apartheid would continue to retain its hold on perhaps most Afrikaners as long as the church continued to endorse the basic idea that God had willed the existence of Afrikaners and, indeed, all nations. As late as 1974 the Dutch Reformed Church synod reaffirmed the stale story of Babel as a parable of God's creation of distinct peoples. On the basis of this it justified apartheid and rejected non-racial membership of the DRC as an unacceptable erosion of the church's ethnic identity. When the government itself wanted to abandon parts of apartheid, the DRC was unable to help it. In the early 1980s it refused to support P.W. Botha when he wanted to abolish the Immorality Act and the Mixed Marriages Act. But the church was becoming isolated. Very few other people had made the happy discovery that God had willed their existence.

The DRC finally broke with apartheid at its 1986 and 1990 synods. In 1986 it declared that the church was open to anyone regardless of colour. It formally decided to base its view of racial policy on the New Testament, in which 'the idea of race plays no part whatsoever'. The church had made a major about-turn, but for some critics this was insufficient: they wanted the church to state that it had acted out of malign and sinful intent in helping to design apartheid in the 1930s and 1940s. The 1986 and 1990 synods refused to make any declara-tion along such lines and explicitly stated that some of those who promoted apartheid also had good intentions. However, it admitted that the church had erred by allowing forced separation to be seen as biblically justified and by not pointing out this error at a much earlier stage. The great majority of the popu-lation, the church declared, had experienced apartheid as a system of oppression and discrimination that violated their human dignity. Such a system clashed with the Bible, and was sinful and a major error.[84]

For more than three centuries there has been a very close connection between the DRC and the Afrikaner community. For much of the time the church put most of its energy into preserving the unity of the church and its bonds with the community despite the existence of obnoxious institutions like slavery and apartheid. Any frontal attack on these institutions would have split the church right through the middle. As a result the church failed to develop. Except for the forty years after the end of the Second World War there was very little Reformed theology in evidence in the official statements of the church; everything was geared towards retaining the unity of the church as the bedrock of Afrikaner nationalist unity. Without a coherent theology the church risked losing its rationale for a large proportion of its membership once power relations in society had changed fundamentally.

In *Devils*, Dostoevsky's novel first published in 1871, the character Shatov says something that is wonderfully applicable to those who belonged to the DRC because it was the semi-official church of the Afrikaner nationalist movement.

> The goal of every national movement . . . is solely the search for God, for their God, for their very own God and belief in Him as the only true God . . . It is a sign of the decay of nations when they begin to have gods in common. When the gods actually become common to nations they die, as does all faith in them, together with the nations themselves . . . Every nation has its own conception, and its own particular good and evil. When these conceptions become common to many nations, the nations begin to die and the very distinction between good and evil begins to fade away and disappear.[85]

The significance of the decisions of the DRC synod in 1986 and 1990 was that they left the Afrikaners without their own national god or their own distinctive conception of good and evil.[86] But while this removed an albatross from the DRC's neck it also created the major crises of identity and relevance with which the church struggles today.

Christian 'realism' and the way forward for the DRC

What is the way forward? In my research for this essay, I was surprised to come across scores of dissertations on DRC history in which the chief source of inspiration is a theologian or philosopher from the continent of Europe, but I have seen none so far which takes seriously the work of Reinhold Niebuhr, the leading and most original Protestant writer on what one could call applied Christianity during the twentieth century.

Niebuhr grasped the fundamental truth that the church can actually do damage in being too idealistic about the resolution of conflicts in society and by being too ignorant about how political power works and how people in power actually operate. Some of the most influential American scholars, including the major liberal historians C. Vann Woodward and Arthur Schlesinger junior, the hugely influential diplomat and analyst of the Cold War George Kennan, and the leading political scientist Samuel Huntington, consider Niebuhr as their spiritual godfather.[87]

Travelling through Germany during the 1930s, Niebuhr sadly concluded that the followers of Karl Barth looked for salvation 'above the area of history' because they lived in an 'old nation' that had suffered repeated defeats. He wanted America and the church to discover its identity so as to come to terms with its peculiar history. As a young nation America had developed delusions of innocence and virtue, which it had carried over to adulthood, at which point it bred the perils of overweening power and overweening virtue.[88]

Niebuhr wrote in times of great uncertainty: the Depression of the 1930s when he briefly became a Marxist, World War II and the Cold War. He saw himself as a Christian realist rather than a Christian idealist, arguing that a vision of impending catastrophe was more realistic than the view held by liberal idealists that there was a kind of necessary underlying harmony in the world, a sort of invisible hand making for good. For liberals, progress was possible if people pursued their true interests rationally and scientifically. They considered all conflicts to be due to a misconception of their interests as a result of false religion, prejudice and superstition.

Niebuhr did not believe that social evils were wholly the result of ignorance or doctrinal error or environmental circumstances; rather they were rooted in the conflict between man's collective behaviour and the moral ideals of an individual life. Niebuhr as a Christian realist urged Christians not to be content with advocating moderation and telling all parties not to stand too firmly on any particular principle.

Niebuhr's key insight was that man as an individual may treat a member of another group in a civil way, but as part of a nation or an ethnic or racial group or a class he is a different animal. He tends to insist on tough methods to advance the cause of his nation, ethnic group or class, he believes in the righteousness of its cause, and will yield only if sufficient power is raised against it. Any idea that the power struggle can somehow be finessed and that people will listen to appeals to 'reason' or the 'broader principles of cooperation' will fall on stony ground until the power balance tilts.

In the early 1930s he observed that the 'white race in America will not admit the Negro to equal rights if it is not forced to do so'. He advocated the nonviolent strategy that Martin Luther King 30 years later adopted.[89] When King's campaign triggered violent resistance he noted frankly: 'We Protestants might begin the new chapter in our national life by contritely confessing that evangelical Christianity has failed to contribute significantly to the solution of the gravest social issue and evil that our nation has confronted since slavery.'[90]

Niebuhr did not think that an aggressive defence of a national group or a country was wrong. He favoured an activist role for the church, because one could not assume that communism would become more democratic or that Nazism would be defeated. He supported the US in the Cold War but strongly opposed the war in Vietnam. He considered as sinful any association of partial or finite national interests with the objective of God. He took as a model the prophet Amos, who showed that Israel's special mission gave it no special security in history. For Amos the very idea that Israel enjoyed special divine favour represented the corruption of pride for which Israel must be punished.

He did not deny the possibility that a nation could formulate a legitimate national mission. His quest to recover an authentic American mission attracted even Martin Luther King. But Niebuhr rejected the idea that any nation could expect favoured treatment from God or connect their mission to the 'destiny of history'. For him history is characterised by irony rather than progress. It is the supreme irony of history that man so often defines security in such a way that the more he pursues this, the more insecure he becomes.

As a lay member of a DRC parish in Stellenbosch I suspect that there is a strong tendency in the church to solve its crisis of relevance in a post-apartheid order by simply reverting to the apolitical Evangelicalism of the Cape church in the late nineteenth century. Apart from religious orthodoxy, Evangelicalism stressed a 'vital religion of the heart', of which the central elements were conversion, the Atonement, and the winning of souls for the Kingdom of God. Evangelicals tended largely to shy away from political or social activism or from a close alliance with a social movement or party. They spelled out broad Christian principles as they saw them, but rarely made their meaning concrete for political life.

Two points can be made about this. Apartheid did not come about because Kuyper's neo-Calvinism was intellectually attractive but because Evangelicalism was politically ineffective. Prior to the Anglo-Boer War the DRC did not concretise the applied political meaning of Christianity and was unprepared for the heady mixture of a *volkskerk* and an ethnic missions policy. The second point is that today the DRC is poorly equipped to compete against the charismatic churches in the market of pietism and religious revivalism.

To me the most important contribution the DRC can make is to spread the message, rooted in its own historical experience, that being too close to power is dangerous, as it undoubtedly was for the DRC in the apartheid period. But there is an equally great danger in avoiding engagement with those in power about the issues of justice and freedom.

The greatest danger in all our history is unchecked political power. In the apartheid era there was a government whose arrogance was born of the knowledge that it had no reason to fear being displaced at the polling booth. Today it is the same, and although the present one is slightly more constrained by a constitution, there is no real balance of power. The political leadership can ignore appeals from the churches about Aids, pornography, Zimbabwe or mass poverty. The legitimate black drive for racial justice has become a headlong rush to empower the black elite.

The poor are helpless not only because they are untrained and uneducated but because they are not allowed to sell their labour at a price below that set by the unions or the government. They are helpless because they are not represented in the corporate triangle of big business, unions and government where decisions are made with a view to their respective interests.

In addressing the Afrikaner Bond in 1999 President Thabo Mbeki said:

> One of the biggest problems facing our people today is that of poverty.
> Our duty is not only poverty alleviation, but also how to end this poverty,
> how to create an enabling environment for all our people to work, eat,
> learn and live their lives to the full . . . The Afrikaners have vast experience
> in these areas; and we challenge everyone today to come into partnership
> with government in making this programme a success.[91]

What the church needs to tell government is that there must be a balance: between the unionised worker and his employer but also between protecting the
employed and offering opportunities to the unemployed, between affirmative
action and offering all people in the country, regardless of their colour, a fair
chance to find work and be promoted in both the public and private sector.
The church needs to tell government that it cannot try to attract skilled people
abroad while some of its own members are jobless or do menial work only because they are too white and have to atone for the sins of apartheid even if they
had no part in it.

The church must also intervene with government, the education departments
and universities to adopt policies that enable Afrikaans to survive as a public
language. If Afrikaans becomes marginalised across the country, the DRC will
face a serious problem in reproducing itself from this generation to the next.

There is a vocal section in our Afrikaans public life that dislikes such talk.
They do not want any mobilisation of Afrikaner economic or cultural interests
because it smacks too much of apartheid or because it distracts from the more
pressing problems they believe the majority of South Africans face. They do
not want any conflict or any pressure to articulate specific collective interests.
If any conflict arises they want the South African Constitution to solve it. They
can be called 'constitution optimists'.

In developing his creed of political realism Niebuhr had little time for the
idealists in the church whose approach to politics was to deprecate all conflict,
to discourage people from mobilisation and to continue to preach brotherly
love. For him justice depends on some balance of power. Without it even the
most loving relationships may degenerate into unjust relations, with love
becoming the screen that hides injustice.

The DRC has little option but to tear down the screen that hides injustice and to organise, along with other sectors of civil society, when its own principles or its members' economic or cultural interests are affected, and try to speak its truth to government. In doing so there is much in its history that it can draw on. In fact, more than is the case in any other church, history *happened* to the DRC – the 'weakness of some' that became the organising principle of the church, the seduction of an ideology that promised to safeguard survival at the expense of others, the sterling role it played in the rehabilitation of the Afrikaner poor, the corruption of power and a too-close relationship with the powers that be, and finally the fall from the pinnacle of power and experiencing first-hand the truth that he who wants to cling to all power will end up with none of it.

In the humble situation in which the church finds itself today, there is no better advice than that given by the Chilean author and human rights activist Ariel Dorfman in talking about the white–black power struggle when the Truth and Reconciliation Commission was in session.[92] 'Shame cannot be the centre of growth and a new life. Both sides need the cleansing process of looking at the past, letting it become a fundamental part of their understanding, and then moving onwards with hope.'

PART TWO

A modern people

In the early 1930s there was a sudden change in South Africa's economic fortunes. After a sharp rise in the gold price from 1933 the country began to experience strong growth. Beginning with Louis Botha and Jan Smuts and ending with P.W. Botha and F.W. de Klerk, Afrikaners dominated the political system between 1910 and 1994. The defeats of the South African Party and the United Party in 1924 and 1948 respectively did not disturb the stability of the political system, a fact which benefited economic growth greatly.

But there were also other factors that contributed to the rapid economic development of South Africa. Firstly, from early in the twentieth century South Africa had a professional civil service that was to a large extent independent of the ruling party. It was instituted after the end of the Anglo-Boer War by Alfred Milner, that bête noire of Afrikaner nationalists. His perspective was that good government is good administration, all the rest is rot. Michael O'Dowd, a writer and member of the board of the Anglo American Corporation, states correctly that from early on the South African state had a better civil service than any country could expect at that stage of its development. For whites, there was effective local government, proper tax collection and a clean civil service.[1]

Apart from a few isolated cases, corruption at the higher levels of the public service was rare. Afrikaners did not insist that the top levels of the civil service had to reflect the ratio of Afrikaners to English in the country. It was only in the early 1960s, more than 50 years after Union in 1910, that the upper half of the central state's civil service reflected the make-up of the white population. After the regime change of 1994 it took only thirteen years to reflect the white–black ratio at these levels.

Secondly, there was consensus among whites that the private sector had to be the engine of growth. No obligation was imposed on the English-speaking business community to 'empower' the Afrikaners or any other group. O'Dowd remarks that South Africa was unique in the sense that there never was any serious threat of nationalisation, despite the fact that by 1939 English-speakers controlled 80 to 90 per cent of the economy, apart from agriculture. The absence of pressure for nationalisation could largely be attributed to the fact that Afrikaners ran the enterprises in the parastatal sector. Iscor and Eskom were soon followed by other state corporations such as the Industrial Development Corporation, which contributed greatly to the rise of a local manufacturing sector and the development of business skills among the Afrikaners.

The 1938 centenary celebrations of the Great Trek provided the spur for Afrikaners to raise capital for Afrikaner enterprises. D.F. Malan and the Free State church leader J.D. ('Father') Kestell suggested that the best tribute to the Voortrekkers would be to save poor Afrikaners through a 'reddingsdaad', an act of rescue. They stressed that only limited help could be expected from the state or the corporate world. Kestell's call, ''n volk help homself' (a people rescues itself), captured the popular imagination. The Afrikaner Broederbond rejected a 'charity plan' and instead preferred deploying Afrikaner savings and capital in Afrikaner enterprises that could 'save' the Afrikaner poor by employing them. It was hoped that by following this route the Afrikaners would also become 'autonomous economically'.[2]

The other aspect of the Afrikaners' advance that needs to be stressed was the improvement of public schools, where the children of poor and rich parents sat next to each other. Helen Zille, who would later become leader of the Democratic Alliance and, prior to that, had headed the education portfolio in the Western Cape provincial government, once wrote: 'There is an aspect in the economic liberation of the Afrikaners that is not emphasised enough. And that is education. For me it was an indispensable part of the reality that for two generations many of the "best and the brightest" of the Afrikaners became teachers and put a premium on education.'[3]

After the National Party victory in 1948 the idea was floated in Afrikaner Broederbond ranks of asking the government's help in promoting the advance of Afrikaner companies in the private sector. In 1956 the Afrikaner Broederbond called a meeting, attended by representatives of branches across the country, to consider asking the government for quotas for Afrikaner companies in the various sectors of the economy. Anton Rupert of Rembrandt and Andreas Wassenaar of Sanlam persuaded the meeting to drop the idea, insisting that 'Afrikaner enterprises have to learn to compete'. I once asked Anton Rupert whether he knew of any cases of Afrikaner businesses being 'empowered' by English corporations. His succinct answer was: 'I cannot think of any and I am grateful for that.'

Thirdly, successive governments provided a stable environment for investment. Investors knew what to expect. The government wanted the economy to grow and the country to develop, but not only so that whites could enjoy a better life. Both liberals and segregationists argued that higher spending on white education was needed to establish a 'healthy core group' to take the lead in economic development and to resolve the problem of widespread white poverty. But there also was an acceptance that addressing the issue of alleviating African and Coloured poverty could not be postponed indefinitely.

The Carnegie Commission appointed to study the poor white issue reported in the early 1930s that black poverty was as acute as white poverty. To justify a focus only on whites, several members of the commission suggested that resolving the problem of dire poverty among a section of the whites would ultimately also benefit other communities. W.M. Nicol, a prominent Dutch Reformed Church minister in Johannesburg, told the 1934 Carnegie Conference: '[We] can do little about a solution for the native question before making progress with the poor-white question . . . Once whites stand firmly on their own feet they would have a better chance to help the native in his turn.'[4]

The ideology of apartheid developed in the 1930s in the competition for African and Coloured souls by the different churches and missions, which were then the main providers of education for people who were not white. The Dutch Reformed Church viewed with increasing concern the steady advance of British and American missions and churches in the battle for African and Coloured souls. They all stressed English as a medium of education and the creed of individual salvation. In response the DRC began promoting the development of the Bantu languages and the need to root the African church in the different African ethnic communities. By the end of the 1930s Afrikaner politicians and academics began proposing apartheid as a superior alternative to segregation, which put little effort into the development of communities.

At the same time South African whites were slowly coming round to the idea that a modern state had the obligation to provide education for all its citizens. By the late 1930s there was still strong opposition to this among white voters. In 1939 R.F.A. Hoernlé, a leading liberal, observed that while a large number of the white voters did not mind 'native education', it would be suicide in most constituencies for a member of Parliament to insist that the government should fund it.[5] Just before the NP won the 1948 election J.G. Strijdom, one of the NP's provincial leaders, warned about the serious danger to white supremacy posed by extending education to the other races on a large scale. It was well known that education, especially the more advanced kind, had a radicalising effect on communities that were oppressed.

In introducing 'Bantu education' in 1953, Hendrik Verwoerd insisted that the better-paid jobs in the so-called white areas would continue to be reserved for whites, but careers in white-collar jobs would be made available to Africans in the administrations of the different homeland governments. But Gwendolen Carter, a well-regarded Africanist from the United States, put this in perspective. She wrote: 'There was much that made sense in the Nationalist arguments. It is obvious that the lack of opportunities in the South African context for Africans with advanced training makes them frustrated and bitter. Moreover, it is hard to deny the importance of basing education on the culture of the particular group.' Carter referred to Verwoerd's vision of the homelands as areas where job opportunities would arise to which blacks could not aspire elsewhere.[6]

Until the early 1970s per capita spending on Coloured and African pupils was much lower than that on whites. Against this stands the fact that state spending on Coloured and African education steadily rose. It has only recently become known that in order to prevent a white backlash, the government hid the capital expenditure on Coloured and African schools in the budget of the Department of Public Works. A fair degree of bipartisan consensus developed in Parliament that African and Coloured education had to be improved and that the racial gap in spending on education had to be reduced as fast as possible.[7]

The process of redistribution of income only started early in the 1960s when the country experienced its first great boom. In 1964 Harry Oppenheimer, head of the Anglo American Corporation, remarked that in the previous five years the average wages of 'non-white' workers in secondary industry had risen by

5,4 per cent (against those of whites at 3,7 per cent) per year. To him this explained why the country was 'so much more stable than many people are inclined to suppose'.[8]

In the course of the 1970s there had developed in the NP leadership a sense of the inclusive nature of South African nationhood and of the obligations the government had to all citizens regardless of their colour. When in the early 1970s black workers in Durban went on strike against their appallingly low wages, John Vorster, the prime minister, told employers that they should see their workers not only as units producing so many hours of service each day for them; they should also see them as 'human beings with souls'.[9]

An important development occurred in the 1970s. As the economist Charles Simkins later observed, it was one that no one in the academic world would have predicted. In government circles the idea had taken root that whites were sufficiently well off, and that the state's priority was to meet its obligations to the disenfranchised.[10] Urban blacks were the great beneficiaries. The 1975–6 budget reduced the personal income of whites by seven per cent but raised that of Indians by three per cent, that of Coloured people by nineteen per cent and that of Africans by eleven per cent.[11] In 1975 it was reported that the wages of a quarter of a million Africans in industry – this was virtually the entire African elite in the common area – had improved on average by fifteen to twenty per cent in the previous year.[12]

In 1978 Vorster warned whites that the abolition of social and economic in-equities would demand significant sacrifices in their living standards and mate-rial aspirations. Three years later the director-general of finance declared that a drastic increase in state spending on blacks at the expense of whites was under way. The government's priority was to satisfy black demands for improved edu-cation and public health services. It would do so by keeping the spending on whites constant until a greater equilibrium was reached.[13]

By the early 1980s the government had come round to recognising that ever better-educated African and Coloured children had to receive some form of effec-tive political representation. In the early 1980s Prime Minster P.W. Botha told his biographers: 'None of my predecessors thought differently than to accept that the Coloured people first had to be uplifted and that the consequences of that have to be accepted.'[14] The same implicitly applied to Africans.

But the Tricameral Parliament introduced in 1984 was a case of too little, too late to attract the better-educated Coloured voters. It also greatly alienated virtually the entire African population. Strong and resourceful black and multi-racial trade unions entered politics, an independent press challenged the government, and Coloured and African numbers increased dramatically in secondary and tertiary education during the 1970s and 1980s. The racial gaps in wages, salaries and pensions narrowed. Black workers streamed to the towns and cities and in the process liberated themselves from the pass laws.

The NP government was unable to transform the apartheid system into one that politically incorporated people from all racial groups. There were deep historical roots for this, which are explained best by Arnold Toynbee, the historian of civilisations. He pointed out that the Spanish also exploited the native peoples in their colonies in Latin America, but the barriers to advancement were not racial, and hence not impermeable. In stark contrast stood the colonies that the Dutch and the British founded. Upward mobility for subordinate races was difficult and intermarriage was virtually ruled out. There was, Toynbee noted, 'no easy way of entry into the . . . dominant caste for an able and adaptable [African]'.[15] In both the Afrikaner family and the political system the racial barriers for African or Coloured people were almost impermeable.

Yet the feared bloodbath in the transition to majority rule did not occur. As a proportion of the population, the incidence of political deaths in South Africa, along with those of Northern Ireland and Israel, was the lowest of all politically motivated deaths in major ethnic or racial conflicts after 1945.[16] As General Jan Smuts famously said in 1949: 'The worst, like the best, never happens [in South Africa].'

In 2003 the South African economy was the twentieth largest in the world measured by purchasing power, the seventeenth largest in terms of market capitalisation, and the twenty-seventh largest with regard to services sector output. It would take quite long for Afrikaner-controlled companies to enter the ranks of the top South African conglomerates. In 1968 there were only four predominantly Afrikaner corporations with assets of more than R1,7 billion (in today's terms). They were the Sanlam-controlled group of companies, Volkskas, Trust Bank and Rembrandt. In 1994, Nasionale Pers was not yet a listed company and had a market capitalisation of only R24 million. Today it is the biggest company in Africa.

In a recent book R.W. Johnson argues that since 1994 the African National Congress has failed to provide South Africa with a new ruling class capable of developing the country. The ANC has become what Johnson calls a 'bureaucratic bourgeoisie', which concentrates on managing its own patronage networks and looking primarily after its own welfare.

The Afrikaners as the old ruling class had many sins but they succeeded in the course of the twentieth century in building a formidable infrastructure, a developed economy, and a series of powerful and efficient institutions – the armed forces, Eskom, Transnet (including a large railway and port system), the civil service, a strong police force and a highly developed water distribution system. 'It kept in check individual or sectional interests and subordinated them to a strong sense of national interests.'[17]

The introduction of a democratic system has opened up the possibility of a great improvement in the performance of African and Coloured pupils and students. So far these expectations have been disappointed. On 16 November 2016 News24 reported the remarks made by the statistician-general, Pali Lehohla, about the state of higher education. He said that progression rates showed that black students were not doing well. In the 1980s, for every black graduate there were 1,2 white graduates. 'Currently, for every one black student who graduates from university, there are six white people who make it through successfully.' He remarked: 'These numbers are declaring a horror, to put it bluntly. It is totally unacceptable.' Lehohla blamed the high dropout rate largely on students lacking sufficient funding. Yet it is difficult to imagine that black students in the 1980s were in a better financial situation than their counterparts are today. It is generally agreed that the greatest obstacles are poor discipline among learners, poor leadership on the part of teachers, and the negative influence of the teacher unions on the profession.

Conclusion

So much of the struggle over the South African state in the final decades of the twentieth century was a propaganda battle that distorted history, especially the course of economic development. Recently John Kane-Berman published a revealing account of the bigger economic picture. He cited the *Monetary Policy Review* published in April 2019 by the South African Reserve Bank, which stated that this country's 'potential growth rate is at long-term lows'. All three of the forecasts cited by the bank for the next few years were 'below the long-run growth rate of 2,5%', the average over the last 50 years. In a recent study the economist Mike Schüssler, using World Bank data, showed that South African income per head in 1990 was 110 per cent of the world figure, but that in 2018 it was only 76 per cent of the world figure. Kane-Berman remarked: 'This spectacular nosedive is quite an achievement for a quarter of a century of rule by the ANC and its communist and trade union allies.'[18]

The highest growth occurred at the height of the apartheid era between 1962 and 1967. This was of little comfort to those black people living on a pittance in the reserves. But for them the glimmer of hope was the prospect of a job, albeit one with a very low wage. In 1965, 73,6 per cent of new entrants to the labour market were absorbed in the formal sector, a rate never achieved before. It would rise to 76,6 per cent in 1970, but would drop to 43,4 per cent in 1998.[19]

Segregation and apartheid were indefensible, and many mistakes were made. But it was not nugatory. A great deal was achieved. The country was steered through a world depression and a world war. By 1994 the country was the most developed in Africa, had the largest manufacturing sector, its own autonomous banks, the best infrastructure in Africa, the lowest electricity prices and a better-housed urban population (of all races) than in any other African country. The ANC inherited the richest and best-run state in Africa, and they did not have to fight a war to do so.

Just as South Africa is a hard country in which to be a farmer, so it is also a difficult and complex country to govern, and the ANC never appreciated this. In 25 years they turned 3,7 million unemployed into 10 million. Inequality and poverty grew. Manufacturing and mining both declined sharply and so did real incomes, year after year. Currently the country, sewn together with so much effort and skill, is falling apart. People of all races look back increasingly at the rule of the Afrikaners and ask the question: How did they achieve such success while their successors have so resoundingly failed?

5.

Alleged and real civil service purges

Article 137 of the Constitution of the Union of South Africa, adopted in 1909, stipulated that Dutch and English would be the official languages and that, if necessary, the government would use compulsion to achieve this. It decreed:

> Both the English and Dutch languages shall be official languages of the Union and shall be treated on a footing of equality and possess and enjoy equal freedom, rights and privileges; all records, journals and proceedings of Parliament shall be kept in both languages, and all Bills, Acts and notices of general public importance or interest issued by the Government of the Union of South Africa shall be in both languages.[1]

Writing in *The State*, Gustav Preller called the Union's promise to place the two official languages on a footing of 'most perfect equality' as essential to Afrikaner support for the Union.[2]

There exists an assumption in the popular press that English-speakers in the public sector were displaced in large numbers after the National Party (NP) victory in 1948 in a manner similar to the ANC's transformation of the public service after 1994. In 1998 Peter Wilhelm stated: 'When the NP attained power in 1948 it immediately and ruthlessly set about displacing English-speakers in key areas such as defence, security and in the public service.'[3] Does this statement stand up to scrutiny?

For an investigation it is necessary to go back to the founding history of the Union of South Africa during the years 1908 to 09 and that of a democratic South Africa in 1992 to 1996. Both represent an attempt to establish a new spirit of

national unity. In the case of Union the main symbolic conflict was over the practical implementation of the status of English and Afrikaans as the official
languages. Many members of the ruling party felt that the equal status that
Dutch (later Afrikaans) enjoyed with English as an official language was mainly
a symbolic concession. The National Party pressed for equal status in the provision of education but did not force the issue in the civil service. It was only in
mid-1960s that the upper levels of the civil service reflected the Afrikaner–
English ratio in the white population group. The retention of skills was one the
strengths of the new South African state that was founded in 1910.

In the case of the transition to an inclusive democratic system during the
1990s whites expected that the transformation of the racial order would be
restricted to those areas specified by the Constitution. The African National
Congress as the new ruling party soon embarked on a radical reconstruction
of the civil service in order to make it 'racially representative'. It greatly weakening the capacity of the state.

After Union was inaugurated, nationalists insisted that the language clause
in the constitution meant that it would be incumbent upon civil servants to be
proficient in both languages. Botha and Smuts, on the other hand, ruled out a
large-scale transformation of the civil service for the sake of reconciliation and
efficiency. Since Hertzog made it clear that he wanted some action in this regard,
the government in 1912 passed legislation which stipulated that civil servants
who knew only one official language would be given five years to learn the other
in order to be considered for promotion.

Progress in bringing Afrikaners into the civil service was slow. There were
two reasons: firstly, the government was not serious about implementing the
arrangement; and secondly, the Afrikaners produced far fewer suitable candidates
than the English community. In 1915 only fifteen per cent of Afrikaner children
proceeded beyond Standard 5 and only four per cent of them progressed far
enough to become proficient in English. As late as 1931 half of the senior civil
servants were not able to communicate with the public in any language but
English.[4]

Shortly after coming to power in 1924 the Pact government announced its
intention to implement the provisions regarding bilingualism in the civil service.
There were strong protests. Jan Smuts, as leader of the opposition, pleaded:
'[Do] it fairly, give proper notice, do not be unjust.'[5] The policy that was now

followed stated that, all things being equal, preference in promotions would be given to bilingual candidates. But in December 1932, just when the final round of the move began towards coalition between the parties of Hertzog and Smuts and the formation of the United Party (UP), P.J.H. Hofmeyr resigned as a member of the Public Service Commission because he felt bilingualism was being neglected. In 1935 D.F. Malan claimed that in his nine years under Hertzog as prime minister he was the only minister who had fought the Public Service Commission when it wanted to promote a civil servant who could speak only English while a bilingual candidate was available.[6]

For Afrikaner nationalists the situation on the railways was a big bone of contention. By the early 1930s Afrikaners made up half the white railway staff, but almost all senior positions were filled by English-speakers. English dominated as a language of communication within the organisation. In 1936 an English-speaking member of the ruling party, Morris Kentridge, called the situation on the railways 'startling'. In his words the proportion of senior Afrikaner civil servants in responsible positions was 'almost infinitesimal'.[7] In 1935 the UP government nevertheless relaxed a regulation relating to bilingualism, which provided Nationalists with the opportunity to claim that the railway administration was favouring English-speakers over Afrikaners in promotion procedures.[8]

While these developments caused some tension, the real politicisation of the civil service dates back to South Africa's entry into World War II. The decision to go to war was taken by a very narrow margin and was in fact a poor basis on which to take the country into a war. The Ossewa-Brandwag (OB), an Afrikaner paramilitary organisation, openly opposed the war. While rejecting any attempt to sabotage the war effort, the NP and Hertzog's Afrikaner Party stated that they would do nothing to assist the war effort.

The Smuts government knew that resistance to the government's policy was great. It announced that no one in the army or police would be compelled to fight abroad. Although Afrikaners formed the greatest part of the South African armed forces abroad, the government and senior civil servants tended to see all Afrikaners and certainly all Nationalists as a security risk. Many Afrikaners were overlooked in appointments or promotions in strategic departments, in particular on the railways and in the ministries of justice, police and defence.

The government also prohibited civil servants and teachers from belonging to the OB, which was understandable in view of its activist opposition to the war. By the end of 1944 civil servants were even prohibited from belonging to the Broederbond. As a result nearly a thousand Bond members resigned. Eight who refused to do so were dismissed under the emergency regulations. Among them were people who would become prominent, like Wennie du Plessis, who would defeat Smuts in his constituency in 1948, Dr H.O. Monnig and A.I. Malan (father of Magnus Malan, who would become chief of the Defence Force). The government's grounds were the Bond's opposition to the war and its political and secret character. There was, however, no evidence that the executive council of the Bond actively undermined the war. It also seemed strange to ban membership of the Bond on account of its political character while civil servants were allowed to become members of political parties. And if secrecy was an issue, the ban should have been extended to other secret organisations such as the Freemasons. Even if one has a strong distaste for secret organisations meddling in democratic politics, one has to concede that this is not in itself seditious. In a debate on this issue in Parliament in 1945, the NP fared rather better than Smuts and his UP supporters.[9]

After the war allegations were rife that during the war years pro-war civil servants were unjustly promoted while promotion was denied to people because they were against the war or simply because they were Afrikaners. There were also stories of unfair transfers and of pressure to take early retirement. The Afrikaner staff on the railways were particularly unhappy. They were bitter about perceived war-time victimisation and because the administration appointed a number of unilingual English-speaking employees to graded posts to replace staff who joined the armed forces. It was the numerous complaints about victimisation that prompted the NP to promise a Grievances Commission if it won the next election to look into cases where people had been unjustly treated.

The Grievances Commission established after the 1948 election heard evidence of some 2 875 railway employees who alleged that, while innocent of anti-war activities, they were nevertheless denied promotion to positions ranging from junior supervisory and clerical posts to that of general manager on these grounds. In many cases the administration suspected staff of anti-war sympathies on the basis of little more than the say-so of an informer.[10]

In the case of the Defence Force it was said that officers who refused to enlist for the war were told that they had no future in the force or anywhere else in the civil service. The NP claimed that even after the war the Defence Force continued to favour those from both language groups who supported the war and to victimise those who had opposed it. Another issue which inflamed relations was the practice of the Department of Military Intelligence to send reports on a regular basis to Louis Esselen, secretary of the UP, who made use of them for party political purposes.

The sharp polarisation continued after the 1948 election. Some senior members of the military command were openly contemptuous of the new government, and even expressed their feelings on an occasion at Roberts Heights in the presence of the new defence minister, Frans Erasmus. To compound matters, war veterans formed a War Veterans' Torch Commando under a highly decorated veteran, 'Sailor' Malan, to oppose segregation. With a membership of over 100 000, some Nationalists feared a *coup d'état* by a combined force of ex-servicemen and disaffected military officers.

Against this background one can review the allegation by Wilhelm that after 1948 the new government 'immediately and ruthlessly' set about to displace English-speakers in the public service and Defence Force. There is little or no evidence for this as far as the period 1948 to 1960 is concerned. Undoubtedly there were individual cases where people of merit were unjustly denied promotion, but if the government had done this on a large scale it would have come up against the powerful Public Service Commission, which could and did block irregular promotions and dismissals. If large numbers of English-speakers voluntarily left the civil service after the war – and there is no evidence for this – the main spurs were the improved job prospects many saw in the private sector and the new government's announcement that the bilingual rule would be strictly enforced in future. But this cannot be seen as 'displacement'. Neither can the strict application of this rule after a reprieve of more than 40 years of Union be deemed unreasonable.

Another spur was a sense among some English-speakers that it was now the Afrikaners' turn in the civil service. A prominent Afrikaner judge, who joined the Justice Department in Pretoria during the 1950s, recollects that considerable numbers of Afrikaners found advancement in the department. 'In some cases it was people who had been overlooked for promotion in the war; in other cases one could speak of "affirmative action" for the Afrikaners.' The judges who were appointed in the Transvaal during the 1950s were overwhelmingly Afrikaners. 'English-speakers who were elevated to the bench could be counted on the fingers of one hand.'[11] (Legal people interviewed by me did not think the same happened in the case of the benches in the Cape Province.) The most blatant case of political favouritism was perhaps the appointment of L.C. Steyn, who at that point was a government law adviser, to the position of chief justice over the heads of some eminent English judges. For more than 30 years the NP government's first instinct was to appoint Afrikaner judges to head commissions of inquiry. Very few English-speakers were ever appointed to head such commissions.

Those who allege that English-speakers were displaced often base their view on three prominent cases in which people were appointed or removed just after 1948. The best-known case involved Marshall Clark, Major-General Evered Poole and Werner Eiselen. In addition there were also certain developments in the Defence Force which must be taken into account. These cases will be discussed briefly.

The most controversial was that of W. Marshall Clark, who had been appointed general manager of the South African Railways and Harbours. Clark worked for the railways before enlisting for the war. He returned in 1942 and rapidly climbed the ladder. When appointed general manager in 1945 at the age of 45, he was the youngest man ever to hold the job, and his salary had trebled in three years. He was a brilliant civil engineer but had no administrative experience. More importantly, the promotion was over the heads of Willem Heckroodt, who was more than ten years his senior and had much more administrative experience, and Danie du Plessis, who also was more senior.

Heckroodt was one of those who alleged in testimony that he had been discriminated against. Paul Sauer, the minister of railways, was unhappy with the idea of a Grievances Commission, since the case presented him with a painful dilemma. Clark's wife and his wife had been roommates at the University of Cape Town. He had proposed the toast at the wedding of the Clarks and the couple were the godparents of the Sauers' daughter.

But Afrikaner railway workers, who formed one of the NP's largest constituencies, were so outraged that it seemed that if Clark did not leave, Sauer would have to be shifted from the railways portfolio. After some vacillation the government declared that Clark was an exceptionally able man, but that his promotion over the head of Heckroodt and Du Plessis constituted an injustice. In 1949 Sauer called in Clark. He told him that he would be removed from his post. He soon retired and was paid £80 000 as a pension, which was a small fortune in those years. (His salary in 1946 was a mere £3 600.[12]) Heckroodt replaced him in the most senior post in the railways and he in turn was succeeded by Du Plessis.

Clark's case was debated in Parliament. A member of the United Party, C.J.M. Abbott, voiced disquiet about *''n algemene uitskuiwery'* of English-speakers but then continued: 'Genl Poole was die eerste om uitgeskuif te word, toe het ons 'n vreemde benoeming in die Departement van Naturellesake gehad en nou Marshall Clark.'[13] Hardly evidence of *''n algemene uitskuiwery'*.

The 'strange appointment' in Native Affairs was that of Werner Eiselen as secretary for native affairs in 1948. He was brought in from the outside to fill a vacancy. Both the under-secretaries were English-speakers and one of them, Fred Rodseth, was particularly aggrieved that he had been overlooked. But a recent study by Ivan Evans has found that Eiselen's appointment was not unreasonable. Eiselen had earlier worked in the department, knew some African languages and had published articles on African society. If anything, the case demonstrated the strength of the Public Service Commission, which first resisted the minister's nomination of Eiselen and only capitulated after the full cabinet insisted on him. Rodseth resigned in 1954 and was replaced by an Afrikaner, but the replacement of the other under-secretary on his retirement was another English-speaker.[14]

In the Defence Force the case of Major-General Evered Poole was something of a *cause célèbre*. As deputy chief of the General Staff, he was first in line to succeed General Sir Pierre van Ryneveld as chief of General Staff by the beginning of 1949. Poole had been an outstanding soldier during the war. One of the reasons he fell foul of the Nationalists was his closeness to Smuts and the fact that in 1946 he became head of the Department of Military Intelligence, which sat on the war-time files of NP politicians. E.C. Erasmus, the NP minister of defence made it clear that he had no intention to promote Poole and offered him the obscure post of head of South Africa's military mission in Berlin. Poole accepted and later rose to the rank of ambassador in Chile.

An abrasive hard-liner, Erasmus harboured some burning resentments from the war years, in particular over matters such as the co-operation between Military Intelligence and the UP. He signalled that he intended to enforce the bilingual rule strictly and that he would attempt to get the Defence Force to display a 'South African spirit' as soon as possible. But he was also faced with tough decisions, having to retrench and to reorganise the Defence Force, which would have made any minister unpopular. In these circumstances the personnel shifts that were announced quickly assumed a political colour. Some 50 members of the senior command of the Army were demoted or received 'Irish promotions' or were unjustly denied promotion for several years. In some cases salaries were lowered. The Army officers affected were mostly English-speakers, but there were also several Afrikaner officers who had clashed with Erasmus. One was Brigadier J.B. Kriegler, who was second in line for the post of chief of General Staff. He was sent from the Witwatersrand Command to a less senior post in Potchefstroom after clashing with Erasmus over the reorganisation of the commandos. He was not close to any political party, and was in fact approached by both the NP and UP to stand for election in 1953.[15]

The Air Force was the branch of the Defence Force most seriously affected by the change-over in 1948. Between 1948 and 1955 English-speakers resigned in droves from the Air Force while Afrikaners did not. The reasons they gave were political influence: they thought that their careers suffered on account of their political views.[16] A detailed study of the Air Force resignations concludes that political interference ended after Erasmus's departure.

> Erasmus in his zeal to remould the South African Air Force was probably unaware of the effect his actions could have on the operational efficiency of the SAAF as wartime operational expertise drained away. His successors have been much more aware of this and have scrupulously avoided even the slightest semblance of political favouritism in the appointments and promotions they have authorised.[17]

The Afrikanerisation of the public sector was in fact a gradual process instead of a sudden take-over. The Afrikaner advance in the security agencies predated the 1948 change in government. Since 1927 the intake of white policemen had

been over 90 per cent Afrikaans-speaking and so were two-thirds of the members of the armed forces during the war. Between 1945 and 1960 the state
appointed Africans at a rate much faster than Afrikaners and by 1960 African
employees would outnumber whites for the first time in history.[18] Table 1 shows
that the increase of Afrikaners employed in the public sector after 1948 was not
dramatic. Over time, however, the civil service acquired an Afrikaner image, or
to be more precise an Afrikaner nationalist image, which reinforced the negative views held by English-speakers. By 1977 one-quarter of English-speakers
worked in the public sector, but they occupied less than ten per cent of the top
positions in the central civil service.[19]

Table 1: Proportion of Afrikaners employed in the public sector

	1936	1960	1977
Afrikaners as a %of white public sector	53,3	58,1	60,8
Afrikaners in public sector as % of Afrikaner labour force	26,1	33,0	36,6

Source: T.J. Steenekamp, "'n Ekonomiese ontleding van die sosio-politieke groepvorming met spesiale verwysing na die Afrikaner", PhD thesis, Unisa, 1989, p. 202.

The NP never had a policy to transform the civil service in such a way that it
became demographically representative of the white population in its upper
levels. Although there was an influx of Afrikaners into the civil service, particularly from the 1930s on, it was only in the 1960s that the senior levels of the
service started to resemble the white population composition. In 1960, 58 per
cent of the white population were Afrikaners, 37 per cent were English-speakers
and the rest gave both languages as their home language. An analysis of the
1960 census found that in the upper levels of the public administration, 57,2 per
cent of civil servants were Afrikaners as against 37,5 English-speakers. The
position was reversed in the private sector. Here only 25 per cent of Afrikaners
were in the upper echelon of the job market as directors, managers and self-
employed owners as against 66 per cent of English-speakers.[20]

Did a large-scale purge of English-speakers occur in the top levels of the
public sector in the first ten years of NP rule? The three major studies of the white

oligarchy published in the 1950s, by Paterson, Marquard and Carter, make no mention of anything of the sort, except for a brief reference by Marquard. He stated: 'Appointment and particularly promotion of civil servants goes on without regard for party-political affiliations,' except when there was a fundamental policy difference. He then mentioned the Smuts government's refusal to promote Nationalists in key positions during the war. These were the notable reversal of Clark's promotion, and the case of people who had been interned and missed promotion.[21]

Ivan Evans, who is the only scholar who so far has done serious research in this field, makes this point:

> A perusal of the Public Service List from 1954–1964, which provides complete lists of all civil servants in the various departments of the state, provides no help in tracing the Afrikanerization of the [Native Affairs] Department. Although the list does break down the department's personnel on the basis of grade and rank, Afrikaner names already heavily dominated the lists for 1947 and 1948, making it difficult to see any marked changes.[22]

The interviews I conducted with Afrikaners who entered the civil service in the decade after 1948 confirm this. The NP victory of 1948 did not herald an abrupt Afrikanerisation of the civil service. It was in fact a much more gradual process, which had already gathered steam by the 1930s and early 1940s, and only culminated in the 1960s and 1970s.

The change of government in 1948 did not represent any rupture in the professional quality of the civil service. There were in all likelihood some cases of discrimination against English-speakers when promotion was considered, but senior officials in the public service were normally people who had come up through the ranks. As far as one can judge from the present state of research there was no loss in economic or administrative efficiency – at least as far as the white oligarchy in a racially structured system was concerned.

6.

The communal nature of the
South African conflict

As the layers of apartheid peel away, the communal essence of the South African conflict becomes ever more visible. The communal conflict is rooted in the history of the country as a settler colony and the resultant black struggle against a political system dominated after 1948 by Afrikaner nationalists, the core group of the larger white community. The huge gap in material wealth between whites and Africans (and, to a lesser extent, Indians and Coloureds) has established a close correspondence between race and class, which makes the conflict much more intractable. But the communal conflict is essentially not a disguised class struggle. It is one between two communities, predominantly Afrikaner and African, whose primary aim is control of the state and possession of a historical homeland. Accordingly, virtually all political parties, trade unions and other public associations are communally based and emphasise the promotion of communal interests rather than purely class objectives.

Many analysts dispute this emphasis on a communal struggle.[1] They stress the pursuit by whites of material rewards and privileges and consider nationalist convictions of lesser importance. The emphasis on material interests as the perceived real purpose of the apartheid system also informs political forecasts. The unspoken assumption of many analysts is that after a cost-benefit analysis of material prospects, the more affluent and secure Afrikaners will settle for majority rule.[2]

No one would deny that the substantially greater rewards and privileges whites enjoy exercise a powerful influence upon the way in which whites (or blacks) think about the system and their political strategies. Yet historians are only too aware that time and again people have acted against what analysts at the time (or retrospectively) considered to be their greater material inter-ests.[3] This is not due to a particular form of short-sightedness. If history teaches one thing, it is that both ruling elites and subordinates attach at least as much weight to socio-political considerations, such as communal or national status, identity and autonomy, as to their evaluation of their immediate material interests and securities.

To investigate the prospects of a possible settlement between the two con-tending nationalisms, it is necessary to analyse briefly the burden of the past and the nature of the two nationalisms. Only then will we be able to assess the prospects of a resolution of the conflicting claims about national status and citizenship identity.

The burden of a settler society

South African history is unique in the way in which post-1870 industrial society adapted to pre-industrial social relations and used a modernised state appara-tus to intensify the forms of oppression established originally by the settler so-ciety. This was the real turning point in South African history: Africans were incorporated into the industrial workforce without undermining white settler domination. This shifts the spotlight to the history of South Africa as a settler society, where the still-powerful racial and national divisions originated. These divisions were mainly the horizontal racial divide between whites and blacks and the vertical one between Afrikaners and English-speakers.[4] The basic an-tagonisms between white and black flowed from slavery and frontier conquest. White settlers increasingly believed themselves to be bearers of a superior so-cial and cultural system which had to be preserved against being swamped and against *gelykstelling* (levelling). The settlers' socio-political dominance enabled them to establish and perpetuate their position of privilege, in the process de-grading slaves, serfs and their descendants. The status, security and ultimate survival of settler society were as vital a concern as reaping the material bene-fits of domination. As George Frederickson concludes: 'The degradation of non-whites frequently served to bind together the white population, or some segment of it, to become a way of life, and not simply a cover for economic ex-ploitation.'[5]

During the accelerated industrialisation that occurred after the 1870s, the interdependence between whites and Africans increased, but this did not dissolve the basic divide between the Afrikaner (and larger white) community and the Africans. In the course of the twentieth century the political system became akin to one of 'nations' interacting within the same territory with highly crystallised, almost caste-like status differences between the two formations.[6]

This, then, is the significance for contemporary South Africa of the failure of industrialisation to alter the basic elements of settler domination and black exclusion. As Sam Nolutshungu cogently observes, the main political cleavages have continued to be ethnic, racial and national. As a result, the state is challenged by the subordinate population primarily in terms of their subordination as a nation rather than in terms of exploitation. Accordingly, blacks issue their challenge primarily in the form of a nationalist movement rather than a class struggle. The white state's attempt to gain widespread black acceptance through reform faces virtually insuperable obstacles. The reason is that the continuing national domination (which corresponds with the racial cleavage) serves to undercut the state's efforts to extend its base by incorporating the vulnerable black middle class and establishing the domination of middle-class people across colour lines.[7]

The National Party, as a 'poor settler' regime in South Africa, has to operate within the constraints imposed by its constituency of settler descendants. Like the Protestants in Northern Ireland or the Jews in Israel, it is concerned with national status and prestige as well as material standing. Since it is ultimately political power which preserves 'colonial birthrights', any dilution of that power, even symbolic political co-optation of the 'natives', raises an outcry from sections who fear betrayal. The conflict in South Africa (like that in Northern Ireland or Israel) is not rooted in religious or racial differences as such. It stems from challenges to the identity – which could be either racially or religiously defined – of the most prestigious community that emerged from the period of settler domination. In South Africa the need for political co-optation is greater, for, unlike Northern Ireland, the country is ruled by a demographically shrinking minority. However, here too historical forces continually undercut parties, such as the Progressive Federal Party, which propose, in the name of enlightened self-interest, the political integration of the subordinates. They also cause the leadership of the governing party to believe that it cannot move much beyond a carefully controlled co-optation policy without encountering major resistance from its right wing.

Despite its fairly recent technocratic gloss, the National Party is still mainly informed by the precepts of Afrikaner nationalism. The nature of this nationalism is discussed briefly below.

Afrikaner nationalism

The rise of Afrikaner nationalism is arguably the single most important political development of the first half of twentieth-century South Africa. Yet the nature of this nationalism, its sustaining power, and its potential for coming to terms with oppositional forces are still poorly understood.

What, indeed, are the chances of this nationalism dissolving itself or committing 'voluntary suicide'? Is there a prospect of national politics being replaced by class-based politics that can accommodate majority rule? To answer this, it is important to know whether nationalism is basically economistic in nature in the sense that material considerations are of overriding importance, or whether non-material or even 'irrational' influences (ideas and sentiments about national identity and status) have acquired a force of their own and play an important, even decisive, role.

Given the National Party government's obsession with ethnicity, almost as if – to use Neville Alexander's terms – it were an elegant variation of divine will, it must be stressed that there is no primordial force called ethnicity that makes groups cohere.[8] It is also not inevitable that competing nationalisms will emanate from a divided society undergoing rapid industrialisation.[9] What prompts a group to choose nationalism rather than, say, socialism as a political strategy is structural forces operating within a particular set of circumstances.

The emergence of nationalism, and the form it assumes, depend on the society's founding history, the population mix, the differential access groups have to power and education, and the nature of the economy. The fact that South Africa has never known a strong socialist movement transcending colour divisions has much to do with its settler origins. Unskilled Afrikaner workers entering the gold or diamond mines never forgot that they, like their fathers, commanded a position of authority and superiority over Africans in the pre-industrial period. That, together with the political power and better education they enjoyed, made them resist the rigid industrial discipline and abuse to which Africans were subjected.[10] It also made them reject industrial *gelykstelling* (social levelling) to cite the words of Dr D.F. Malan in the 1930s: 'The white man, because he is white, is expected – whatever his chances in the labour market – to maintain a white standard of living . . . you can understand that in the circumstances, the competition for the white man is killing.'[11] The cheap wages that black workers had to accept for a variety of reasons, especially in the mining and agricultural sectors, made the development of common worker interests impossible.

Thus, there were powerful reasons for a basic divergence of racial identities, which has continued to manifest itself in the us–them syndrome. This was reinforced by the segregation policies of the nineteenth and twentieth centuries. But all this does not explain the particular form of nationalism that arose among Afrikaners. Theorists usually distinguish between territorial nationalism, associated with Western Europe, where the thrust was to create out of the people living in a particular state a culturally homogeneous nation which governed itself, and ethnic nationalisms (or ethno-nationalisms), occurring in multi-ethnic states such as those of Eastern Europe. Here members of cultural groups develop for various reasons a vivid sense of oneness of kind. Their identification with their ethnic group drives them to claim full political control in the name of ethnic self-determination. If successful, they set themselves up as the nation while relegating others to the position of subordinate minorities. Unlike territorial nationalisms which have been built on a high culture (for example German or Italian), ethno-nationalisms usually have to embark on social engineering and ideological invention to create a high culture and establish a close linkage between state and culture.[12]

Afrikaner nationalism obviously fits the category of ethno-nationalism, but why did Afrikaners over time develop such a vivid sense of oneness of kind? The answer seems to lie in the great advantage ethno-nationalism enjoys as a form of political mobilisation. It combines a strategy to promote or defend the discrete interests of classes within the group with a dimension that relates to ethnic or communal power and status. The latter dimension is explicitly political and emotional. On occasion, outsiders even consider it irrational, something to be dismissed as reflecting a 'frontier' or 'laager' mentality, rather than subjecting it to dispassionate analysis.

Recent analyses of Afrikaner nationalism concentrate on economistic explanations, and in some cases virtually exclude the political and emotional dimension.[13] There certainly was a profound economic dimension in the rise of Afrikaner nationalism. The fact that it originally manifested itself during the first phases of industrialisation is hardly coincidental. Industrial development is always uneven, leaving some groups behind or with a sense of relative deprivation. If inequalities are of an ethnic or cultural nature – as they were in the case of Afrikaners and English-speakers – groups with access to power and education often mobilise themselves under ethnic banners.

Industrialisation also tends to generate ethno-nationalism for another reason. As Ernest Gellner has pointed out, industrialisation requires workers to have shared generic skills. This in turn demands a standardised, homogeneous and centrally sustained high culture. In the South Africa of the late nineteenth century, English and Dutch functioned as high cultures. English would have established a monopoly had it not been for the Dutch-Afrikaner intellectuals and 'clerks' (teachers, church ministers, attorneys, civil servants, etc.) who found their careers blocked by English high culture. They became 'language manipulators':[14] people whose livelihood depended on the mastery of a language. It is they who turned an ethnic dialect into a modern language and then insisted that the state help elevate it to a high culture. They also made it their particular concern to minister to the sense of estrangement and exclusion which the uprooted, urban Afrikaners experienced in the rough early phases of South African industrialisation. This gave rise to a highly charged romantic nationalism which emphasised Afrikaner history and traditional values.[15]

It is also not difficult to give economic reasons why Afrikaner nationalism had such a sustaining power even after the 1940s when the early phase of industrialisation had passed and most Afrikaners had become urbanised. The Nationalist government promised to promote a variety of interests – better producer prices and stricter labour controls for farmers, job reservation for workers, state contracts for businessmen, and an insistence on bilingualism for civil servants. Partly as a result of state aid, Afrikaners experienced a dramatic economic advance between 1946 and 1977. By 1946, only a third of Afrikaners could be considered middle class (being in white-collar urban jobs or reasonably secure farmers); by 1977 this had increased to close to 70 per cent.[16]

But had nationalism merely been a disguised form of class politics, occurring particularly during early industrialisation, one would expect it to have waned once the income gap between Afrikaners and English-speakers started to narrow, lifestyles began to converge, and the sharp polarisation of the early stages disappeared. And one would expect businessmen and workers across racial and ethnic divides to have been drawn towards a form of class-oriented politics. Had ethno-nationalism merely been masked class politics, there would indeed have been a chance of 'voluntary (ethnic) suicide' in order to promote class interests under different banners. However, if one looks at white politics over the past twenty years most trends point the other way. The PFP, as the only party committed to integrative politics, never attracted more than seven per cent of the Afrikaner vote, declining to four per cent in the 1987 election. White English-speakers have increasingly considered South Africa to be their homeland and a place where whites have considerable control over their political destiny. The support for parties and candidates to the left of the NP and right-wing 'white homeland' parties declined from 30 per cent in 1977 to 27 per cent in 1981 and to 18 per cent in 1987.

In the literature there has been a strong tendency to present the NP and the government as the vehicle of the upper middle class and particularly of big business. However, the NP has in fact retained a fair spread in its class composition. According to a 1986 poll, the party derived 20 per cent of its support from people in the 'upper middle' category of household income, 45 per cent from the 'middle' and 35 per cent from the 'lower middle' or 'lower' category. (The figures for the HNP and Conservative Party are 10, 49 and 41 per cent respectively.) In a crude fashion, these figures display the extent to which the National Party will have to square upper-middle-class, middle-class and working-class interests. In recent extensive interviews with NP parliamentarians and ministers, Lawrence Schlemmer found that the vast majority of these politicians were, above all, sensitive to the wishes of party supporters. Most politicians wanted to achieve a balance between the variety of interest groups within the Afrikaner national community and the broader white community. None suggested that business interests and the large corporate sector had a particular influence on government.[17]

Ethno-nationalism, then, clearly cannot be explained in purely economistic terms. In his astute general observations on communal conflicts, Walker Connor remarks that statesmen and scholars (particularly Americans) err in assuming that economic considerations will be decisive in human affairs under conditions of communal strife. Connor concludes that economic factors 'are likely to come in a poor second when competing with the emotionalism of ethnic nationalism'.[18]

It was invariably emotive issues relating to national identity and status which triggered the major electoral shifts in South African political history. The Rebellion of 1914–15 (on the issue of South Africa's participation in World War I) paved the way for the NP's first breakthrough in the election of 1915, when it unexpectedly captured 27 seats. Fusion between Hertzog's NP and Smuts's South African Party, which was perceived as a threat by some Afrikaners to national sovereignty, led to the establishment of Malan's 'Purified' NP. This party may well have remained in the wilderness had South Africa's participation in World War II not destroyed the white middle ground. The NP won the 1948 election mainly on the platform of establishing Afrikaner control over their homeland.

Once in power, the NP government on several occasions made decisions which were 'irrational', judged purely on economic grounds. In the 1950s it barred many skilled immigrants from English-speaking countries who could have contributed greatly to economic growth. The government took the country out of the British Commonwealth in 1961, despite dire predictions about economic disaster, because it did not want to compromise national 'autonomy' and 'honour'. In 1986 the NP government deliberately invited sanctions and disinvestment (again disregarding dire predictions) in order to demonstrate its immunity to foreign pressure. Despite this, English-speaking support for the NP increased to over 50 per cent in the 1987 election, compared to below thirty per cent in 1981.

This suggests that the political and emotional dimensions of the ethno-national strategy – issues relating to ethnic or communal power and status – are crucial and, indeed, decisive. It is important to realise why this is so. In his study, Elie Kedourie warns against dismissing nationalist ideology as hardly worthy of analysis. In fact, nationalist identity is the creation of a nationalist doctrine rather than the other way round.[19] Nationalism builds on the Kantian doctrine that self-determination is the supreme political good. This leads to the central nationalist claim that self-determination can only be realised in a world 'naturally' divided into nations.[20] This forms the basis for both Afrikaner nationalism and its ideological instrument, apartheid. President P.W. Botha, as leader of the moderate wing of Afrikaner nationalism, has clearly internalised the doctrine of the 'group' or 'nation', making it the guiding principle of his approach to politics.[21]

The NP's insistence on self-determination is no longer cast in narrow Afrikaner terms, but rather has a broader, white-community orientation. It embraces a combination of elements such as a distinctive lifestyle, a sense of origin and identity, the psychological satisfaction of in-group community life (which includes schools), standards of public order, behaviour and respectability, and sufficient control over the allocation of resources and the maintenance of security to ensure the continuation of these benefits.[22]

National Party interviewees nowadays seldom mention threats to the Afrikaans language and its culture as among the most pressing problems or salient issues.[23] However, this does not mean that Afrikaner ethnicity is no longer an issue. It is because the culture is so well protected within the dominant white community that it does not surface as a concern. This may change rapidly the moment political control is threatened, not to speak of a possible take-over by the ANC as the vanguard of African nationalists. As Gellner observed in a general context: 'The high (literate) culture in which they have been educated is, for most men, their most precious investment, the core of their identity, their insurance, and their security.'[24] Ultimately ethno-nationalism goes beyond culture and involves a close emotional identification with the state, national institutions such as Parliament and the Army, and national symbols and values. Much of the talk about a peaceful transfer of power in South Africa misses the fundamental point: that Afrikaners and the larger white nation consider their sovereignty as precious. It is not something to be bartered away.

African nationalism

In a new study of nationalism, Benyamin Neuberger makes a useful distinction between various approaches to nationalism on the African continent. There is the liberal-democratic approach to national self-determination, which demands respect for basic human rights, protection of minorities, equality for all individuals and groups, free elections, and the right to participate in government. It found best expression in French West Africa during the 1950s when the African elite was ready to transcend national self-determination for the sake of the full democratisation of the French Empire.

There was also the national approach to self-determination. This was pursued under the banner of anti-colonial nationalism, which aimed to restore, albeit in modified form, a golden age which had come to an abrupt end through foreign conquest. Neuberger declares: 'The national school of self-determination defines the achievement of independence as the goal of national self-determination. National self-determination is perceived as fulfilled as long as the citizens of the nation are ruled by their "kith and kin".'[25] In white-ruled South Africa, the crucial question was and is: 'who are the people in the territory who constitute the appropriate self for self-determination?'[26]

The question, then, is how Africans in South Africa see the political self. In meetings such as that in Dakar in July 1987 with a group of internally based South Africans, the ANC leadership strongly emphasised its liberal-democratic credentials. This is based in the first place on the Freedom Charter, adopted in 1955, and the secession of some Africanists who established the Pan Africanist Congress (PAC) in 1959. In fact, the Charter's use of the term 'national' is ambiguous. One of the key phrases reads, 'All national groups shall have equal rights', which, some of the Charter's critics claim, suggests the creation of four nations – Africans, Coloureds, Indians and whites.[27] Another clause states: 'The national wealth of our country, the heritage of all South Africans, shall be restored to the people.' Charter supporters argue that the word 'national' refers to all South Africans,[28] but the word 'restore' may suggest that it has primarily Africans in mind. And then, of course, there is the Charter's ringing opening phrase: 'South Africa belongs to all who live in it, black and white, and . . . no government can justly claim authority unless it is based on the will of the people.' This again suggests a liberal-democratic approach to self-determination.

The Charter is such a synthesised document that too much weight should not be attached to individual clauses. It reflects the three main strands which characterised the ANC during the 1950s, namely Charterist, workerist and Africanist. The Charterist position was aimed at constructing a broad-based movement transcending race and class to oppose apartheid. The workerist strand sought to build a political trade union movement that would 'harness workers' demands for economic amelioration to a political cause'.[29] It was to participate in the political struggle against pass laws, Bantu education and other forms of oppression.[30] The third strand was Africanism. This was for the first time openly expressed by the ANC's Programme of Action of 1949 and then again by the PAC. The PAC argued that the Programme of Action had proposed an ethnically assertive nationalism, which the ANC subsequently diluted by its alliance with the white-dominated Congress of Democrats and by the strategic influence of white communists within the ANC. In the PAC's view this influence expressed itself in the Charter's recognition of the rights and status of all national groups.

In the view of the Africanists an emphasis on 'multiracialism' was dangerous because it would deprive them of the most effective ideological means of inspiring a mass following and would perpetuate the African dependence on whites on which minority domination rested.[31] The PAC itself was ambiguous about the degree to which it wanted whites to be excluded. In his 1959 presidential address, Robert Sobukwe called for a government by Africans for Africans – and specified that 'everybody who owes his loyalty to Africa has to be regarded as African'. In a newspaper article, Sobukwe exhorted whites to adjust their outlook in such a fashion that 'Africa for the Africans could apply to them even though they are white'. Sobukwe also stated, however, that whites were for the present unable to pledge their loyalty to Africa, even if they were intellectual converts to the cause of African freedom, 'because they benefit materially from the present set-up', and so 'cannot completely identify themselves with that cause'.[32] The crucial question is whether the ANC–PAC split involves a fundamental disagreement over goals and ideology, or whether it is one at a lower level about discipline, strategy and tactics to promote nationalist goals.

The NP's shifts over the past ten years have provided a classic case of a nationalist movement adapting its strategy, image and rhetoric without wishing to abandon its nationalist claims. No serious analyst has argued that the breakaway of Dr Andries Treurnicht's Conservative Party (CP) in 1982 'proved' that the NP was less committed to Afrikaner rule or that it genuinely intended to share power with the Coloured and Indian communities. In the case of the

ANC, however, there is a surprising willingness to accept clauses in the Freedom Charter and the break with the PAC as sufficient proof that it is not in the first place committed to African nationalism but rather to an inclusive South African liberal democracy.

Like other nationalist movements, the ANC has above all been committed to building an all-class front in its primary community, the Africans. Its goal is national self-determination in which the 'self' would undoubtedly be the Africans in the majority. Nelson Mandela spelled out this position in the Rivonia Trial: 'The ideological creed of the ANC is, and always has been, the creed of African nationalism. It is not the concept of African nationalism expressed in the cry "drive the white man into the sea". The African nationalism for which the ANC stands is the concept of freedom and fulfilment for the African people in their own land.'[33]

The ANC's split with the PAC stemmed predominantly from struggles at leadership level on the Witwatersrand during the 1950s. At times, this threatened to destroy the movement. Bogged down by bannings, the Treason Trial, and inexperienced or incompetent office-bearers, the Transvaal ANC was vulnerable to challenges. In a manner similar to the manoeuvres of Treurnicht's men during the two or three years prior to the 1982 NP–CP split, some Africanists exploited ideological differences in their struggle to gain control of the Transvaal ANC. Only when that failed did they break away, declaring, very much like Treurnicht in the case of Afrikaner nationalism, that they would form an organisation of their own to function as a 'custodian of traditional ANC policy'.[34] The PAC never succeeded in establishing followings in the Transvaal or the Eastern Cape, which either meant that there were no Africanists there – which is unlikely – or that they did not have any major ideological differences with the ANC.

The ANC enlistment of white support in the 1950s was a matter of strategy rather than principle. It realised that sympathetic whites were necessary to educate other whites on the evils of the pass system and to lead deputations to the government and local authorities. Apart from the communists, however, very few whites were integrated into the organisation and activities of the ANC. Jack Simons, an academic with a long association with the movement, states that while the ANC has had open membership since 1943, it made no considered attempt during its period of legitimacy to integrate non-Africans. After the movement had been driven into exile in the early 1960s, a substantial number of Indians, Coloureds and whites were absorbed into the ANC. Nevertheless, until 1985 non-Africans were not included in the National Executive Committee of the ANC. Prior to the movement's consultative conference of that year, an ANC leader made a stand against non-African inclusion on the grounds that the ANC's struggle was first and foremost against white domination, and that Africans should liberate themselves under their own leadership. Commenting on this, Simons writes that there was 'an obvious contradiction between the approved policy of enlisting militants from all national groups and the proposed exclusion of non-Africans from the leadership'. He adds that 'an even more serious contradiction existed between this Africanist approach and the claims of Congress to represent all national groups in the struggle for a single South African nation'.[35] The conference of 1985 resolved the issue in favour of the participation of all South Africans in the work of the ANC at all levels.

In the ANC's ideology the same contradictions are evident. Two themes dating back to the late 1920s vie with each other. On the one hand the ANC proposes a non-racial struggle of all the classes (with the workers as a leading force), while on the other hand it calls for an Africanist struggle against white colonisation. Until very recently the latter theme dominated. The ANC slogan *Mayibuye iAfrika* is a demand for a return of the land of Africa to its indigenous inhabitants. There is little ambivalence about the issue of the appropriate self for self-determination. In a 1982 discussion of two basic ANC documents, the Freedom Charter and the ANC's 'Strategy, Tactics and Programme', the ANC journal *Sechaba* stated clearly: 'Our notion of the people identifies the African people as the main revolutionary force and the African people as a decisive component in it.'[36] The mainspring of the struggle is the mobilisation of African people as a dispossessed and racially oppressed nation. In certain instances the ANC's actions deliberately coincide with Afrikaner nationalist events. In response to the Afrikaners' celebration of 16 December as the day symbolising their victory over Africans at Blood River, the ANC formed its military wing, Umkhonto we Sizwe, on the same day in 1961 and still celebrates it as the historic 'turning point in the long march to freedom'.[37]

The degree to which the ANC as a nationalist movement adopts an inclusive approach to its membership (as opposed to the PAC's exclusion of whites) is the result more of strategic considerations imposed by its existence in exile than of any unified ideological commitment. In an analysis published in 1962, Edward Feit wrote that the ANC had at all times sought to include all shades of African opinion. It was struggles over leadership, not ideology, that led to expulsions and splits. The disunity of the movement was so great that Nelson Mandela felt that should the ANC ever achieve its aims, it would probably split into a number of political parties.[38] Exile, in contrast, enforced discipline and also strengthened the ANC's commitment to an inclusive nationalism and non-racialism. Some African countries disliked the ANC's inclusion of whites as members, but the movement's main concern was winning Western diplomatic recognition and support. In this struggle it made much more sense to grant South African whites a place in the sun than to acquire an image similar to that of the PAC, which sometimes appeared as if it wanted to drive the whites into the sea.

As a nationalist movement in exile, the ANC has had few problems with incorporating other organisations in its broad front despite ideological differences. Thus, the leadership could laud the Black Consciousness movement for its organisational achievements and absorb part of the movement despite, as Oliver Tambo delicately phrased it, its 'limitations in seeing our struggle as racial'.[39] It was also able to welcome the establishment in 1983 of the United Democratic Front, a movement with a great many non-African members. On the other hand, the ANC displays a typical nationalist suspicion of working-class mobilisation that may over time pose a challenge to its leadership. This probably accounts for the expulsion in the late 1970s of a group of workerists who felt that the ANC had failed by not having built the movement on the working class. These suspicions are also reflected in the ANC advice to the 1987 Congress of South African Trade Unions (Cosatu) national conference against adopting socialism as Cosatu policy.[40]

Building a broad front of allies does not mean that the ANC is no longer a nationalist movement at its core. Yet a broad front almost inevitably has an effect on ideology. The ANC no longer uses the term 'non-racial struggle of all classes' primarily in a Marxist sense but rather as liberals would do so in a stand against apartheid's enforced group membership. The degree to which this dimension can be strengthened will determine whether the ANC is prepared to enter the arena of multi-party competition. For the moment, however, the nationalist temptation to assert hegemonic control over all oppositional forces remains very strong.

What route to nation-building the ANC and its allies will follow if they win power also depends on the values forged during the struggle for their liberation. The fight against apartheid rules out the building of a nation on the basis of distinct ethnic groups. Except for its earlier stages, the ANC never favoured the Afrikaners' brand of ethno-nationalism. Instead, the ANC insists on the forced unification of ethnic groups in a homogeneous nation. Like mass parties elsewhere on the African continent, it envisages this nation-building project as occurring under the direction of a highly centralised government. However, if the ANC in the course of its struggle is compelled to forge alliances and make political compromises, the Jacobin tendencies within this nationalism may be softened. A kind of political and cultural pluralism could take root and yield a form of nationalism that is *sui generis* on the continent.

Disputed territories and communal claims

In South Africa the divisions between whites and blacks, and between Afrikaner and African nationalism, remain deep and strongly felt. Recent times have witnessed a slight but not insignificant blurring of the divisions. The political barriers between Afrikaners and English-speaking whites have largely disappeared and the government is increasingly drawing black civil servants into the administration and defence of the state. On the ANC side some strides have been made in the past years to redefine its struggle ideologically in non-racial, rather than nationalist, terms. However, this does not mean that the essence of either the NP or the ANC has changed. On occasion their core thinking is revealed, for example when Chris Heunis, minister of constitutional development, stated that 'it is in the long-term interest that the Afrikaner should always have the privilege of the leadership role'.[41] The ANC, on the other hand, while stressing that it is not exclusivist, insists that its primary task is the 'national liberation of the largest and most oppressed group – the African people'.[42] In a statement by the ANC's National Executive Committee in December 1986 the struggle is seen primarily in terms of the continuity of African resistance from the Battle of Isandlwana in 1879, through the Bambatha uprising in 1906, up to the present time.

There does not appear to be much evidence that there will be a disintegration of communal lines because of class interests. In the first place comparative studies show that ethnic and communal antagonisms are exacerbated by rapid urbanisation – and millions of Africans will become urbanised during the next two decades. Whites will attempt, against considerable odds, to preserve the lifestyles to which they are accustomed. Blacks will challenge the head start whites continue to enjoy by virtue of their access to virtually all the resources of the state – economic, educational, political, administrative and social. Expanded black education seems to be strengthening the black demand for equality in state services rather than weakening it. The tensions will greatly intensify once whites sense that the state may fall and their 'homeland' may be lost.

Once the conflict reaches this stage, it may well become non-negotiable. Then the struggle truly will be one of survival, involving the basic issue of personal and communal identity and integrity. It is not a question of the dominant group being massacred or driven into the sea: of this there is virtually no chance in South Africa. It is rather a question of dominant groups in deeply divided societies identifying so strongly with the ethnic homeland and state that they become part of their extended self. To lose control over the homeland 'is to risk the fragmentation of the self, an eventuality which people will resist with their very lives'.[43] Not much store should be put on rationality when dominant groups are driven to the wall. In a comparative study of Lebanon and South Africa, Theodor Hanf remarks: '[It] is by no means certain that economic considerations would govern the behaviour of a dominant group if it felt that its existence was threatened. A scorched-earth policy is hardly an economically rational concept. Nevertheless it is one often, and particularly, practised in civil wars between ethnic and religious groups.'[44]

Conclusion

Robert McNamara has summed up well the 'magic' political formula for peace in South Africa. It must, he declared, assure black people of full participation in genuine political power. And it must protect whites against a winner-takes-all form of majority rule. At the moment the NP government is insisting on considerably more. The least the government would settle for – after well-directed pressure and incentives – is co-equality or a form of dualism. On the one hand, one would have a white-led political group stressing group rights and choosing their own representatives. On the other hand, one would have a political bloc headed by African nationalists stressing individual rights and representation. A system built on freedom of association, with every person having the freedom to decide which bloc to support, would constitute a decisive break with apartheid. Once there is mutual acceptance, these two blocs would be able to negotiate a system in which they have parity of representation at legislative and executive levels, and with a chief executive appointed on a rotating basis. The challenge would be to build a new nation over time that would transcend both Afrikaner and African nationalism.

Such a system is far less than what black people are struggling for, but also much more than they currently enjoy. It may be the only realistic intermediate goal for those wanting peaceful change in South Africa. Only a government with a clearly representative black and white component will have the moral authority to use force and to meet the security and identity needs of both whites and blacks.

To arrive at a compromise, a strategy of gradualism is necessary to de-escalate tensions. Useful insights can be gleaned from studies advocating de-escalation in the US–Russian conflict: Etzioni's *The Hard Way to Peace* and Osgood's *An Alternative to War or Surrender*. The central principle in this approach involves a series of unilateral actions that induce – or at least provide – an opportunity for the adversary to reciprocate. Above all, it needs an attitude shift with respect to the realistic possibilities of change. Whites and blacks have no option but to find a way of living with one another that meets the crucial need for identity, dignity and security of all. The alternative is Afrikaner and African nationalism becoming locked into a struggle to the bitter end over national identity and sovereignty.

7.

Apartheid 'grand corruption'? The ABSA lifeboat and the demand for repayment

Between 1985 and 1995 the Reserve Bank provided bail-outs to the heavily indebted bank Bankorp, which was first owned by Sanlam and subsequently by ABSA, which acquired it in 1992. After an initial outcry and a debate in Parliament in which this essay was also cited, it was decided that the beneficiaries were Sanlam policy-holders and recovery of the money was not possible. The issue suddenly resurfaced in 2017 when a report by the new public protector, Busisiwe Mkhwebane, who investigated the issue, was leaked. She recommended that ABSA repay an amount of R2,25 billion plus interest. The South African Communist Party called for extending the investigation to cover 'the entire apartheid era's state looting'.[1]

My essay was first posted on the blog Politicsweb on 18 November 2013 when the issue was still a topic of heated public debate. The blog's editor, James Myburgh, introduced the essay with the words 'Hermann Giliomee takes on the claim that the rescue of the bank was a case of "apartheid grand corruption"'. The essay appears unchanged here.

During the late 1980s and early 1990s the Reserve Bank rescued Sanlam-controlled Bankorp, the fourth largest bank in the country. The gravity of the bank's troubles, occurring at a point where the political system faced its greatest political crisis, was not the only reason for the intense speculation at the time and since about the issue. Adding flavour was the fact that Afrikaner nationalists headed up the three institutions involved, namely the South African government, the Reserve Bank and Sanlam. It would almost become a show trial of the NP-controlled state and its financial probity.

Because of the secrecy that invariably accompanies central banks' bail-outs, the Bankorp rescue has never been properly examined in the literature. Yet there has been no shortage of rumours and indictments. In 2002 a financial commentator called it 'the biggest fraud ever perpetrated on the South African taxpayer'.[2] Ten years later Hennie van Vuuren put the 'lifeboat scandal' at the centre of 'apartheid grand corruption', 'implicating the South African Reserve Bank in malfeasance'. According to him, the Reserve Bank gave loans to commercial banks 'that were essentially converted into gifts or lifeboats'.[3] My analysis strongly disagrees with these interpretations.

The Bankorp crisis occurred within the context of a major political and financial crisis. South African financial institutions and parastatal corporations, particularly Eskom, had run up major financial obligations abroad. In the first half of the 1980s short-term loans surged ahead from 18 per cent of all loans to 39 per cent. Patti Waldmeir, correspondent of the *Financial Times*, described the view of foreign banks: 'South Africa was unstable and small; small, unstable countries (unlike large ones) do not borrow money.'[4]

The crisis was greatly exacerbated by President P.W. Botha's Rubicon speech in August 1985, which put a damper on the expectations of major political reforms. As a result, foreign banks refused to roll over loans to South Africa, forcing the government to declare a unilateral moratorium on the repayment of foreign debt. Both Barclays Bank and Standard Bank disinvested.

The Bankorp crisis, seen within the context of the debt standstill, represented a financial crisis of a very grave kind. The loss of billions of rands of deposits would have had a major domino effect on the other banks and on business in general. It would have plunged the country into a severe systemic financial crisis at the very point when the political crisis had reached its climax.[5]

During the twentieth century bank rescues took place in many other countries, but because of the stability of the South African financial system over a long period people were poorly prepared for the local banking crises that erupted during the 1970s and 1980s. Because almost everything in South Africa is politics, many people mistakenly assumed that the Bankorp rescue was somehow driven by Afrikaner nationalist interests and not by financial considerations. At the most bizarre level it was even suggested that the Broederbond membership of some Reserve Bank senior managers made them look more kindly on a bank within the Sanlam group, which also had several Broederbond members among its senior managers.

The Bankorp lifeboat was only one of several banking crises that occurred between 1976 and 1990. Others included the rescue of African Bank in the 1970s and of Nedbank in the early 1980s. Instead of investigating all the cases of banks that had received Reserve Bank assistance, the ANC government singled out the Bankorp case for an investigation. Trevor Manuel, minister of finance, repeatedly stated that the Bankorp rescue was funded by taxpayers' money, which Sanlam had to pay back. He and others like him persevered despite the fact that in the budget documents there was never any suggestion of taxpayers' money being used.

To recap the Bankorp story briefly. The Bankorp group was established between 1975 and 1984 after Sanlam had acquired control of Trust Bank and several other banks. In an aggressive attempt to build up a large bank as quickly as possible, many of the loans that were granted were of a poor quality. The Bankorp group soon ran into major problems. By 1985 Bankorp's troubles were serious enough for the bank's management to approach the Reserve Bank for assistance. In response, the latter provided a low-interest loan of R300 million that had to be repaid in 1990.

In March 1989 Fred du Plessis, CEO of both Sanlam and Bankorp, died in a car crash. In August 1989 Dr Chris Stals succeeded Dr Gerhard de Kock as governor of the Reserve Bank. Shortly afterwards Derek Keys became chairman of Bankorp.

Bankorp's troubles were still far from solved, as it was unable to repay its loan to the Reserve Bank and to meet the prescribed capitalisation requirements for a bank. Bankorp now announced a rights issue of R350 million, underwritten by Sanlam. The issue, which took place in November 1989, was not very successful. It required Sanlam to invest R230 million, including the rights not taken up.

In June 1990 Bankorp notified the Reserve Bank that it was unable to repay its 1985 loan. The Reserve Bank first requested the external auditors to investigate the financial position of Bankorp and then decided to become 'the lender of last resort' by providing Bankorp with a repayable loan to the amount of R1 billion at one per cent interest per annum. Bankorp then lent out the money at substantially higher rates than then prevailed. The surplus which Bankorp made as a result enabled it to write off its substantial bad debts.

The purpose was to stabilise the Bankorp group and to avoid the severe systemic risk that would occur should the Bankorp group fail to meet its obligations to its depositors. The Reserve Bank secured the capital sum by demanding that the loan be reinvested at the central bank. Sanlam repaid the loan to the Reserve Bank in 1995.

As part of the rescue package the Reserve Bank set stiff conditions. Sanlam had to arrange a second rights issue for Bankorp. The issue, which took place in November 1990, amounted to R526 million. Sanlam as underwriter was compelled to take up 80 per cent of the issue and in the process had to invest a further R420 million in Bankorp.

In June 1991 it became clear that further assistance was required to write off more bad debts. The Reserve Bank agreed to increase its assistance but demanded that Sanlam provide a ten-year low-interest loan of R500 million to Bankorp. In effect, this meant a further Sanlam 'investment' in Bankorp of R510 million. Thus, in the period between November 1989 and September 1991 Sanlam put in money and incurred obligations that ultimately would cost it more than R1 billion. This assistance, together with the Reserve Bank's help, avoided a major financial and banking crisis that would have seriously jeopardised the establishment of an inclusive democracy.

In 1992 ABSA acquired Bankorp and bought out the minority shareholders. No criticism has been expressed about this deal with ABSA.

With the details of the negotiations kept a tight secret, there was intense speculation in banking circles about the contribution the Reserve Bank required of Sanlam as part of the rescue package. Some bankers outside the circle of the Afrikaner *volksbeweging* simply could not believe that Reserve Bank officials would not extend preferential treatment to Sanlam. Those inside the circle could not understand how one could doubt the personal and business integrity of those who negotiated the rescue. The following exchange in an interview I conducted with Dr Anton Rupert reflects this:

> HG: A top manager of a major bank told me that the Reserve Bank was perhaps extra kind to Sanlam as an Afrikaner institution by asking it to make an interest-free loan of R300 million available. The bank could have told Sanlam to make the amount of R500 million available. What can one say to that?

> AR: One can say that Sanlam could declare that R300 million is as far as
> it is prepared to go. If that is not acceptable, Sanlam would let the bank
> collapse. What would the top manager of your so-called major bank
> say then?[6]

As I have indicated, the actual amount Sanlam contributed far exceeded the
amounts referred to in my interview with Dr Rupert.

The ANC-led government was not prepared to let the matter die. It first
instituted an inquiry into the entire Bankorp history led by Justice Willem Heath.
This produced no evidence of any malfeasance.

In 2000 the ANC government appointed a panel, chaired by Judge Dennis
Davis, to investigate the Bankorp bail-out and the transaction with ABSA. The
Davis panel found that ABSA paid fair value for Bankorp. It expressed no criticism of this transaction. The government did not ask the panel to investigate
the assistance to other banks. Nedbank, for instance, precipitated the country's
financial crisis in 1985 by recklessly failing to take cover in foreign transactions.
Hence the question arises why the new government focused only on the Bankorp rescue effort.

The answer is that the ANC after 1994 did not stop its propaganda campaign
against the NP-controlled state. In the financial press there was speculation that
Broederbond members in the Reserve Bank and the Sanlam group had sought
to resolve the crisis in a way that benefited Afrikaner business. These allegations
fed on the stereotype that had been built up in some circles of the Afrikaner
Broederbond as a secret cabal at the heart of the previous government, one
that was prepared to do anything to promote the welfare of its cause.

The Davis panel criticised some 'individual undesirable features' of the assistance given to Bankorp and other banks, but also found that the intervention in
the case of Bankorp was 'justified'. It stated that 'there is absolutely no evidence
to suggest that the [Reserve] Bank concluded any of the relevant contracts with
an element of turpitude. The available evidence indicates that the Bank genuinely and honestly believed that it was so empowered to act.'[7]

On the issue of Afrikaner favouritism the Davis panel formulated the matter
as follows: 'Some commentators have implied that, instead of merely aiming
to protect the financial system, the SA Reserve Bank conferred benefits on the

shareholders of Bankorp and ABSA for unspecified reasons . . . One version of the hypothesis in the public domain is that the close personal ties were linked to other forms of association within the Afrikaner elite such as the Broeder-bond.'[8] The panel stated that it was not required to investigate this particular issue and had found no evidence to enable it to reach such a conclusion about the alleged role of the Broederbond.

In discussing with me the case of Bankorp, Reserve Bank officials are adamant that there was nothing improper about the rescue package. They point out that the bank's interventions with other banks in trouble followed a similar pattern. The governor of the Reserve Bank had acted within his rights.

Viewing the entire saga dispassionately, one might say Sanlam could have followed a totally different route when it discovered in the mid-1980s that Bankorp was in grave trouble. It could have put the bank in liquidation and walked away from what was at that point one of the country's four big banks. None of the Reserve Bank's critics seems to favour this route.

8.

An exceptional editor

The challenge of ethnic survival confronts virtually all small nations that live close to more powerful nations. For much of the twentieth century the Afrikaners had to find a way of co-existing with the wealthier, better-educated white English community and the far more numerous African community. Piet Cillié, editor of *Die Burger* from 1954 to 1978 and chairman of the Nasionale Pers board from 1977 to 1992, frequently referred to the vulnerability of the Afrikaners, which drove them to such extreme measures to ensure their survival that they had become, in his words, the 'polecat of the world'.

Cillié was without doubt the most influential editor in the South African press during the second half of the twentieth century. In 1965 *The Times* of London included *Die Burger* in a series of articles on the most outstanding newspapers of the world. Peregrine Worsthorne, editor of the London *Sunday Telegraph*, who had visited South Africa five years earlier, wrote in his memoirs that no journalist of any nationality impressed him as much as Cillié. He was especially struck by Cillié's argument that what was happening in South Africa should not be judged in moral terms but as a true tragedy – 'an irreconcilable struggle not between right and wrong, but between right and right'.[1]

One of the main themes of Cillié's writings is indeed his attempt to reconcile the quest for survival of the Afrikaners, which can be described as a quintessential 'small nation', with an attempt to find an ethically just solution for South Africa's political problems. To do this he appealed to Afrikaners to be true to their historical heritage as the first people who became involved in an anti-colonial struggle in the twentieth century.

The second half of Cillié's term as editor (1966–78), which almost exactly coincided with John Vorster's term of office as prime minister, was marked by major advances in the provision of secondary education for children in the disenfranchised communities, a concerted effort to narrow the racial wage gap, the introduction of trade union rights for all, and the relaxation of the colour bar in sport and diplomacy. There was, however, very little progress in grasping the nettle of political rights for Africans and Coloured people. During the early 1980s P.W. Botha once formulated the core belief of the National Party (NP) leadership as follows: 'All my predecessors believed the Coloured people first had to be uplifted and that the consequences of this had to be accepted.'[2] Virtually no NP leader at the time advocated the incorporation of African people as full citizens in a common country.

In 1960 Cillié supported the idea of parliamentary representation of Coloured people by Coloured people but he allowed himself to be won over by Vorster's personal overtures to accept the exclusion of Coloured people from any form of representation in 'white' structures and to deny South African nationality to those Africans whose leaders had accepted 'independence' from South Africa. Cillié returned to the intra-white politics of the 1950s by accusing the opposition parties of '*Boerehaat*' (fomenting hatred of the Afrikaners) in order to bring about the National Party's defeat. He failed to come to terms with the fact that as a result of strong population growth among Africans, the Afrikaners had to adapt their survival strategies radically.

Small nations

Uriel Abulof's *The Mortality and Morality of Nations* is a recent comparative study of the historical struggle for survival of Afrikaner nationalists, French Canadians and Jewish Israelis. All three are small nations harbouring existential fears about their survival. The book's epigraph is a passage from *Testaments Betrayed* by Milan Kundera, who was born a Czech. During the nineteenth century the Czech nation's demands for liberation from the empire of Austria-Hungary were constantly frustrated by the more powerful Austrian Germans and Magyars. Kundera, as translated by Abulof, wrote:

> Small nations. The concept is not quantitative; it points to a condition, a fate; small nations lack that felicitous sense of an eternal past and future; at a

given moment in their history they all passed through the antechambers of death . . . they see their existence as perpetually threatened or with a question mark hovering over it; for their very existence *is* the question.[3]

The Dutch refreshment station at the Cape of Good Hope, founded in 1652, was never meant to be the cradle of a new European nation but rather to serve the material interests of the largest trading company in the world. Beyond the first mountain ranges the Afrikaner trekboers were interested mainly in subsistence farming on an extensive scale. In the pre-industrial period the Afrikaners above all craved land.

Unlike the Brazilians who encouraged large-scale immigration from Europe in the nineteenth century to ensure the European character of the nation, the Afrikaner trekboers rejected the idea of assisted immigration in favour of having enough land for themselves and their sons. By 1900 the Afrikaner population of 532 500 had spread out over most of the Cape Colony and the Boer republics in the Free State and the Transvaal.

The Afrikaners passed through 'the antechambers of death' both in the Great Trek into the interior (1834–44) and in the South African War (1899–1902), which was fought over the Transvaal gold mines against the might of the British Empire. A tenth of republican Afrikaners died as a result of the war and more than two-thirds of the stock on farms in the Boer republics was destroyed. In the eastern part of the Cape Colony many Afrikaner farmers suffered from the raids of British troops. If the British forces had managed to smash the Boer republics within a short period of time, English would almost certainly have become the sole national language of a new South African state.

It was the *bittereinder* struggle of the last two years of the war that changed the fate of the Afrikaner community. In May 1902, 60 officers representing about 17 000 men – the *bittereinders* – who were still in the field met at Vereeniging to discuss whether to surrender unconditionally or to continue the battle against the overwhelming British military force. On this occasion General Jan Smuts, who was to become one of the most famous Afrikaners in the world, clinched the argument by declaring that political independence was not the highest value in the struggle for survival. Smuts continued: '[We] must not sacrifice the *Afrikaansche volk* on the altar of independence.' Once the chance of maintaining independence had gone, it was the duty of the *bittereinders* to stop. Smuts warned: 'We must not run the risk of sacrificing our nation and its future to a mere idea which can no longer be realised.'[4] For Smuts the obvious approach was for the Afrikaners to forge a coalition with like-minded English people to build a white supremacist state and strong economy.[5]

But if independence was lost, on what other issue could the Afrikaners unite to remain a people? Only one of the delegates of the *bittereinders* at the Vereeniging assembly of May 1902 proposed the Dutch language as the basis for future survival. He was Jozua François Naudé, a 29-year-old Transvaal teacher, later a co-founder of the Afrikaner Broederbond. Naudé reminded delegates that one of the conditions set by the *bittereinders* in the field was to have the right of the Dutch language guaranteed. Dutch 'was of great significance to the *volk*, forming a channel through which the *volk* could again become *volk*'. He refused to sign the peace treaty.

These two interventions, by Smuts and Naudé, presaged the different responses of Afrikaners to the challenge of maintaining themselves as a people in the twentieth century. On the one hand there was Smuts, who sought allies to build a new South Africa and yet retain a private Afrikaner identity. On the other hand there was Naudé, who argued that without a language as the symbol of their national identity the Afrikaners would not survive as a people.

In numerical terms the Afrikaners remained a small nation. In 1936 their numbers stood at 1 121,200 and they formed 55,6 per cent of the white population. Africans totalled 6,5 million, Coloured people 769 000 and Indians 220 000. By 1996 there were 3 037 000 Afrikaners. They made up just under 60 per cent of the white population but their numbers were only a tenth of the black population.[6]

From the early days of the Union this issue of the survival of the Afrikaners and of Afrikaans as a public language was debated more in Afrikaans newspapers than in Parliament. In 1948 A.I. Malan, a Nationalist MP and father of Magnus Malan, who would become head of the Defence Force and minister of defence, acutely articulated the survival fears of the Afrikaners as a small nation. '[The Afrikaner] belongs to a small nation . . . If he should vanish from the stage, who remains to perpetuate his way of life, his culture? . . . Can it thus be wondered at that, for the Afrikaner, the matter of survival has become an irresistible life force, a veritable obsession.'[7]

A journalist in the making

Born in 1917, Piet Cillié grew up in Stellenbosch, the son of G.G. Cillié, who was professor of education and for six years rector of Stellenbosch University. His father was also a well-known and influential figure in the Cape National Party and Nasionale Pers, which both had their offices in Keerom Street in Cape Town.

In 1933, J.B.M. Hertzog of the National Party and J.C. Smuts of the South African Party merged their organisations into the United Party (UP) under Hertzog's leadership. Dr D.F. Malan, the first editor of *Die Burger*, broke away to form the Gesuiwerde (Purified) National Party in opposition to the UP. From the start the Cape NP and *Die Burger* would fight the political struggle as comrades in arms. Until 1954, when power in the NP migrated to the north, a journalist from *Die Burger* regularly attended the NP's parliamentary caucus.

Cillié studied at the University of Stellenbosch from 1933 to 1935. He received a BSc degree with distinction. He was attracted to journalism and the Afrikaans popular movement from the start. Initially he was more sympathetic to Hertzog than to Malan, whom he considered dour and uninspiring. A crucial event that changed his entire political outlook was Parliament's decision with a majority of thirteen to declare war on the side of Britain in 1939.

The governor-general refused Hertzog's request that a general election be called despite the fact that there was a real chance that a party favouring neutrality would win. Leading Afrikaans intellectuals such as the poet N.P. van Wyk Louw called the decision to go to war a 'great defeat' and vowed to devote themselves to an uncompromising spiritual commitment to the Afrikaner *volk*.

Much later Cillié explained why the vote to enter the war alienated him and others so profoundly. South Africa was the only predominantly non-British state that right from the start voluntarily entered the war. Locally the parliamentary majority acted as if South Africa were still a British colony. The vote had made clear to the Afrikaner nationalists that the fight for independent statehood had not yet been won.[8]

The Smuts government implemented highly controversial war measures. Many Afrikaners were interned despite the fact that South Africa's own security was not at stake. 'Security requirements' also led to the dismissal of or denial of promotion to a large number of Afrikaner civil servants suspected of anti-war sympathies, often on the basis of unsubstantiated allegations.

So widespread were complaints from Afrikaners on the railways about being wronged that the NP government after 1948 had to appoint a Grievances Commission to investigate the claims of some 2 875 railway employees who had laid formal complaints. They testified that, although innocent of anti-war activities, they had been denied promotion for posts ranging from clerk to general manager.[9] This was the background to the words of Dr Malan, NP leader, after his party's victory in the 1948 election: 'Today South Africa belongs to us once more.'[10]

The essence of the crisis

Piet Cillié became foreign editor of *Die Burger* in 1944, assistant editor in 1945 and editor in 1954, in which position he would remain until 1977. He was the first professor of journalism at Stellenbosch University. He served as chairman of Nasionale Pers from 1977 to 1992 and died in 1999.

Three major issues occupied Cillié in his work as thought leader:

> To spell out the extent to which the Afrikaner–English conflict in the electorate greatly complicated efforts to find a solution for the larger and much more intractable racial conflict.
>
> To move beyond mere Afrikaner survival as an end in itself and to seek a just form of survival.
>
> To promote Afrikaans as a public language by attracting all speakers of the language, regardless of colour, while still retaining the NP's coherence as a predominantly white party.

In the hurly-burly of party politics some of the NP's opponents claimed that South Africa did not actually have a political problem, but only a racial problem, stemming from what was called the Afrikaners' 'frontier mentality' and an 'archaic, Calvinist-inspired' racism. A perspective that transcended the narrow ethnic squabble between the two white communities was urgently required.

In the early 1950s Piet Meyer, who would later become the chairman of the board of the South African Broadcasting Corporation, conducted an interesting exercise of asking some of the great minds in the West how they viewed South Africa as a 'problem'. Martin Heidegger, one of the most important twentieth-century philosophers, replied that the problem was not really a racial question. It was in fact an intractable political question that had to be approached in a much more thoughtful way.[11]

The great liberal historian, C.W. de Kiewiet, said something similar. He had grown up in South Africa, but spent virtually his entire academic career in the US. He visited South Africa in the mid-1950s and then again in the mid-1960s. He recorded his impressions first in a book, entitled *The Anatomy of South African Misery* (1956), and then in an article in *Foreign Affairs*, one of most prestigious journals in the US. 'Apartheid', he wrote in the mid-1950s, 'is no subject for mockery or facile comment.' The liberal, De Kiewiet wrote, 'seeks in vain for an acceptable alternative between economic chaos and human despair'.[12] He was not impressed by the proposals of Afrikaner academics who advocated the dynamic political and economic development of the homelands. Yet he added: 'Apartheid has within it the basis for re-education and a new recognition of the realities of South African life.'[13]

An important issue that De Kiewiet did not discuss was the electoral system. Scholars concur that the voting systems used on the continent of Europe tend to promote reconciliation and coalition-building much better than the first-past-the-post electoral system used in Britain and the United States. In 1910 the new state of South Africa took over the latter system without much debate.[14]

The Westminster system encourages politicians representing a large ethnic community or a powerful corporate group in the electorate to join together by excluding any marginal community that holds the balance of power. In the Southern states of the US most black voters were excluded from the vote between the 1890s and mid-1960s. It took Lyndon Johnson, a Southern Democrat, to persuade Congress to give blacks the vote.

In South Africa the Westminster system favoured the Afrikaners, who formed between 57 and 59 per cent of the white community between 1946 and 1996. But this demographic advantage did not mean that it was assured of victory at the polls. Between 1939 and 1966 very few white English-speakers supported the NP and a significant proportion of Afrikaners first voted for the South African Party and later for the United Party.

The NP victory in 1948 came as a profound shock to white English-speakers in the country. While there was very little difference between Afrikaners and

English-speakers in their support for a system of white domination, English-speakers resented being suddenly shut out from power after the NP victory in 1948. Patrick Duncan, the son of a governor-general, wrote:

> English South Africans are today in the power of their adversaries. They are the only English group of any size in the world today that is, and will remain for some time, a ruled, subordinated minority. They are beginning to know what the great majority of all South Africans have always known – what it is to be second-class citizens in the land of one's birth.[15]

For Duncan the blow that relegated the English-speakers to a position of seemingly permanent opposition seemed almost as harsh as the NP's much more rigid exclusion of Africans from the privileges of citizenship. Coloured voters had the potential of holding the balance of power between the two main parties in several Cape Province seats. In Cape Town they formed almost a block vote against the NP. In the rural areas of the western Cape the situation was more fluid.

The NP won the 1948 election with only five seats, but it attracted 100 000 fewer votes than the UP. Approximately 40 000 Coloured voters went to the polls. In the elections for the provincial councils in 1949 the NP's victories in the seats of Paarl and Bredasdorp in the previous year were reversed. According to Cillié, it was never proved that this reversal was the result of 'extra' Coloured voters being registered in order to clinch a UP victory, but for the NP leadership it became an issue of great importance to eliminate the Coloured franchise as a swing vote that could help the UP to regain power.[16]

In 1952 *Forum*, a liberal journal, asked Cillié to predict the NP's strategy and tactics in the 1953 general election, which the NP was fighting on the plank of removing Coloured voters from the voters' roll and putting them on a separate roll to elect a limited number of white representatives. Cillié wrote that 'English political liberalism has always seemed to the Nationalists to be more English than liberal and more concerned with power for the English-speaking section than the vote for non-Europeans'. Cillié predicted that the NP would contest the election as a battle for its own survival.[17]

Cillié, who became editor of *Die Burger* in 1954, dismissed racist or religious justifications for the Afrikaners' claim to govern themselves in what they saw as their land, or their part of the land, as it was later reformulated. At the same time he challenged those who questioned the importance of the national issue in societies where different ethnic or racial communities coexisted.

In 1952 Cillié wrote to Ben Marais, a Dutch Reformed Church minister, whose comprehensive *Die Kleur krisis en die Weste* (The Colour crisis and the West) had just been published: 'I agree wholeheartedly with you that any attempts to find a Scriptural justification for apartheid . . . is doomed to fail . . . I know only one old gentleman who believes that the Coloured people as children of Ham are cursed eternally. No coherent pseudo-scientific myths about race are being intentionally propagated in South Africa.'

But Cillié also rejected any attempt to treat ethnic, national or racial differences as mere myths that could be easily refuted with rational explanations. He expressed doubt whether statistics quoted by Marais, to prove that races and ethnic groups differed very little inherently, would have any practical value in addressing South Africa's problems. How, Cillié asked, did it help the Jews and Arabs in Palestine to know that people were more similar than different?

Colour in South Africa was for Cillié important only because it constituted in his mind the border between 'peoples' or 'nations'. Politics was essentially a matter of 'national instincts'. He criticised Marais because he did not investigate the issue of political power which lay at the base of race relations. Apartheid had to enable Afrikaners and the broader white community to maintain power over themselves.[18] The heart of the matter was the national issue. The very future of the Afrikaner people depended on whether the national question could be resolved in a way that ensured the survival of the Afrikaner people and the Afrikaans language.

In South Africa it was not only Cillié who made this point. L.E. Neame, a liberal editor of the *Cape Argus* and author of a book about apartheid, rejected the view that apartheid was based purely on the assertion that the white race was superior. For him colour prejudice was not at the heart of the matter. The problem was 'national rather than pigmental. Differentiation is not enforced as a brand of inferiority but as a bulwark against the infiltration of people of another civilisation. The motive is not detraction but defence.'[19]

Comparative perspectives

Cillié entered the senior editorial ranks of his paper when the Afrikaner government was seemingly standing alone at a time when the Western colonial powers were falling over their feet to retreat from their colonies. Inside South Africa the Afrikaners had precious few allies. In 1950 Cillié wrote: 'There is a feeling of catastrophe in the air. We are governing the country in the face of resistance by all sections, except the Afrikaners. How long can this continue?'[20]

Apartheid developed out of segregation but added a new dimension that initially stressed ethnic churches and, later, ethnic homelands and governments. The word was first used in print in 1929 in a Dutch Reformed Church publication and remained confined to the church's missionary circles until the early 1940s. As policy, it was a strange combination of extreme racial exclusion and discrimination, on the one hand, and an idealistic commitment to uplift and promote the development of the Coloured and African communities, on the other.

Cillié and other proponents of apartheid sincerely believed that enabling African and Coloured communities to take over their 'own affairs' represented an approach that was superior to the policy of segregation. According to NP thinkers, the latter amounted to little more than *afhok*, by which was meant ghettoising people in their own townships and reserves without any effort to improve their education and social development.

Like almost all other white thought leaders, Cillié remained blissfully unaware of the cruelty and hardship that implementing the policy inflicted on those who were on its receiving end. He continued to see the racial issue as subordinate to the national conflict between whites and blacks fighting for control over the same land. He felt that without a settlement of the national issue no real progress on developmental issues could be made.

A conference that Cillié attended in Pakistan in 1954 strengthened his view that the conflict in South Africa was of a national rather than a racial kind. Shortly before Indian independence deadly clashes had broken out between Hindus and Muslims, and as a result Pakistan became independent. In his speech to the conference Cillié referred to the work of Philip Mason, a researcher of the Royal Institute of International Affairs, who had studied several multiracial countries including Southern Rhodesia. Mason argued that South African whites should consider becoming a 'creative minority' who in their own interests should integrate the black majority with a view to ceding power to them over the short to medium term.

Cillié wrote to a colleague at Nasionale Pers that he listened to these words with great dismay but also found some of the other speeches very instructive. In his own speech to the conference he said that Pakistanis were confronted with the same demand as whites in South Africa to become integrated with the majority but found an alternative by seceding and drawing their own national borders. Pakistan and India became separate countries and as such could coexist.[21]

Cillié's analogy between South Africa and the Indian subcontinent was not quite sound. The Pakistanis had a genuine claim to the part of India where they lived at the time that India received independence. Until the 1960s it was commonly believed that South Africa was an empty land at the time of the arrival of white settlers in the mid-seventeenth century with the exception of limited numbers of Khoikhoi and San, who lived dispersed across the subcontinent. The prevailing interpretation was that African groups migrating from the north crossed the Limpopo only by the seventeenth century, almost at the same time that Jan van Riebeeck's party came ashore in Table Bay. This perspective evolved into a historical tradition that was later called 'the myth of the empty land'.

This myth was refuted in the academic literature during the 1960s. Archaeologists and historians established that black people had moved across the Limpopo many centuries before the whites arrived and then spread over the northern and eastern part of South Africa. The problem of the Afrikaners as a small nation was not so much their small numbers but their dispersal over a great area between the mid-seventeenth and the end of the nineteenth century.

In suggesting at the 1954 conference that South African whites become a 'creative minority' under a black government, Philip Mason drew on his experiences in Southern Rhodesia, which he had visited during the early 1950s. Another British scholar who also worked in Southern Rhodesia between the mid-1950s and 1960s remarked on the racial problem in southern Africa in strikingly different terms. He was Lewis Gann, whose article 'The Liberal Interpretation of South African History' appeared in 1959. It is not known whether Cillié ever read it, but if he did, he probably would have warmly endorsed Gann's views.

Gann was born in a Jewish family in Germany who escaped to Britain in 1938. He studied at Oxford and spent the period from 1954 to 1963 as an archivist in what was then Salisbury, Southern Rhodesia. Here the prospects for a stable, multiracial democracy were a live issue, with a constitution being drawn up for the federation of Southern Rhodesia, Northern Rhodesia and Malawi.

Gann argued that liberals in South Africa incorrectly took nineteenth-century Britain as their model with its belief in the invisible hand making for the greatest good of the greatest number. In this view the fact that the unskilled workers mostly belong to a different ethnic group is irrelevant and the different parties all seek to pursue their political ambitions without wishing to overthrow the political order. Furthermore, political and social emancipation was thought compatible with the maintenance of something like the existing class structure in South Africa. But, as Gann pointed out, the analogy was all wrong. Britain was a wealthy country and a well-established, homogeneous society without important ethnic, racial or religious divisions. Protest movements were not reinforced by national or cultural demands.

Gann concluded that the history of Britain was of no relevance to South Africa. In his view liberals in South Africa should rather interest themselves in the history of states with national minority problems, where class divisions coincide with ethnic divisions, as was the case in many states in Eastern Europe and the Middle East. Here national minorities can expect rough treatment when they become subject to a nationally distinct majority. This would be especially true if the minorities appear to be possessed of more than their fair share of economic wealth. They might even be liable to expulsion or outright dispossession.[22]

The chaos surrounding the withdrawal of the Belgians from the Congo in 1960 seemed to confirm all the fears of privileged minorities in Africa and Asia. In his work on the first 50 years of black independence in Africa, Martin Meredith succinctly describes the unravelling of order in the Belgian Congo. Two weeks after Independence Day on 30 June 1960 'internal security had collapsed; the army had degenerated into a rabble and the exodus of whites had left the administration bereft. Leopoldville was in turmoil and the secession of Katanga threatened to break the country apart.'[23]

On 9 July 1960 Cillié wrote in the 'Dawie' column:

We must not mislead ourselves about this catastrophe. For the first time since the 'winds of change' started blowing, a white minority is fleeing from black terror head over heels. It sends shivers through Kenya and the Federation and it ought to have done the same throughout the Western world had it not become intoxicated with negrophilism. It does something more; the powers that wish the white man to be expelled from Africa are celebrating. The Congo is to them a signal in the sky. For them even craven abdication is not enough; the settled whites must be expelled.[24]

On 11 July 1960 *Die Burger* asked this question in an editorial: 'Can one expect that blacks in countries like Rhodesia and Zambia would be prepared to take whites as partners in a system of joint government?' It replied: 'We can find in all of Africa not a shred of evidence that black nationalists would be prepared to pull together in a single yoke with white *volksgroepe* [communities]. Nothing that has happened since the introduction of the policy of partnership in the Federation of Rhodesia and Nyasaland offers any evidence that the black man would accept partnership except perhaps as a transition phase in the march to black *baasskap*.'[25]

In the early 1990s another academic with links to central Europe expressed the same bafflement as Gann and Cillié about the inability of liberal and Marxist scholars to understand the nature of ethno-national conflicts in multinational states. He was the Hungarian political scientist George Schöpflin who, like Gann, later moved to the West, where he became a political science professor in London. In 1991 Schöpflin wrote that, with the collapse of communism, nationalism was very much an ideology with a future. He argued that both Marxist and liberal scholars have a poor understanding of nationalism because both firmly believe that an individual's class interests must transcend all other interests. For nationalists the key point is that nationhood constitutes a political category that derives from cultural rather than economic concerns. He defined culture as 'the sum total of the subjective perceptions in a community, the rules by which it orders its life, its sense of a common past and shared future, and its socially constructed picture of the world'.[26]

A radical survival plan

Although the urban African community over the longer term posed the greatest challenge to white rule, Cillié, like the NP leaders, devoted very little time to discussing it. Almost all their energy went into addressing the problem of developing the reserves into homelands for Africans and of accommodating the Coloured community, with a separate homeland for them being ruled out from the start.

In 1956 a commission headed by Professor F.R. Tomlinson proposed developing the reserves, now called 'Bantu homelands', by investing R7 819 billion (in 2011 terms) over ten years. Cillié warmly endorsed the commission's recommendations. He added: 'The time has come to decide what we are going to do about it. A policy that is not converted into acts is not much better than no policy.'[27] Cillié strongly supported the Tomlinson report and believed Hendrik Verwoerd, who was minister of native affairs, was the right person to drive its implementation. But Cillié misjudged the intentions of Verwoerd, who allocated only a paltry sum to the economic development of these territories and did not permit private investment.

Initially Western governments showed some interest in Tomlinson's recommendations as forming at least part of a solution, with the West German ambassador calling it a 'Marshall plan' for South Africa. The London *Sunday Times* wrote that the ruling Afrikaner minority seemed intent on finding an alternative to resisting a multiracial democracy to the death. If there had to be apartheid, the paper continued, the Transkei homeland represented a courageous step as a visible alternative.[28] *The Guardian* accepted the principle of separate viable white and black spheres of influence, leading ultimately to full partition.

But the idea of the homelands, as at least part of the solution, progressively faded. There were two main reasons. In the Cold War the Soviet Union sided with African states, which generally rejected the policy out of hand. This prompted the West after 1970 to make its rejection of apartheid policy clear. Secondly, the socio-economic development of the homelands was sluggish. Between 1960 and 1972 only 85 544 jobs were created in the homelands and border areas – well below the number the Tomlinson Commission had considered necessary. In 1974 Tomlinson remarked that the economic development of the reserves had to date been small-scale and fragmentary.[29] In 1981 he ruefully observed that his commission had been highly successful, but only as an ideological exercise. For fifteen years after the tabling of the report in 1956 hardly anything was done. Yet, Tomlinson added, 'There has not been a single parliamentary session since [1956] in which the report has not been referred to.'[30]

A stand for non-racial rights

In 1960 Cillié reconsidered *Die Burger*'s stand on parliamentary representation for Coloured people. From insisting on the exclusion of Coloured people in the competition between the two white communities, he shifted to proposing a system under which Coloured people would be allowed to elect their own representatives in Parliament. The reasons for this change of mind were complex.

The NP had now become firmly entrenched as the dominant political party and was unlikely to lose power soon. Secondly, international pressure had intensified. During his visit to South Africa Harold Macmillan, British prime minister, in addressing the South African Parliament, told whites unambigiously that they would forfeit the sympathy of the Western powers if they continued to deny political representation to all people who were not white.

In 1958 N.P. van Wyk Louw, the premier Afrikaner intellectual, returned to South Africa after a spell of eight years in the Netherlands. Later that year his book *Liberale nasionalisme* appeared which included some essays he had previously published in popular journals. Anthony Delius, a perceptive English journalist, immediately recognised that Louw's writing represented the very cogent beginning of an Afrikaner nationalist attempt to reform from within. Cillié wrote a positive review in which he called Louw an intellectual midwife 'much more adept and subtle than others who pretend to pose as thinkers about these issues'.[31]

Louw's most seminal idea was that the Afrikaners had to strive towards a form of *voortbestaan in geregtigheid*, which meant surviving in a way that would be considered just. In principle Louw had no problem with the homeland policy with respect to Africans, but saw no justification for pursuing such a policy in respect of the Coloured community. In a preface to David Botha's *Die opkoms van ons derde stand* (1960), he wrote: 'The Coloured people are our people, belong with us . . . It is my most passionate wish that my nation [*volk*] and the language that we speak survive in this land.'[32]

Within NP ranks, particularly those outside the western Cape, Cillié attracted strong criticism for proposing in 1960 that the government allow the Coloured community to elect their own parliamentary representatives, who could be either white or Coloured. Cillié seriously considered resigning, but after some reconsideration decided to stay on.

The declining credibility of the homeland policy as a solution for white–black relations prompted Cillié in 1964 to write an extended essay in the literary journal *Standpunte*. It can be regarded as his most outstanding contribution. In the article Cillié argued that Western imperialism, by which he meant the direct domination of one nation of another, had irreparably collapsed. Nations now had to govern themselves. The Afrikaners, he went on, ought to be the last people to oppose in principle the idea of national freedom. They were the descendants of a people who fought the first anti-colonial war of the twentieth century. By taking up arms, they demonstrated that colonialism was everything but a divine and lasting order.

Cillié wrote:

> We rejected others dominating us but we did not reject our domination of other peoples as equally objectionable . . . With little protest we endorsed sucking in masses of black labourers without any plan to grant them expanding political rights that would correspond with their expanding economic might . . . This is a colonialist frame of mind. It was condemned not only by the world but should also be condemned in terms of our best Afrikaner principles.[33]

The next battleground was in the Afrikaans churches. Matters came to a head at an ecumenical conference organised by the World Council of Churches which took place in December 1960 in Cottesloe, Johannesburg. The three affiliated Afrikaans churches, the Cape DRC, the Transvaal DRC and the Hervormde Kerk, had set up study groups consisting of senior church ministers and theological professors to formulate their position.

At the end of the Cottesloe conference the DRC delegations accepted the resolutions that drew largely on the memorandum of the Cape DRC, stating that everyone had the right 'to own land where he is domiciled and to participate in the government of his country'. They also stated that the banning of mixed marriages was not grounded in the Scriptures, that migrant labour had 'disintegrating effects' on family life, that job reservation had to be replaced by a more equitable system of labour, and that Coloured people had to be directly represented in Parliament.[34]

In a sympathetic review of Cottesloe, Cillié frankly admitted that the resolutions constituted an acute crisis of confidence for Afrikaner nationalists, who now had to resolve 'some of the deepest and gravest questions that touched on everyone's existence in South Africa'. But he emphasised that the Afrikaner church leaders involved could not be dismissed as liberals and that the DRC, through its massive involvement in missions, knew more about race relations in a practical sense than the NP did. For him two major tendencies were now battling for predominance in the minds of Afrikaner people – a noble aspiration to move away 'from self-preservation in a narrow sense and from living only for ourselves' and an evil urge 'to grow back into ourselves, back into our own bitterness and sourness, and back to the assumed safety of proven old emotions and attitudes'.[35] He asked: 'Must church leaders interpret the will of God in the way it is expected of an Afrikaner political party or do they have to attempt to interpret God's will as purely as possible?'[36]

Prime Minister Verwoerd wasted little time in urging the Afrikaans churches to distance themselves from the church leaders and the Cottesloe resolutions. His New Year's Message for 1961 referred only obliquely to announcements by 'individual churchmen', but in his speech there was a pointed remark that the churches themselves, in fact, had not yet spoken but were expected to do so at their respective synods of lay members and clergy.

In the months to come the Afrikaans churches, along with Afrikaner Broederbond, came out in support of Verwoerd. The episode made Cillié very sceptical about whether sustained support from the Afrikaans churches would be forthcoming were he to use moral arguments to criticise apartheid.

Vorster's 'co-worker'

Unlike his relationship with Verwoerd, which was distant, formal and sometimes frigid, Cillié and John Vorster found each other almost immediately on a personal level and as allies. In 1976 Cillié wrote of his relationship with Vorster:

'More than before and also more often I felt like a fellow worker [of the NP leader].' Vorster cultivated Cillié and asked his assistance in helping to consolidate Afrikaner power. In 1976 Cillié wrote tellingly about Vorster: 'His priority is not victory for his dogma but to win people over – not people as an abstract mass, but YOU.'[37]

What tied Vorster and Cillié together was their common rejection of white conservatives, who opposed any reforms, and the increasing demands of Western powers and South African liberals for the political integration of white and black South Africans under a system of majority rule. But both understood that the shrinking white demographic base was constantly undermining Afrikaner power. In 1969 it became known that the population projections of the early 1950s on which Verwoerd had based his apartheid policy were wrong. Instead of 19 million people, the African population was now expected to reach 28 million. But even the revised projections were wrong. In reality, by 2000 there were 34 million black South Africans, with some 15 million living in the 'white' cities instead of the 2–3 million projected in 1951.[38]

Both Vorster and Cillié questioned the idea that the Afrikaners and the Afrikaans language could survive under a liberal constitution, given such numbers. They also both believed that it would be better to dispel any notion of the NP government moving towards power-sharing. A CIA assessment of 1977 correctly noted that Vorster 'throughout his career has shown a strong inclination towards actions which project power and tough-mindedness and has made no secret of his personal contempt for world opinion'. The report warned of the real possibility that the Vorster government might develop and ultimately test nuclear weapons as part of a conscious decision to defy the world. 'Threats would have the opposite effect on the Afrikaners to that intended.'[39]

It is quite possible that soon after becoming prime minister Vorster identified Cillié as someone who could be recruited as an ally. Influential editors and columnists tend to find it difficult to reject out of hand a call for help by political leaders who are confronting highly divisive political problems. A famous case is that of Walter Lippmann, one of the most eminent American commentators, who backed the US war in Vietnam after being dined and fed wrong information by President Lyndon Johnson. Lippmann later claimed that Johnson had misled him.[40]

Cillié was not 'used' by Vorster. It was rather a case of both recognising that they needed each other as allies. The Cape Town-based Nasionale Pers had entered the Transvaal newspaper market in the mid-1960s in the face of bitter opposition from the Afrikaner right. The protective hand of Vorster was a great asset. Vorster had studied at Stellenbosch and his wife's father was chairman of Nasionale Pers. Although his constituency was in the Transvaal he was more at home in the Cape NP than the Transvaal NP.

Vorster shunned those Afrikaners he knew he could not win over. Frederik Van Zyl Slabbert once told me that Vorster never returned his greetings even if he looked him straight in the eye as they passed each other in the lobby in Parliament. By contrast Vorster treated Helen Suzman courteously and responded promptly, either in Parliament or his office, to questions she asked about various issues, including the treatment of political prisoners on Robben Island. I once asked her for her blunt assessment of each of the NP leaders she had observed up close in Parliament. She responded: 'John Vorster had a mind. I liked listening to him.'

After becoming prime minister, Vorster's priority was to talk with African heads of states to ward off foreign pressure on South Africa and to persuade them to block the spread of Soviet influence in southern Africa. His assumption was, as the historian Jamie Miller phrases it, that self-interest would persuade these states to embrace mutually advantageous co-operation rather than assume a posture of futile confrontation with the South African regime. He offered several African states financial and economic assistance.

Miller shows how John Vorster tried to reinvent the Afrikaners as an African nation seeking peace, acceptance and coexistence with other nations in Africa. In talking to leaders of African states to the north of South Africa's border he redefined the Afrikaners as an African *volk* that was as rooted in the continent as any other nation. They were, moreover, a people who had fought the first anti-colonial war on the continent between 1899 and 1902.[41]

Soon after coming to power Vorster signalled that he planned to abolish the existing forms of representation of Coloured people in the House Assembly and the Cape Provincial Council. In their place would come a Coloured Persons Representative Council with extremely limited powers, consisting of nominated and elected members. Cillié told Vorster he had serious objections to the plan, which he thought was more drastic than his proposal in 1960 that the Coloured community elect their own representatives to Parliament. Vorster replied that despite objections he was determined to press ahead with his plan. Cillié responded that he considered the proposal a negative step but that he did not plan to throw *Die Burger* in front of a steamroller.[42]

Conservative NP circles in the Transvaal almost gleefully spread the rumour that Cillié had caved in to Vorster.[43] According to Piet Meyer, head of the South African Broadcasting Corporation, Vorster told Cillié shortly after coming to power that he was going to abolish the franchise of the Coloured people and that it was up to Cillié to decide whether to support him or not. Meyer alleges that as Cillié was leaving, he turned to Vorster and said: 'John, you bastard.'[44]

A partial citizenship

By the early 1970s any open-minded NP supporter had to face the fact that apartheid was no longer a credible solution. None of the homelands had become economically viable states. With the homelands clearly incapable of sustaining their populations, black people streamed to the white areas. In the black townships there was no proper system of local government. The main political function of the homelands had changed radically. The plan was no longer to build economically viable states, but to use independence granted to a homeland as sufficient justification for denying non-white people in the white areas the right to vote. No homeland attained meaningful independence.

No significant enterprises were established in the Coloured townships and not a single one was able to become financially self-sufficient. A Coloured Persons Representative Council was introduced but it was little more than a consultative body, which enjoyed very little popular support. Cillié made little or no comment about this.

But there was some real progress under both Vorster and his successor, P.W. Botha. Much less noticed than the failure to extend a common form of political citizenship to people of different racial communities was the steady extension of a common form of what can be called industrial citizenship. After 1970 there was a dramatic increase in the number of African, Coloured and Indian children in secondary and tertiary education. The government steadily reduced the share that white education received from the budget.[45]

After major strikes in 1973 against low wages, Vorster implored employers to consider their workers as 'human beings with souls' and to pay them proper wages. In the mid-1970s he started the process that would lead to the Wiehahn Commission, which would propose a non-racial system of industrial relations. In the course of the 1980s black unions would slip from the reins of control which the state still tried to maintain. Cillié backed Vorster in all these initiatives.

On 30 July 1971 a group of 29 academics in the north rejected the government's segregation of the Coloured community and asked that it grant members of this community full and equal citizenship. Shortly afterwards 109 Stellenbosch academics backed this call. In the western Cape the signatories of the petition all asked the question: What would Cillié do? In 1964 he wrote the essay 'Back to Our Belief in Freedom' in which he argued that the Afrikaners fighting the war in 1899–1902 were 'the pioneers of anti-colonialism' and went on to say that Afrikaners ought to be the last people to condone or practise colonialism.

In 1970, André du Toit, a lecturer at Stellenbosch, wrote an open letter to Cillié in the hope that he would publish it and open up a debate. Du Toit stated that among a younger generation of academics concern had mounted about a shift in Cillié's approach. The appeal in his 1964 article in *Standpunte* to be true to the Afrikaners' 'anti-colonialist tradition' had given way to 'a cynical preoccupation with party politics'. The political issues had become ever more urgent but no one knew where *Die Burger* took its stand.[46] Cillié did not publish the letter.

Unlike the aftermath of the 1948 election, the NP's control of the political system was no longer precarious. In the 1970 election it won 70 more seats and attracted 300 000 more votes than the UP. The two white communities had grown much closer together. More English-speakers were enrolled at Afrikaans universities than Afrikaners at English universities. Youths from both white communities were conscripted for military service. The British flag and national anthem, which for 50 years enjoyed equal status as symbols of South African nationhood, had long since been phased out.

Yet Cillié fought the political battles of the 1950s against the UP all over again. In a by-election in Oudtshoorn in 1974 he pulled out all the stops in claiming that the United Party was inspired by *Boerehaat*. The only plausible explanation for abandoning his 'loyal resistance' was the desire to buttress Vorster's position in the face of right-wing opposition.

Cillié also supported Vorster in 1975 when the latter stumbled into a war in Angola, hoping to drive out Russian and Cuban auxiliary forces and to establish South Africa as a major African player in the Cold War. Cillié supported this incursion almost without qualification and gloried in the victories of the South African Defence Force during the early stage of the war. It was in fact a major political blunder to fight an undeclared war without clear objectives and to try to keep it secret.

In a visit to Germany in 1977 Vorster met Henry Kissinger, who described the former later as an intelligent political leader. He told Kissinger that he expected his policy to evolve into a series of self-governing black states and one or two white homelands. Kissinger replied that such an outcome would be unacceptable to the US.[47]

During this visit Vorster also met the West German Chancellor Helmut Schmidt, who urged him to consider introducing majority rule despite the risks this might entail. Germany, Schmidt told Vorster, had survived two catastrophic world wars in the twentieth century, yet 30 years later West Germany was the richest country in Europe. 'You don't understand,' Vorster replied. 'For us Afrikaners there won't be a second chance if we lost power.'[48]

The arrival in 1975 of increasing numbers of Cuban soldiers and Soviet advisers in Angola and the Western refusal to provide any direct assistance to South Africa prompted Vorster to warn the US government that he would use extreme measures if pushed into a corner. In 1978 an all-South African team produced the first enriched uranium and in 1979 the first fully assembled nuclear device. A total of six nuclear devices, which could be delivered by aircraft or missile, were completed. This was considered to be the minimum for deterrent purposes. They were not stockpiled in assembled form but instead the nuclear and non-nuclear components were stored separately in concrete steel vaults.

From the outset, everyone involved in the programme knew that the government did not intend or foresee an offensive application of the bomb. Assembling nuclear bombs revealed a can-do mentality and the desire by the white community in South Africa to be taken seriously by the great powers. Chester Crocker, US assistant secretary of state for Africa during the 1980s, observed that while the Afrikaner elite behaved as if the country belonged to them, they displayed a strange mix of ethnic insecurity and arrogance. Loyalty and solidarity were the supreme virtues, and outsiders were distrusted. The government had largely cut itself off from the advice of outsiders, but craved Western acceptance.[49] (A Soviet Union insider described the ruling elite in his own country as guided by the same mix.[50])

'A painful reassessment'

In 1982 Cillié finally gave up hope that the Afrikaners could retain control over a homeland of their own. The occasion was a speech he gave at the launch of the book Swart verstedeliking (Black urbanisation), written by Flip Smit and Jan Booysen. It was the first Afrikaans work that spelled out the magnitude of black urbanisation and all its socio-political implications.

Cillié referred to the book's 'strong and ominous message for the Afrikaner'. The NP had procrastinated for too long in implementing a policy of separation between white and black. For Cillié the foundation of Afrikaner nationalism had always been the dream of a 'promised land: a piece of land which irrevocably is, or must be, his'. Economic forces, however, had shattered the dream of separate homelands in South Africa, and because the Afrikaners had refused to accept this, there was no strategy for black urbanisation. 'We are now being forced by the facts, the irrefutable facts . . . to undertake a painful reassessment so deep and far-reaching that we might pray for this cup to rather pass us by.'[51]

Cillié's last comprehensive essay was published in 1985 in the quarterly journal Die Suid-Afrikaan, which I coedited. I proposed that I would write an indictment of apartheid to which he could respond in as much space as he wanted.[52] The article of more than 5 000 words was vintage Cillié. It provided a unique perspective on the origins of apartheid in the 1940s. He also traced the origins and evolution of apartheid between the mid-1940s and the mid-1960s in terms of realpolitik.

Cillié rejected the view that it was the apartheid policy that secured victory for the NP in 1948. To him the immediate impetus was the decision of Parliament in 1939 to side with Britain in declaring war against Germany. During the war many Afrikaners felt they had been discriminated against for being anti-war. After the 1948 election the NP government feared that if it lost power, the anti-Afrikaner political forces would, by way of mobilising the vote of Coloured and African people against the Afrikaners, make sure that they never lost power again.

Cillié's analysis placed South Africa in the context of societies and regions characterised by severe ethnic conflicts such as Palestine, Cyprus, India and Pakistan, Northern Ireland, Nigeria, Ethiopia and Lebanon where the death toll tended to be much higher than in South Africa. This perspective was singularly lacking in much contemporary discussion of post-1948 South Africa. Apartheid was usually portrayed as uniquely wrong-headed or disastrous without much effort to place it in the context of ethnic conflicts elsewhere.

Cillié touched on another problem. It was the tendency to idealise pre-1948 race relations in South Africa. In his article for *Die Suid-Afrikaan* he wrote a parody of what can be called 'the rosy view of pre-1948 race relations':

> The pre-1948 period of relatively good and relaxed race relations were suddenly disrupted by a regime change in 1948, South Africa was dumped in four senseless decades of increased racial tension and racial hatred. An evil ethnic ideology was imposed on an unsuspecting land. A society on its way to developing friendly relations was divided, fragmented and uprooted by a sectional, authoritarian regime. The poisonous fruits are now being picked, in the form of venom, unrest and sanctions that threaten everyone's standard of living. The call now is: Break apartheid down, dig up its roots and begin building the New Jerusalem.[53]

Cillié reflected on the true nature of apartheid as the NP started to implement it after the 1948 election:

> A system? An ideology? A coherent blueprint? No, it was rather a pragmatic and meandering process aimed at consolidating the leadership of a nationalist movement. It was an attempt to secure the Afrikaner's self-determination not against a force of people of colour but to prevent the return of a United Party government. If the UP were to recapture power it would make certain that the NP would never get another chance. All that would remain was an uprising in an attempt to seize power by force.[54]

The question is: Why did the NP government not move towards a credible democratic alternative to apartheid well before the onslaught against it began to gather momentum in the mid-1970s? An important reason often over-looked is the existence of two sizeable white communities competing for power. It made a solution much more difficult to find. Under universal franchise a significant section of the English community would try to form a catch-all party with Coloured people, Indians and 'moderate blacks'. Such a coalition could well entrench itself in power and keep the Afrikaners out of power.

A federal solution was another possibility. The Afrikaners' main problem is not, as Solidarity's Flip Buys has pointed out, that they are too few in numbers, but that they live too dispersed across the country – a third in the Western Cape, a third in the present-day Gauteng province and a third spread out all over the rest of the country. Outside the Western Cape the Afrikaners would be isolated.

Conclusion

Apartheid made South Africa 'the polecat of the world', a phrase that Cillié coined in 1965 in an article commissioned by the *New York Times*. The world indeed found the policy appalling. Many commentators in the West thought that a solution was readily available, namely democracy. But few gave heed to the advice of Donald Horowitz, an American scholar who made an impressive contribution to understanding the problems surrounding the challenge of consolidating democracy in multi-ethnic societies. The problem is not democracy, he writes, 'but ascriptive majority rule with skin colour the determinative factor. It kills democracy by turning elections into "censuses" in which the election result reflects the population mix rather than any policy preferences. It entrenches the largest ethnic or racial group in power, locking minorities out.'[55]

9.

Leaders and the citizenry

This chapter focuses on how the National Party (NP) leadership treated members of the different racial groups as citizens and on its conception of the citizenry in general. Under citizenry I include all the permanent inhabitants of South Africa and I see citizenship as comprising three components: a political component concerned with the franchise, formal participation in the decision-making process, and the more informal process of influencing policy through party membership and the mass media; a civil component dealing with rights such as the security of the individual and of property, freedom of speech and of association, and equality before the law; and a social component, which involves the provision of education, health and other social services to enable citizens to derive the maximum benefits possible from the exercise of political and civil rights.[1]

This chapter will not discuss the dismal record of the apartheid state on each aspect of citizenship,[2] but will instead describe how the leadership mediated the different rights and claims of the various groups in the citizenry. To do so, it is necessary to look beyond the ideological pronouncements of the NP leadership or its black opponents.

Apartheid with its utopian ideal of separate nations, each with its own separate citizenship, fell far short of its ideological ambition to create a white state. Despite the divisions in the country there remained a common political and economic order which made it impossible to treat black people as non-citizens in all the different components of citizenship. For example, for all the apartheid state's rejection of *gelykstelling* (levelling) between races, the principle of legal equality was a fundamental part of legal procedures and practice. As a recent analysis remarks: 'That blacks had access to the courts, that in principle (though not, of course, often in practice) they had equal standing as legal subjects, that whites could be held accountable in law for misdemeanours towards blacks . . . these principles became progressively established as uncontroversial aspects of the legal system and of a public order.'[3]

Just as there was tension between the formal legal position and apartheid ideology, the NP leadership was constantly torn between a commitment to apartheid as a goal in itself and apartheid as a mere instrument to preserve the state and the capitalist order. In the period under discussion, the latter conception increasingly predominated. Whereas the dictates of Afrikaner nationalism had earlier impelled the government to deny citizenship to blacks, the demand for stability called for the recognition of the common citizenship of all South Africans.

This chapter will discuss three main periods during NP rule. The first is 1948 to 1968, when the prime ministers were Afrikaner leaders above all else; the second is 1966 to 1989, when B.J. Vorster and P.W. Botha tried to transform themselves from Afrikaner leaders into leaders of whites in general and, as imperial presidents, leaders of the entire South African people; and the final period is the rule of F.W. de Klerk, who projected himself as the leader of all 'minorities'.

From 'volksleier' to white leader, 1948–1968

The NP, which won power in 1948, saw the Afrikaners as the core group of the citizenry. Afrikaners formed its primary constituency and it was they who would become the main beneficiaries of state privilege and protection. For the Afrikaners the state was 'their' state and the ministers 'their' ministers. Although white English-speakers enjoyed full citizenship, their relationship to the government and the state under NP rule was much more formalistic. Under the Westminster system their parties had little opportunity to influence the political decisions of the executive and they soon tended to eschew employment in the civil service in favour of the private sector.

During the period 1948 to 1968 the NP leadership tried first to cement the movement of ethnic mobilisation; secondly, it sought to win English-speaking support for the socio-political order and in particular for a republican form of government; and, finally, it attempted to deprive blacks of the political component of citizenship. The second and third trends prompted Afrikaner *volksleiers* (ethnic leaders) to assume also the role of leadership of all whites, but for most of the 1950s the leadership was concerned with the task of consolidating the Afrikaner *volksbeweging* (ethnic movement) behind it.

Consolidating the ethnic movement

Close associates of D.F. Malan report that after he had led the NP to victory in 1948 he exclaimed: 'At last we can feel at home again in our own country.'⁴ 'We' referred to the Afrikaner nationalists. Malan's party saw the Smuts government (1939–48) as being dominated by unilingual English-speakers, most of whom had a stronger commitment to the British Empire than to South Africa. It also claimed with some justification that Afrikaner nationalists were kept out of high civil service positions during the war years on account of their political affiliations.

In winning the election narrowly (by a majority of five seats) the NP attracted only 38 per cent of the vote against the United Party's 48 per cent. For Malan as leader, the highest priority was to cement the relationship between government, the NP and other Afrikaner political and cultural associations. Almost as much as being prime minister, Malan wanted to be the unquestioned *volksleier* – the leader of a unified Afrikanerdom which accepted the authority of the NP as the vanguard of the *volksbeweging* or national movement. The constituent parts of the *volksbeweging* – the Broederbond, the Afrikaans press, the Reformed churches and organised Afrikaner business – all served the Afrikaner people but at times tended to pull in different ways. Now the challenge was to consolidate Afrikaner rule through securing common acceptance of the political leadership of the NP. Malan depicted the party as the 'mother' of Afrikaner national consciousness and of the Afrikaners' language rights, their press, the broadening of their freedom, and their determination to preserve white civilisation.⁵

For many years Afrikaner political unity was more an ideal than a reality. However, during the war years the NP had crushed the two pro-Nazi organisations, the Ossewa-Brandwag and the Nuwe Orde, which had set themselves up in opposition to the NP. Through an election pact with the Afrikaner Party in 1948 and the subsequent absorption of that party into the NP, Malan drew General J.B.M. Hertzog's supporters into the NP fold. Still on the outside, until as late as 1960, stood between a quarter and a third of the Afrikaners, who continued to support the United Party. They had to be won over through persistent appeals to Afrikaner interests and ideals. Ben Schoeman, a member of Malan's first cabinet, frankly states that he advised NP candidates at election time to concentrate on Afrikaner voters and not to rely on the vote of English-speaking whites. If English-speakers did vote for the party, it was a bonus.[6]

During the first ten years of NP rule, Malan and Strijdom had great difficulty in establishing Afrikaner political and ideological coherence under NP leadership. Contrary to the impression given in many accounts, apartheid by 1948 was far from a ready-made system which the NP could purposefully propagate and implement. Looking back in 1985, Piet Cillié, doyen of Afrikaner journalists, gave an apt description of how NP rule unfolded. 'A system? An ideology? A coherent blueprint? No, rather a pragmatic and tortuous process aimed at consolidating the leadership of a nationalist movement in order to safeguard the self-determination of the Afrikaner.'[7]

Mindful of the Afrikaner schisms of the early 1940s, the leadership guarded against anything which could undermine the authority of the *volksleier* and of the party. The Broederbond was a case in point. Malan was a leading member of the Bond but his closest confidant, Paul Sauer, was not and on occasion expressed his dislike of secret organisations. Rather than turning to another Broederbond member, Malan appointed Sauer in 1946 and 1947 to head up important party commissions to formulate the NP's apartheid policy. Malan's successor, Strijdom, was also determined to prevent the Broederbond encroaching on his or the party's political turf. In 1954 he rejected a request from the Broederbond executive council to establish a special branch of the Bond during the parliamentary session for out-of-town MPs. Strijdom subsequently told an executive council delegation 'with great emphasis' that the Bond should stay out of the political arena and refrain from interfering in political policy, which was the prerogative of the NP. In 1957 Strijdom even refused a Broederbond request to arrange a discussion about the form a future republic should take.[8]

In the light of this it is baffling that a recent author can write: 'It was the Broeders who were the real authors of apartheid', and 'No Nationalist prime minister would dream of taking a major policy step without first checking it out with the Broederbond'.[9] In fact, the Broederbond during the 1950s clearly lacked a sense of purpose and direction. An authorised study of the Bond states that the organisation during this period was gripped by indecisiveness. In 1956 the Potchefstroom branches of the Bond told the executive council that the Bond no longer had a task or a vision. They had formed the impression that the NP kept the organisation on a leash, with the result that interest in the Bond was waning. They added that many members were troubled by the fact that the authorities could not be criticised.[10]

The Bond received a fresh lease of life in 1959 when the new prime minister, Hendrik Verwoerd, instructed it to accept co-responsibility with the party to prepare the electorate for a republic. Verwoerd's intellectual strength, his long association with the Bond and close personal ties with its leadership made it easy for him to turn the body into his staunchest support organisation. It was Verwoerd who finally developed apartheid into a fully fledged, rigid ideology which could be applied to virtually any contingency. In the early 1960s the Bond appointed fourteen 'expert task groups' (later expanded to nineteen), which covered virtually the entire field of political, economic and social policy.[11] Since Verwoerd was at this stage in unquestioned control of the *volksbeweging*, it can be safely assumed that the task groups accepted the ideological leadership of Verwoerd on all vital issues.

An uneasy relationship also existed between the *volksleier* and the Afrikaans press. This was closely linked to the conflict over the issue of provincialism. The NP was in fact not one but a coalition of four (or five, if South West Africa – later Namibia – is added) provincial parties, each with its own leader, separate party organisations and congresses. The Afrikaans newspapers in Cape Town, Johannesburg and Bloemfontein were allies of their respective provincial parties rather than the national NP. To prevent the conflict from getting out of hand, the *hoofleier* (leader or chief) had to project himself as transcending provincial rivalries. Malan, however, was closely aligned both to the Cape Town paper *Die Burger*, of which he was the founding editor, and the Cape party. As a result strong resentment built up in the Transvaal against the 'Keerom Street clique'. (The offices of Nasionale Pers, which publishes *Die Burger*, and of the Cape NP were both in Keerom Street at that time.)

With Strijdom and Verwoerd in power, the Transvaal began to dominate Afrikaner politics. This shift threatened to isolate Nasionale Pers both politically and financially. To regain its predominant position it had to publish its own newspaper in Johannesburg, the powerhouse of South Africa. This was inimical to the political and financial interests of the Transvaal leadership, who had begun to build up their own stake in newspapers. To block Nasionale Pers, Strijdom even resorted to rejecting the company's application for an increased import quota for paper.

Nasionale Pers found an even more formidable opponent in Verwoerd. On becoming prime minister, Verwoerd succeeded Strijdom as chairman of the company that published the Sunday paper *Dagbreek* and also became chairman of the board of Voortrekkers Pers, which published the daily *Die Transvaler.* Thwarted, Nasionale Pers delayed expansion into the Transvaal market until the mid-1960s, when it sprang a Sunday paper, *Beeld*, on a resentful Verwoerd. With Vorster in power (his wife was the daughter of a Nasionale Pers director), *Beeld* quickly served notice that it would ignore the unwritten rule not to publicise differences in NP ranks in the Transvaal. With relish *Beeld* exposed right-wing attempts under the leadership of Dr Albert Hertzog to undermine Vorster's adaptations of apartheid policy. This brought into the open serious tensions within the Transvaal party and between the Cape and Transvaal press groups.

Perhaps anticipating problems of a similar nature, Verwoerd in 1959 opposed the introduction of television in South Africa. In cabinet he argued that it would be 'to the detriment of the Afrikaners'.[12] He was more confident of controlling the radio service and in fact turned it into an NP instrument by appointing Piet Meyer, head of the Broederbond, as chairman of the South African Broadcasting Corporation.

The NP leadership's efforts to promote unity depended ultimately on whether it could raise the Afrikaners to the position of a secure middle class and a racially entrenched status group. When the NP won power in 1948 some 40 per cent of economically active Afrikaners were still blue-collar workers, while another 20 per cent were financially insecure farmers or agricultural workers. The NP's policy in the first two decades of power was designed to give whites and Afrikaners in particular a protected position in society. The concerns of the leadership were well expressed by Malan in his 'Quo vadis?' speech:

> Through the urbanisation of our *volk* Afrikanerdom has largely lost its protected position spiritually as well as economically. White poverty, coupled

with the advance of non-whites and taken together with manifold daily contacts in all fields and on virtually an equal footing, makes the struggle for racial purity ever more difficult . . . What hovers threateningly above us is nothing less than the modern and ostensibly civilised *heidendom* as well as the descent into semi-barbarism through blood mixing and the disintegration of the white race.[13]

During the first five years of NP rule, this matter was addressed through legislation such as the Mixed Marriages Act (1949), the Immorality Act (1950), the Population Registration Act (1950) and the Reservation of Separate Amenities Act (1953). In this legislation two considerations were inextricably linked: without a privileged position the Afrikaners could not survive as a separate people; without safeguarding the racial separateness of the people a privileged position could not be maintained. The following words of Strijdom illustrate the connection:

> If the European loses his colour sense he cannot remain a white man . . . On the basis of unity you cannot retain your sense of colour if there is no apartheid in everyday social life, in the political sphere or whatever sphere it may be, and if there is no residential separation. South Africa can only remain a white country if we continue to see that the Europeans remain the dominant nation; and we can only remain the dominant nation if we have the power to govern the country and if the Europeans, by means of their efforts, remain the dominant section.[14]

Verwoerd elaborated on this theme but cast apartheid in a more modern idiom. He also persuaded an astonishingly large number of his followers that it was morally defensible. Realising just how important this element was, Verwoerd promptly secured the rejection by the Dutch Reformed Church of the concluding statement of the Cottesloe conference in 1960. Convened by the World Council of Churches in the aftermath of the Sharpeville shootings, the conference opposed all unjust discrimination (specifically migrant labour, job reservation and the ban on racially mixed marriages) and recognised all racial groups as part of the total population of South Africa. Delegates from the

Transvaal and Cape DRC had supported the Cottesloe statement, but as a result of Verwoerd's appeal and strong lobbying by the Broederbond the synods fell into line, repudiating their own elected representatives. Subsequently no NP leader had to fear any attack on apartheid from the DRC or other Afrikaner churches.

The leader's position was greatly strengthened by the economic advance of the Afrikaners, which in turn was facilitated by the 'affirmative action' policy applied by the government to Afrikaners. After 1948 Afrikaners rose rapidly into senior positions of the civil service and public corporations like Eskom, Iscor and Sasol. By the mid-1960s they completely dominated the upper and middle echelons of the central state and parastatal organisations. Through protective policies and subsidies the NP government made the position of farmers and workers much more secure. Afrikaner business also benefited from the close association with the NP government, seeing their share in the private sector rise from 9,6 per cent in 1949 to 20,8 per cent in 1975. This Afrikaner economic advance expressed itself in a general movement away from less-skilled, poorly paid labour towards skilled, better-paid, usually well-protected careers. This general trend was accelerated as the government, bodies like the Broederbond and institutions like the church assiduously promoted Afrikaner education.[15] The movement can be discerned in the accompanying table.

Table 1: Percentage of Afrikaners in the broad categories of occupation, 1936–77

Occupational category	1936	1946	1960	1977
Agricultural occupations	41,2	30,3	16,0	8,1
'Blue collar' and manual workers	31,3	40,7	40,5	26,7
'White collar'	27,5	29,0	43,5	65,2
	100,0	100,0	100,0	100,0

Source: J.L. Sadie, published originally in Adam and Giliomee, *Ethnic Power Mobilized*, p. 169.

Afrikaner ethnic entrepreneurs always stressed that a people cannot (and must not) live by bread alone. Malan, Strijdom and Verwoerd all constantly promoted Afrikaner nationalist symbols and ideals. Under Strijdom the Union Jack and 'God Save the Queen' lost their official status, leaving 'Die Stem van Suid-Afrika' and the South African tricolour as the sole national anthem and flag. The NP leadership also decided to test support for a republic by way of a referendum. It recognised that imposing a change on the form of the state by way of a simple parliamentary majority would cause great tensions among the white citizenry. To achieve its ultimate goal, the *volksbeweging* was prepared to recognise its limits. Starting with the referendum on the republican issue, the NP leadership increasingly tried to secure English-speaking support for the state as the guarantor of the interests and political survival of whites as a whole.

Securing English-speaking support

After the 1948 election Malan thanked the 'thousands' of English-speaking supporters who had made the victory possible. However, in the first ten years of NP rule virtually no English-speakers from the business community, professions or universities were prepared to support publically the NP as an ethnically exclusive party with undercurrents of anti-Semitism (it was only in 1950 that the Transvaal NP removed a clause barring Jews from party membership). Throughout the 1950s the English-speaking middle class was largely repelled by the NP's racial explicitness, which substituted legislation for convention. The business community feared declining stability and profitability. Just after the 1948 election Smuts had warned: 'South Africa has lost the confidence of the world, the flood of capital and people that had been coming in has suddenly stopped. They can no longer trust South Africa.'[16] In 1949 the United Party established the United South Africa Trust Fund under the chairmanship of Harry Oppenheimer with the goal of raising £1 million to fight the NP in the forthcoming election. Capping all this was the fear among English-speakers that the NP would strip them of their language rights (which Verwoerd and others had proposed to do in the Republican Constitution of 1942) and that it would lead South Africa out of the British Commonwealth.

Verwoerd's decision in 1959 to hold a referendum on the republican issue was a bold gamble, given that the UP was confident of a 'no' vote from 25 per cent of Afrikaners and more than 90 per cent of English-speakers. Since every vote counted, the only effective change the NP proposed was that the governor-general would be replaced by a state president as the head of state. Verwoerd also promised to apply for South Africa's continued membership of the Commonwealth.

In addressing the white electorate Verwoerd presented a republic as the best way to achieve unity between the two white groups and so avoid the danger of their separate cultures being used to establish separate nationhoods. White unity was also presented as essential for economic growth. Verwoerd stated explicitly that the republic would be organised on the basis of apartheid. In effect this meant Coloured or Indian or African voters would not be allowed a say in 'white politics'.[17] He argued that to allow Coloured people or Africans to vote in elections for Parliament, the provincial councils or 'white' city councils would inflame the relationship between the two white groups and between whites and blacks. The Coloured vote, so his argument ran, was used by the UP for the cynical purpose of 'ploughing the nationalist Afrikaners under'. This was the NP's main justification for removing the Coloured people from the common voters' roll in 1956 and for abolishing the indirect representation of Africans in Parliament.

In the 1960 republican referendum the government excluded all people who were not white from the vote. Illiterate whites, however, could participate. Commenting on this, a UP parliamentarian declared: 'While we hold a referendum to alter our constitutional form to a republic and do not even consult the Coloured people or the Natives, we cannot be said to aim at real national unity.'[18] To this Verwoerd replied that it was only because the anti-republicans were afraid of losing that blacks were being 'dragged into the struggle'. He added: 'It had always been generally acknowledged that the white man must decide his own affairs but now that point of view was being contested. It had always been the white man who decided on the affairs of South Africa and there had never been any objection to that.'[19]

After having led the NP to victory in the referendum on the republic and later, under pressure, having removed South Africa from the Commonwealth, Verwoerd sought to heal the divisions in white ranks. However, ruling elites in divided societies often find it difficult to suppress the temptation to go ever further in their attempts to homogenise the citizenry. Leading figures in the Broederbond were concerned that the blurring of intra-white divisions would undermine Afrikaner exclusivity and power. They were particularly concerned that a wrong interpretation could be placed on Verwoerd's call to relegate to the past all the historical differences which could impede white co-operation. In 1962 the Broederbond head office sent a circular to all branches that the prime minister's call should not be misunderstood: co-operation had to come from the English-speakers, while Afrikaners would not deny them the opportunity to do so. The circular went on: 'It is not they who should absorb us in their circles but we should absorb them in ours.'[20]

In 1966 Broederbond chairman Piet Meyer, in a secret meeting with the highest organ of the body, spelled out his quest for undiluted Afrikaner hegemony. He pointed to the danger of a steady anglicisation of Afrikaners while English influence was so pervasive in virtually all walks of life. In his view, the political realm was dominated by the specific contribution the English section had made. This included the parliamentary system and an emphasis on 'citizenship as a collectivity of all state subjects, irrespective of differences of origin or culture, everyone potentially equal'.

In contrast to this nation-state approach the Afrikaner emphasis on an ethnically homogeneous state, which formed the basis of the homeland policy, had not yet received 'full development'.[21] What Meyer now proposed was nothing less than the homogenisation of the white citizenry through 'the Afrikanerisation of the English-speaker'. He believed that this task would have to be achieved primarily through the educational system and would mean:

> that the English-speaker has to make the Afrikaans world-view his own; that he will integrate his ideals and life style with those of the Afrikaner; that he will adopt Afrikaans history as his own; that he will accept Afrikaans as his national language, alongside English as the international community language . . . We shall then be able to speak of Afrikaans- and English-speaking Afrikaners.[22]

Meyer was such a close associate of Verwoerd that it is difficult to believe that he could develop these ideas without sounding his leader out. In public, however, Verwoerd tended to preach Afrikaner–English reconciliation while warning about the dangers of the *Engelse geldmag* (the English money power). After Sharpeville the executive committee of the Associated Chambers of Commerce (ASSOCOM) pleaded for Africans to be granted freehold tenure in townships, greater freedom of movement and permission to bargain collectively. Verwoerd charged that this intervention was part of an organised campaign against the state. He also openly opposed the United States–South Africa Leader Exchange Program (USSALEP) in which prominent American and South African business leaders and academics worked towards peaceful change and reducing the racial conflict in South Africa. He was also deeply suspicious of the South Africa Foundation, established in 1961 by South African business leaders to improve the country's image abroad and to act as an informal lobby for changes to apartheid policy. In 1964 Verwoerd refused the Foundation permission to recruit black members.

Verwoerd also allowed cabinet ministers to depict Harry Oppenheimer and his Anglo American Corporation as no friend of the Afrikaner and a bitter enemy of apartheid. According to a right-wing extremist, Professor Piet Hoek, Verwoerd was greatly concerned about the stranglehold which Oppenheimer, through his conglomerate, had on the South African economy and was looking for ways to break it. In 1965 Verwoerd warned that the South African 'money power' was becoming entangled with an international 'money power' alien to South Africa. The Nationalists would have to guard against the threat this posed to their ideals and security.[23]

The background to this speech was the increasing interpenetration since the early 1960s of Afrikaner and English capital, a development which was given great impetus by Harry Oppenheimer when he enabled Afrikaner capital in 1964 to take over the mining house General Mining. Verwoerd and his allies feared that Oppenheimer had changed tactics. Rather than continuing with the ineffectual attempts of the 1950s to unseat the NP, he was now using his influence to forge a political alliance of all-white moderates which could oust the intransigent prime minister.[24]

Nevertheless, Verwoerd's position was bolstered by the fact that the English-speaking business elite no longer directly opposed him. In addition he benefited from the success that tough security measures had in restoring stability after Sharpeville. In the 1966 general election Verwoerd led the NP to a landslide victory. The party won a majority of all votes cast (57,8 per cent, as against 46,2 per cent in 1961). In the predominantly English-speaking province of Natal its share of the vote was 40,6 per cent, up from 16,7 per cent in 1961. This 1966 victory was won a mere six years after Douglas Mitchell, UP leader in Natal, had declared: 'We do not accept the Republic in Natal . . . We live under a hostile government and this is tyranny and rule by force . . . We will seek the first opportunity to make our own laws.'[25]

This growing unity among the white citizenry calls to mind the observation that 'nations are the creation not of their historians but of their enemies'.[26] Whites, who were the government's first-class citizens and the 'state nation', were united by common threats and challenges to their position of power and privilege. For example, the South African Defence Force developed as an institution which was exclusively white in its ethos and in the composition of its officer corps. While it accepted blacks who volunteered, compulsory military service was restricted to medically fit young white men, under the terms of the Defence Amendment Act of 1967.[27] A sense of white nationhood was also fostered by prosperity. The move to a republic did not turn out to be as costly as English-speakers had feared. The economy entered a boom period which lasted ten years. Moreover, the attraction of being tied to the British Commonwealth steadily faded as that body became increasingly black and as Britain applied sanctions to Rhodesia after its white government had declared unilateral independence.

Although only two of the NP's 126 elected representatives in 1966 were English-speaking, Verwoerd and the NP had for the first time become acceptable to English-speakers. The Afrikaners had arrived and had mellowed in the process. Their rapid, often traumatic urbanisation was behind them. By 1970 some 90 per cent lived in the towns and cities, compared to 50 per cent in 1936. Nearly 60 per cent found themselves in white-collar occupations, as against fewer than 30 per cent in 1936. The republican ideal had been achieved and Afrikaner culture was secure. The NP leadership saw its great task now as harnessing the support of all whites to make the republic invincible and prosperous.

The leadership and the black population

The NP policy towards the African population took as its point of departure the idea that whites had an undeniable historical right to all the land except those concentrations of black settlement known as the reserves. This 'white' land had to be safeguarded for future generations in the face of a steady increase in the African population. Unlike General Smuts, who declared that white supremacy 'will last forever'[28] but refused to take any further measures to safeguard it, Malan and his followers believed that drastic steps were necessary to prevent black liberation some day in the future. Along with the mainstream of the UP, the NP was a racist party which believed in the social and biological superiority of whites. However, developments such as the independence of India forcefully brought home the point that a belief in white supremacy was by itself not sufficient to guarantee continued white domination. As one contemporary writer put it: 'The European assumption that the mere biological inferiority of the non-Europeans is sufficient to prevent them from displacing the Europeans, particularly in a predominantly non-European country, is an assumption that is found wanting.'[29]

During the 1930s and 1940s the NP leadership directly challenged the UP government's attempts to improve conditions for black people, which took place in a political vacuum. In particular it questioned the money spent on education for Africans in white areas. As J.G. Strijdom put it, this would inexorably lead to Africans becoming developed and civilised, a process which would erode the distinguishing line of colour and would bring about equality step by step.[30] To forestall this, Malan, Strijdom and their successors had little compunction in denying blacks political rights. In this respect Malan and Strijdom were nothing but hard-core segregationists, like their counterparts in the American South. But apartheid was not the same as segregation. Its distinguishing feature was the combination of paternalism and a peculiar rationalisation of racial discrimination.

The specific character of apartheid in its earlier phase is particularly striking in the pronouncements of Malan, an ex-minister of the Dutch Reformed Church. When an African deputation presented him with an address in October 1948, Malan expressed himself in the following terms: 'I regard the Bantu not as strangers and not as a menace to the white people, but as our children for whose welfare we are responsible, and as an asset to the country. My government has no intention of depriving you of your rights or oppressing you. Nothing will be taken from you without giving you something better in its place.'[31] In another speech, given two weeks after the NP's electoral victory, Malan spoke in similar terms about Coloured people: 'The days when people . . . speak . . . of racialism are past. We will get the co-operation of the various races.

There will be no discrimination against any section. We have a policy in regard to non-Europeans, but this involves no oppression or removal of any other rights. We shall protect them against oppression.'[32] Likewise Hendrik Verwoerd, in addressing the Natives Representative Council in 1950, declared that apartheid meant exactly the opposite of oppression.[33]

These statements must be understood within the context of the constraints with which the NP leadership had to contend. It was impossible for it to deny black people citizenship in all its components – political, civil and social. Indeed, the South African Citizenship Act of 1949 reaffirmed the common citizenship of all South Africans. On the other hand, the NP leadership believed the white voters in South Africa's *herrenvolk* democracy were powerful enough to block any attempt to grant black people equal civil rights in a common political and social system. Even a gradualist approach would be met by ever fiercer resistance.[34]

The way the NP leaders thought they could resolve this dilemma was by offering 'something better' than segregation, to use the words of Malan in his October 1948 speech. In Malan's thinking, segregation also discriminated but offered nothing in return. While segregation had for Malan the connotation of *afhok* (separation or isolation), the NP proposed in its place apartheid, 'which could mean equality but each on its own terrain', according to Malan. It was he who used the word 'apartheid' for the first time in Parliament when, in 1944, he called for a policy which would give to Africans and Coloured people the opportunity to develop under white leadership 'according to their character and ability'.[35]

In the NP leadership's thinking, the discrimination which blacks suffered as citizens would be compensated for by a policy promoting the national development of the different black ethnic groups as segregated political entities. In typically paternalistic fashion, the leadership decided that this policy was in the best interests of blacks and was what they themselves actually wanted. In his October 1948 speech to an African delegation Malan stated: 'What you want is a rehabilitation of your own national life, and not competition and intermixture and equality with the white man in his particular part of the country.'[36]

For the Coloured people, the 'something better' was an explicit policy of granting them a position of privilege over Africans in the white part of the country and more opportunities to serve their 'own people' in the civil administration and in their own communities.[37] Apartheid policy would also promote the social upliftment of Coloured people, a large part of whom were trapped in acute poverty and illiteracy.

The promise of black upliftment and human development was for the NP leadership the essence of what it called 'positive apartheid' and, as such, a commitment to the social component of citizenship. This developmental aspect was considered a sufficient counter-balance to negative apartheid, which denied blacks political citizenship in common political institutions. Hence the leadership's belief that apartheid did not really entail discrimination or racialism.

The problem was that the black leadership saw politics in starkly different terms. This was highlighted in the responses on two separate occasions by the leadership of the African National Congress (ANC) and by Dr Richard van der Ross, a prominent Coloured educator. Before embarking on its passive resistance campaign in 1952, the ANC declared that its action was not directed against any national group or race. It called attention to its efforts 'by every constitutional method to bring to the notice of the government the legitimate demands of the African people . . . in particular, their inherent right to be directly represented in parliament, the provincial and municipal councils and in all councils of state'. In reply Malan disputed the claim to inherent rights of Africans, who, he said, differed from Europeans in ways which were 'permanent and not man-made'. He continued:

> If this is a matter of indifference to you and if you do not value your racial characteristics, you cannot in any case dispute the Europeans' rights, which in this case are definitely an inherent right, to take the opposite view and to adopt the necessary measures to preserve their identity as a separate community. It should be understood clearly that the government will under no circumstances entertain the idea of giving administrative or executive or legislative powers over Europeans, or within an European community, to Bantu men and women, or to other smaller non-European groups.[38]

In response, the ANC leadership observed that when it objected to discriminatory laws it did not refer to biological differences but to 'citizenship rights which are granted in full measure to one section of the population and completely denied to the other by means of man-made laws artificially imposed, not to preserve the identity of Europeans as a separate community, but to perpetuate the systematic exploitation of African people'.[39] In 1960, when mobilising mass action against the advent of the republic, Nelson Mandela contrasted the exclusive 'Boer republic' with a 'democratic republic where all South Africans will enjoy human rights without the slightest discrimination'.[40] The banning of the ANC as the most important organ of black resistance silenced this voice for nearly two decades.

Also in 1960, Van der Ross expressed the profound alienation of those Coloured people who had once enjoyed political rights but were now excluded from the republican referendum. Writing just after Referendum Day, he remarked that 5 October 1960 was 'a double R-day: Referendum Day for whites, Rejection Day for non-whites'. White South Africa had a chance to interpret citizenship in a grand manner but chose not to do so. In fact it made it quite clear to the non-white people of South Africa that they had no part in running the affairs of the country. Van der Ross concluded: 'We were excluded from partaking in the referendum, and by this very exclusion we understand that the term citizen is reserved for whites only . . . It is important for us, too, that this was an exclusion of all non-Whites, African, Coloured, Indian, Malay, Chinese.'[41]

Van der Ross's statement was remarkably prescient. The growing white unity of the 1960s had as its corollary a widening of the gulf between whites and blacks. Three months after the republic was established, Verwoerd declared: 'Let me be very clear about this: When I talk of the nation, I talk of the white people of South Africa.'[42] In Verwoerd's eyes Coloured people were destined to become a nation in their own right. Van der Ross commented: 'It means that in future no non-white South African need regard "Die Stem" as his national anthem, or the South African national flag as his flag.'[43] In effect this was Verwoerd's view as well. In 1965 he argued that as much as Ceylon was the land of the Sinhalese, regardless of the presence of the Tamils, South Africa was a white state despite the presence of other groups. After all, in Verwoerd's reasoning, Africans were being eliminated from the political life of the state, and the Coloured people and Indians were mere marginal minorities.[44]

From this line of thinking followed the denial of political citizenship for blacks. The government abolished the indirect Coloured representation in Parliament and prohibited racially mixed political parties. In the apartheid form of political compensation, the Union Coloured Advisory Council was upgraded and became the Coloured Persons Representative Council, which was partly elected by universal franchise. Designed to be the 'mouthpiece of the Coloured population', it was also given limited powers to administer Coloured local government, education, communal welfare and rural areas. The government contended that the funds allocated to the council were roughly equal to the amount contributed by Coloured taxpayers.

In the case of Africans, the denial of citizenship went even further. All political representation had to be channelled through their respective homelands. The NP leadership insisted that there 'can be no permanent home or permanency for even a section of the Bantu in the area of white South Africa'.[45] The recognition of civil and social citizenship of Africans was reduced to a minimum. The state's contribution to funding for African education was pegged and money for other services was linked to the African capacity to pay. Africans were also denied the right to own property, form companies or establish African-controlled financial institutions and wholesale concerns. Intensified influx control severely restricted their right of free movement. The pass law regulations spun an Orwellian web of control, preventing the influx of rural people to the towns except in terms of rigidly defined procedures and expelling non-productive 'surplus' people to the homelands.

The apartheid state, in paternalistic fashion, continued to insist that it was committed to the socio-economic upliftment of the people under its care. However, with vast funds committed to shoring up the position of the white citizenry, the state always lacked funds to spend sufficiently on social welfare for all. In fact, the basic pattern of taxation and state expenditure did not change much. In 1949–50 whites paid 81,1 per cent of the taxes; this figure declined slowly to 76,9 per cent in 1975–6, while the African share of taxes rose from 11,4 per cent to 16,2 per cent in the same period. In 1949–50 whites received 61 per cent of state expenditure directly allocated by racial group, while the Coloured, Indian and African shares were 11 per cent, 3 per cent and 25 per cent respectively. The proportions stayed fairly constant for quite some time. By 1975–6 the white share had declined to 56 per cent, while that of Africans had risen to 28 per cent. The proportions for Coloureds and Indians stood at 12 per cent and 4 per cent respectively.[46]

In justifying the continuing racial disparities in state spending, the NP leadership was unwilling to state openly that the government discriminated against black people because they were inferior. Instead it argued on the one hand that the state needed to spend on whites to preserve a white nation in a black continent, and on the other that since whites carried the lion's share of the taxes they could expect preferential treatment. Indeed, they also had the right to expect gratitude for what was spent on black people out of their taxes. As Malan wrote to an American clergyman in 1954, 'It is computed that every European taxpayer in our country "carries" more than four non-whites in order to provide the latter with the essential services involving education, hospitalisation, housing etc.'[47]

Rationalisations such as these helped to fortify the NP leadership in its belief that apartheid was offering 'something better' than segregation and was even in the interests of all the people in the country. Confronted by widespread resistance to apartheid by the mid-1980s, the NP political leadership and the Nationalist press found it difficult to admit that the basic point of departure of apartheid was wrong or unjust. In a series of articles analysing the legacy of apartheid, a senior journalist of *Die Burger* wrote that apartheid was to a large extent 'a tale of frustrated idealism'. He went on to say that there were idealists who supported the NP who did not want to humiliate or oppress but wanted to create new opportunities for development.[48] P.W. Botha answered in the same mould when asked what was the greatest mistake the NP had made. In his view it was the failure to give expression to the positive content of apartheid. He added: 'There was a time when we could have done much more with respect to housing, social upliftment and development. I don't know but we delayed for one reason or another and time caught up with us.'[49] There is no recognition here that the apartheid state failed in its obligations to black citizens because it excluded blacks from political participation. John Stuart Mill observed in his essay 'Representative Government' that in the absence of its natural defenders the interests of the excluded are always in danger of being overlooked and, when looked at, are seen with very different eyes from those of the persons whom they directly concern. So it was with African and Coloured citizens of South Africa, particularly in the first three decades of apartheid.

From white leader to imperial president, 1966–1989

In the twenty-odd years between the death of Verwoerd and the coming to power of F.W. de Klerk, the NP leadership set itself three goals. Firstly, it wanted to consolidate the white citizens in a political community which would anchor the South African state. Secondly, it sought to narrow the gap between white and black citizens in the treatment they received from the state in order to gain some black acquiescence in the political order. Thirdly, it attempted to co-opt leadership strata in the three black groups to administer 'their own people' and also to discuss matters of general concern, though always within the apartheid framework. In the first of these objectives – cementing white unity – the leadership was relatively successful, but in the other two its efforts were largely frustrated by the swelling tide of black resistance.

Consolidating the white nation

John Vorster, unlike Verwoerd, was no intellectual. Nevertheless he was a formidable debater who asserted himself strongly in Parliament. He shunned the ideological flights of fancy of a Verwoerd or the Broederbond's Meyer. As a senior cabinet minister recounted, Verwoerd projected apartheid as a goal in itself. Even if the grand designs of apartheid were impractical, they had to be held up to the white citizenry as an ideal. Vorster, by contrast, had come to the position of prime minister after having been minister of justice and police, where he had fought the security threats to the state. He had developed a more pragmatic sense of what was essential for the political survival of a shrinking white minority. In private he expressed the view that apartheid was simply not a goal in itself but an instrument in the service of stability and security.[50] In public he gradually began to curb the ideological overreach of apartheid.

Vorster came to power in a period of surging NP confidence, owing to the 1966 landslide electoral victory, the economic boom and black political quiescence in the wake of draconian security measures. He understood that the time had come to consolidate white unity rather than pursue Meyer's absurd plans for the Afrikanerisation of the white people. In a major speech at the secret jubilee celebrations of the Broederbond, Vorster explicitly rejected the view that the support of English-speakers could be dispensed with. He made it clear that he had no intention of 'cheating' the English-speakers.[51]

In public Vorster paid tribute to the contribution of the English-speaking section, declaring that he respected their traditions and monuments as much as his own. He repudiated a speech by Dr Hertzog in which the latter argued that English-speakers could not be trusted in the battle for white survival in Africa because they were infused with liberalism. Vorster became the first leader since the NP had won power in 1948 to declare that white unity was thwarted as much by 'super-Afrikaners' as by jingoes.[52]

Unlike Verwoerd, who in his own words was a conviction politician demanding that co-operation take place according to his principles, Vorster's pursuit of white unity was characterised by the politics of (white) reconciliation. He told all English newspaper editors (except Laurence Gandar of the *Rand Daily Mail*) that his door was open to them. He addressed gatherings of English-speaking business people in exclusive clubs and, while a quintessential Afrikaner politician, he won many over with remarkable ease. As the *Rand Daily Mail* remarked, Vorster introduced a more humane and relaxed touch which took some of the steam out of the body politic.[53] As anxious as his predecessors to maintain his Afrikaner base, Vorster nevertheless projected himself more as prime minister than as leader of the ruling party.[54]

Under Vorster and his successor, P.W. Botha, the NP managed to win the electoral support of between a quarter and a third of English-speakers. This put paid to any hope the United Party had of winning power. The UP self-destructed in the mid-1970s, as Vorster had anticipated. More importantly, while English-speakers never displayed enthusiastic support for the NP, few joined the liberation struggle. Resistance within their ranks to military conscription remained limited. Most English-speakers supported the Progressive Federal Party, the official opposition from 1977 to 1987, and its successor, the Democratic Party. Both parties espoused majority rule, but the great bulk of English-speakers remained solidly opposed to the kind of majority rule the ANC envisaged. In a 1989 poll only seven per cent (as against five per cent of Afrikaners) supported a unitary state with one Parliament and one person, one vote.[55] A 1991 poll found that only eight per cent of Democratic Party supporters agreed with the statement that an ANC government was capable of running South Africa.[56] What English-speakers wanted was a pro-capitalist state which steadily absorbed educated blacks as political managers while safeguarding stability. To them the NP still seemed essential to helping manage this process.

In the sphere of culture and public morality, the ethos of the *volksbeweging* lingered for quite some time. A leading Afrikaner thought leader, Schalk Pienaar, wrote in 1969 that the NP government 'cannot, will not and does not want to rule South Africa as if only Afrikaners live in the country'.[57] Pienaar was only partly correct. The government, through its censorship machinery, continued to impose Afrikaner norms of public morality. The easing and eventual scrapping of apartheid in the fields of sport, entertainment and public facilities occurred only after a critical mass of Afrikaner support had been won. In the economic field, by contrast, the NP gave up on this quest for Afrikaner income parity with the English-speaking section and shed its fears of Anglo American and 'international money power'. The Carlton meeting of 1979 between top government people and business leaders symbolised the end of the public antagonism which had long characterised the relationship between government and the English-speaking business elite. This Afrikaner–English rapprochement inevitably produced great strains within the ranks of Afrikaner nationalists.

From the mid-1960s sharp differences arose in Afrikaner ranks about the strategies and methods by which the political survival of Afrikaners and the larger white group could be realised. During the 1970s these differences began to manifest themselves in the Afrikaans press and in the party, church and Broederbond, which all struggled to maintain ideological coherence. Yet despite internal discord the leadership could count on a great deal of implicit support. During the 1970s upwards of 60 per cent of NP supporters declared that they would support the leadership even if things were done which they did not understand or approve of.[58]

However, as Afrikanerdom became more stratified the leadership found it ever more difficult to impose discipline on Afrikaner institutions and organisations. Just after he had come to power, Vorster expressed the view that in Afrikaner life only the party and the church had an independent right to exist and that there was a place for other organisations only if they were prepared to act in support.[59] Vorster soon ran up against resistance to this belief. Confronted with a major public squabble between the northern and southern Afrikaans newspapers, he failed to persuade the newspaper publishers to sign an undertaking not to try to formulate policy or criticise the party's policies. Even a threat to resign as prime minister if the press war was not resolved failed to produce results.

In the 1970s the Afrikaans press, particularly the Sunday newspaper *Rapport*, struck out on a more independent path. As a result both Vorster's and Botha's relationship with the paper and its editors became strained. The trend towards a more independent stance was reversed when Botha became the leader. He had been a director of Nasionale Pers and used close personal ties to forestall any criticism of him by newspapers in this group until his very last year or two in office. His notorious temper was sufficient to moderate any criticism of him as leader in the Afrikaans press.

The worsening security situation after 1976 greatly increased the tendency of leaders to manipulate news for the sake of maintaining unity. This put the Afrikaans press in a particular dilemma, since it posed a conflict between defending the state and remaining autonomous. Botha, as the spokesman for the security establishment when he was minister of defence and then prime minister and state president, demanded a range of curbs on reports of unrest, acts of sabotage and strikes. His argument that this was imperative for the defence of the state struck a responsive chord in Afrikaans press circles. Ton Vosloo, editor of the Nasionale Pers paper *Beeld* and later managing director of the group, remarked in the early 1980s that the political struggle had become a matter of conflict between white and black nationalism in which the press was being employed by both parties. 'It is us or them,' he declared.[60]

Despite threats and intimidation by Botha, both the Afrikaans and the English press managed to avoid becoming too subservient to the state. As a result Botha increasingly instructed the television and radio service to broadcast news about the security situation within the context of his view of a 'total onslaught' against the state. Botha even intervened directly when the television news did not give his interpretation of his sacking of the first Coloured minister in the cabinet, Allan Hendrickse.

Both Vorster and Botha continued to employ the Broederbond to broaden their own power base and to gain acceptance for the NP's tortuous move away from apartheid. Vorster used secret meetings of the Broederbond to isolate Dr Hertzog and his followers in the party, before driving them from both the party and the Bond. Suspicious of 'experts' who were not also staunch nationalists, Vorster allowed the Bond to develop proposals for multiracial sport, changes in Coloured policy and a new constitution. Under Botha the Bond's usefulness in this regard began to wane: it had now become necessary to negotiate reforms with black representatives instead of just handing down policy. The Bond nevertheless remained influential in educational policy. Botha appointed Gerrit Viljoen, ex-chairman of the Bond, to deal with educational reform, while prominent Bond members Pieter de Lange (also a former chairman) and Tjaart van der Walt headed investigations into the crisis in African and Coloured schools.

The leadership recognised that the Afrikaans churches, and in particular the largest one, the Dutch Reformed Church (DRC), had an important role to play in legitimising both apartheid and reform. Both Vorster and Botha tried to use the church for this purpose. Vorster was in a particularly strong position since his brother served as moderator of the DRC, as did a close friend, the Rev. J.S. Gericke. When right-wingers in the caucus objected to a proposal for a new policy for multiracial sport, Vorster told them that a respected church leader (probably Gericke) had underwritten this, as had the full cabinet.[61]

Confronted by divisions in party ranks about contentious issues like the racial sex laws, Vorster and Botha tried to get the DRC family (the white together with the three black DRC churches) to speak out with one voice. It was, after all, the DRC which in the 1940s had put pressure on government to prohibit sexual contact across racial lines and to adhere rigidly to the principle of racial apartheid. The church leadership could not help the political leadership in its tentative moves towards reform. How closely the former remained aligned to apartheid became clear in 1979 when it was revealed that the church leadership had received secret funds to counteract the campaign of the World Council of Churches against apartheid. Vorster's brother was unrepentant, arguing that the church had acted honourably because it had accepted the money for use against the 'enemies of our *volk*' – thus blurring the distinction between church and *volk*. In 1982 an overwhelming majority in a DRC synod meeting rejected a motion that the Mixed Marriages Act and section 16 of the Immorality Act were scripturally unjustifiable and should be revoked.[62] While the DRC became more sophisticated in its terminology, its basic support for the principles of apartheid remained the same until mid-1986, by which time the government had already moved away from it.

In the end two developments fundamentally changed the ethos of the *volksbeweging* and the leader's relationship to it. On the one hand there were political splits within the party that cost it its position as the sole authentic representative of the *volk*. During the late 1960s Vorster's support for a white nation and the relaxation of apartheid in sport led to the founding of the Herstigte (Reconstituted) National Party under the leadership of Albert Hertzog. Although it failed to win a single parliamentary seat, it soon became clear that large numbers of Afrikaner workers, farmers and civil servants in the lower-income groups had become disaffected.

In 1982 Andries Treurnicht and seventeen NP parliamentary representatives broke away on the issue of power-sharing under the proposed new constitution, to form the Conservative Party (CP). In the general election of 1987 the CP won the support of more than a third of Afrikaners. A full 43 per cent of votes for the NP in this election came from English-speakers. By now it was clear that it was futile for the NP leadership to attempt to mobilise support in all Afrikaner institutions as a precondition for reform. The demise of the *volksbeweging*-style of politics in fact considerably increased the government's freedom of action.

The other development was the rise in the 1970s of the executive state, headed after 1983 by a president on whom the constitution conferred vast powers. The route to power of the first president, P.W. Botha, passed through the ministry of defence, which strengthened his personal inclination towards authoritarian leadership coupled with administrative teamwork. The severe challenges to the state in the mid-1980s, together with Botha's temperament and vast powers, conspired to bring about an imperial presidency.[63]

As in so many other countries, the executive state in South Africa pushed the political parties and Parliament into the background as institutions through which the support of the citizenry could be mobilised. In their place came a large bureaucracy reared on the principles of non-accountability, secrecy and the use of technical knowledge to mystify the citizenry. Leaders now demanded large discretionary powers to deal with pressing political and economic crises. If legitimation was required it occurred in the form of television addresses, thereby sidelining the press, the political parties and Parliament.

These trends had already manifested themselves under Vorster. The watershed event was South Africa's invasion of Angola in 1975, about which the public was kept in ignorance for several weeks. The Information Scandal of the latter half of the 1970s revealed a disturbing lack of accountability. These tendencies were still somewhat tempered by Vorster's leadership style, which resembled that of a chairman of a board rather than an executive director. He was unwilling to act unilaterally and on most major policy decisions waited for consensus to develop in the cabinet and caucus before he acted.[64]

Botha, by contrast, was a technocrat through and through. He became as domineering as Verwoerd in cabinet and used the State Security Council as a forum where vital decisions about security, regional destabilisation and a settlement in South West Africa were taken. These were later referred to cabinet for rubber-stamping, while the caucus was left largely out in the cold. In the final years of his period in office Botha was a remote figure, feared by office-holders in the party and largely out of touch with a citizenry who themselves remained ignorant of much that was happening in the struggle between the state and the ANC.

The leader and the black citizenry: Insiders and outsiders

In the twenty years after Verwoerd's death, apartheid was steadily broken down by the inexorable drift of black people to the cities, the economy's demand for better skilled and stabilised black labour, and the black quest for human dignity and freedom. Verwoerd wanted, in his own words, 'to be a rock of granite'[65] in resisting any concessions to his policy of maximum separation between race groups in all spheres of life. His successors, by contrast, had to go ever further in adjusting to the exigencies of the situation. All of them agonised before ultimately saying their farewell to a particular aspect of apartheid. Often they attempted to replace apartheid with policies which still bore the stamp of apartheid thinking.

The homelands are a case in point. For Verwoerd it was an open question whether blacks had the capacity to develop the homelands to the point where they could become politically autonomous. Vorster, by contrast, declared that the government would grant independence to any African homeland which demanded this right under the apartheid policy. But independence had an ominous catch as far as citizenship was concerned. The Bantu Homelands Citizenship Act of 1970 stipulated that every African person in the Republic of South Africa had to be a citizen of a homeland but that they and their children remained citizens of the republic. However, citizens of homelands that took independence, as the Transkei did in 1976, lost their South African citizenship. They became aliens who could be deported. Children of these citizens born after the granting of independence would be denied the opportunity to establish a claim to section 10 exemptions, which allowed for permanent residence in the 'white' areas. In 1978 Dr Connie Mulder, who was narrowly beaten by Botha in the same year's leadership contest, formulated the goal as follows:

> If our policy is taken to its logical conclusion as far as black people are concerned, there will not be one black [African] man with South African citizenship . . . Every black man in South Africa will eventually be accommodated in some independent new state in this honourable way and there will no longer be a moral obligation on this parliament to accommodate those people politically.[66]

Even the labour reforms which were first introduced in 1979 did not represent a bold break with the past. They were passed only with reluctance. The government's original idea had been to deny the new industrial rights to migrant workers and citizens of independent states. When the government accepted that influx control had broken down, it tried to limit freedom of movement to those who had jobs and houses. And when the government finally came to write a new constitution in the early 1980s, it sought to erect a firm barrier between Africans, who were left out, and the Coloureds and Indians, who were now seen as members of the same nation as whites.

In general the government pursued a double-edged policy between the mid-1960s and the mid-1980s. On the one hand it pushed the 'outsiders' away and tried to limit their claims on the state and their access to the cities. On the other hand it tried to draw nearer the 'insiders' – the urban Africans, Coloureds and Indians – by slowly turning the state into something which was racially neutral.

It was the Coloured people, the group most intimately interwoven with the whites, who shattered Verwoerd's policy of separate nations developing in perpetuity in parallel to each other.[67] Both Vorster and Botha assumed that improved education and training would inevitably yield irresistible demands for integration. Vorster conceded in a private conversation with Van der Ross that an injustice was being done to Coloured people. He suggested that they mobilise themselves as the Afrikaners had done with respect to the English-speakers to win recognition as *volle mense* (full human beings).[68] Vorster was clearly using as an analogy the two-stream policy articulated by General Hertzog between 1910 and 1940. He had envisaged the merger of the Afrikaner and English streams after the former had the opportunity to develop to the full. Botha declared that, unlike in the 1950s, the Coloured people of the 1980s had to be accommodated; the consequences of the policy of social upliftment had to be accepted.[69]

Yet NP policy remained ambiguous throughout the 1970s and 1980s. The leadership rejected appeals by Afrikaner academics in 1971 for full citizenship for Coloured people because it would lead to political integration and because the state lacked the means to provide for parity in welfare spending. The state slowly eliminated discriminatory salaries, but in general Coloured people were denied the means to mobilise in the way that the two-stream analogy presupposed.

In general, the crude racism which characterised apartheid's public discourse in the 1950s was replaced by the less offensive rhetoric of good neighbourliness and separate development. Verwoerd was a transitional figure who straddled the two versions of apartheid. Although he spoke of a potential nation of separate but coequal racial groups, he still propagated racist views. When he clashed with *Die Burger* about Coloured policy he told his wife that he was not the man who would lead the Afrikaners to 'bastardisation'.[70] Vorster, by contrast, from the beginning stated explicitly that there were no inferior people in South Africa and that the government had to treat black diplomats and political representatives of black states (including homelands) in exactly the same way as their white counterparts.

It was, of course, Vorster more than anyone else who was associated with the remorseless suppression of radical opposition to apartheid. It was also he who allowed a cabinet minister to stay on in office after he had uttered the infamous words that Steve Biko's death left him cold. It is difficult to avoid the impression that a black enemy of the apartheid state was much more vulnerable than a white one. It was, however, also Vorster, first as minister of justice and police and then as prime minister, who signalled clearly that the days were over when white citizens could take the law into their own hands against black citizens. In 1965 Vorster was asked by a delegate at the Orange Free State NP congress to reconsider the law of assault because farm labourers had become too easily inclined to lay a charge if their employers had given them 'a little slap'. Vorster replied as follows:

> I issue many licences but one licence I cannot issue and that is for one man to assault another. I cannot do what the resolution asks me by implication to do. One general principle we must always maintain in all circumstances: nobody has the right to assault anybody else. Congress has my assurance that, if such assaults take place, I and the police will act accordingly.[71]

Given the racial character of the state, it was unlikely that more than a small proportion of blacks who had been assaulted would lay charges. And in the courts equal justice remained a distant ideal. A study undertaken in the late 1960s of the perceptions of practising advocates found that half felt that a black person tried on a capital charge stood a stronger chance of being sentenced to death than a white. Of those holding this opinion 41 per cent believed that such differentiation was conscious and deliberate.[72] Nevertheless, the overall trend, however weak and incoherent at times, was in the direction of equality before the law of all citizens.

The leader and the apartheid institutions for blacks

Within Vorster's first five years in power all black representation in Parliament, the provincial legislatures and local government had been removed. The NP now saw the task at hand as making sure that the apartheid institutions created as substitutes would work. It was here that its policies failed most abysmally.

A steadily deteriorating relationship characterised the association between the NP leadership and the Coloured Persons Representative Council (CPRC), which operated between 1969 and 1980. The (Coloured) Labour Party's declared objective was to participate in the council only to destroy it. In response the government packed the council with nominated members to prevent Labour becoming the dominant party. In 1975 Labour succeeded in this objective, but its rejection of the council's budget was an impotent gesture of despair, for the government had the power to override it.

In the mid-1970s Vorster made a half-hearted effort to establish a consultative cabinet council which would be composed of the CPRC executive and an equal number of white cabinet ministers under the prime minister's chairmanship. The Labour Party rejected this and pressed for full representation in Parliament. Constitutionally the council would have created an impossible situation. As a recent study remarks: 'Cabinet council decisions would automatically be imposed on the CPRC. This raised the question, that if the Coloured members of the cabinet council had the final say in what laws would be made and what laws done away with, what was the purpose of debating the issues in the CPRC?'[73]

The Tricameral Parliament was an effort to transcend the substantive and symbolic weaknesses of the CPRC and the Indian Council. Although the houses sat separately to discuss their respective 'own affairs', the scope for Coloured and Indian participation was considerably widened, especially in joint committees and by the representation in cabinet of the leaders of the Indian and the Coloured houses. The Tricameral Parliament helped to break down the racially exclusive character of Parliament. However, it failed to transcend apartheid. By temperament Botha was not the kind of leader who was prepared to turn the system into a genuine form of consociational government, and Coloured power in the tricameral structure was too weak to force him to do so. Botha also wrongly assumed that Coloured people would accept a segregated position in the political system as a trade-off for the sectional advantage they had over the African 'outsiders'.[74] During a stormy session in the House of Representatives Botha exclaimed: 'Let me tell members something now: If it were not for [the] very Afrikaner and the National Party, the Coloured population would not be in the privileged position it is in today.'[75]

What Botha failed to realise was that the Coloured people had increasingly rejected their definition as a distinct group under the apartheid system. A study based on two surveys undertaken in 1976 and 1983 in the Cape Peninsula found a striking change in Coloured self-perception. In 1976 some 81 per cent considered themselves primarily Coloured; by 1983 this figure had dropped to 35 per cent. In 1976 less than 1 per cent thought of themselves as South Africans first of all, but by 1983 the proportion had risen to 49 per cent.[76] As South Africans they wanted a common citizenship in common institutions. Only once this was granted would they generate pressure as a communal group on the basis of self-association.

As far as Africans were concerned, both Vorster and Botha considered the homelands the keystone of apartheid. While Verwoerd put the emphasis on their separation from the white state, both Vorster and Botha tried to reincorporate them into some larger apartheid framework. In the first half of the 1970s Vorster convened a series of meetings with homeland leaders to discuss matters of common concern. These meetings were largely ineffectual and in 1976 the homeland leaders asked that full human rights be granted to black people, instead of mere concessions. It was the Soweto uprising of 1976 which greatly accelerated the disintegration of the apartheid system. Already in 1977 the process had gone so far that M.C. Botha, the minister responsible for the homelands, asked in a memorandum: 'Does the limitation of black numbers and a secondary status for blacks in white South Africa not remain our basic aim?'[77]

Under P.W. Botha the Verwoerdian goal of separate viable homeland economies was abandoned. In its place Botha announced a new regional economic strategy, transcending the borders of the republic and the homelands. Economic regions would be functionally defined to meet the requirements for economic development, and compensating growth points would be developed in the regions to counteract the powerful attraction of the large metropolitan areas. A development bank would play a key role in implementing the new plans for economic development.

However, this attempt to bring the segregated white and black institutions together failed to make much headway. No political dispensation could have a chance of even minimum black acceptance before the issue of a common South African citizenship was resolved. Secondly, the fact that some homelands were independent, while others (particularly KwaZulu) were not, created conflict among the homelands' leaders and made it all but impossible to bring them into a federation on an equal basis. Lastly, the fragile economies of the homelands demanded an increased commitment of resources to ensure that the building blocks of the government's projected confederation – the separate white and black homelands – did not disintegrate.[78]

De Klerk and the new South Africa: From imperial pretensions to minority group

F.W. de Klerk's normalisation of South African politics came as a great surprise to many outside observers, for he had been known as one of Botha's more conservative ministers. In NP deliberations over the constitution of 1983 he argued for diverting as many governmental functions as possible to the 'own affairs' (racially based administrative) machinery. When the tricameral constitution came into operation, De Klerk favoured retaining the racial sex laws for some time.

In retrospect there were indications from the early 1980s onwards that De Klerk displayed quite different characteristics from his predecessors. In the first place he was not subject to the personal delusions of power and grandeur that afflicted Botha in his last years in office. When he assumed the leadership of the NP in Transvaal in 1982, De Klerk stated: 'I want to commit myself to frank and reticent [beskeie] leadership. I want to be a leader who serves – not only on platforms but as one man to another [van mens tot mens], I want to be a leader of a team . . .'[79]

Secondly, De Klerk recognised better than Botha that time was running out for reaching an accommodation with the other groups in South Africa. In 1982 he declared: 'We do not want to live permanently in a state of siege in which hatred and blood reign supreme. If he wishes to survive, the white person will have to reveal the pioneering vision of his forefathers and create a future for himself which does not block the vision of the 25 million who are not white.'[80]

Finally, De Klerk's road was made easier by the fact that the NP decided in 1986 to accept the principle of a single citizenship and nationhood for all South Africans (except those living in the independent homelands). In the five years before his election as leader De Klerk carefully retained a balance in which he spoke both of own affairs and of a common destiny in shared political institutions. In 1986 he said: 'There is a new generation of educated black people, Coloured people and Indians. They want to be genuinely free.'[81]

Under Botha the government was still committed to race classification. The implication was that it wanted to construct the nation on the pillars of the four apartheid communities – Africans, whites, Coloureds and Indians. Under De Klerk the NP government moved away from group identities based on statutory classification. Minority rights as articulated by the NP leadership no longer had an explicitly racial dimension. There was no longer talk of white group rights but rather of rights which all minorities laid claim to, regardless of colour.

These claims as articulated by the NP fell into several broad categories. Firstly, there were its political claims, which stressed the need for multi-party competition, regular elections, power-sharing and representation of minorities at all levels of government. Secondly, there were economic claims. These ranged from a firm demand that property rights be inviolable to the insistence that the free-market system be retained and expanded. Thirdly, there were claims related to communal life and culture. For instance, the state should provide schools for each community on an equal basis, with parents having the option of sending their children to the school of their choice. Moreover, people should have the right to a separate community life, if they so wished, but without any statutory compulsion underpinning this. Fourthly, there were individual rights, such as freedom of speech and religion and of cultural expression, which would be protected by a bill of rights and an independent judiciary.

The NP articulated these demands and claims in terms of the project of nation-building. After the historic Groote Schuur talks in May 1990 between the government and a delegation from the ANC, Gerrit Viljoen, minister of constitutional development, remarked that while the NP did not question the principle of majority rule, it demanded to know whether stability and nation-building would be served by a majority governing all by itself. The NP's own conviction was that a common South African nationhood would best be promoted by the recognition of diversity.[82]

The NP was not alone in its concern for the protection of minority rights. Inkatha leader Mangosuthu Buthelezi warned that failure to provide minority group rights in a new South African constitution would 'invite a white backlash far worse than that inflicted by Unita and Renamo on Angola and Mozambique respectively'.[83] This warning showed the very high stakes involved. What was at issue was not a set of small, vulnerable minority groups asking for protection to ensure the survival of an endangered culture and way of life. In fact, there were powerful subnational groups with the capacity to wreck the economy and destroy any sense of a common citizenship and nationhood if they should find themselves in the position of a beleaguered minority.

Conclusion

In the 45 years since the NP's 1948 electoral victory, its leadership presided over the rise and the demise of the apartheid system. The tentative and fumbling efforts to construct the system in the 1950s were followed by the years of polit-ical hubris in the 1960s and 1970s. When South Africa entered a period of pro-longed economic stagnation in the mid-1970s, the leadership began to curb the overreach and excesses of the system. This tendency was accelerated by the ris-ing tide of black economic integration and resistance.

Citizenship was the core issue in the entire project of apartheid. During much of the apartheid era the NP leadership believed it could deflect black citi-zenship claims upon the state by introducing a separate political citizenship in the 'autonomous' states and other subordinate institutions. Yet for all the attempts to maintain a fiction of international relations with the homelands, the apartheid system was unable to continue to deny the reality of black citizen-ship and the demand for equal treatment by the state regardless of race.

10.

The broken heart of the Afrikaners

In 1947, the year in which the Afrikaans poet C. Louis Leipoldt died, he wrote a remarkable English poem entitled 'Chess in South Africa'.

> The much belauded Fool
> Looked wise
> And pondered what he saw:
> 'I think' he said, 'that if
> He tries
> White still might make a draw!'
>
> The Master smiled and
> Shook his head:
> 'You've left it all too late.
> There is no doubt of it' he said
> 'It's black to move and mate.'

The poem has been published only in John Kannemeyer's biography of Leipoldt.[1] Kannemeyer's own comment on the poem is the rather bland statement: 'clearly [the poem] has bearing on race relations on South Africa'. He also does not mention the poem in his authoritative *Die Afrikaanse literatuur in Suid-Afrika*. There is no reference to it in André Brink's three-volume anthology of Afrikaans poetry comprising 1 299 pages.

Predictions and warnings

Forgotten in the history of Afrikaans literature is the bleak prediction, made in
the late 1950s, by the premier Afrikaans novelist Etienne Leroux. He wrote to
the writer Jan Rabie, who had just published a searing indictment of apartheid
in his novel *Ons, die afgod* (We, the idol). Leroux wrote:

> And now, Jan, I'll tell you what will happen. Our god has been vanquished,
> the knight lies emasculated in the cellar, the foundation of the fortress begins
> to crumble and there are only three different outcomes possible:
> - to put on a sackcloth and step out to meet the enemy
> - to defend the fortress with blood, tears and shame
> - to withdraw and think back longingly about a glorious past while awaiting
>   the death-blow.

Leroux continues:

> To be honest I do not know if there is any solution. In fact, the word solu-
> tion is wrong. A natural process is unfolding: the substitution of one civilisa-
> tion by another, the supremacy of numbers. Who has the right to condemn
> the new civilisation? But who has the right to condemn a civilisation that is
> waning? Don't talk about justice. Rather talk about multi-colouredness and
> social dynamics, if you wish. I like the sentence in your letter: 'We are a
> young nation asked to do a superhuman thing: to recognise that our will to
> survive can contain something evil.'[2]

Like Graham Greene, the French politician and philosopher Jean-François Revel
visited Leroux on his farm in the Free State. Leroux, who was impressed by
Revel's book *Without Marx or Jesus* (1970), wrote to him:

> Africa is a puzzle. After years of colonial rule, really very little of the best of
> Pax Britannica, the French connection, the Flemish touch etc. remained. This
> is a Dark Continent in the Jungian sense. So much of the collective un-
> conscious is smouldering under the surface – a primordial racial memory
> that is trying to break through in new and meaningful symbols that can
> be reconciled with a world of the mind and technology and peaceful

co-existence in a materialistic sense. I do not know how the people of Africa will tame this Black Bitch – because Africa has a feminine darkness of things unknown, dangerous and creative . . .

When Robert Sobukwe mentioned to you that the whites are not realistic and when the whites (unknown) expressed the same belief with regard to 'reality' to you, they only expressed their wish for a universal conformity in terms of their 'tribal' beliefs. Africa has no inkling of democracy. Or the freedom of the individual. Africa's only claim to freedom lies in the fact that the rulers are allowed to be unpredictable.[3]

The great Afrikaans poet and essayist N.P. van Wyk Louw identified the defection of the intellectuals as one of the major survival crises of the Afrikaners. Writing in the early 1950s, he introduced the evocative phrase *'voortbestaan in geregtigheid'* – survival in justice – and insisted that national death might be preferable to a form of ethnic survival based on injustice.

His most important essay, 'Kultuur en krisis', first published in August 1952 in the popular magazine *Die Huisgenoot*, was triggered by the policy of the new NP government towards the Coloured people, which drove a deep wedge between the two communities. He refused to believe that this legislation was necessary for Afrikaner survival, but he did not voice any public criticism, particularly since he was teaching in Amsterdam in the Netherlands at that time. It was in this context that he wrote the haunting passages that would constantly echo in the Afrikaner debate about survival over the next four decades.

He identified three kinds of *volkskrisisse*, or national crises, which represent situations in which the Afrikaners' very existence was at stake.

- When the Afrikaners were overwhelmed by external military might or by the prospect of being 'ploughed under' by mass immigration, as some pro-British politicians proposed. Louw was referring to the defeat of the Boer republics at the hands of the British in the Anglo-Boer War of 1899–1902, and the subsequent attempt by Lord Milner to establish an English-speaking majority among the white population by way of state-sponsored mass immigration.

- When a great number of the Afrikaner people doubted in themselves 'whether we ought to survive as a *volk*'. Afrikaners might still
  survive individually and some might even prosper, but they would
  no longer constitute a distinctive *volk*: they 'would be absorbed in
  either an Anglo-Saxon or Bantu-speaking nation'.
- 'When some time in the future a great number of our people would
  come to believe that we need not live together *in justice* [Louw's
  emphasis] with other ethnic groups; when they come to believe that
  mere survival is the chief issue, not a just existence.'

Particularly in the third crisis, the response of a few intellectuals was critically
important. He did not believe that the Afrikaner *volk* had some metaphysical or
inherent right to continue to exist. The Afrikaners formed a small group of
people and their survival was at risk if a mere thousand among them, people
who 'were intelligent enough to *think*', gave up on the *volk*. This could happen
when the spiritual and cultural life of Afrikaners became too barren. It could
also happen if the Afrikaners maintained their dominant position by unacceptable means.

In a vivid passage he posed this question: 'Can a small *volk* survive for long,
if it becomes hateful, even evil, in the eyes of the best of its members and also
to people outside its fold?' The *volk*, he warned, ran the risk of the withdrawal
of allegiance by a critical number of intellectuals if it yielded to the 'final temptation' of abandoning the quest for 'survival in justice' and preferred 'mere survival'. In the case of a small *volk* like the Afrikaners, such defection could have
a fatal effect. But he did not despair that ultimately Afrikaner survival would
come to be based on moral values. As he phrased it: 'I believe that the greatest,
almost mystical crisis of a *volk* is that in which it is reborn and re-emerges
young and creative; the "dark night of the soul" in which it says: "I would rather
go down than survive in injustice."'[4]

The question is whether the views of these three can be considered as representative of the Afrikaners as a whole. Hennie Aucamp, perhaps the leading
short story writer in Afrikaans, makes an interesting distinction between the
political experiences of 'Boers' in the ex-republics and the 'Bolanders' in the south-
western Cape. Aucamp, who grew up on a farm in Dordrecht in the eastern Cape,

wrote that the history and ways of thinking of Afrikaners in the eastern Cape differed starkly from those of the Afrikaners in the Boland. During the Anglo-Boer War there was strong support for the Boers from some Afrikaner farmers in the eastern Cape Colony, which led to British soldiers ransacking the farms of suspected Boer supporters. The western Cape Afrikaners offered virtually no resistance to the British war effort.

In a short story, published in 1975, Aucamp tells how moved he was reading Johannes Meintjes's biography of President M.T. Steyn of the Republic of the Orange Free State. He explains why. 'We may in the near future yet again witness the death of the Boer – a death that may exact everything and even the death of that which is most treasured – the Boer's language.' He concluded: 'The Boer in the interior and the Afrikaners of the Boland are two different species. The Boland's beautiful mountains form the shield which keeps out the stink of the spilled blood of Boers in the war. That is why the Cape remains so Dutch, which in fact means British.'[5]

•

Stellenbosch University opened its doors in 1918 with a specific ideological purpose. Like the Victoria College, which preceded it, it wanted to become 'the emblem of a particular, vigorous, growing national life for the Afrikaners seeking to express itself . . . It stands for an idea.' The only vice-chancellor who interpreted this 'idea' in nationalist terms was H.B. Thom, who occupied the position from the mid-1950s to the mid-1960s. Only during his term could Stellenbosch University be described as a '*volksuniversiteit*'. But it is not only the founding idea that imposes an obligation on the university to use Afrikaans as language of instruction. Unlike the other Afrikaans-medium universities, it is located in an area where the majority of the population is Afrikaans-speaking. Lastly, there is the fact that in terms of admission to university and successful completion of studies the Coloured Afrikaans-speaking community, which forms the biggest language community in the province, scores lowest of all communities in the country.

Switching to English

If one surveys the fate of Afrikaans between 1998 and 2018 as a medium of instruction at tertiary level, one is struck by how little prepared the two largest

Afrikaans-medium universities were with respect to preserving Afrikaans. Van Wyk Louw warned that the very existence of Afrikaner people was imperilled if a thousand people in strategic positions gave up on being Afrikaners and on preserving Afrikaans as a medium of instruction.

In the early 1990s the Suid-Afrikaanse Akademie vir Wetenskap en Kuns submitted a memorandum to Dr Gerrit Viljoen, the NP's chief constitutional negotiator, on the measures required to preserve Afrikaans at university level. But Dr Viljoen had to retire for health reasons and his successor, Roelf Meyer, in response to an inquiry from the Akademie, replied that he knew nothing about such a document.

From 1998 the University of Pretoria introduced parallel-medium instruction without any undue pressure from government. The steady decline of Afrikaans at the university until its abolition as a medium of instruction eighteen years later was fairly predictable.

Stellenbosch University turned itself into an English-medium university in 2017. The role of the ANC government in the anglicisation of Stellenbosch University was only marginal. It did exert pressure but not of the kind that would cow any university council or management with a backbone. The truth is that the university for a variety of reasons willingly embraced the English language as the main medium of instruction, while at the same time relegating Afrikaans to an inferior position.

As I explain in my book *The Rise and Demise of the Afrikaners* (2019), the process started in the late 1980s. The trigger was the introduction of the ranking system that graded universities and lecturers predominantly in terms of their research output. Stellenbosch University was found to be far behind the University of Cape Town and Witwatersrand University and well below the University of the Orange Free State in this respect.

Firstly, the university appointed English-speakers with a good research record and put no real pressure on them to become sufficiently proficient in Afrikaans to be able to teach in it. Secondly, the administration offered no incentives to staff to publish in Afrikaans. The proportion of Stellenbosch University staff publishing scientific articles in Afrikaans was the lowest of all Afrikaans-medium universities.

In 2018 I attended a conference at Leuven University, Belgium, which is ranked among the top 50 universities in the world. Lecturers here were expected to become proficient in Dutch in order to teach in it. The organiser of the conference, who is a law professor at Leuven, stressed how important it is that universities provide special incentives for the staff to publish at least some of their scientific contributions in the national language.

Thirdly, there was at Stellenbosch no incentive for English-speaking students to become proficient enough to follow lectures in Afrikaans. The so-called T-option (using both Afrikaans and English as medium in the same lecture) was widely employed. Dr Van Zyl Slabbert, an alumnus who earlier had taught at Stellenbosch University, appropriately described this method as 'a pedagogic absurdity'.

While black students were flocking to the former liberal universities, many English-speaking students fled to Stellenbosch after being assured that they would be under no compulsion to become proficient in Afrikaans. They could simply wait for the lecturer to repeat in English what had been said in Afrikaans. After studying the Stellenbosch language policy, Jean Laponce, a French-Canadian authority on language displacement, predicted that 'Afrikaans would survive at Stellenbosch but only as a decoration'.

Fourthly, Stellenbosch University ignored studies that found Afrikaans-speaking students preferred Afrikaans-medium instruction. In 2007 the council authorised me to investigate student preferences by way of a poll conducted by a professional company and supervised by professional people. It was found that more than 80 per cent of Afrikaans students preferred the option of predominantly Afrikaans-medium instruction, while more than 40 per cent of English-language students said the same.

Instead of taking the poll seriously, the university greatly increased the intake of English-language students, both white and Coloured. From 2008 to 2017 the number of white English-speakers grew by more than a quarter, while that of Coloured English-speakers more than doubled. White Afrikaans-speakers declined by ten per cent and the number of Coloured Afrikaans-speakers only slightly improved. The numbers of African students who spoke either English at home or one of the nine official Bantu languages rose from 830 to over 2 300.

Overall the university increased its intake of undergraduates between 2003 and 2017 by nearly half from 13 875 to 19 880. During this period the number of white English-speaking students increased from 2 384 to 5 458 and that of Coloured English-speakers from 512 to 2 588. White Afrikaans-speakers dropped in this period from 8 210 to 6 926, while Coloured Afrikaans students increased from 1 329 in 2004 to 1 433 in 2017. The participation of Coloured Afrikaans-speaking students in tertiary education and in successfully completing their university studies is the lowest among all communities in the country. That Stellenbosch University is doing almost nothing about this constitutes the real betrayal that is being perpetrated by the Stellenbosch authorities and academics.

By 2017 most of the undergraduates were English-speaking. It was widely claimed that Afrikaans students indicated their preferred language of instruction as English in the hope of improving their chances of being admitted. It is still unclear why Stellenbosch University increased its total intake of undergraduates so dramatically between 2008 and 2017. An ex-vice-chancellor, who is considered an authority on the subject, expressed the view that as far as the state's subsidy formula goes, the optimum undergraduate number for Stellenbosch University is 10 000.

At Stellenbosch University the number of teaching staff who could not lecture in Afrikaans steadily increased. In 2016 the university was forced to admit in the Cape High Court that despite presenting itself as a bilingual university, a fifth of its lecturers were unable to teach in Afrikaans and that in the case of 268 modules the university violated its own language policy as specified in the University Yearbook.

Between 2002 and 2016 office-bearers at Stellenbosch University continued to assure the public that Afrikaans was safe at Stellenbosch. Having followed the process closely and having served as a council member for four years, I was prepared to testify in the 2016 court case that nowhere had I seen a university so blatantly misleading the public about a vital service it was offering as Stellenbosch University did with respect to its language policy.

The demise of Afrikaans?

What are the prospects for Afrikaans in general, now that there is only one Afrikaans campus (Potchefstroom) left among all 37 campuses in the country? A reply must take both the present 'consumption' of Afrikaans and the reproduction of a language community into account.

At the moment there still is a vibrant consumption of Afrikaans, measured in terms of the output of books, music, radio and television programmes, and the arts and literary festivals. By contrast, the prospects for the reproduction of an Afrikaans-speaking community are bleak. By reproduction I mean well-functioning Afrikaans-medium schools and universities capable of producing new generations of Afrikaans writers, poets, readers and listeners. With very few places where prospective Afrikaans-medium teachers can finish a degree and receive a teaching diploma in Afrikaans, more and more of the leading Afrikaans-medium secondary schools will become English-medium.

What is so heart-breaking about the demise of Afrikaans at Stellenbosch University is the leading role of Afrikaners (or, to use the more neutral term, white Afrikaans people) in the downgrading and marginalisation of Afrikaans. Many of the council members are white Afrikaans-speakers educated at Afrikaans schools and Afrikaans universities. But other members are on the university's payroll or are nominated by government or institutions that have no interest in preserving Afrikaans.

The first to defect was the business elite, who welcomed the new opportunities that have opened up after 1994. For them Afrikaans was dispensable. They saw the issue exclusively in market terms. Using English as the medium of instruction enlarges the pool from which the university can draw students and lecturers. A fundraiser told me that only a minute proportion of business people prepared to provide funding objected to the university becoming predominantly an English institution.

Joining the business elite in the support for English were white Afrikaans academics. To them the greatest threat was being forced to give their lectures in both languages without receiving extra remuneration. Among the Afrikaans-speaking staff who abandoned Afrikaans as a medium of instruction (or remained silent) were members of the Afrikaner Broederbond.

Writers' words

There were also highly respected people who expressed their opposition to the folly of Stellenbosch. In mid-2016, J.M. Coetzee, a Nobel Prize winner for literature, made the following observation in an email message: 'Universities have been fully absorbed into the neo-liberal economy. Young people don't think of them as cultural institutions any longer . . . The English language is not thought of as the bearer at a deep level of a particular Anglo-Saxon view of the world; it is thought of simply as medium of communication.' But Coetzee was prepared to take a stand on behalf of Afrikaans. After reading the submission of the executive committee of convocation of Stellenbosch University, which objected to the downscaling of Afrikaans, Coetzee wrote: 'My sympathies are all on your side. The crucial fact, for me, is that the official "Taalbeleid" document does not once use the word "kultuur". The university management seems to conceive of language as an instrumental communication system without any culture-bearing role.'[6]

What would the iconic Afrikaans writers mentioned at the start of this chapter have said about about Stellenbosch University's abandonment of Afrikaans? Leipoldt would probably have remarked that in a chess game in which Afrikaans and English are expected to play on the same field, English would win hands down and that this outcome was just a matter of time. Leroux would probably have seen the abandonment of Afrikaans in terms similar to those suggested in the third of his options for the Afrikaners: thinking back longingly about the glorious Afrikaans past 'while awaiting the death-blow'.

As an academic Van Wyk Louw would probably not be all that surprised by the 'treason of the intellectuals' at Stellenbosch. Today it is the system of ratings and rankings according to publication in English journals or books that is of paramount importance. There is also government pressure to transform the racial profile of the university. Stellenbosch University has never explained properly why it has failed to address the challenge of narrowing the huge gap between white and Coloured Afrikaans-speakers in the composition of the teaching staff and in the admission of students. The university's neglect of the Coloured Afrikaans-speaking community is shameful.

I wish to end by quoting an email message I received from Joan Kruger, a teacher at Paternoster on the West Coast.

> For me it is of particular importance to put the emphasis on instruction in the mother tongue. Here at Paternoster we are involved in the development of the reading skills of fishermen's children. What has happened at Stellenbosch University is to me a case of high treason perpetrated against

children of a rural community. Universities are there to serve communities. The university must not only teach them in their mother tongue but must also empower them to serve the community in Afrikaans to become teachers, librarians, bookkeepers, nurses . . . Why is that so difficult to understand?[7] Why indeed? One may ask.

Conclusion

If academics are allowed a fairly free hand, which is largely what Stellenbosch University's language policy enabled them to do between 2002 and 2017, many would pursue their own particular interests. For most of them it is finding the time for research and publishing their work – the key to promotion. Coming second or third are the interests of Afrikaans students and of the community out of which the university grew. And, of course, since its inception in 1918 Stellenbosch has most of the time been inordinately loyal to whatever regime rules the country.

Books by Hermann Giliomee

ENDNOTES

Part One: An Exceptional History and the Growth of a Maverick Community

1. Charles Feinstein, *An Economic History of South Africa: Conquest, Discrimination and Development* (Cambridge: Cambridge University Press, 2005), pp. 1–3.
2. O. Schreiner, *Thoughts on South Africa* (London, 1923; reprinted Johannesburg: Ad Donker, 1992), p. 175.
3. This is drawn from Olive Schreiner's 1890 essay 'The Boer Woman and the Modern Woman's Question' in *Thoughts on South Africa*, pp. 168–93.
4. P.J. van der Merwe, *Die noordwaartse beweging van die Boere voor die Groot Trek, 1770–1842* (The Hague: Van Stockum, 1937), p. 52.
5. Hermann Giliomee, *Die Kaap tydens die Eerste Bewind, 1795–1803* (Cape Town: HAUM, 1975), pp. 266–7.
6. P.J. van der Merwe, *Die Noordwaartse Beweging van die Boere voor die Groot Trek, 1770–1842* (Den Haag: Van Stockum, 1937) p.p.52; Hermann Giliomee, *Die Kaap tydens die eerste Britse Bewind* ((Cape Town: HAUM, 1975), pp.266–67.
7. Van der Merwe, *Noordwaartse beweging*, pp. 78–9.
8. Robert Ross, 'The Rise of the Cape Gentry', *Journal of Southern African Studies*, vol. 9, no. 2 (1983); Leonard Guelke, 'Freehold Farmers and Frontier Settlers', Richard Elphick and Hermann Giliomee (eds.), *The Shaping of South African Society, 1652–1840* (Cape Town: Maskew Miller, 1989), pp. 80–94.
9. C.W. de Kiewiet, *A History of South Africa: Social and Economic* (London: Oxford University Press, 1941), p. 17.
10. Timothy Keegan, 'The Making of the Orange Free State, 1846–1854', *Journal of Imperial and Commonwealth History*, 17,1, 1988; Timothy Keegan, *Colonial South Africa and the Origins of the Racial Order* (Cape Town: David Philip, 1996).
11. James Bryce, *Impressions of South Africa* (London: Macmillan, 1899), p.314.
12. Leonard Thompson, 'Constitutionalism in the South African Republics', *Butterworths South African Law Review*, vol. 1, 1954, pp. 50–71.
13. C.T. Gordon, *The Growth of the Boer opposition to Kruger, 1890–1899* (Cape Town: Oxford University Press, 1970), p. 10.
14. J.H. Hofmeyr, 'Introduction' in Edgar Brookes et al. (eds.), *Coming of Age: Studies in South African Politics and Citizenship* (Cape Town: Maskew Miller, 1930), pp. 6–9.

15. Jon Lewis, 'The Germiston By-Election of 1932', in P. Bonner (ed.), *Working Papers in Southern African Studies* (Johannesburg: Ravan Press, 1981), pp. 97–120.

1. 'Allowed Such a State of Freedom': Women and Gender Relations in the Afrikaner Community before Enfranchisement in 1930

1. From the late eighteenth century the term 'Afrikaners' was widely used for colonists of Dutch, German and French descent. During the nineteenth century the term was sometimes restricted to white Dutch or Afrikaans-speaking people living in towns, while the farming population was called Boers. To simplify matters, I refer to all white colonists who spoke Dutch or a form of Dutch as Afrikaners.

2. Karel Schoeman's biographies include *Olive Schreiner: 'n Lewe in Suid-Afrika, 1855–1881* (1989); *Die wêreld van Susanna Smit, 1799–1863* (1995); *Dogter van Sion: Machtelt Smit en die 18de-eeuse samelewing aan die Kaap, 1749–1799* (1997); and *Armosyn van die Kaap: Die wêreld van 'n slavin, 1652–1733* (2001). All were published by Human and Rousseau in Cape Town.

3. I wish to thank especially Andreas van Wyk, whose work on the legal position of Afrikaner women under Roman-Dutch law has opened up a fundamentally new perspective.

4. M. Waller, *The English Marriage* (London: John Murray, 2010), back cover.

5. E. Morgan, 'Subject Women', *New York Review of Books*, 31 October 1996, p. 67. Morgan discusses here the following books: C. Berkin, *First Generation: Women in Colonial America* (New York: Hill and Wang, 1996) and M.B. Norton, *Founding Mothers and Fathers: Gendered Power and the Forming of American Society* (New York: Knopf, 1996).

6. I wish to thank Margaret Lenta for some of the points in this paragraph.

7. J. Israel, 'A Great, Neglected Victory', *New York Review of Books,* 8 April 2010, p. 44. See also S. Schama, *An Embarrassment of Riches: An Interpretation of Dutch Culture in the Golden Age* (London: Fontana, 1987), pp. 405–6.

8. L. Guelke, 'Freehold Farmers and Frontier Settlers', in R. Elphick and H. Giliomee (eds.), *The Shaping of South African Society* (Middletown: Wesleyan University Press, 1988), p. 81.

9. W. Dooling, *Slavery, Emancipation, and Colonial Rule in South Africa* (Pietermaritzburg: University of KwaZulu-Natal Press, 2007), pp. 31–41.

10. Tannie Sannie, a crass character in Olive Schreiner's *The Story of an African Farm*, had inherited a farm from her deceased husband, and was planning to marry a young man in a loveless match. See also R. Shell, *Children of Bondage: A Social History of the Slave Society at the Cape of Good Hope* (Johannesburg: University of Witwatersrand Press, 1994), pp. 289–92.

11. A.H. van Wyk, 'The Power to Dispose of Assets of the Universal Matrimonial Community of Property: A Study in South African Law with Excursions on the Laws of Brazil and the Netherlands', PhD thesis, Leiden University, 1976, pp. 110, 195–213, 262.

12. P. van Heerden, *Die sestiende koppie* (Cape Town: Tafelberg, 1965), p. 7.

13. K. Schoeman, *Armosyn van die Kaap: voorspel tot vestiging, 1415–1651* (Cape Town: Human and Rousseau, 1999), pp. 251–4.

14. C.P. Thunberg, *Travels at the Cape of Good Hope, 1772–1775* (Cape Town: Van Riebeeck Society, 1986), p. 36.

15. F. Valentyn, *Description of the Cape of Good Hope, 1726* (Cape Town: Van Riebeeck Society, 1971), p. 209.

16. P. Coertzen, *Die Hugenote van Suid-Afrika* (Cape Town: Tafelberg, 1988), p. 94.

17. Email communication of author with H.C. Viljoen, chairman of the Huguenot Society of South Africa, 5 August 2010. A fairly comprehensive list of South African *stamvaders* and *stammoeders* can be found at http.www.stamouers.com.

18. G.D. Scholtz, *Die ontwikkeling van die politieke denke van die Afrikaner* (Johannesburg: Voortrekkerpers, 1967), vol. 1, p. 241.

19. D. Visser, 'Die beveiliging van die Kaap teen binnelandse bedreiging', in C. de Wet, C. Hattingh and J. Visagie (eds.), *Die VOC aan die Kaap, 1652–1795* (Pretoria: Protea, 2017), p. 219.

20. J.A. Heese, *Die herkoms van die Afrikaner* (Cape Town: Balkema, 1971).

21. H.F. Heese, *Groep sonder grense: die rol en status van die gemengde bevolking aan die Kaap, 1652–1795* (Bellville: University of the Western Cape Institute for Historical Research, 1984); J.L. Hattingh, 'Die blanke nageslag van Louis van Bengale en Lijsbeth van de Kaap', *Kronos*, 3 (1980), pp. 5–51.

22. Heese, *Groep sonder grense*, pp. 6, 20–1, 41, 45, 53, 54.

23. K. Schoeman, *Dogter van Sion: Machtelt Smit en die 18de-eeuse samelewing aan die Kaap, 1749–1799* (Cape Town: Human and Rousseau, 1997), pp. 51–6.

24. O.F. Mentzel, *Description of the Cape of Good Hope* (Cape Town: Van Riebeeck Society, 1944) vol. 3, pp. 58, 103, 112–13, 120.

25. Mentzel, *Description of the Cape*, vol. 3, p. 120.

26. R. Semple, *Walks and Sketches at the Cape of Good Hope* (Cape Town: Balkema, 1968 [1803]), pp. 31–2.

27. F. MacCarthy, 'The First Feminist', *New York Review of Books*, 1 December 2005, p. 56. Wollstonecraft lived from 1759 to 1797.

28. Shell, *Children of Bondage*, pp. 289–329.

29. Semple, *Walks and Sketches*, p. 30.

30. Andrew Bank argues that Shell exaggerates the incidence of wet-nursing. See his 'Slavery without Slaves', *South African Historical Journal*, 33 (1995), pp. 190–1.

31. R. Shell, '"Tender Ties": The Women of the Cape Slave Society', *Societies of Southern Africa*, papers presented at the Institute of Commonwealth Studies, University of London, vol. 17 (1992), p. 14.

32. Mentzel, *Description*, vol. 3, p. 120.

33. G. Botha, *Social Life in the Cape Colony* (Cape Town: Struik, 1973), pp. 50–1.

34. Schama, *Embarrassment of Riches*, p. 406.

35. Semple, *Walks and Sketches*, p. 28.

36. N. Penn, *Rogues, Rebels and Runaways: Eighteenth-Century Cape Characters* (Cape Town: David Philip, 1999), pp. 9–12.

37. J. Mason, '"Fit for Freedom": The Slaves, Slavery and Emancipation in the Cape Colony, South Africa', PhD thesis, Yale University, 1992, p. 215.

38. P. van der Spuy, '"Making Himself Master": Galant's Rebellion Revisited', *South African Historical Journal*, 34 (May 1996), pp. 20–1.

39. G. Freyre, *The Masters and Slaves: A Study in the Development of Brazilian Civilization* (New York: Knopf, 1956), p. 349.

40. Mentzel, *Description*, vol. 2, pp. 109–10.

41. Mentzel, *Description*, vol. 3, p. 115.

42. H. Giliomee, *The Afrikaners: Biography of a People* (Cape Town: Tafelberg, 2009), pp. 33–4.

43. R. Elphick and H. Giliomee, 'The Origins and Entrenchment of European Dominance at the Cape', in Elphick and Giliomee (eds.), *The Shaping of South African Society*, pp. 521–66.

44. Ibid., p. 525.

45. R. Percival, *An Account of the Cape of Good Hope* (London, 1804), pp. 286–92.

46. H. Giliomee and R. Elphick, 'The Structure of European Domination at the Cape, 1652–1820' in Elphick and Giliomee (eds.), *The Shaping of South African Society, 1652–1820* (Cape Town: Longman, 1979), p. 374.

47. L. Guelke, 'The Anatomy of a Colonial Settler Population, 1657–1750', *International Journal of African Historical Studies*, 21, 3 (1988), pp. 462–63.

48. For a further five per cent of the sample, one of the grandparents was of unknown (and possibly European) descent. See G.F.C. de Bruyn, 'Die samestelling van die Afrikaner', *Tydskrif vir Geesteswetenskappe*, 16, 1 (1976) and personal communication; Heese, *Die herkoms van die Afrikaner*, and personal communications.

49. G.C. de Wet (ed.), *Resolusies van die Politieke Raad, vol 10: 1740–43* (Pretoria: Government Printer, 1984), p 226; *De Gereformeerde Kerkbode 1854*, pp. 11, 169.

50. A.W. Biewenga, 'De Kaap de Goede Hoop, een Nederlandse vestigingskolonie, 1680–1730', PhD thesis, Vrije Universiteit, 1998, pp. 174–82.

51. H. Lichtenstein, *Travels in South Africa, 1803–1805* (Cape Town: Van Riebeeck Society, 1928), vol. 1, p. 116.

52. Biewenga, 'De Kaap de Goede Hoop', p. 180.

53. P.B. Borcherds, *An Autobiographical Memoir* (Cape Town: African Connoisseurs Press, 1963 [1861]), pp. 196–7.

54. P.J. van der Merwe, *The Migrant Farmer in the History of the Cape Colony, 1657–1842* (Athens, OH: Ohio University Press, 1995), p. 166.

55. R. Shell, 'The Family and Slavery at the Cape, 1680–1808', in Wilmot James and Mary Simons (eds.), *The Angry Divide: Social and Economic History of the Western Cape* (Cape Town: David Philip, 1989), p. 24.

56. S. Trapido, 'Household Prayers, Paternalism and the Fostering of a Settler Identity', paper presented at LSE, London, 8 December 2000.

57. Anonymous [W.W. Bird], *State of the Cape of Good Hope in 1822* (London: John Murray, 1823), p. 74. The complex intimacy and tensions in the paternalistic relationship between a white woman and her servant during the apartheid years are sensitively portrayed in Marlene van Niekerk's novel *Agaat* (2006).

58. See particularly Shell, *Children of Bondage* and P. Scully, 'Liberating the Family? Gender, Labour and Sexuality in the Western Cape, South Africa', PhD thesis, University of Wisconsin, 1993.

59. E. Genovese, *Roll, Jordan. Roll: The World the Slaves Made* (London: André Deutsch, 1974), p. 364.

60. Genovese, *Roll, Jordan, Roll*, p. 363.

61. Shell, *Children of Bondage*, p. 53.

62. C.F.J. Muller, *Die oorsprong van die Groot Trek* (Cape Town: Tafelberg), pp. 371–3; J.C. Visagie, 'Die Katriviernedersetting, 1829–1839', PhD thesis, Unisa, 1978, p. 323; J.C. Visagie, *Die trek uit Oos-Rietrivier* (Stellenbosch: Private publication, 1989), p. 55.

63. J.C. Visagie, *Voortrekkerstamouers* (Pretoria: Unisa, 2000); interview with J.C. Visagie, 7 August 2010.

64. *Die dagboek van Anna Steenkamp* (Pietermaritzburg: Natalse Pers, 1937), p. 47.

65. O. Schreiner, *Thoughts on South Africa* (London, 1923; reprinted Johannesburg: Ad Donker, 1992), p. 235.

66. E.A. Walker, *A History of Southern Africa* (London: Longmans Green, 1957), p. 200.

67. K. Schoeman, *Die wêreld van Susanna Smit, 1799–1863* (Cape Town: Human and Rousseau, 1995), p. 113.

68. She was the sister of Gert Maritz, who at the time was chairman of the Volksraad, and the wife of Erasmus Smit. He was not an ordained minister but a missionary-cum-teacher. The couple were in a precarious financial and social position.

69. This section on the meeting in Pietermaritzburg is based on Schoeman, *Die wêreld van Susanna Smit*, pp. 112–59.

70. J. Markoff, 'Origins, Centers, and Democracy: The Paradigmatic History of Women's Suffrage', *Signs: Journal of Women in Culture and Society*, 29, 1 (2003).

71. Schreiner, *Thoughts on South Africa*, p. 176.

72. Ibid., p. 175.

73. This is drawn from Olive Schreiner's 1890 essay 'The Boer Woman and the Modern Woman's Question' in *Thoughts on South Africa*, pp. 168–93.

74. Schreiner, *Thoughts on South Africa*, p.175.

75. H. Bradford, 'Gentlemen and Boers: Afrikaner Nationalism and Colonial Warfare in the South African War', in G. Cuthbertson et al. (eds.), *Writing a Wider War: Rethinking Gender, Race and Identity in the South African War* (Cape Town: David Philip, 2002), pp. 44–55.

76. Cited by Bradford, 'Gentlemen and Boers', p. 47; A.M. Grundlingh, *Die 'Hendsoppers' en 'Joiners': die rasionaal en verskynsel van verraad* (Pretoria: HAUM, 1979), p. 142.

77. S.B. Spies, 'Women and the War', in Peter Warwick (ed.), *The South African War* (London: Longman, 1980), p. 168.

78. M. Marquard, *Letters from a Boer Parsonage* (Cape Town: Purnell, 1967), p. 78.

79. Grundlingh, *'Hendsoppers' en 'Joiners'*, p. 142.

80. J.R. MacDonald, *What I Saw in South Africa* (London: The Echo, 1902), p. 24.

81. M.A. Fischer, *Tant Miem Fischer se kampdagboek, 1901–1902* (Cape Town: Tafelberg, 1964), p. 32.

82. H. Bradford, 'Gendering Afrikaner Nationalism', unpublished paper, p. 10; Marquard, *Letters*, p. 39.

83. Scholtz, *Die ontwikkeling van die politieke denke van die Afrikaner*, vol. 5, p. 101.

84. A. Grundlingh, 'The National Women's Movement', in Cuthbertson et al. (eds.), *Writing a Wider War*, pp. 22–5.

85. For a stimulating experience from a gender perspective, see Bradford, 'Gentlemen and Boers', pp. 37–66.

86. W.K. Hancock and J. van der Poel, *Smuts Papers* (Cambridge: Cambridge University Press, 1966), vol. 1, p. 469.

87. *Hertzog-toesprake, 1900–1942* (Johannesburg: Perskor, 1977), vol. 3, pp. 232, 246, 257.

88. A. Grundlingh and S. Swart, *Radelose rebellie: dinamika in die 1914–15 Afrikanerrebellie* (Pretoria: Protea Boekhuis, 2009), pp. 63–4.

89. Grundlingh, *'Hendsoppers' en 'Joiners*, p. 142.

90. Dooling, *Slavery, Emancipation and Colonial Rule*, p. 36.

91. J.J.F. Joubert, 'Die geskiedenis van Bloemhof', MEd dissertation, University of Stellenbosch, 1945, p. 10.

92. University of Stellenbosch Library, Manuscripts Collection, M.E. Rothmann Papers, Speech given to Women's Enfranchisement League, 1926: MER, *My beskeie deel* (Cape Town: Tafelberg, 1972), pp. 58–62.

93. I.H. Weder, 'Die geskiedenis van die opvoeding van meisies in Suid-Afrika tot 1910', MEd thesis, University of Stellenbosch, 1938, pp. 104–5.

94. T. Mayer (ed.), *Gender Ironies of Nationalism: Sexing the Nation* (London: Routledge, 2000), pp. 1–24.

95. S.J. du Toit, *Nehemia as volkshervormer* (Paarl: D.F. du Toit, 1985), p. 19.

96. E. Britz and D. Pienaar, 'Die representatie van die vrou in die verse van die Eerste Afrikaanse Taalbeweging', *Stilet*, 16, 2 (2002), pp. 217–38.

97. M. du Toit, 'The Domesticity of Afrikaner Nationalism: Volksmoeders and the ACVV, 1904–1929', *Journal of Southern African Studies*, 29, 1 (2003), p. 175.

98. J.L. McCracken, *The Cape Parliament, 1854–1910* (Oxford: Clarendon Press, 1967), p. 29.

99. L.M. Thompson, *The Unification of South Africa* (Oxford: Clarendon Press, 1960), p. 344.

100. K. Schoeman, *In liefde en trou: Die Lewe van Pres. en Mev. M.T. Steyn* (Cape Town: Tafelberg, 1983), p. 124.

101. S.B. Spies, 'Women and the War', in Warwick (ed.), *The South African War*, p. 162.

102. O. Schreiner, *Women and Labour* (London: T. Fisher Unwin, 1911), pp. 13–14.

103. J.C. Steyn, *Die honderd jaar van MER* (Cape Town: Tafelberg, 2004), pp.177–80; MER, *My beskeie deel*, p. 226.

104. L. Vincent, 'Afrikaner Nationalist Women's Parties', *South African Historical Journal*, 40 (1999), p. 84.

2. Afrikaner Frontiers

1. The term 'Afrikaner' is used somewhat anachronistically since the frontiersmen did not consistently and self-consciously refer to themselves as Afrikaners. But it is more convenient to use this term than something like 'Dutch-Afrikaner settlers'.

2. Gerrit Harinck, 'Interaction between Xhosa and Khoi: Emphasis on the Period 1620–1750', in L. Thompson (ed.), *African Societies in Southern Africa* (London: Heinemann, 1969), pp. 145–69; J.B. Peires, 'A History of the Xhosa, c.1700–1835', MA thesis, Rhodes University, 1976, pp. 81–4, 105–6.

3. Charles C. Ballard, 'The Natal Frontier Experience: A Case Study of Cultural and Political Change', paper presented to the Association for Sociology in Southern Africa, Maseru, 26–28 June 1979.

4. R.G. Wagner, 'Coenraad de Buys in Transorangia', in *The Societies of Southern Africa in the 19th and 20th Centuries* (University of London, Institute of Commonwealth Studies), vol. 4, pp. 1–8.

5. I have discussed this in detail in 'The Eastern Frontier, 1770–1812', in Richard Elphick and Hermann Giliomee (eds.), *The Shaping of South African Society, 1652–1820* (Cape Town: Maskew Miller, 1979), pp. 291–337.

6. Martin Legassick, 'The Griqua, the Sotho-Tswana and the Missionaries, 1780–1840: The Politics of a Frontier Zone', PhD thesis, University of California, Los Angeles, 1969, pp. 2–3.

See also his chapter 'The Northern Frontier to 1820: The Emergence of the Griqua People', in Elphick and Giliomee, *The Shaping of South African Society*, pp. 243–90.

7. Leonard Guelke, 'The White Settlers, 1652–1780', in Elphick and Giliomee, *The Shaping of Southern African Society*, p. 49.

8. Ibid., pp. 57, 64. For a fuller discussion, see Leonard Guelke, 'The Early European Settlement of South Africa', Ph.D thesis, University of Toronto, 1974. In Afrikaans there are the classic studies of P.J. van der Merwe, *Die trekboer in die geskiedenis van die Kaapkolonie, 1657–1842* (Cape Town: Nasionale Pers, 1938) and *Trek: studies oor die mobiliteit van die pioniersbevolking aan die Kaap* (Cape Town: Nasionale Pers, 1945). More controversial is S.D. Neumark, *Economic Influences on the South African Frontier* (Stanford: Stanford University Press, 1957).

9. J.F.W. Grosskopf, 'Rural Impoverishment and Rural Exodus', in Report of the Carnegie Commission, *The Poor White Problem in South Africa*, 5 vols. (Stellenbosch: Pro Ecclesia, 1932), vol. 1, pp. 35–6; Van der Merwe, *Trek*, pp. 43–61, 99–106.

10. For an elaboration of this argument, see Leonard Guelke, 'European Expansion and the Meaning of Frontier Settlement', paper presented to an international conference for historical geographers, Los Angeles, 1979, pp. 4–5.

11. Cited by Van der Merwe, *Die Trekboer*, p. 185.

12. Report of the Commission of Circuit, 28 February 1812, in G.M. Theal, *Records of the Cape Colony*, 36 vols. (London, 1897–1905), vol. 8, pp. 298–9.

13. Grosskopf, *Rural Impoverishment and Rural Exodus*, p. 38.

14. Guelke, 'The Early European Settlement', p. 313.

15. Giliomee, 'The Eastern Frontier', in Elphick and Giliomee, *The Shaping of South African Society*, p. 300. The statement by the Khoikhoi client is in D. Moodie, 'Deposition of Platje Swartland, c.1836', *Afschriften*, vol. 11.

16. See also the analysis of Khoikhoi cultural change in the south-western Cape by Richard Elphick in his *Kraal and Castle: Khoikhoi and the Founding of White South Africa* (New Haven: Yale University Press, 1977), pp. 179–81.

17. H.W. Struben, *Recollections of Adventures* (Cape Town, 1920), p. 86. This section on the Soutpansberg is based on an illuminating study by R. Wagner, 'Soutpansberg: The Dynamics of a Hunting Frontier, 1848– 1867', in A. Atmore and S. Marks (eds.), *Economy and Society in Pre-Industrial South Africa* (London: Longman, 1980).

18. Hermann Giliomee, *Die Kaap tydens die Eerste Britse Bewind, 1795–1803* (Cape Town: HAUM, 1975), pp. 258–9.

19. For a selection of documents which illustrate attitudes toward labour, see André du Toit and Hermann Giliomee (eds.), *Afrikaner Political Thought, 1780–1854* (Berkeley: University of California Press, 1981), ch. 2. The relationship which existed until very recently between the 'farm Bushmen' of the Ghanzi district of Botswana and the Afrikaner farmers is strongly reminiscent of that which existed on the pioneering frontier. For an analysis, see Margo Russell, 'Slaves or Workers? Relations between Bushmen, Tswana and Boers in the Kalahari', *Journal of Southern African Studies*, 2, 3 (1976), pp. 178–97; Mathias G. Guenther, 'Bushmen Hunters as Farm Labourers', *Canadian Journal of African Studies*, 11, 2 (1977), pp. 195–203.

20. Cited by B.J. Liebenberg, *Andries Pretorius in Natal* (Pretoria and Cape Town: Academica, 1977), p. 117.

21. This is a controversial issue in South African historiography. See the argument of P.J. van der Merwe, *Die noordwaartse beweging van die Boere voor die Groot Trek, 1770–1842* (The Hague: Van Stockum, 1937), pp. 168–75.

22. Liebenberg, *Andries Pretorius in Natal*, pp. 117–20.

23. For indentureship, see W. Kistner, 'The Anti-Slavery Agitation against the Transvaal Republic, 1852–1868', *Archives Year Book for South African History (1952)*, vol. 2, pp. 226–43; J.A.I. Agar-Hamilton, *The Native Policy of the Voortrekkers: An Essay in the History of the Interior of South Africa, 1836–1858* (Cape Town: Maskew Miller, 1928), pp. 164–95; Stanley Trapido, 'Aspects in the Transition from Slavery to Serfdom: The South African Republic, 1842–1902', *Societies of Southern Africa*, vol. 6 (1976), pp. 24–31.

24. See Du Toit and Giliomee, *Afrikaner Political Thought*.

25. Ibid.

26. See especially J.P.F. Moolman, 'Die Boer se siening van en houding teenoor die Bantoe in Transvaal tot 1880', MA thesis, University of Pretoria, 1975, pp. 30–51, 70–89, 122.

27. Cited in J.D. Huyser, 'Die Naturelle-politiek van die Suid-Afrikaanse Republiek', DLitt thesis, University of Pretoria, 1936, p. 235.

28. For a fuller exposition, see Hermann Giliomee and Richard Elphick, 'The Structure of European Domination at the Cape, 1652–1820', in Elphick and Giliomee, *The Shaping of South African Society*, pp. 359–86.

29. This is well argued in Guelke, 'European Expansion'.

30. Giliomee, 'The Eastern Frontier', p. 298.

31. Alden T. Vaughan, *New England Frontier: Puritans and Indians, 1620–1675* (Boston: Little, Brown, 1965), p. 62.

32. This argument is expanded in Giliomee and Elphick, 'The Structure of European Domination', pp. 359–86.

33. Martin Legassick, 'The Frontier Tradition in South African Historiography', *Societies of Southern Africa*, vol. 2 (1971), p. 19.

34. D.G. van Reenen, *Die joernaal van Dirk Gysbert van Reenen*, ed. W. Blommaert and J.A. Wiid (Cape Town: Van Riebeeck Society, 1937), p. 209.

35. Wagner, 'Soutpansberg'. For another case study, see Philip Bonner, 'Factions and Fissions: Transvaal–Swazi Politics in the Mid-Nineteenth Century', paper for the Biennial Conference of the South African Historical Society, Cape Town, 1977.

36. Coenraad Beyers, *Die Kaapse Patriotte* (Pretoria: Van Schaik, 1967), p. 326.

37. Hermann Giliomee, 'The Burgher Rebellions on the Eastern Frontier, 1795–1815', in Elphick and Giliomee, *The Shaping of South African Society*, pp. 348–54.

38. Leonard Thompson, *Survival in Two Worlds: Moshoeshoe of Lesotho, 1786–1870* (Oxford: Oxford University Press, 1975), pp. 142–4, 236–7.

39. Wagner, 'Soutpansberg'; see also Legassick, 'The Frontier Tradition', pp. 18–19.

40. Allen Isaacman and Barbara Isaacman, 'The Prazeros as Transfrontiersmen: A Study in Society and Cultural Change', *International Journal of African Historical Studies*, 8, 1 (1975), pp. 1–39.

41. For a discussion of such an Afrikaner society, see W.G. Clarence-Smith, 'The Thirst-land Trekkers in Angola', *Societies of Southern Africa*, vol. 6 (1976), pp. 42–51. See also Alistair Hennessy, *The Frontier in Latin American History* (London: Edward Arnold, 1978), pp. 19–25, 43–5.

42. David M. Potter, *People of Plenty: Economic Abundance and the American Character* (Chicago: University of Chicago Press, 1954).

43. Monica Wilson, 'The Growth of Peasant Communities', in Monica Wilson and Leonard Thompson (eds.), *Oxford History of South Africa*, 2 vols. (Oxford: Clarendon Press, 1969–71), vol. 2, pp. 49–72.

44. W.S. van Ryneveld, 'Beschouwing', *Het Nederduitsch Zuid-Afrikaansch Tydschrift*, 8, 4 (1831), p. 293.

45. John Barrow, *Travels into the Interior of Southern Africa*, 2 vols. (London: Cadell and Davies, 1806), vol. 2, p. 331.

46. Guelke, 'The Early European Settlement', p. 260.

47. See the exchange between William Norton and Leonard Guelke on subsistence and commercial farming, in *Annals of the Association of American Geographers*, 67, 3 (September 1977), pp. 463–7. Norton points out that a fundamental difference between the North American and the southern African experiences is the willingness of southern African settlers to locate on farms at distances from markets not compatible with commercial development. Guelke explains that in doing this the southern African settlers were not acting in a 'noneconomic' way. The frontier offered people without much capital a reasonable subsistence, generally outside the exchange economy, combined with a measure of independence which many found preferable to wage labour.

48. Cape Archives, Acc. 447, pp. 21–4.

49. Giliomee, 'The Eastern Frontier', p. 317; Van der Merwe, *Trek*, pp. 54–5.

50. D. Moodie, *The Record; or, A Series of Official Papers Relative to the Condition and Treatment of the Native Tribes of South Africa*, 5 vols. (Cape Town, 1838–42), vol. 5, pp. 23–6 (Report of Colonel Collins, 1809).

51. *Records of the Cape Colony*, vol. 23, p. 196 (Report of the Commissioners of Enquiry, 30 September 1825).

52. Gubbins Collection, University of Witwatersrand, Replies to questions on the importation of slaves by W.S. van Ryneveld, 29 November 1797.

53. Cape Archives, GR 6/15, Stockenström – Plasket, 1 December 1825.

54. *Records of the Cape Colony*, vol. 8, p. 299 (Report of the Commission of Circuit, 28 February 1812).

55. A. Steedman, *Wanderings and Adventures in the Interior of Southern Africa*, 2 vols. (London, 1835), vol. 1, p. 124.

56. H.B. Thom, *Die geskiedenis van die skaapboerdery in Suid-Afrika (Amsterdam:* Swets and Zeitlinger, 1936), pp. 272–330.

57. For a full and perceptive analysis of Graaff-Reinet, see Kenneth Wyndham Smith, 'From Frontier to Midlands: A History of the Graaff-Reinet District, 1786–1910', DPhil thesis, Rhodes University, 1974, pp. 115–17 (published as Occasional Paper no. 20, Rhodes University Institute of Social and Economic Research, 1976).

58. Ibid., p. 125.

59. D. Hobart Houghton, 'Economic Development, 1865–1965', in Wilson and Thompson, *Oxford History of South Africa*, vol. 2, p. 4.

60. Robert Ross, *Adam Kok's Griquas: A Study in the Development of Stratification in South Africa* (Cambridge: Cambridge University Press, 1976).

61. G.J. Lamprecht, 'Die ekonomiese ontwikkeling van die Vrystaat van 1870 tot 1899', DPhil thesis, University of Stellenbosch, 1954.

62. Cited in ibid., p. 33.

63. Hennessy, *The Frontier in Latin American History*, p. 48.

64. For detailed discussions, see F. J. Potgieter, 'Die vestiging van die Blanke in Transvaal (1837–1886) met spesiale verwysing na die verhouding tussen die mens en die omgewing', *Archives Year Book for South African History* (1958), vol. 2, pp. 1–208; A.N. Pelzer, *Geskiedenis van die Suid-Afrikaanse Republiek: wordingsjare* (Cape Town: Balkema, 1950); R. Cornwell, 'Land and Politics in the Transvaal in the 1880s', *Societies of Southern Africa*, vol. 4 (1974), pp. 29–40.

65. Francis Wilson, 'Farming, 1866–1966', in Wilson and Thompson, *Oxford History of South Africa*, vol. 2, p. 123.

66. Cornwell, 'Land and Politics', p. 30.

67. D.M. Goodfellow, *A Modern Economic History of South Africa* (London: George Routledge, 1931), pp. 132–3.

68. For an unconvincing attempt to explain this phenomenon by portraying the Afrikaners as prisoners of their culture, see Randall G. Stokes, 'Afrikaner Calvinism and Economic Action: The Weberian Thesis in South Africa', *American Journal of Sociology*, 81, 1 (1975), pp. 62–81.

69. C. van Onselen, 'Reactions to Rinderpest in Southern Africa, 1896–97', *Journal of African History*, 13, 2 (1972), pp. 437–88.

70. A.N. Pelzer, 'Die arm-blanke verskynsel in die Suid-Afrikaanse Republiek tussen die jare 1882 en 1899', MA thesis, University of Pretoria, 1937, p. 118.

71. Elphick, *Kraal and Castle*, pp. 179–81.

72. Moodie, *The Record*, vol. 5, p. 22 (Report of Colonel Collins, 1809).

73. See the argument of S. Newton-King in her chapter, 'The Labour Market of the Cape Colony, 1806–1828', in Atmore and Marks, *Economy and Society in Preindustrial South Africa*.

74. Imperial Blue Book no. 50 (1836), Aborigines Committee Report, question 2310. For a discussion of the significance of Ordinance 50, see Leslie Clement Duly, 'A Revisit with the Cape's Hottentot Ordinance of 1828', in Marcelle Kooy (ed.), *Studies in Economics and Economic History* (London: Macmillan, 1972), pp. 26–56.

75. Colin Bundy, 'The Abolition of the Masters and Servants Act', in A. Paul Hare et al. (eds.), *South Africa: Sociological Analyses* (Cape Town: Oxford University Press, 1979), pp. 373–9.

76. Cited by H.J. van Aswegen, 'Die verhouding tussen Blank en Nie-Blank in die Oranje-Vrystaat, 1854–1902', D.Phil thesis, University of the Orange Free State, 1968, p. 634.

77. The labour question in the Orange Free State is discussed at length in ibid., pp. 467–643.

78. Colin Bundy, 'The Emergence and Decline of a South African Peasantry', *African Affairs*,

71, 285 (1972), pp. 369–88. For a full statement, see Bundy, *The Rise and Fall of the South African Peasantry* (London: Heinemann, 1979).

79. Van Aswegen, 'Die verhouding tussen Blank en Nie-Blank', p. 640; see also pp. 576, 581.

80. See the fascinating discussion on 'The Labour Question' by R.J.F. in *The Friend* (Bloemfontein), 2 and 5 April 1895.

81. For the constraining influence of the fear of British intervention, see Barend Johannes Kruger, *Diskussies en wetgewing random die landelike arbeidsvraagstuk in die Suid-Afrikaanse Republiek met besondere verwysing na die plakkerswette, 1885–1899* (Pretoria: Unisa, 1966).

82. Ibid., p. 47.

83. Stanley Trapido, 'Landlord and Tenant in a Colonial Economy: The Transvaal 1880–1910', *Journal of Southern African Studies*, 5, 1 (1978), pp. 26–58. This is a major reinterpretation of class relationships in the Transvaal.

84. Kruger, *Diskussies en wetgewing*, pp. 12, 45, 56–7.

85. Cited by Trapido, 'Landlord and Tenant', p. 28.

86. Stanley Trapido, 'The South African Republic: Class Formation and the State, 1850–1900', *Societies of Southern Africa*, vol. 3 (1973), p. 58.

87. Kruger, *Diskussies en wetgewing*, p. 30.

88. Ibid., p. 10.

89. Ibid., p. 209.

90. G.C. de Wet, 'Die vrybevolking in die Kaapse nedersetting 1657–1707', DPhil thesis, University of Stellenbosch, 1978, pp. 213–15.

91. For a full discussion, see Guelke, 'The European Settlement of South Africa', pp. 335–6.

92. W.S. van Ryneveld, 'Beschouwing', p. 124.

93. Van der Merwe, *Trek*, p. 60.

94. H. Blink, *De Zuid-Afrikaansche Republiek en hare bewoners* (Amsterdam, 1890), p. 98.

95. W. Grosskopf, 'Plattelandsverarming en plaasverlating', in Report of the Carnegie Commission, *The Poor White Problem in South Africa*, 5 vols. (Stellenbosch: Pro Ecclesia, 1932), vol. 1, p. 121.

96. R.W. Wilcocks, 'The Poor White' (Report of the Carnegie Commission), vol. 2, p. 60.

97. Ibid., p. 63.

98. A.M. Grundlingh, *Die „Hendsoppers' en „Joiners': die rasionaal en verskynsel van verraad* (Pretoria: HAUM, 1979), pp. 232–6; Thomas Pakenham, *The Boer War* (Johannesburg: Jonathan Ball, 1979), pp. 566–8.

99. Quoted in Muller, *Die oorsprong van die Groot Trek*, p. 193.

100. John S. Galbraith, 'The "Turbulent Frontier" as a Factor in British Expansion', *Comparative Studies in Society and History*, 2 (1959–60), pp. 150–68.

101. F.A. van Jaarsveld, *Die eenheidstrewe van die Republikeinse Afrikaners, 1836–1864* (Johannesburg: Impala Educational, 1951); J.A. du Plessis, 'Die ontstaan en ontwikkeling van die amp van die Staatspresident in die Zuid-Afrikaansche Republiek, 1858–1902', *Archives Year Book* (1955), vol. 1, pp. 1–271.

102. Free State Archives, GS 292, pp. 16–18.

103. Cited by Duly, 'A Revisit with the Cape's Hottentot Ordinance of 1828', p. 38.

104. J.S. Marais, *The Cape Coloured People, 1652–1937*, 2nd ed. (Johannesburg: CNA, 1957), p. 183; Muller, *Die oorsprong van die Groot Trek*, p. 187.

105. J.C. Visagie, 'Die Katriviernedersetting, 1829–1839', DLitt et Phil thesis, University of South Africa, 1978, p. 120.

106. *The South African Directory and Almanac for the Year 1834*, p. 204.

107. G. Tylden, *The Armed Forces of South Africa* (Johannesburg: Africana Museum, 1954), p. 58.

108. Trapido, 'Aspects in the Transition from Slavery to Serfdom', p. 26.

109. For an extensive treatment, see G.N. van den Bergh, 'Die polisiediens in die Zuid-Afrikaansche Republiek', DPhil thesis, Potchefstroom University, 1971.

110. A. Atmore and S. Marks, 'The Imperial Factor in South Africa in the Nineteenth Century: Towards a Reassessment', *Journal of Imperial and Commonwealth History*, 5, 3 (1974), pp. 125–6.

111. Van den Berg, 'Die polisiediens in die ZAR', pp. 459–62.

112. Trapido, 'Landlord and Tenant', pp. 52–8.

113. Ibid., p. 55; Tim Keegan, 'Peasants, Capitalists and Farm Labour: Class Formation in the Orange River Colony, 1902–1910', *Societies of Southern Africa*, vol. 9, pp. 18–26.

114. S.T. Plaatje, *Native Life in South Africa*, 2nd ed. (London: P.S. King & Son, n.d.), p. 66.

115. *Die groot vlug* is the title of a pamphlet published in 1916 by D.F. Malan, the Afrikaner nationalist leader.

116. Louis B. Wright, *Life on the American Frontier* (New York: Capricorn Books, 1971), p. 13.

117. Significantly, in the Afrikaans language there is only the word *grens*, meaning border. To translate the American sense of the word 'frontier', one would probably have to use terms such as grensgebied or pionierswêreld.

3. Becoming Afrikaners

1. D. Welsh, 'The Political Economy of Afrikaner Nationalism', in A. Leftwich (ed.), *South Africa: Economic Growth and Political Change* (London: Allison and Busby, 1974), pp. 249–86; H. Giliomee, 'The Afrikaner Economic Advance', in H. Adam and H. Giliomee, *Ethnic Power Mobilized: Can South Africa Change?* (New Haven: Yale University Press, 1979); D. O'Meara, *Volkskapitalisme: Class, Capital and Ideology in the Development of Afrikaner Nationalism, 1934–1948* (Cambridge: Cambridge University Press, 1983).

2. F.A. van Jaarsveld, *The Awakening of Afrikaner Nationalism, 1868–1881* (Cape Town: Human and Rousseau, 1961), especially pp. 214–15.

3. E. Gellner, *Nations and Nationalism* (Oxford: Oxford University Press, 1983), pp. 47–8.

4. M. Bloch, 'The Idol of Origins', cited by C. Vann Woodward, *Thinking Back: The Perils of Writing History* (Baton Rouge: Louisiana State University Press, 1986), pp. 60–1.

5. Van Jaarsveld, *The Awakening*, p. 215; T.R.H. Davenport, *The Afrikaner Bond: The History of a South African Political Party, 1880–1911* (Cape Town: Oxford University Press, 1966).

6. A. du Toit and H. Giliomee, *Afrikaner Political Thought: Analysis and Documents, vol. 1: 1780–1850* (Cape Town: David Philip, 1983), pp. 4–27, 132–4, 195–204, 230–46.

7. A.B. du Toit, 'No Chosen People: The Myth of the Calvinist Origins of Afrikaner Nationalism and Racial Ideology', *American Historical Review*, 88, 4 (1983), pp. 920–52.

8. This term is used to indicate that the concept of 'Afrikaner' had not become crystallised before the second half of the nineteenth century.

9. J.C. Visagie, 'Willem Frederik Hertzog, 1793–1847', *Archives Year Book of South African History*, 37 (1974), pp. 55–72.

10. J.H. Hofmeyr, *The Life of Jan Hendrik Hofmeyr (Onze Jan)* (Cape Town, 1913), p. 42.

11. *Cape Times*, May 1877, editorial.

12. E. van Heyningen, 'Social Evil in the Cape Colony, 1868–1902: Prostitution and the Contagious Diseases Act', *Journal of Southern African Studies*, 10, 2 (1984), p. 182.

13. See the comments of Olive Schreiner, *Thoughts on South Africa* (London, 1923), p. 17.

14. A. Atmore and S. Marks, 'The Imperial Factor in South Africa in the Nineteenth Century: Towards a Reassessment', *Journal of Imperial and Commonwealth History*, 3, 1 (1974), pp. 120–5.

15. M.A. Basson, 'Die Britse invloed in die Transvaalse onderwys, 1837–1907', *Archives Year Book of South African History,* 2 (1956), pp. 63–75.

16. S.F. Malan, *Politieke strominge onder die Afrikaners van die Vrystaatse Republiek* (Durban: Butterworth, 1982), pp. 54–5.

17. For an analysis of rural Transvaal society, see S. Trapido, 'Landlord and Tenant in a Colonial Economy: The Transvaal, 1880–1910', *Journal of Southern African Studies*, 5 (1978), pp. 27–58, and his 'Aspects of the Transition from Slavery to Serfdom, 1842–1902', *Societies of Southern Africa*, 6 (1976), pp. 24–31. On the role of the field-cornet, see F.A. van Jaarsveld, 'Die veldkornet en sy aandeel in die opbou van die Suid-Afrikaanse Republiek tot 1870', *Archives Year Book of South Africa*, 2 (1952), pp. 187–352.

18. *De Tijd*, 25 March 1868, letter from 'Vrystater'; *De Tijd*, 15 April 1868, letter from 'Een Eigenaar . . . en een Afrikaander'.

19. A.M. Grundlingh, *Die 'Hendsoppers' en 'Joiners': die rasionaal en verskynsel van verraad* (Pretoria: HAUM, 1979), pp. 232–6.

20. Van Jaarsveld, 'Die veldkornet', p. 332.

21. C.W. de Kiewiet, *The Imperial Factor in South Africa* (Cambridge: Cambridge University Press, 1937), p. 95.

22. J.E.H. Grobler, 'Jan Viljoen, 1912–1893: 'n Transvaalse wesgrenspionier', MA thesis, University of Pretoria, 1976, pp. 83–99.

23. C.J. Uys, *In the Era of Shepstone* (Lovedale: Lovedale Press, 1933), p. 283.

24. Ibid., pp. 421–2.

25. Grobler, 'Jan Viljoen', pp. 67–82, 147–8.

26. Malan, *Politieke strominge*, pp. 25–6.

27. A. Smith, *The Ethnic Revival* (Cambridge: Cambridge University Press, 1981), pp. 77–8.

28. Malan, *Politieke strominge*, pp. 24–30, 37–42, 56–7.

29. Van Jaarsveld, *The Awakening*, pp. 79–80.

30. T.E. Kirk, 'Self-Government and Self-Defence in South Africa: The Interplay between British and Cape Politics, 1846–54', DPhil thesis, Oxford University, 1972, pp. 490–508.

31. J.L. McCracken, *The Cape Parliament, 1854–1910* (Cape Town: Oxford University Press, 1967), pp. 36–7, 52; *Hofmeyr, Hofmeyr*, p. 42.

32. A.J. Purkiss, 'Politics, Capital and Railway Building in the Cape Colony, 1870–1885', DPhil thesis, Oxford University, 1978, pp. 32, 55.

33. *De Zuid-Afrikaan*, 21 May 1857, editorial.

34. T.N. Hanekom, *Die liberale rigting in Suid-Afrika: 'n kerkhistoriese studie* (Stellenbosch: Christen-Studentevereniging-Maatskappy, 1957). For a full account of one minister's campaign against liberal tendencies, see M.C. Kitshoff, Gottlieb Wilhelm Antony van der Lingen: *Kaapse predikant uit die negentiende eeu (Amsterdam: Free University of Amsterdam, 1972)*.

35. R. Robinson, 'Non-European Foundations of European Imperialism: A Sketch for a Theory of Collaboration', in R. Owen and B. Sutcliffe (eds.), *Studies in the Theory of Imperialism* (London: Longmans, 1972), p. 124.

36. J. du P. Scholtz, *Die Afrikaner en sy taal* (Cape Town: Nasou, 1965).

37. Smith, *Ethnic Revival, pp. 97–8*.

38. See Kitshoff, *Van der Lingen, chs. 6–10*.

39. H.J. Hofstede, *Geschiedenis van den Oranje-Vrijstaat* (The Hague, 1876).

40. F.A. van Jaarsveld, *The Afrikaner's Interpretation of South African History* (Cape Town: Simondium Publishers, 1964), p. 36.

41. *De Tijd*, 8 July 1868, letter from 'Opmerker'; J.A. Henry, *Die eerste honderd jaar van die Standard Bank* (Cape Town: Oxford University Press, 1963), pp. 10–13, 28, 47; Standard Bank Archives (SBA), Henry's précis of general managers' letters to London, letter of 12 March 1882.

42. Cited by Van Jaarsveld, *The Awakening, p. 123*.

43. *De Graaff-Reinet Courant*, 7 April 1876, editorial.

44. Uys, *In the Era of Shepstone*, pp. 421–2; De Kiewiet, Imperial Factor, pp. 105–6.

45. 'Onze Wyn', *Het Zuid-Afrikaansche Tijdschrift*, February 1878, pp. 26–39.

46. Ibid., p. 32.

47. G.T. Amphlett, *The History of the Standard Bank of South Africa Limited, 1862–1913* (Glasgow: Robert Maclehose, 1914), pp. 202–3.

48. Purkiss, 'Politics, Capital and Railway Building', p. 28.

49. *De Zuid-Afrikaan*, 6 October 1853, 3 May 1866; Andre du Toit, 'Constitutional Politics: Franchise and Race', unpublished paper.

50. A. Mabin, 'Class as a Local Phenomenon: Conflict between Cape Town and Port Elizabeth in the Nineteenth Century', unpublished paper presented at the University of the Witwatersrand, 1984.

51. S. Trapido, '"The Friends of the Natives": Merchants, Peasants and the Political and Ideological Structure of Liberalism in the Cape', in S. Marks and A. Atmore (eds.), *Economy and Society in Pre-Industrial South Africa* (London: Longman, 1980), pp. 247–74.

52. A.R. Zolberg, 'Political Conflict in the New States of Tropical Africa', *American Political Science Review*, 68 (1968), p. 4.

53. A. Wilmot, *The Life and Times of Sir Richard Southey* (London, 1904), pp. 202–3.

54. For a discussion, see S. Dubow, *Land, Labour and Merchant Capital: The Experience of Graaff Reinet District in the Pre-Industrial Rural Economy of the Cape, 1852–1872* (Cape Town: Centre for African Studies, UCT, 1982), *p. 59*; C. Bundy, 'Vagabond Hollanders and Runaway Englishmen: White Poverty in the Cape before Poor Whiteism', *Societies of*

Southern Africa (London, 1983), pp. 1–10; K.W. Smith, *From Frontier to Midlands: A History of Graaff Reinet District. 1786–1910* (Grahamstown: Institute of Social and Economic Research, 1976), *pp. 389–92;* for an analysis of conditions of the poor in Cape Town, *see* E. Bradlow, 'Cape Town's Labouring Poor a Century Ago', *South African Historical Journal*, 9 (1977).

55. 'Our Agricultural Population', *Cape Monthly Magazine*, 6, 33 (March 1873), p. 130.

56. *De Zuid-Afrikaan*, 12 April 1873, 'Die Bijbel in Afrikaans'. The foregoing two paragraphs draw on an excellent student essay by Jean du Plessis, 'Notes on Political Consciousness on the Periphery: With Specific Reference to the Issue of Language in the South Western Cape during the 1870s', unpublished paper, University of Stellenbosch, 1983.

57. *De Zuid-Afrikaan*, 8, 15, and 22 July 1874, articles by 'A True Afrikaner'.

58. *Het Volksblad*, 19 August 1875, editorial.

59. Genootskap van Regte Afrikaners, *Die Afrikaanse Patriot, 1876* (facsimile edition, Cape Town: Tafelberg, 1974), pp. 35, 41, 82, 113–14. *See also* G.D. Scholtz, *Die ontwikkeling van die politieke denke van die Afrikaners, vol. 4: 1881–1899* (Johannesburg: Perskor, 1977), pp. 169–71, 298–300.

60. Davenport, *The Afrikaner Bond*, pp. 35–6.

61. De Kiewiet, *Imperial Factor*, p. 95.

62. J.G. Kotze, *Biographical Memories and Reminiscences* (Cape Town: Maskew Miller, n.d.), vol. 1, p. 501.

63. Van Jaarsveld, *The Afrikaner's Interpretation*, pp. 40–42.

64. For these and similar statements, see Van Jaarsveld, *The Awakening*, pp. 150–213; Malan, *Politieke strominge, pp. 70–92*. For the Hofineyr quotation, see Hofmeyr, p. 164.

65. P. van Breda, 'Die geskiedenis van de Zuid-Afrikaansche Boerenbeschermingsvereeniging in die Kaapkolonie, 1878–1883', MA thesis, University of Stellenbosch, 1981, pp. 178–84.

66. Hofmeyr, *Hofmeyr, p. 164*.

67. G.J. Schutte, 'Nederland het stamland van de apartheid?', unpublished essay, p. 5.

68. Malan, *Politieke strominge*, pp. 53–5, 117–18.

69. L. Chisholm, 'Themes in the Construction of Free Compulsory Education for the White Working Class on the Witwatersrand, 1886–1907', unpublished paper delivered to the University of the Witwatersrand History Workshop, 1984.

70. *De Zuid-Afrikaan*, 23 April 1879.

71. Malan, *Politieke strominge*, p. 92.

72. *De Zuid-Afrikaan*, 21 September 1878.

73. Purkiss, 'Politics, Capital and Railway Building', pp. 1–84, 137–46, 451; for an in-depth analysis of the collaborating relationship, see D.M. Schreuder, *The Scramble for Southern Africa, 1877–1895* (Cambridge: Cambridge University Press, 1980).

74. P. Lewsen, *John X. Merriman: Paradoxical South African Statesman* (New Haven: Yale University Press, 1982), p. 95.

75. Hofmeyr, *Hofmeyr*, pp. 330–1.

76. Davenport, *Afrikaner Bond*, pp. 129–30.

77. Hofmeyr, *Hofmeyr*, p. 406.

78. Ibid., *p. 488.*

79. *Zuid-Afrikaan,* 14 April 1885, editorial; Hofmeyr, Hofmeyr, pp. 42–3.

80. James Rose Innes, *Autobiography* (Cape Town: Oxford University Press, 1949), p. 3.

81. Lewsen, *Merriman,* p. 139.

82. E.T. Cook, *Edmund Garrett* (London: Edward Arnold, 1909), p. 109.

83. C.T. Gordon, *The Growth of Boer Opposition to Kruger, 1890–1895* (Cape Town: Oxford University Press, 1970), p. 10.

84. Van Breda, 'Die geskiedenis van de ZABBV', pp. 26, 29.

85. Bun Booyens, *'Ek heb gezeg': die verhaal van ons jongeliede en debatsverenigings* (Cape Town: Human and Rousseau, 1983); *Malan, Politieke strominge,* pp. 186–206.

86. G.J. Hupkes, 'Die Stellenbosche Distriksbank', MCom thesis, University of Stellenbosch, 1956, p. 99.

87. A. Mabin, 'The Making of Colonial Capitalism: Intensification and Expansion in Economic Geography of the Cape Colony, South Africa, 1854–1899', PhD thesis, Simon Fraser University, 1984, pp. 222–3.

88. The paragraphs on the Standard Bank and local financial institutions are based on primary research in the Standard Bank archives, and draw particularly on the inspection reports for Stellenbosch and Paarl between 1880 and 1930. Specific references are given in my paper 'Farmers and Politics', presented to the conference of the Economic History Society, University of Natal, July 1984.

89. S.W. Pienaar (ed.), *Glo in u volk: dr. D.F. Malan as redenaar* (Cape Town: Tafelberg, 1964), p. 175.

90. G.J. Pretorius, *Man van die daad* (Cape Town: Tafelberg, 1959), pp. 62–3.

91. A leaguer is a large cask originally used to transport liquids in ships.

92. Hupkes, *Die Stellenbosch Distriksbank;* Adam and Giliomee, *Ethnic Power Mobilized,* ch. 6.

93. Malan, *Politieke strominge,* pp. 238–9.

94. Ibid., pp. 199–206.

95. Ibid., p. 262.

96. See particularly A.N. Pelzer, 'Die De Wildt-toesprach van General Hertzog', in P.J. Nienaber (ed.), *Gedenkboek Generaal J.B.M. Hertzog* (Johannesburg: Afrikaanse Pers-Boekhandel, 1965), pp. 259–60.

97. Gordon, *The Growth of Boer Opposition to Kruger,* pp. 184–204.

98. See the succinct analysis by D. Denoon, *A Grand Illusion: The Failure of Imperial Policy in the Transvaal Colony during the Period of Reconstruction, 1900–1905* (London: Longman, 1973), pp. 59–95.

99. Cited by N.G. Garson, '"Het Volk": The Botha–Smuts Party in the Transvaal, 1904–1911', *Historical Journal,* 9, 1 (1966), p. 128.

100. A.R. Colquhoun, *The Africander Land* (London: John Murray, 1906), pp. xii–xiv.

101. On the state–capital symbiosis, see D. Yudelman, *The Emergence of Modern South Africa: State, Capital and the Incorporation of Organized Labour on the South African Gold Fields, 1902–1939* (Cape Town: David Philip, 1984), pp. 3–12, 52–123.

102. Cited by E.C. Pienaar, *Die triomf van Afrikaans* (Cape Town: Nasionale Pers, 1973), p. 274.

103. Isabel Hofmeyr, 'Building a Nation from Words: Afrikaans Language, Literature and "Ethnic Identity", 1902–1924', in S. Marks and Stanley Trapido (eds.), *The Politics of Race, Class and Nationalism in Twentieth Century South Africa* (London: Longman, 1987), pp. 95–123.

104. I. Hexham, *The Irony of Apartheid: The Struggle for National Independence of Afrikaner Calvinism against British Imperialism* (New York: Edwin Mellen Press, 1981).

105. Hofmeyr, 'Building a Nation from Words', p. 106.

106. C. van Onselen, *Studies in the Social and Economic History of the Witwatersrand, 1886–1914, vol. 2: New Nineveh* (London: Longman, 1982), pp. 111–70.

107. Hofmeyr, 'Building a Nation from Words', p. 101.

108. For an illuminating case study, see R. Morrell, 'A Community in Conflict: The Poor Whites of Middelburg, 1900–1930', paper presented to the University of the Witwatersrand History Workshop, 1984.

109. Bun Booyens, *Die lewe van D.F. Malan: die eerste veertig jaar* (Cape Town: Tafelberg, 1969), pp. 273–95.

110. J. du Plessis, *The Life of Andrew Murray of South Africa* (London: Marshall Brothers, 1919), pp. 431–3.

111. Lewsen, *Merriman*, p. 369.

112. J.H.H. de Waal, *Die lewe van David Christiaan de Waal* (Cape Town: Nasionale Pers, 1928), pp. 303–8.

4. 'The Weakness of Some': The Dutch Reformed Church and White Supremacy

1. D.F. Malan, 'Op die wagtoring', unpublished MS, University of Stellenbosch Library, Documents Collection.

2. M.A. Schwartz, *Trends in White Attitudes towards Negroes* (Chicago: Chicago University Opinion Research Centre, 1967); H. Hyman, and P. Sheatsley, 'Attitudes towards Desegregation', *Scientific American*, 211 (1964).

3. Gwendolen Carter, *The Politics of Inequality: South Africa since 1948* (London: Thames and Hudson, 1958), p. 78.

4. D.N. Noel, *The Origins of American Slavery and Racism* (Columbus, OH: Charles Merrill, 1972), p. 184.

5. G. Thompson, *Travels in Southern Africa* (London: Colburn, 1827), p. 324; *Transactions of the [London] Missionary Society* (London: Bye and Law, 1804), p. 324.

6. G.D. Scholtz, *Die ontwikkeling van die politieke denke van die Afrikaner* (Johannesburg: Perskor, 1978) vol. 5, pp. 282–3.

7. H.S. Smith, *In His Image but …: Racism in Southern Religion, 1780–1910* (Durham, NC: Duke University Press. 1972), p. 11.

8. Ibid., p. 248.

9. Robert Shell, *Children of Bondage: A Social History of the Slave Society of the Cape of Good Hope, 1652–1838* (Johannesburg: Wits University Press, 1994), p. 342.

10. *Transactions of the [London] Missionary Society*. 1804.

11. N.J. Hofmeyr, 'Het zendingwerk', series of articles in *De Gereformeerde Kerkbode*, 5 March, 28 May and 25 June 1853.

12. Ibid.

13. J.G. Botha, *Gedenkuitgawe van die Nederduitse Gereformeerde Sendinggemeente van Malmesbury in die eeufeesjaar 1981* (Malmesbury: NG Sendingkerk, 1981), pp. 16–18.

14. D.P.M. Huet, *Een kudde en een herder* (Cape Town: N.H. Marais, 1860).

15. D.P.M. Huet, Commentary, *Elpis*, 4 (1860).

16. Richard Elphick, *The Equality of Believers: Protestant Missionaries and the Racial Politics of South Africa* (Scottsville: University of KwaZulu Natal Press, 2010), p. 45.

17. Ibid., pp. 107–15.

18. J. du Plessis, *The Life of Andrew Murray* (London: Marshall Bros., 1919).

19. R. Elphick, 'Evangelical Missions and Racial Equality in South Africa, 1890–1914', unpublished paper, 1999.

20. J. du Plessis, 'The South African Problem', *International Review of Missions*, XV, 59 (1926).

21. D. Bosch, D. 1986. 'Johannes du Plessis', in J. du Preez (ed.), *Sendinggenade* (Bloemfontein: NG Kerkuitgewers, 1986).

22. H. Bradford, *A Taste of Freedom: The ICU in Rural South Africa* (Johannesburg: Ravan Press, 1987), p. 4.

23. J.C. du Plessis, 'Die ideale van ons kerk in die sendingwerk', in *Die NG Kerk in die OVS en die Naturellevraagstuk* (Bloemfontein: NG Kerkuitgewers, 1929), pp. 22–5; L. Louw (comp.). *Dawie, 1946–1964* (Cape Town: Tafelberg, 1964), p. 49.

24. F. Geldenhuys, *In die stroomversnellings: vyftig jaar van die NG Kerk* (Cape Town: Tafelberg, 1982), p. 34.

25. J.G. Strydom, *Die NG Kerk in die OVS en die Naturellevraagstuk*, pp. 34–5, Preface.

26. J.A. Lombard, 'Die sendingbeleid van die NGK in die OVS', PhD thesis, University of the North, 1985, pp. 308–13.

27. J. Kinghorn, 'Die groei van 'n teologie', in J. Kinghorn (ed.), *Die NG Kerk en apartheid* (Johannesburg: Macmillan, 1986), pp. 86–9.

28. H. Giliomee, *The Afrikaners: Biography of a People* (Charlottesville: University of Virginia Press, 2003), p. 460.

29. Cited by A.J. Botha, *Die evolusie van 'n volksteologie* (Bellville: University of Western Cape, 1984), p. 149.

30. T.D. Moodie, *The Rise of Afrikanerdom: Power, Apartheid and the Afrikaner Civil Religion* (Berkeley: University of California Press, 1975), pp. ix–x.

31. P.F. Theron, 'Natuur en genade, kerk en volk', in C.J. Wethmar and C.J.A. Vos (eds.), *'n Woord op sy tyd* (Pretoria. N.G. Kerkboekhandel, 1988); J. Durand, 'Afrikaner piety and dissent', in C. Villa-Vicencio and J.W. de Gruchy (eds.), *Resistance and Hope* (Cape Town: Davis Philip, 1985); J. Durand, *Ontluisterde wêreld: die Afrikaner en sy kerk in 'n veranderende Suid-Afrika* (Wellington: Lux Verbi, 2000).

32. *Ons Land*, 6 July 1915.

33. C.C. O'Brien, *God Land: Reflections on Religion and Nationalism* (Cambridge: Harvard University Press, 1988), pp. 2–3.

34. Du Plessis, *The Life of Andrew Murray*, p. 416; F.A. van Jaarsveld, *The Awakening of Afrikaner Nationalism, 1868–1881* (Cape Town: Human and Rousseau, 1961).

35. A. du Toit, 'No Chosen People: The Myth of the Calvinist Origins of Afrikaner Nationalism and Racial Ideology', *American Historical Review*, 88 (1983), p. 4.

36. Botha, *Die evolusie van 'n volksteologie*; I. Hexham, *The Irony of Apartheid* (Toronto: Edward Mellen, 1981).

37. Du Toit, 'No Chosen People', p. 952.

38. J.N. Gerstner, *The Thousand Generation Covenant: Dutch Reformed Covenant Theology and Group Ideology in Colonial South Africa* (Leiden: E.J. Brill, 1991).

39. W.W. Collins, *Free Statia* (Bloemfontein: The Friend, 1907).

40. O'Brien, *God Land*, pp. 41–2.

41. Malan, 'Op die wagtoring'.

42. C. Hattingh (comp.), *Hy was groot en gelief: roudienste by die afsterwe van dr. H.F. Verwoerd* (Johannesburg: Voortrekkerpers, 1967).

43. J.S. Gericke, 'Wees sterk', in Hattingh (comp.), *Hy was groot en gelief*, p. 19.

44. Moodie, *The Rise of Afrikanerdom*, p. 57.

45. Van Wyk 1991, pp. 39–53.

46. J.A. Loubser, *The Apartheid Bible: A Critical Review of Racial Theology in South Africa* (Cape Town: Maskew Miller Longman, 1987), p. 58.

47. G. Schutte, 'The Netherlands: Cradle of Apartheid?', *Ethnic and Racial Studies*, 10, 4 (1987).

48. J.D. du Toit, 'Die godsdienstige grondslag van ons rassebeleid', *Inspan*, December 1944.

49. W. Jordan, *White over Black: American Attitudes towards the Negro, 1550–1812* (Baltimore: Johns Hopkins University Press, 1976), pp. 245, 538.

50. Moodie, *The Rise of Afrikanerdom*, p. 71.

51. E.L.P. Stals, 'Die geskiedenis van die Afrikaner Broederbond, 1918–1994', unpublished MS, 1988, pp. 203–8.

52. Giliomee, *The Afrikaners*, pp. 444–79.

53. D.F. Malan junior, 'Biographical Notes on My Father', 1965, University of Stellenbosch Library, Documents Collection.

54. R. Millar, 'Science and Society in the Early Career of H.F. Verwoerd', *Journal of Southern African Studies*, 19, 4 (1993), p. 650.

55. H. Giliomee, *From Apartheid to Nation-Building* (Cape Town: Oxford University Press, 1989), p. 47.

56. *Die Transvaler*, 16 February 1947.

57. Kinghorn, 'Die groei van 'n teologie', p. 92.

58. Stals, 'Die geskiedenis van die Afrikaner Broederbond, 1918–1994', pp. 234–6.

59. G.B.A. Gerdener, *Die Afrikaner en die sendingwerk* (Cape Town: NG Kerkuitgewers, 1959), p. 127.

60. D. Bosch, *Kerk en wêreld* (Bloemfontein: N.G. Sendingkerk, 1961), p. 35.

61. C.H. Badenhorst, 'Die ontwikkeling van die Bantoe op godsdienstige en maatskaplike gebied, soos uit die oogpunt van die drie Afrikaanse kerke gesien', in *Volkskongres oor die toekoms van die Bantoe* (Bloemfontein, 1956), p. 89.

62. *Die Transvaler*, 12 June 1940; Cronjé et al., 1947, pp21–22. 39.)

63. G. van der Watt, 'G.B.A. Gerdener: koersaanwyser in die Nederduitse Gereformeerde Kerk se sending en ekumene', PhD thesis, University of the Free State, 1990, p. 292.

64. Ibid.; G.B.A. Gerdener, *Reguit koers gehou* (Cape Town: NG Kerkuitgewers, 1951).

65. P.J. Coertze, F.J. Language and B.C. van Eeden, *Die oplossing van die Naturellevraag-stuk in Suid-Afrika* (Johannesburg: Publicité, 1943).

66. G.B.A. Gerdener, 'Van die redaksie', *Op die Horison*, 5, 1 (1943).

67. Elphick, 'Evangelical Missions and Racial Equality in South Africa, 1890–1914'.

68. Gerdener, *Reguit koers gehou*, p. 102.

69. D.F. Malan, Account of D.F. Malan's reply to the Transvaal Delegates, 5 February 1947, University of Stellenbosch Library, Documents Collection.

70. Sauer Report, 'Verslag van die Kleurvraagstuk-kommissie van die Nasionale Party' (Cape Town, 1947), p. 13.

71. J.G. Strydom, 'Christelike apartheid', *Die Kerkbode*, 22 September 1948.

72. B.J. Marais, 'Kritiese beoordeling van die standpunt van ons kerk in sake rasseverhoudings met die oog op die gebeure oorsee', *Op die Horison*, 9, 2 (1947), pp. 76–9.

73. B.J. Marais, 'Die Skrif en rasse-apartheid', *Die Kerkbode*, 14 July 1948, pp. 15, 96.

74. Gerdener, *Reguit koers gehou*, pp. 1–5.

75. D.F. Malan junior, 'Biographical Notes on My Father'.

76. *House of Assembly Debates*, 1950: cols. 4141–2.

77. Elphick, 'Evangelical Missions and Racial Equality in South Africa, 1890–1914'.

78. J. Brits, *Op die vooraand van apartheid: die rassevraagtuk en die blanke politiek in Suid-Afrika, 1939–1948* (Pretoria: Unisa, 1994); Giliomee, *The Afrikaners*, pp. 455–6.

79. The source of the data is a survey conducted and published by the Cape Town-based Institute for Reconciliation and Justice (www.ijr.org.za). This survey was undertaken at the end of 2000 and the beginning of 2001 and involved 3,727 interviews. The interviews were conducted in the language of choice of the respondent.

80. H. Fagan, *Ons verantwoordelikheid* (Stellenbosch: Universiteitsuitgewers, 1959), pp. 42–4.

81. D. Botha, 'Historiese agtergrond van die stigting van die afsonderlike etniese NG kerkverbande', unpublished paper.

82. J.M. du Preez, *Africana Afrikaner* (Alberton: Liberatius, 1983).

83. L. Schlemmer, 'Factors in the Persistence or Decline of Ethnic Group Mobilisation: Afrikaners in Post-Apartheid South Africa', PhD thesis, University of Cape Town, 1999, p. 184; L. Schlemmer, 'Between a Rainbow and a Hard Place', *Fast Facts*, December 2001.

84. W. Jonker, *Selfs die Kerk kan verander* (Cape Town: Tafelberg, 1998); Nederduits Gereformeerde Kerk, *Kerk en samelewing* (1986); Nederduits Gereformeerde Kerk, *Church and Society* (1990).

85. F. Dostoevsky, *Devils* (Oxford: Oxford Paperbacks, 1992 [1871]), p. 264.

86. D. Akenson, *God's Peoples: Covenant and Land in South Africa, Israel and Northern Ireland* (Ithaca, NY: Cornell University Press, 1992).

87. C. Vann Woodward, *American Counterpoint: Slavery and Racism in North-South Dialogue* (Boston: Little, Brown, 1971).

88. C. Coloured, *A Reinhold Niebuhr Reader* (Philadelphia: Trinity Press, 1992); R.W. Fox, *Reinhold Niebuhr: A Biography* (New York: Pantheon Books, 1985); R. Stone, *Reinhold Niebuhr: Prophet to Politicians* (Nashville: Abingdon Press, 1972).

89. R. Niebuhr, *Moral Man and Immoral Society* (New York: Charles Scribner's Sons, 1934), pp. xi–xxv, 253.

90. Coloured, *A Reinhold Niebuhr Reader*, p. 110.

91. T. Mbeki, Address to the Afrikanerbond, 1999, at www.polity.org.za/govdocs/speeches/1999/spo727b.html.

92. A. Dorfman, 'If you would change the world, change yourself', *Cape Times*, 1 July 1997.

Part Two: A Modern People

1. Michael O'Dowd, 'An Assessment of the English-Speaking South Africans' Contribution to the Economy', in André de Villiers (ed.), *English-Speaking South Africans Today* (Cape Town: Oxford University Press, 1976).

2. Hermann Giliomee, *The Afrikaners: Biography of a People* (Cape Town: Tafelberg, 2003), p. 436.

3. Email message from Helen Zille, 17 January 2017.

4. *Verslag van die volkskongres oor die armblanke vraagstuk, 1934* (Cape Town: Nasionale Pers, 1934), p. 13.

5. *Cape Times*, 18 May 1939.

6. Gwendolen Carter, *The Politics of Inequality* (London: Thames and Hudson, 1958), pp. 102–5.

7. Hermann Giliomee, *The Rise and Demise of the Afrikaners* (Cape Town: Tafelberg, 2019), pp. 115–35.

8. Anglo American Corporation, Chairman's Statement in 1964 Annual Report, p. 2.

9. *House of Assembly Debates*, 9 February 1973, col. 346.

10. Charles Simkins, *Liberalism and the Problem of Power* (Johannesburg: SA Institute of Race Relations, 1986), p. 16.

11. For an extended discussion, see J.L. Sadie, 'The Economic Demography of South Africa', PhD thesis, University of Stellenbosch, 2000, pp. 316–85.

12. *South African Digest*, 29 August 1975, p. 7.

13. Personal communication from Jan Sadie, 23 July 2002. For an extended discussion see Sadie, 'The Economic Demography of South Africa', pp. 316–85.

14. Dirk and Johanna de Villiers, *PW* (Cape Town: Tafelberg, 1983), p. 90.

15. Arnold Toynbee, 'History's Warning to Africa', *Optima*, 9, 2 (1959), pp. 55–6.

16. See the table in Hermann Giliomee and Bernard Mbenga, *New History of South Africa* (Cape Town: Tafelberg, 2007), p. 398.

17. R.W. Johnson, *Fighting for the Dream* (Johannesburg: Jonathan Ball, 2019), p. 122.

18. John Kane-Berman, 'Enemies of Entrepreneurship', first posted on 14 July 2019 on www.politicsweb.co.za.

19. Personal communication from Jan Sadie, 23 July 2002.

5. Alleged and Real Civil Service Purges

1. Henry John May, *The South African Constitution* (Cape Town: Juta, 1955).

2. Gustav Preller, 'The Union and the Boer', *The State*, 1, 6 (1909), p. 638.

3. *Financial Mail*, 2 October 1998, p. 44.

4. S.S. Pauw, *Beroepsarbeid van die Afrikaners* (Stellenbosch: Pro-Ecclesia, 1946), pp. 188–9.
5. G.D. Scholtz, *Die ontwikkeling van die politieke denke van die Afrikaners* (Johannesburg: Perskor, 1979), vol. 7, p. 125.
6. J.H. le Roux and P.W. Coetzer, *Die Nasionale Party, vol. 3: 1924–1934* (Bloemfontein: INEG, 1982), p. 472; *Die Burger*, 16 November 1935.
7. Pauw, *Beroepsarbeid*, p. 224.
8. Rob Davies, *Capital, State and White Labour in South Africa, 1900–1960* (Brighton: Harvester Press, 1979), pp. 285–6.
9. *House of Assembly Debates*, 21 March 1945.
10. Davies, *Capital, State and White Labour*, p. 298.
11. Off-the-record interview, 28 April 1999.
12. Dirk and Johanna de Villiers, *Paul Sauer* (Cape Town: Tafelberg, 1977), p. 99.
13. *House of Assembly Debates* (Afrikaans edition), 1949, col. 1886.
14. Ivan Evans, *Bureaucracy and Race: Native Administration in South Africa* (Berkeley: University of California Press, 1997), pp. 72–3.
15. Interview with person wishing to remain off the record, 28 April 1999.
16. Annette Seegers, *The Military in the Making of Modern South Africa* (London: Tauris Academic Studies, 1996), p. 96.
17. W.H. van den Bos, 'An Investigation into Resignation of Officers from the South African Air Force (Permanent Force) during the Period 1946–1971', MA thesis, Unisa, 1978, p. 155.
18. Seegers, *Military*, p. 93.
19. The calculation of J.L. Sadie quoted in Heribert Adam and Hermann Giliomee, *Ethnic Power Mobilized: Can South Africa Change?* (New Haven: Yale University Press, 1979), pp. 165–6.
20. S. Van Wyk *Die Afrikaner in die beroepslewe van die stad.* (Pretoria: Academica, 1971.)
21. Leo Marquard, *The Peoples and Policies of South Africa* (London: Oxford University Press, 1952).
22. Evans, *Bureaucracy and Race*, p. 87.

6. The Communal Nature of the South African Conflict

1. I prefer 'communal' to 'ethnic'. Ethnic is too narrow a category for it refers to a group with a common belief in a shared ancestry and history. This would fit the Afrikaners, but not the larger white community or, for that matter, the African or larger black community. Moreover, the ethnic style of politics is linked more particularly with the efforts to define a group exclusively and to give vivid expression to its historic heritage and cultural symbols. Communalism, by contrast, operates within less rigid boundaries and is more geared to the politics of group entitlement which makes special claims upon the state for rewards and services on the basis of past performance (or exploitation). However, the emotional bond sustaining communalism and its implicit nationalist claims should not be underestimated. I use the terms 'communal' and 'nationalist' interchangeably, although Afrikaner nationalism in the past had a much stronger insistence on exclusive 'possession' of the land than the present-day communalism.
2. See for instance the perspective of an influential scholar: Heribert Adam, *Modernizing*

Racial Domination (Berkeley: California University Press, 1971), p. 53; Heribert Adam and Hermann Giliomee, *Ethnic Power Mobilized: Can South Africa Change?* (New Haven: Yale University Press, 1979), pp. 3–4, 301–2; Heribert Adam and Kogila Moodley, *South Africa without Apartheid: Dismantling Racial Domination* (Berkeley: University of California Press, 1986), p. 262.

3. See Barbara Tuchman, *The March of Folly: From Troy to Vietnam* (New York: Ballantine Books, 1984).

4. For analyses of the development of stratification in the pre-industrial period, see Robert Ross (ed.), *Racism and Colonialism: Essays in Ideology and Social Structure* (The Hague: M. Nijhoff Publishers, 1982); and Richard Elphick and Hermann Giliomee (eds.), *The Shaping of South African Society* (Cape Town: Maskew Miller Longman, 1979), ch. 10.

5. George Frederickson, *White Supremacy: A Comparative Study in American and South African History* (New York: Oxford University Press, 1998), pp. 42–3.

6. L. Schlemmer, 'South Africa's National Party Government', in Peter Berger and Bobby Godsell, eds., *A Future South Africa* (Cape Town: Human and Rousseau, 1980), pp. 40–4.

7. Sam Nolutshungu, *Changing South Africa* (Manchester: Manchester University Press, 1982), pp. 147–50, 204–7.

8. For an excellent discussion of this in the Northern Ireland context, see Michael Mac-Donald's *Children of Wrath* (Cambridge: Cambridge University Press, 1986), particularly pp. 147–8. Also relevant is a recent comparative study of the decisive role of settlers in Algeria and Ireland in wrecking integrative policies which aim to extend political participation rights to wider strata. See Ian Lustick's *State Building Failure in British Ireland and French Algeria* (Berkeley: Institute of International Studies, 1985).

9. Neville Alexander, *Sow the Wind* (Johannesburg: Skotaville, 1985), pp. 126–53. There is an interesting debate about the emergence of nationalism between Ernest Gellner, *Nations and Nationalism* (Oxford: Basil Blackwell, 1983), who insists on a connection with early industrialisation as something of a sociological law, and Elie Kedourie, who in *Nationalism* (London: Hutchinson, 1985) emphasises the force of ideas and gives examples of nationalism occurring outside the context of early industrialisation.

10. Rob Turrell, 'Kimberley: Labour and Compounds, 1871–1882', in Shula Marks and Richard Rathbone (eds.), *Industrialisation and Social Change in South Africa: African Class Formation, Culture and Consciousness, 1870–1930* (London: Longman, 1982), pp. 45–76.

11. Cited by J. Lever, 'White Strategies in a Divided Society: The Development of South African Labour Policy', unpublished paper.

12. This paragraph draws on Anthony Smith's *The Ethnic Revival* (Cambridge: Cambridge University Press, 1981), pp. 18–19; Gellner, *Nations and Nationalism,* pp. 97–101; Kedourie, *Nationalism,* pp. 131–3.

13. A case in point is Dan O'Meara, *Volkskapitalisme: Class, Capital and Ideology in the Development of Afrikaner Nationalism, 1934–1948* (Cambridge: Cambridge University Press, 1983). For a more sophisticated social history approach, see the volume edited by Shula Marks and Stanley Trapido, *The Politics of Race, Class and Nationalism in Twentieth Century South Africa* (London: Longman, 1986).

14. The term is that of Hugh Seton-Watson, *Times Higher Educational Supplement,* 27 August 1982, pp. 12–13.

15. I deal in greater detail with the origins of Afrikaner nationalism in two articles, one published in *South African Historical Journal*, 17 (1987) and the other in *Journal of Southern African Studies*, 14, 1 (1987).

16. I discuss this more fully in Adam and Giliomee, *Ethnic Power Mobilized*, pp. 145–76.

17. Schlemmer, 'South Africa's National Party Government', pp. 19–28.

18. Walker Connor, 'Nation-Building or Nation-Destroying', *World Politics*, 24 (1972), p. 343.

19. Kedourie, *Nationalism*, p. 146.

20. Ibid., pp. 9–27.

21. Koos van Wyk and Deon Geldenhuys, *Die groepsgebod in PW Botha se politieke oortuigings* (Johannesburg: RAU, 1987).

22. Schlemmer, 'South Africa's NP government', p. 27.

23. Ibid., p. 24.

24. Gellner, *Nations and Nationalism*, p. 111.

25. Benyamin Neuberger, *National Self-Determination in Post-Colonial Africa* (Boulder, CO: Lynne Rienner, 1986), pp. 12–13.

26. Neuberger, *National Self-Determination*, p. 41.

27. No Sizwe, *One Azania, One Nation* (London: Zed Press, 1979).

28. Raymond Suttner and Jeremy Cronin, *30 Years of the Freedom Charter* (Johannesburg: Ravan Press, 1985), p. 136.

29. E. Feit, *Workers without Weapons* (Hamden, CT: Archon Books, 1975).

30. Paul Maylam, *A History of the African People of South Africa* (London: Croom Helm, 1986), pp. 188–9.

31. Tom Lodge, *Black Politics in South Africa since 1945* (Johannesburg: Ravan Press, 1983), pp. 82–6.

32. Ibid., pp. 84–5.

33. Nelson Mandela, *Long walk to Freedom* (Randburg: Macdonald-Purnell,1994), p.438.

34. Peter Raboroko, 'The Africanist Case', *AfricaSouth*, April–June 1960.

35. Jack Simons, 'The Freedom Charter: Equal Rights and Freedoms', in *The Freedom Charter: A Commemorative Publication* (London: ANC, 1985), pp. 102–66.

36. Cited in *The Freedom Charter*, pp. 75–6.

37. ANC pamphlet, 'Born of the People', Statement by O.R. Tambo, 16 December 1986.

38. Edward Feit, *South Africa: The Dynamics of the African National Congress* (London: Oxford University Press, 1962), pp. 11–12.

39. Documents of the Second National Consultative Conference of the ANC, Zambia, 16–23 June 1985, p. 13.

40. *Financial Mail*, 24 July 1987, 'Political Game Plan'.

41. I expand on this in the articles 'The Botha Quest: Sharing Power without Losing Control', *Leadership SA*, 2, 2 (1983), pp. 27–35 and 'Apartheid, Verligtheid and Liberalism', in Jeffrey Butler, Richard Elphick and David Welsh (eds.), *Democratic Liberalism in South Africa* (Middletown: Wesleyan Press, 1986), pp. 363–83.

42. See the critical comments of Robert Fatton, 'The African National Congress of South Africa: The Limitations of a Revolutionary Strategy', *Canadian Journal of African Studies*, 18, 3 (1984), pp. 593–608.

43. These comments apply to a future South Africa although they were made in the Israeli

context: Group for Advancement of Psychiatry, *Self-Involvement in the Middle East* (New York, 1978), pp. 489–503.

44. Theodor Hanf, 'Lessons Which Are Never Learnt: Minority Rule in Comparative Perspective', in Heribert Adam (ed.), *The Limits of Reform Politics* (Leiden: E.J. Brill, 1983), p. 27.

7. Apartheid 'Grand Corruption'? The ABSA Lifeboat and the Demand for Repayment

1. Apartheid Grand Corruption. As a citation toucan state This appeared first on 18 November 2013 on the blog politicsweb.co.za
2. David Gleason, *Business Day*, 4 March 2002. The view is also expressed in a book by an aggrieved former ABSA banker. See Bob Aldworth, *The Infernal Tower* (Johannesburg: Contra Press, 1996).
3. Hennie van Vuuren, Letter to *Business Day*, 22 August 2013.
4. Patti Waldmeir, *Anatomy of a Miracle* (New York: Norton, 1997), p. 56.
5. Apart from the sources below, this assessment is based on my private interviews with people who held senior positions at time in the Reserve Bank and in Sanlam. I also conducted an extended interview with a person who is now a director in a US-based bank. All the interviews were given on the condition of confidentiality.
6. Interview with Anton Rupert, 3 May 1999.
7. 'Report of the Governor's Panel of Experts to Investigate the SA Reserve Bank's Role with Regard to the Financial Assistance Package to Bankorp Limited', pp. 5, 141.
8. Ibid., p. 74.

8. An Exceptional Editor

1. Jaap Steyn, *Penvegter: Piet Cillié van 'Die Burger'* (Cape Town: Tafelberg, 2002), p. 211.
2. Dirk and Johanna de Villiers, *PW* (Cape Town: Tafelberg, 1984), p. 90.
3. Uriel Abulof *The Mortality and Morality of Nations* (Cambridge: Cambridge University Press, 2015), p. vii.
4. Leaders like Smuts and Gen. J.B.M. Hertzog did not always use the term '*volk*' in an ethnic or nationalist sense. In this particular case Smuts appeared to be using it in an ethnic sense, referring to white Afrikaans-speakers.
5. I discuss the debate in my *The Afrikaners: Biography of a People* (Cape Town: Tafelberg, 2003), pp. 259–63.
6. Jan Sadie, *The Fall and Rise of the Afrikaners in the South African Economy* (Stellenbosch University, 2002/1), pp. 30–1.
7. René de Villiers, 'Political Parties and Trends', in G.H. Calpin (ed.), *The South African Way of Life* (Melbourne: William Heinemann, 1953), p. 137.
8. Steyn, *Penvegter*, p. 42.
9. R. Davies, *Capital, State and White Labour in South Africa* (Brighton: Harvester Press, 1970), p. 298.
10. J. Robinson, *Liberalism in South Africa, 1948–1963* (Oxford: Oxford University Press, 1971), p. 3.
11. P.J. Meyer, *Nog nie ver genoeg nie* (Johannesburg: Perskor, 1984), p. 64.

12. C.W. de Kiewiet, *The Anatomy of South African Misery* (Oxford: Oxford University Press, 1956), pp. 40–5.

13. C.W. de Kiewiet, 'Loneliness in the Beloved Country', *Foreign Affairs*, 42, 3 (1964), p. 424.

14. I deal with the issue of the 'Coloured vote' in the first 40 years of Union in my *The Rise and Demise of the Afrikaners* (Cape Town: Tafelberg, 219), pp. 3–31.

15. Patrick Duncan, *The Road through the Wilderness* (Johannesburg: n.p., 1953). See also G.D. Scholtz, *Het die Afrikaanse volk 'n toekoms?* (Johannesburg: Voortrekkerpers, 1955), pp. 126–31.

16. Piet Cillié, 'Bestek van apartheid', *Die Suid-Afrikaan*, Spring 1985, p. 17.

17. P.J. Cillié, 'The National Party's Possible Line of Attack', *Forum*, 1, 7 (1952), pp. 13–14.

18. Steyn, *Penvegter*, pp. 69–71.

19. L.E. Neame, *The History of Apartheid* (London: Pall Mall Press, 1962), p. 80.

20. Steyn, *Penvegter*, p. 67.

21. Ibid., p. 82.

22. Lewis Gann, 'Liberal Interpretations of South African History', *Rhodes-Livingstone Journal*, 1959, p. 51.

23. Martin Meredith, *The State of Africa: A History of Fifty Years of Independence* (London: Free Press, 2006), p. 103.

24. Louis Louw (comp.), *Dawie: 1946–1964* (Cape Town: Tafelberg, 1965), p. 181.

25. Steyn, *Penvegter*, p. 138.

26. George Schopflin, 'Nationalism and National Minorities in East and Central Europe', *Journal of International Affairs*, 45, 1 (1991), pp. 51–2.

27. Louw, *Dawie*, p. 114.

28. Cited by *Die Burger*, 29 January 1962 and Steyn, N.P. *Van Wyk Louw*, p. 978.

29. *Die Volksblad*, 24 October 1974, cited by J.C. Steyn, *Van Wyk Louw: 'n lewensverhaal* (Cape Town: Tafelberg, 1998), p. 1165.

30. Adam Ashforth, *The Politics of Official Discourse in Twentieth Century South Africa* (Oxford: Clarendon Press, 1991), pp. 152–3.

31. Die Burger 16 August 1959.

32. Steyn, *N.P. van Wyk Louw*, pp. 906–7.

33. Louw, *Dawie*, pp. 285–6.

34. A.H. Luckhoff, *Cottesloe* (Cape Town: Tafelberg, 1978).

35. Ibid., pp. 205–6.

36. Ibid., p. 204.

37. P.J. Cillié, *Tydgenote* (Cape Town: Tafelberg, 1980), p. 25.

38. Email from Servaas van der Berg, 21 November 2010. For a detailed demographic study of black urbanisation, see F. Smit and J.J. Booysen, *Swart verstedeliking: proses, patroon en strategie* (Cape Town: Tafelberg, 1981); according to the 1951 census there were 2,3 million blacks in the cities and 614 000 in towns, p. 36.

39. Nic von Wielligh and Lydia von Wielligh-Steyn, *Die bom: Suid-Afrika se kernwapenprogram* (Pretoria: Litera, 2014), pp. 142–3.

40. Ronald Steel, 'Walter Lippmann backing LBJ in Vietnam', *New York Review of Books*, 25 September 1980.

41. Jamie Miller, *An African Volk: The Apartheid State and the Search for Survival* (Oxford: Oxford University Press, 2016).

42. Steyn, *Penvegter*, p. 225.

43. Meyer, *Nog nie ver genoeg nie*, p. 88.

44. Ibid.

45. Hermann Giliomee and Lawrence Schlemmer, *From Apartheid to Nation-Building* (Cape Town: Oxford University Press, 1898), pp. 103–9.

46. Steyn, *Penvegter*, p. 254.

47. Henry Kissinger, *Years of Renewal* (London: Weidenfeld and Nicholson, 1999), p. 963.

48. Communication by Marion Donhoff, publisher of *Dje Zelt* Final Corrections to me in 1984.

49. Chester A. Crocker, *High Noon in Southern Africa* (New York: W.W. Norton, 1992), pp. 87, 111.

50. George Arbatov, *The System: An Insider's Life in Soviet Politics* (New York: Times Books, 1992), pp. 189–219.

51. Piet Cillié, 'Preface' to Smit and Booysen, *Swart verstedeliking*.

52. The indictment appeared under the title 'Die erfenis van apartheid', *Die Suid-Afrikaan*, Spring 1985, pp. 14–15.

53. Cillié, 'Bestek van apartheid', p. 17.

54. Ibid., p. 18.

55. Donald Horowitz, *A Democratic South Africa? Constitutional Engineering in a Divided Society* (Cape Town: Oxford University Press, 1991), p. 98.

9. Leaders and the Citizenry

1. This distinction between the different components of citizenship is derived from the work of T.H. Marshall, *Class, Citizenship and Social Development* (Garden City: Doubleday, 1964) and Talcott Parsons, *The Social System* (New York: The Free Press, 1964). See S.P. Cilliers, 'Industrial Progress: Its Social, Political and Economic Implications', in A. Paul Hare, Gerd Wiendieck and Max H. von Broembsen (eds.), *South Africa: Sociological Analyses* (Cape Town: Oxford University Press, 1979), pp. 209–18.

2. See John Dugard, *Human Rights and the South African Legal Order* (Princeton: Princeton University Press, 1978); J.P. Verloren van Themaat and Marinus Wiechers, *Staatsreg* (Durban: Butterworths, 1981), pp. 344–96.

3. André du Toit, 'Understanding Rights, Discourses and Ideological Conflicts in South Africa', in Hugh Corder (ed.), *Essays on Law and Social Practice in South Africa* (Cape Town: Juta, 1988), p. 261.

4. Personal communication by Piet Cillié, ex-editor of *Die Burger*, 30 January 1991.

5. D.F. Malan (compiled S.W. Pienaar), *Glo in u volk: Dr. D.F. Malan as redenaar* (Cape Town: Tafelberg, 1964).

6. Ben Schoeman, *My lewe in die politiek* (Johannesburg: Perskor, 1978), p. 225.

7. Piet Cillié, 'Bestek van apartheid', *Die Suid-Afrikaan*, Spring 1988, p. 18.

8. B.M. Schoeman, *Van Malan tot Verwoerd* (Cape Town: Human and Rousseau, 1973), pp. 120–1. Schoeman's book is based on the diary kept by Albert Hertzog, who was on the Bond's executive council and became a cabinet minister in 1959.

9.   Allister Sparks, *The Mind of South Africa* (London: Heinemann, 1990), p. 177.

10. A.N. Pelzer, *Die Afrikaner-Broederbond: Eerste 50 jaar* (Cape Town: Tafelberg, 1979), p. 177.

11. J.H.P. Serfontein, *Brotherhood of Power* (London: Rex Collings, 1979), pp. 84–8.

12. Dirk Richard, *Moedswillig die uwe: Perspersoonlikhede van die noorde* (Johannesburg: Perskor, 1985).

13. Malan, *Glo in u volk*, p. 136.

14. C.M. Tatz, *Shadow and Substance: A Study in Land and Franchise Policies Affecting Africans, 1910–1960* (Pietermaritzburg: University of Natal Press, 1962), p. 113.

15. I deal with this extensively in Heribert Adam and Hermann Giliomee, *Ethnic Power Mobilized: Can South Africa Change?* (New Haven: Yale University Press, 1979), pp. 145–76. The calculations are by Professor J.L. Sadie.

16. Schoeman, *My lewe in die politiek*, p. 158.

17. For some of Verwoerd's most prominent speeches, see the *Cape Argus*, 8 August, 18 August and 1 October 1960.

18. *Cape Argus*, 18 August 1960, speech by J. Hamilton Russell.

19. *Cape Argus*, 8 August 1960.

20. Pelzer, *Die Afrikaner-Broederbond*, pp. 101–2.

21. Serfontein, *Brotherhood of Power*, p. 323.

22. Ibid., p. 238.

23. B.M. Schoeman, *Die geldmag: Suid-Afrika se onsigbare regering* (Pretoria: Aktuele Publikasies, 1980), p. 10; see also pp. 23–45, 78–82.

24. Ronald Segal claims to have had an interview with Oppenheimer in which he said as much. See R. Segal, 'Portrait of a Millionaire', *AfricaSouth*, 4, 3 (1960).

25. Schoeman, *My lewe in die politiek*, p. 271.

26. Kenneth Boulding, *The Image* (Ann Arbor: Michigan University Press, 1956), p. 114.

27. Kenneth Grundy, *Soldiers without Politics: Blacks in the South African Armed Forces* (Berkeley: University of California Press, 1983), p. 106.

28. 'The Doctrine of Apartheid', *Round Table*, 39 (December 1948), p. 32.

29. Eugene P. Dvorin, *Racial Separation in South Africa: An Analysis of Apartheid Theory* (Chicago: University of Chicago Press, 1952), p. 193.

30. H.B. Thom, *D.F. Malan* (Cape Town: Tafelberg, 1980), p. 279.

31. Dvorin, *Racial Separation*, p. 95.

32. Ibid., p. 64.

33. H.F. Verwoerd, *Verwoerd aan die woord: toesprake, 1948–1962* (Johannesburg: Afrikaanse Persboekhandel, 1963), p. 121.

34. Ibid., pp. 20–1.

35. *House of Assembly Debates (HAD)*, 25 January 1943, col. 75. For the first use of 'apartheid' by *Die Burger* see Louis Louw (comp.), *Dawie: 1946–1964* (Cape Town: Tafelberg, 1965), pp. 48–50.

36. Dvorin, *Racial Separation*, p. 95.

37. Thom, *Malan*, pp. 250–1.

38. The exchange of letters is published in Leo Kuper, *Passive Resistance in South Africa* (New Haven: Yale University Press, 1957), pp. 233–41.

39. Ibid., p. 240. In a letter to an American clergyman, also published in this volume (pp.

217–26), Malan also refers to the fundamental difference between the two groups, white and black. Here he states: 'The difference in colour is merely the physical manifestation of the contrast between two irreconcilable ways of life, between barbarism and civilization, between overwhelming numerical odds on the one hand and insignificant numbers on the other.'

40. Mary Benson, *Nelson Mandela* (Harmondsworth: Penguin Books, 1986), p. 100.
41. R.E. van der Ross, 'Coloured Viewpoint', 6 October 1960, republished in R.E. van der Ross, *Coloured Viewpoint* (Bellville: University of the Western Cape, 1984), p. 133.
42. Ibid., p. 102.
43. Ibid., p. 181.
44. *HAD*, 1965, cols. 4403–10.
45. *HAD*, 16 April 1964, col. 4337, speech by P.W. Botha.
46. Michael McGrath, 'The Racial Redistribution of Taxation and Government Expenditures', unpublished paper, University of Natal, 1979; Norman Bromberger, 'Government Policies Affecting the Distribution of Income, 1940–1980', in Robert Schrire (ed.), *South Africa: Public Policy Perspectives* (Cape Town: Juta, 1982), pp. 172–86; Hermann Giliomee and Lawrence Schlemmer, *From Apartheid to Nation-Building* (Cape Town: Oxford University Press), pp. 103–7.
47. Letter from Malan to the Rev. John Piersma, republished in Kuper, *Passive Resistance*, p. 222.
48. J.J.J. Scholtz, 'Apartheid: verhaal van verydelde idealisme', *Die Burger*, 18 November 1985.
49. Dirk and Johanna de Villiers, *PW* (Cape Town: Tafelberg, 1984), p. 91.
50. Compare Schoeman, *My lewe in die politiek*, pp. 224–34, and Richard, *Moedswillig die uwe*, p. 135.
51. B.M. Schoeman, *Vorster se 1000 dae* (Cape Town: Human and Rousseau, 1974), p. 41.
52. Ibid., pp. 254–7; John D'Oliveira, *Vorster: The Man* (Johannesburg: Ernest Stanton, 1977), pp. 224–43.
53. Cited by D'Oliveira, *Vorster*, pp. 212–13.
54. J.H.P. Serfontein, *Die verkrampte aanslag* (Cape Town: Human and Rousseau, 1970), p. 72.
55. Giliomee and Schlemmer, *From Apartheid to Nation-Building*, p. 157.
56. Rory Riordan, 'Consolidating Negative Attitudes', *Monitor*, December 1990, p. 61.
57. Cited by *The Star*, 17 February 1969.
58. Theodore Hanf et al., *South Africa: The Prospects of Peaceful Change* (London: Rex Collings, 1981), pp. 400–2.
59. Schoeman, *Vorster se 1000 dae*, p. 37. See also Schalk Pienaar, *Getuie van groot tye* (Cape Town: Tafelberg, 1979), pp. 95–106, 126–32.
60. For a fuller discussion see Hermann Giliomee and Heribert Adam, *Afrikanermag: Opkoms en toekoms* (Stellenbosch: UUB, 1981), pp. 214–15.
61. Schoeman, *Vorster se 1000 dae*, p. 42.
62. For an account see F.E. O'Brien Geldenhuys, *In die stroomversnellings: Vyftig jaar van die Kerk* (Cape Town: Tafelberg, 1982).
63. Brian Pottinger, *The Imperial Presidency. P.W. Botha – The First Ten Years* (Johannesburg: Southern Book Publishers, 1988), esp. pp. 34–44. For a discussion from a more sympathetic perspective, see Dirk and Johanna de Villiers, *PW*.

64. R.A. Schrire, 'The Formulation of Public Policy', in Anthony de Crespigny and Robert Schrire (eds.), *The Government and Politics* (Cape Town: Juta, 1978), pp. 176–94.
65. G.D. Scholtz, *Dr Hendrik Frensch Verwoerd, 1900–1966* (Johannesburg: Perskor, 1966), vol. 2, p. 162.
66. *HAD*, 7 February 1978, col. 579.
67. Verwoerd did make the 'concession' that once full separation had been achieved contact could again be allowed. See Scholtz, *Verwoerd*, vol. 2, p. 173.
68. Van der Ross remembers Vorster as saying: 'Hy wou my sê dat die Afrikaners deur 'n era gegaan het waarin hulle maar so goed kon wees as hulle wou, maar nie as volle mense erken is nie omdat hulle Afrikaans was.' (He wanted to say that the Afrikaners passed through a phase in which they could be as good as they wanted to be, but were nevertheless denied recognition as full human beings because they were Afrikaners.) *Rapport*, 17 February 1991, p. 10.
69. De Villiers and De Villiers, *PW*, pp. 89–90.
70. Scholtz, *Verwoerd*, vol. 2, p. 171.
71. D'Oliveira, *Vorster*, p. 169.
72. B.D. van Niekerk, 'Hanged by the Neck until You Are Dead', *South African Law Journal*, 86 (1969), p. 467.
73. Roy Howard du Preez, 'The Role and Policies of the Labour Party of South Africa, 1965–1978', MA thesis, Unisa, 1987, p. 157.
74. For a full discussion, see Gerd Behrens, 'The Other Two Houses: The First Five Years of the Houses of Representatives and Delegates', PhD thesis, University of Cape Town, 1989.
75. *Debates of the House of Representatives*, 1987, col. 2286.
76. J.P. Groenewald, 'Reaksies op minderheidsgroepstatus by Kleurlinge', PhD thesis, University of Stellenbosch, 1987, p. 241.
77. J.A. du Pisani, 'Die ontplooing van afsonderlike ontwikkeling tydens die B.J. Vorster-era: die tuislandbeleid, 1966–1978', PhD thesis, University of the Orange Free State, pp. 261–301; the quote is on p. 301.
78. Hermann Giliomee, 'The Political Functions of the Homelands', in Hermann Giliomee and Lawrence Schlemmer (eds.), *Up Against the Fences* (Cape Town: David Philip, 1985), pp. 52–6.
79. Alf Ries and Ebbe Dommisse, *Leierstryd* (Cape Town: Tafelberg, 1990), p. 101.
80. Ibid., p. 106.
81. Ibid.
82. *Die Burger*, 15 May 1990.
83. For a review of Buthelezi's negotiating position see Ben Temkin, *Buthelezi: A Biography* (London: Frank Cass, 2003), p. pp.249–88.

10. The Broken Heart of the Afrikaners

1. J.C. Kannemeyer, *Leipoldt: 'n Lewensverhaal* (Cape Town: Tafelberg, 1999), p. 650.
2. J.C. Kannemeyer, *Leroux: 'n Lewe* (Pretoria: Protea Boekhuis, 2008), p. 245.
3. Ibid., pp. 505–6.
4. N.P. van Wyk Louw, *Versamelde prosa*, vol. 1 (Cape Town: Tafelberg, 1986), pp. 460–3.

5. H. Aucamp and M. Bakkes, *'n Baksel in die môre: boerestories uit die Stormberge* (Cape Town: Tafelberg, 1973), pp. 1–3.

6. Email message from J.M. Coetzee, 16 April 2016.

7. Email message from Joan Kruger.

INDEX

communal interests of Afrikaners and
Africans 191-
Congress of Democrats 203
Congress of South African Trade Unions
(Cosatu) 206
Connor, Walker 200
Cottesloe Conference 231-232, 247-248
Conservative Party (CP) 199, 203, 265
Crocker, Chester 237
Currie, Walter 83

Dagbreek 246
Dakar meeting (1987) 202
Davenport, Rodney 90
Davis, Dennis 214
De Buys, Coenraad 46, 60
Defence Amendment Act (1967) 253
Defiance campaign (passive resistance) 256
De Kiewiet, CW 11, 111, 222
De Klerk, FW 175, 242, 260, 271-272
De Kock, Gerhard 212
De Lange, Pieter 264
De la Rey, Koos 128
Delius, Athony 230
Democratic Alliance 176
Democratic Party 261
De Savoye, Marguerite 23
De Villiers, Bruckner 124
Devils 166
De Waal, JHH 133
De Wet, CR 38, 156
Difaqane 55-56, 76
Dingane 60
Dönges, Eben 135
Dorfman, Ariel 171
Dostoevsky, Fyodor 166
Duncan, Patrick 223
Du Plessis, Danie 188-189
Du Plessis, Fred 212
Du Plessis, Jan Christoffel 144
Du Plessis, Johannes 142-143
Du Plessis, Wennie 186
Durand, J 146

Dutch 11, 20, 39, 89, 91-93, 96-111, 113-124,
126, 129-133, 147, 183, 198, 219, 279, 281,
288, 292
Dutch East India Company 11, 18, 21-22,
29, 57, 63, 65, 68, 74, 90, 136, 146, 148,
152
Dutch Reformed Church (NG Kerk) 1, 7-8,
15, 39-40, 42, 92, 95, 98-99, 107, 109-110,
121, 124, 128, 131, 134, 137-138, 140-146,
151, 153-159, 161, 163-166, 169-171, 177,
224-225, 231-232, 247-248, 254, 264
Dutch Reformed Church (Hervormde
Kerk) 95, 128, 159, 231
Dutch Reformed Sendingkerk (Mission
Church) 157-158, 163-164
Du Toit, AF 94
Du Toit, André 147-148, 236
Du Toit, Gertruida 21
Du Toit, JD 151-152, 155
Du Toit, SJ 41-42, 107-109, 111-116, 119, 133

education
of Afrikaners/Dutch 2, 23-24, 39-40, 91,
98-99, 106-109, 111, 114-115, 119, 123,
126-127, 135-136, 144-145, 170, 176-178,
181, 184, 196, 198, 203, 248, 251, 254, 259,
264, 267, 282; of Africans and Coloureds
142, 144-145, 158, 177-180, 196, 203, 208,
217, 225, 235, 251, 254, 258, 267, 282;
secularisation of 98-99, 107-108, 144-145,
153, 155-158, 160
eiesoortige ontwikkeling (autochthonous
development) 157
Eiselen, Werner 156, 159, 188-189
Eloff, FG (Nettie) 38
Elphick, Richard 15, 143, 160
Equality of Believers, The 143
Erasmus, Frans 153, 187, 189, 190
Eskom 176, 181, 211, 248
Esselen, Louis 128, 187
Ethiopianism 143-144
ethno-nationalism 197-201, 207
Etzioni, Amitai 209